MW01275068

PHILOSOPHY IN DIALOGUE

Topics in Historical Philosophy

General Editors David Kolb
John McCumber

Associate Editor Anthony J. Steinbock

PHILOSOPHY IN DIALOGUE

Plato's Many Devices

Edited by Gary Alan Scott

Northwestern University Press
Evanston, Illinois

Northwestern University Press
www.nupress.northwestern.edu

Copyright © 2007 by Northwestern University Press. Published 2007. All rights
reserved.

Printed in the United States of America

10 9 8 7 6 5 4 3 2 1

ISBN-13: 978-0-8101-2354-0 (cloth)
ISBN-10: 0-8101-2354-1 (cloth)
ISBN-13: 978-0-8101-2356-4 (paper)
ISBN-10: 0-8101-2356-8 (paper)

Library of Congress Cataloging-in-Publication Data
   Philosophy in dialogue : Plato's many devices / edited by Gary Alan Scott.
      p. cm. — (Topics in historical philosophy)
   Includes bibliographical references and index.
   ISBN 0-8101-2356-8 (pbk. : alk. paper) —
   ISBN 0-8101-2354-1 (cloth : alk. paper)
   1. Plato. 2. Dialectic. I. Scott, Gary Alan, 1952– II. Series: Northwestern
University topics in historical philosophy.
B398.D5P45 2007
184—dc22

                                                            2007007863

Contents

Acknowledgments

We would like to express our appreciation for all of the editorial, production, and marketing staff at Northwestern University Press for their professionalism and dedication in the production of this volume. The project editor, Serena Brommel, shepherded the book through its various phases, and it has been my pleasure as the book's editor to work with her. We also appreciated the careful work of Northwestern's marketing and sales department in facilitating the marketing questionnaires and other aspects of publicity for the book.

Paul Mendelson was meticulous and thorough in copyediting the book, which surely saved us from innumerable errors.

We also want to thank Susan Betz, acquisitions editor and editor in chief, for guiding the manuscript through the review process and for placing the book well in Northwestern University Press's Topics in Historical Philosophy series, and we wish to thank the series editors, David Kolb and John McCumber.

All the contributors to this collection and its editor owe a debt of gratitude to Hilde Roos, who was, in effect, the editorial assistant for the book throughout its various stages of production. And finally, we wish to acknowledge Ms. Lisa M. Flaherty, administrative assistant to the philosophy department at Loyola College in Maryland. Her coordination and facilitation in getting the chapters to the contributors and back to the press, on top of her many other duties, were indispensable.

Introduction

Gary Alan Scott

Questions concerning Plato's many and varied devices arise almost immediately upon beginning to read one's first Platonic "dialogue." Just
what kind of work is a "dialogue," and how do such works communicate
their author's philosophical views? To what sort of literary genre or philosophical "school" do Plato's dialogues belong? Readers new to Plato
quickly notice that there is something peculiar about his philosophical
texts: they are decidedly not first-person essays or treatises, the standard
form in which most modern and contemporary philosophy has been
presented. These "dialogues" are also not "critical" works (such as Kant's
three "critiques"), nor are they archaeologies or genealogies, polemics,
meditations, confessions, consolations, letters, handbooks, or autobiog-
raphies. Plato's dialogues are not written in the first person, because
in them Plato never speaks in his own voice (though he might be said
to speak in his own voice in the oft-disputed letters attributed to him).
Instead, there are often several voices heard, and frequently others (including various poets and historians) echoed in a single dialogue.

Plato's audience is indeed presented with a variation on the first-
person voice in a dialogue such as the *Apology of Socrates,* but the voice
one hears is the voice of Socrates and not the voice of Plato. The *Apology*
is a "direct" dialogue, rather than a "reported" (or "narrated") dialogue.
Socrates delivers his speech directly to his large jury and audience, and
his speech is not mediated by any narrator or "narrative frame." Therefore, the reader has the impression that Socrates is speaking directly to
her. But of course, Socrates is not the author of this work. So the fact
that Socrates speaks directly to the reader does not create the kind of
first-person point of view that would permit one to read off what the
author, Plato, thinks from what is said in the first person by a character,
Socrates, in the drama Plato immortalized.

The new reader quickly notices that it is characters (such as
Socrates, Euthyphro, Laches, Crito, Phaedo, Gorgias, and some seventy
others) who speak and interact in little plays, in which the talk quickly
turns to questions at the heart of human life. Since the nineteenth cen-

tury, our modern conceptual framework allows scholars to distinguish, if not to isolate, philosophical components from literary or dramatic ones, but we should be clear that such categories would not have occurred to Plato's ancient audiences, nor would such distinctions have been applied to "philosophy," since philosophy would not yet have been relegated to a narrow subject field, or "discipline."[1] Nor would it have surprised Plato's ancient audiences to find yet another author writing "conversations with Socrates" (*sokratikoi logoi*), since Plato is supposed to have been a relative latecomer to a genre that could already count half a dozen or more contributors by the time Plato threw his hat into the ring, and since, in the ancient world, one would have written within an existing genre, rather than attempting to be "original."[2] However, it certainly occurred to Plato to have Socrates in the *Republic* tell of an ancient quarrel between philosophy and poetry, a discussion that provides a warrant for the distinction between philosophy and literature, which would not be formalized until more than two millennia later. Scholars have recently argued that it seems harder to believe that Plato was the mere heir to this "ancient quarrel" than it is to believe that he "invented" this "quarrel" (along with philosophy itself) as a way of setting philosophy apart from other paths to wisdom.[3]

Whatever the case, the dialogue form has the benefit of showing audiences something at the same time as the characters in these little dramas tell them things. The conversations in Plato's dialogues are often devoted to matters such as courage, wisdom, moderation, justice, piety, virtue in general, and what human beings can know concerning these matters. There are also discussions about what is right and good in human life, about standards of measure and qualifications for judging, about appearance and reality, and many other issues.[4]

Readers new to Plato might next discover that most of Plato's characters are modeled on actual historical people, so they might try to determine how closely, or in what specific respects, Plato's characters resemble what we know of the historical personae.[5] One might also notice that certain dramatic clues permit Plato's audiences to know (more or less) when many dialogues were supposed to have taken place, and all of the dialogues that supply such clues are set somewhere between the middle and the end of the fifth century B.C.E., almost a full generation ahead of Plato, who would have been only twenty-seven or twenty-eight years old when Socrates drank the hemlock in 399 B.C.E.[6] Of the thirty-five dialogues attributed (at one time or another) to Plato, only one explicitly states that Plato was in attendance. Only in the *Apology of Socrates* does Plato write himself into the dialogue, but the first-time reader of the *Apology* quickly learns that Plato's dramatic depiction of

Socrates' trial is no mere transcript or "court report"; and moreover, in the *Phaedo,* Plato intriguingly writes himself out of the last conversation between Socrates and the members of his circle. An industrious first-time reader might have already searched the casts of characters in a collected edition of Plato's dialogues only to discover that there is no character named "Plato" who puts forth the author's views against other characters in any of the dialogues. Indeed, nowhere does a character named "Plato" defend a thesis or construct an argument, and therefore whatever Plato might "mean" and whatever the historical Plato might have believed, his dialogues do not express directly his beliefs or state his meaning in a first-person voice. Therefore, it would seem to be prima facie false for commentators to say loosely, "Plato says," for Plato does not "say" anything in these dramas.[7] Many characters make assertions and put forth arguments in Plato's texts, but none of them is named "Plato." One is therefore quickly forced to wonder: What kind of philosophical argument is required to ascribe views to Plato? How should one go about discerning the author's thought? And what might Plato have wished his audiences to take away from these (more or less) dramatic, philosophical works? In short, how should one go about interpreting a Platonic dialogue?

It would seem that the task of discerning Plato's thoughts or "meaning" from the words and actions of his characters is a task that more closely resembles the interpretation of the works of Shakespeare or Sophocles than the interpretation of the works of almost any modern philosopher. (And here it is noteworthy that commentators on Elizabethan drama do not say: "Shakespeare says, 'To be or not to be—that is the question: / Whether 'tis nobler in the mind to suffer / The slings and arrows of outrageous fortune, / Or to take arms against the sea of troubles / And by opposing, end them' "; they say that Hamlet asks himself this question!) Now since Plato's dialogues are more or less dramatic, and since they make or do something in the course of the work, one wonders how this dramatic element might complicate the task of justifying inferences about what Plato thought (or might have wanted his audiences to think or to "get") from the words of his characters. How should one begin to determine what Plato would have his audience think or believe, much less what he himself thinks or believes? To be sure, this cannot be determined a priori. How then might one show that because character *X* says *Y*, Plato believes (or wants us to believe) *Y*? Doesn't this very way of formulating the question presuppose that philosophy consisted, for Plato, in a set of problems and positions, arguments and inferences?

One would need to begin interpreting any one of Plato's dialogues by asking what was exhibited or enacted through the course of the dialogue's dramatic action. Is there something about a particular character's motivation or way of life that is expressed (or contravened) in what he says? Is there anything in a character's particular psychology that might suggest a certain logical tack in dealing with him? What can Plato's audience learn by comparing the *logoi* of the dialogue with the *ergon* of the dialogue? Where is the dialogue set? How does it end? How does the philosophical questioning arise? How do the issues discussed bear on the existential occasion that gives rise to them?

The "reported" dialogues utilize a narrator (and at least in one case—the *Symposium*—more than one). This is another way in which the dialogues can express something, even if this saying is not done by one of the characters in real time, but rather through narrators of the real-time events. In many cases, the narration functions partly to supply information directly to Plato's audience. In the five dialogues that Socrates narrates (*Republic, Lysis, Protagoras, Euthydemus,* and *Charmides*), the narrative frame is employed to supply information about his emotional state or his inner thoughts, or to announce something he was about to do but decided against doing, as Anne-Marie Bowery shows in chapter 4 of the present volume.[8] In other instances, the narrators function to provide commentary on the dramatic action, and even on the mood of those gathered, as Phaedo does in the middle of the *Phaedo*. Some of this information would not have been available to the characters in the dialogues, since it is given at the level of the narrative. Those gathered at Agathon's house during that infamous night when Socrates debated the poets, for example, would not have been privy to Apollodorus' comment at *Symposium* 222c: "Alcibiades' frankness provoked a lot of laughter, especially since it was obvious that he was still in love with Socrates."

We noted earlier that dialogues such as the *Apology* are "direct" or entirely "enacted," and so no narrator is used. This is why we could call Socrates' voice in the *Apology* "first person." Socrates speaks directly to his jury and Plato's audience is able, as it were, to "listen in" on his unmediated (if frequently interrupted) defense speech.

An author may choose to create a character who is clearly identifiable as propounding the author's viewpoint; for example, the character called "Dante" in Dante's *Divine Comedy* or the character of Philonous in Berkeley's *Three Dialogues Between Hylas and Philonous*. Some foil, some hero or heroine, or some character who dominates all comers within the drama would clearly indicate that the author wishes his audience to regard this superlative character as representing him. (This is no less true in cases where authors clearly champion "antiheroes" rather than heroes.) The philosophical equivalent of a superhero might be someone knowledgeable, virtuous, compassionate, able to dispense ad hoc sage-like advice, and someone willing and able to teach would-be students of philosophy. But is such a character to be found in Plato's dialogues?

By definition, all writers of *sokratikoi logoi* feature a character named "Socrates" who may or may not reflect well or accurately the historical Socrates, and the three extant examples of this once-popular genre—those of Plato, Xenophon, and Aristophanes—vary considerably. As far as one can tell, Plato's Socrates is far and away the most complex, para-doxical, unclassifiable, and ironic character in these dialogues. If this characterization of Socrates were even partially correct, then how would saying that Socrates represents Plato's views of philosophy or of the phi-losopher help us to identify and understand Plato's deeply held views?

Let us consider briefly whether Plato's Socrates is really capable of carrying the mantle of the philosophical superhero, with whom ev-ery reader would identify the author himself. If one focuses solely on Socrates' missionary role in many (though not all) dialogues and on his stature as a martyr (both erotic and religious) who dies for his beloved pursuit of wisdom—condemned to this fate by many men whom he had questioned and found wanting—a reader new to Plato might then be led to conclude that Socrates is precisely such a superhero, albeit a tragic one. Yet if we consider the complex portrait of Socrates that Plato draws, one might note vital aspects of Socrates' character that would seem to make him unfit for, or at least miscast in, the role of superhero. I would note five such features:

1. Throughout the dialogues, Socrates insists that he does not have knowledge of the most important things (some of which are things he thinks people in certain positions need to, and should, know). If the conditions for knowledge are made strict enough, then we must regard him as entirely sincere in his general disclaimers of knowledge and his insistence that his "small" human wisdom is worth little or nothing (*Apology* 22e–23b).

2. Socrates' ironic stance keeps him at arm's length from others and makes it impossible in some cases to know exactly what he is saying or meaning. This ironical "shield" (as D. C. Muecke calls it) appears hubristic to others, such as Alcibiades and Agathon in the *Symposium*, or entirely *pseudos*, as with Thrasymachus in the *Republic* and Callicles in the *Gorgias*, or seemingly impenetrable, as in the case of Socrates' response to Alcibiades' offer of sexual favors (*Symposium* 218e–219a). I agree with Alexander Nehamas that irony, at its most complex level, is not simply a way of speaking, but is rather a mode of being. Plato's Socrates doesn't just "use" irony; he *is an ironist*.[9] And as Nehamas has

noted, the dialogues employ a double irony: on the one hand, irony is characteristic of Socrates' posture toward many interlocutors, but it is also a feature of Plato's posture toward his audience, so that "as we watch Socrates manipulate his interlocutors, we ourselves are being manipulated by Plato."[10]

3. Socrates may fairly be regarded as sometimes preachy and at other times as unfair to his interlocutors, and he appears patently stubborn in arguments with some people.[11]

4. One might conclude from reading some or all of Plato's dialogues that Socrates learns very little about justice, piety, courage, moderation, rhetoric, or friendship from his interlocutors. But he does learn one important thing about wisdom, and this is that he is apparently better off as he is, knowing what he does not know, rather than thinking that he knows (see *Apology* 22e–23b). Dialogues such as *Symposium* and *Menexenus* may present counterexamples in which Socrates does seem to learn from female teachers; but this learning is set in the distant past and, by and large, if Socrates learns anything in the course of a Platonic dialogue, one must look for what he has learned somewhere other than in the conversation's express content.

5. Finally, Socrates might be judged culpable by Plato's readers (though it is doubtful that this reflects Plato's own view) for his treatment of his wife and children, both on account of his absenteeism at home and because of his willingness to sacrifice himself for his cause, whether or not his principled action was best for his family and friends.[12] This last point forces Plato's audience to wonder whether Socrates' life is livable, whether it is amenable (as a whole) to imitation, or whether Socrates is one of a kind, as is implied by the descriptions of him as *atopos* (in all of its senses: unclassifiable, strange, and without place).

Yet the difficulty in regarding Plato's dominant philosophical characters as philosophical exemplars or role models is not limited to Socrates. It would seem that all of the philosophical characters in the dialogues—Socrates, Parmenides, the visitor from Elea, the Athenian Stranger, Timaeus, and Diotima—confess to a gulf between their own wisdom and the wisdom they desire and believe they need. Many, if not all of them, thus say things that downplay their knowledge or distance themselves from the highest and most desirable kind of knowledge.[13] Add to this the fact that many investigations end in aporia (and in the ones that do not, no one appears on the scene to tie together in summary form what has been learned through the conversation), and the task of ascertaining Plato's views is rendered even more difficult. In Plato's dialogues, gods don't appear or speak and there is no obvious "messenger" or "chorus," as one often finds in tragedy, to supply the audience with crucial information or to comment on the action of the play. Most conclusions reached in the dialogues are established in merely presumptive and provisional terms, so they are open to further discussion, as the philosophical characters, especially Socrates, engage in discussion after discussion to test their opinions, beliefs, and hypotheses, amassing evidence for the best views on various subjects. (This has been termed "Socrates' evidentialism.") [14] Despite what Socrates appears to know compared to others, he never claims knowledge of anything except his ignorance.[15] Likewise, Plato writes his dialogues so that difficulties among the various positions are left unresolved, philosophy does not always get the last word, and more than a few dialogues end inconclusively. So it is not only that Plato wrote richly textured, heterogeneous, open-ended, quasi-historical fictions, but also that those key conclusions which seem to be reached in them are presented as only tentative and subject to reexamination.

At some point, a first-time reader attempting to unpack and understand her first Platonic dialogue would be justified in wondering whether there wasn't a simpler, less ambiguous, more direct way in which Plato might have written if he just wanted his readers to understand his "teachings" or his own "beliefs." If this author's aim had truly been to communicate a set of "doctrines" to his audience—especially if those doctrines were central beliefs that he held deeply or strongly, and he wished to disseminate them—another form of writing would seem to have been simpler, more straightforward, and much more prima facie successful than the open-ended dialogue form. Even if a first-time reader was diligent and faithful and worked through a dialogue carefully and critically, she might still feel at the end of the day that all of the fine grains of sand she had mined and collected were in danger of slowly slipping through her hands. Confidence in one's understanding, like Socrates' "shadowy wisdom," is here as ephemeral as a dream.

At this point the first-time reader will either give up or persevere, either returning to the "gateway" dialogue, tackling another one, or throwing up her hands. Going on to a second dialogue raises new problems, since it inevitably entails attempting to reconcile what is said in one dialogue with what is said in another. How should one resolve apparent discrepancies, or even seeming contradictions, between (or among) what is said in one dialogue and what is said in others, even by the same character? For example, Socrates argues in the *Gorgias* that pleasure is not the Good; in the *Protagoras*, he defends the view that pleasure is the Good; and in the *Philebus*, he argues that pleasure is part of the Good. Can these three positions be reconciled? Is Socrates tailoring his statements to different interlocutors? (After all, don't human beings speak differently to different people in real life?) Or might different contexts explain discrepancies in what a character says? Could it be the case that different conversations stress different aspects of the whole, and so different emphases are highlighted in different places? Or is Socrates simply trading on the equivocity in phrases such as "the Good" and "the pleasurable"? Or is it to accomplish different ends that a character such as Socrates will speak differently to different people? Or is it rather that Plato changes his mind from dialogue to dialogue (or at least—as the school of interpretation known as "developmentalism" would have it—from compositional period to compositional period: early, middle, and late)? Of course, these questions can only be pursued concretely once one has discovered a way to ascertain Plato's views in the first place. So we must make a new beginning.

Readers may ask: If Plato is not aiming to tell his audience his deepest beliefs or convictions, what other reasons for writing might he have had? Perhaps he just wanted to entertain people with his fictional dramas. Maybe he wanted to display the human condition in all of its tragic and all of its comic dimensions, as that delicious suggestion near the close of the *Symposium* gestures toward. Perhaps he wished to hold up a mirror to his fellow Athenians as they engaged in the search for scapegoats after their defeat in war, the overthrow of the city by the so-called Thirty Tyrants, and the trial and execution of Socrates. Perhaps he wanted to preserve a sense of what it was like to talk to Socrates, by means of a way of writing that sacrifices (or at least subordinates) his own voice in order to keep alive the voice of Socrates. Maybe he wanted to provide exercises, "likely stories" (*Timaeus* 29c–d), philosophical exemplars, and new topoi for human beings inclined toward philosophy. Or perhaps he wished to convert more people to the practice of philosophy than just those who could attend his school, extending his reach so that kindred philosophical spirits could be reached across time and space. Or perhaps he wanted to examine philosophical issues by placing them in question in a way that would allow their fullest complexity to be grasped without resolving anything, but instead trying out a series of hypotheses, or thought-experiments. It is soon apparent that the question, "Why write?" is a very different (and somehow more fundamental) one than the question: "Why write in this way?" "Why write dialogues?"

With a renewed sense of purpose, a new reader might now begin to think about the various ways in which the dialogues of Plato work, which might also entail coming to understand how Plato's writings differ from the other forms of writing from which we distinguished them earlier. One might begin to pay attention to the characters featured in a given dialogue and to the way Plato "sketches" them. Many of the characters' names are significant and suggestive, so this is another way in which Plato may choose to exhibit something important in a dialogue.[16] The dialogue's mise-en-scène would also be worthy of examination, as would any other clues supplied about the setting, dramatic date, and dramatic personae at the beginning of a dialogue. One need only recall the opening of the *Phaedo,* where Socrates shifts from a prone position to sitting upright with his feet on the ground, to see such dramatic effects. Add to this the Theseus imagery and the way the removal of Socrates' leg irons sparks the discussion of the contraries, pleasure and pain, and it should be clear to all readers that Plato took great care in crafting these little dramas. Many dialogues can be regarded as using a kind of prologue to prefigure the themes with which the ensuing conversation will be concerned.[17]

If there were some dramatic pretext for the discussion, this detail would be especially noteworthy. One might notice, for example, that the inquiry into the immortality of the soul in the *Phaedo* is motivated not only by the existential occasion, namely, that Socrates is about to die, but also by his empathetic concern for the general mood among his friends, which must first be addressed before Socrates will be able to engage them in philosophical conversation for the last time, on this solemn day. As the various interlocutors in a dialogue pursue some question or discussion point, Plato's audience must then note the position defended by each character, the kind of argument he presents, and the objections his interlocutors raise. In many dialogues, different interlocutors maintain different positions on a question, so it is rarely, if ever, the case that only one argument is presented in a given dialogue or that the "argument" of a particular dialogue is homological and seamless, though the conversation may have only one theme or topos. One might then be led to examine the relations between various characters (given each one's particular "psychology"), and the logical line Socrates (or another character) takes with each one respectively in argument.

Crucially worthy of consideration, in addition, is the way that various aporiai function in the dialogues to indicate an impasse in the discussion or to announce a positive accomplishment on the part of one of the characters: namely, that he has come to recognize his ignorance and has thereby become teachable. Astute readers might then notice that in some dialogues a reason for the apparent perplexity, inconclusiveness, or outright failure is supplied in the dialogue. In the *Euthyphro,* for example, Socrates seems to be criticizing Euthyphro for setting out to prosecute his father for impiety when Euthyphro clearly does not even know what piety and impiety are. One might also notice that the dialogue's aporia concerning the question of piety is not a complete aporia.

Socrates suggests (at 11e–12a) that piety is a part of justice, but he and Euthyphro are unable to determine the part of justice to which piety belongs because Euthyphro is in too big a hurry to get on with his prosecution, despite the fact that he still does not know what piety is. This shows that the dialogue's ending is probably not meant to suggest that there is no way in principle to know what piety and impiety are. Similarly, in the *Lysis,* Socrates explicates the reason for the inadequacy of the inquiry into friendship when he expresses the need to find older interlocutors with whom to carry on the discussion begun with the two pubescent boys (*Lysis* 223a). Such dialogues compel one to move from the level of the drama to the level of the impact of the drama on the audience. This two-level approach, as Holger Thesleff termed it, introduces another series of questions about how the dialogues work. Readers or auditors can learn from the mistakes of characters in conversation, or they may be able to see why a given conversation stalls or a particular line of argument runs into difficulty.

The more one studies Plato's dialogues, the more one has the gathering sense that Plato "knows" more than he reveals in his works. This leaves the impression that Plato is cryptic, sphinxlike, reticent, or (to borrow Diskin Clay's word) silent. All serious schools of Plato interpretation have to address this issue. Plato might have taken this approach because he wanted his readers to do a great deal of difficult work on their own (if they are truly to harbor any hope of understanding his conception of philosophy), or because he has no dogmatically held doctrines that he wants his readers to share, or because the most important things he knows—as the *Seventh Letter* suggests—are not things he will write down, at least not in simple, pithy phrases or maxims, even if he could, because the deepest insights are inexpressible in any simplistic or formulaic fashion. This may be the principal reason why Plato cultivates a pregnant silence in his dialogues, remaining immanent but ubiquitous and forsaking the authorial prerogative to appear and speak as a character, as Dante will later do.

It is not only that Plato chose the dialogue form in which to present his philosophy and his conception of the philosopher, but also that the kinds of dialogues he wrote do not lend themselves to straightforward exoteric readings. Plato chose to write open-ended, often aporetic, dialogues in which the various positions taken and the many arguments made are heterogeneous and always context-dependent; that is, the views expressed are always tied to particular people acting in particular situations. So one must justify or legitimate any attempt to detach these views from their native context and render them absolute or abstract.[18]

So why did Plato write dialogues? The simple answer may well be that Socratic conversations (*sokratikoi logoi*) were already quite popular as a genre when Plato decided to compose some sort of philosophical works. No doubt, in his Academy, many other kinds of writing were used: handbooks on rhetoric, and some standard problems and exercises (something like the *Dissoi Logoi*) that one could work through to perfect debating skills, develop logical acumen, and practice dialectic (here understood as arguing the two sides of a thesis) or *antilogia*.[19] We know that mathematics was also an integral component of the curriculum in Plato's school. Yet Plato did not choose to write a geometry textbook, or a logic workbook, or a catalogue of rhetorical examples or analyses of oratorical styles, any more than he dedicated himself to composing treatises on various topics. Instead he decided to try his hand at *sokratikoi logoi*, though he was neither the first nor the last to do so.[20] But why did he choose to write the *kinds* of dialogues he wrote?

The availability of a genre is not a sufficient explanation for an author's decision to write in the first place. So although the "Socratic dialogue" was already fashionable among the first generation of Socrates' followers, Plato must also have wanted to communicate something in some way. But in what way do dramatic works "communicate"? They certainly do not communicate in the same way as the writings of most modern philosophers communicate, employing the argumentative or expository essay to defend a thesis. It is not at all clear that a dramatist must defend a thesis or take a position on some issue or other. Yet to acknowledge that Plato did not invent either the genre in which the bulk of his work is presented nor the character of Socrates, who appears in most of these works, is not to suggest that Plato may not at the same time be the master of the craft. Indeed, Nehamas suggests that this is part of Plato's seduction, in that readers regard his Socrates as the real Socrates, and this allure is compounded for philosophers who see themselves as more like Socrates than the interlocutors, when we are in fact positioned as victims of Socrates' impenetrability, just as much as Socrates' interlocutors are. Worse, as Jay Farness has noted, whereas one might assume that Plato's dialogues function to provoke one to reexperience the sting of the gadfly philosopher, as Friedländer suggested, many readers are, in fact, comforted into complacency by the notion that Socrates doesn't really die insofar as his life has been transferred onto the stage of world history by the Socratic authors.[21]

When judging Plato's dialogues against the other two extant examples of the genre, however, Plato's dialogues are clearly superior philosophically. Aristophanes' comic lampoon of the philosopher, albeit a lampoon that rightly makes claims to its own kind of truth from the perspective of the non-philosopher, bears little resemblance to a

Platonic dialogue and does not really purport to be philosophically sophisticated (despite the fact that it sometimes is). And although we can
learn much from Xenophon's Socratic conversations, for we see a more
Cynic-like Socrates in these writings than most readers find in Plato's
dialogues, Xenophon's dialogues have neither the literary and dramatic brilliance nor the philosophical genius of Plato's dialogues. What
is more, Xenophon regularly offers his own judgments about Socrates
in his dialogues, something Plato never does in his own voice; and
Xenophon places himself within Socrates' inner circle, which Plato does
only nominally in the "trial and death" dialogues, *Apology of Socrates* and
Phaedo. Plato does not tell his audience where his own views are to be
found, which characters articulate positions that he would agree with,
and what his audiences are supposed to take away from his philosophical dramas. Pierre Hadot puts the point this way:

> Plato in his own individuality never appears in [the dialogues]. The
> author doesn't even intervene to say that it was he who composed the
> dialogues, and he does not include himself in the discussions, which
> take place between the interlocutors. On the other hand, neither does
> he specify what, in the remarks that are recorded, belongs to Socrates
> and what belongs to him.[22] Plato, unlike Xenophon, remains recondite
> within these dialogues.

The present anthology aims to reinvigorate scholarly examination
of the way Plato's dialogues "work" and to prompt a reconsideration of
how the form of Plato's philosophical writing bears on the Platonic conception of philosophy. Is the dialogue form, in all its literary and dramatic richness, integral to Plato's conception of philosophy, or is the
form in which he dramatizes philosophical discussions merely an accidental feature of his conception of philosophy?[23] The question, "Why
did Plato write dialogues rather than choosing some other kind of philosophical approach?" raises fundamental questions for interpreters. For
interpretive schools that ignore the characteristic form of Plato's writing, its form or style poses no problem, because the arguments are their
primary, if not exclusive, concern.

The essays gathered here each examine vital aspects of Plato's
method. "Method" here has at least three senses: (1) the myriad devices through which Plato presents his philosophy; (2) the tools and
practices employed by philosophical characters in Plato's writings; and
(3) the interpretive methods Plato would have his audiences employ as
auditors or readers of his works or as practitioners of the fledgling vo-
cation he called "philosophy." Let us be clear from the outset that the

word "method" must not be construed in a modern, "proto-scientific" sense, where "method" refers to "objective" and uniform procedures for testing hypotheses or theories. Instead, "method" must be understood here in its original Greek sense of *methodos*, a mode of expression that foregrounds the connotation of being on a road or pathway. When this original meaning of *methodos* becomes "scientific method," it ceases to be applicable to Plato without violence or anachronism.

A similar and related problem concerns the meaning of the term "philosophy" (*philosophia*). Pierre Hadot and Monique Dixsaut have shown that this word arises only in the fifth century B.C.E., probably first in Herodotus, but that the noun *philosophia* is distinctively defined by Plato, in whose hands it means "the love of wisdom" (as opposed to the possession of such wisdom). Hadot also shows that the term *philosophia* was broad enough to cover both the connotation of "wisdom" and the connotation of "knowledge," more specifically "know-how" of one type or another. Modern readers must remain mindful of the fact that Plato's conception of philosophy would not have resembled our own academic, "professional sense" of the term. It seems rather more likely that Plato believed that philosophy consisted of a set of discourses and a set of practices that aimed primarily at transforming one's entire way of life. Hadot thinks that for Plato the most important thing was choosing a philosophical way of life, or as Luc Brisson puts it, "learning to live philosophically."[24] To paraphrase Viktor Goldschmidt's hyperbolic pronouncement that Plato's dialogues aim to "form rather than to inform," I would say that they aim to form one as a person every bit as much as they aim to inform one about the author's approach to philosophy.[25] This way of formulating the point preserves the equilibrium of content and form, theory and practice, information and transformation.

Whereas a "school" today is determined by one's intellectual affiliation to some doctrine or approach to a set of problems, in antiquity, by contrast, philosophy was first and foremost a way of life constructed around the pleasure and interest one took in wisdom, and no fewer than six distinct "schools"—each with its own emphases, its own spiritual exercises, and its own model of self-transformation—have been identified and characterized by Hadot.[26] This reminder is necessary because I suspect that many modern readers as well as commentators assume that Plato's objectives in composing his philosophical works would have been the same as those of a modern philosopher who writes an argumentative essay to convince readers that his or her view is right and true. (Who knows, after all, what Plato imagined himself to be doing, or how he might have understood the process of composing and "publishing"?) But we may be able to determine his conception of philosophy from the way he crafts his dialogues. It is well also to keep in mind that Plato's "texts" were crafted, one might say, between orality and literacy, and that they are set in the previous generation, in the fifth century, when only 5 to 10 percent of the population could read and the rest would still have been quite mistrustful of letters. So the dialogues are "between" orality and literacy in at least two ways: (1) they are set at a time when the oral culture still flourished; and (2) they are between oral and literate traditions because they are written works in which characters recite, compose, and rehearse aloud, but also discuss problems associated with the written word (most notably at *Phaedrus* 274c ff.). Plato's (written) dialogues depict characters reciting long passages from memory, rehearsing old myths and stories, or composing or memorizing long speeches. The facile textbook treatments of Plato's dialogues make a reconsideration of Plato's many devices all the more urgent. The richness, open-endedness, and literary brilliance of the dialogues are too often lost in the reduction of these finely textured dramas to the set of arguments and "doctrines" that are expressed in them by one character or another. Even the obvious fact that Plato chose to write dramatic dialogues in the tradition of *sokratikoi logoi,* rather than compose treatises or straightforward essays, has often been lost on readers and commentators alike. Such interpreters proceed as though the many disclaimers, apparent contradictions, Plato's anonymity, or a dialogue's inconclusiveness pose no problem for understanding or interpreting the author's "doctrines." So although it has been often noted, it bears repeating that Plato not only wrote dramatic philosophical conversations, but if they champion anything, it is the primacy of dialogue in the care of the self, because dialogue is a fundamental human activity that forms and shapes one's character and thought.[27] This is perhaps Plato's way of assigning pride of place to the process over the product. Dialogue is itself a kind of spiritual exercise (an *askēsis* or *technē tou biou*) that, at one and the same time, is focused on the questions concerning how best to live, while exercising one's character and thereby improving it.

Because philosophy, in Plato's time, was still very much a way of life and therefore an inherently ethical activity, self-transformation needed to be supported by a set of practices that functioned as "spiritual exercise." Paul Rabbow has shown that various forms of such exercise were practiced in Plato's Academy.[28] And the dialogues depict some of these practices, perhaps most prominently the role of dialogue itself in forming and shaping human beings.

Yet the care of the self in Plato's time was certainly not divorced from the philosophical content or subject matter of thought either, so it would be a mistake to conclude that the philosophical content did not matter. It is simply that philosophy today has moved so far away from practice that it is necessary to remind modern readers that spiritual exercises were very much a part of the way of life called "philosophy" in antiquity. In Plato's dialogues, particularly, ethics and metaphysics seem to interpenetrate on ever-higher levels of understanding and expression. Work on one's behaviors and practices was an integral part of the practice of philosophy, as I suspect Plato understood it. This is why the philosophers Plato features in his dramas are chiefly concerned with what they regard as fundamental human concerns. Central among these concerns were the questions: "What is the best way to live?" and "What is the Good?" Not surprisingly, then, Plato's philosophical exemplars are often concerned in his dialogues with practical, existential questions rather than solely speculative ones. Or to put it another way, we might better say that the speculative inquiries are motivated by, and brought to bear upon, pressing fundamental human concerns.

Whereas Plato in his dialogues seems to have been thoroughly engaged in wresting a distinctive meaning for *philosophia* by carving out its signification from, and contrasting it with, rival paths to wisdom, contemporary philosophy has become increasingly narrow and more specialized. It consists primarily in the study of texts. Far from being a way of life, contemporary philosophy has become primarily academic philosophy, a training of specialists by specialists. Most philosophers today are employed by a college or university, are required to teach and to publish, and, as a result, both the ancient tradition of philosophy as a way of life and that tradition's guiding questions have given way to the study of myriad philosophies and the texts that express them.

It would hardly be surprising, then, if our modern understanding of philosophy colored the way Plato is now read and interpreted. It should also not be surprising if contemporary philosophy, no longer connected to any way of life except "the way of life of a university professor," as Hadot puts it, has become a highly technical and overly abstract endeavor. Through the centuries since Plato lived and wrote, philosophy has differentiated itself from history, from literature (including mythology, drama, and poetry), from rhetoric, theology, political science, the natural sciences, and psychology.

It is to the dramatic, literary, interdisciplinary Plato described above that the textbooks could hardly do justice. Hence it is this Plato that is reexamined in this collection of original essays. Several of the essays included here suggest new models for thinking about what Plato is doing in his dialogues and for adumbrating his conception of philosophy itself. Others focus on Plato's use of Socrates as a character in his dramas. The overwhelming majority of Plato's dialogues feature

Socrates as the philosophical exemplar, perhaps also advanced as the paradigmatic philosopher, or the philosopher par excellence. Still other essays in this collection reread and reconsider Plato's use of Homer; his notion of dialectic; the employment of medical imagery; the figure of the midwife; the "pairing" of speeches, characters, or dialogues; the role of laughter, divine madness, and play; and many other devices that enrich the meaning of *methodos*. We believe that the result is an engaging, provocative, and highly readable volume on some of the most important issues in Plato interpretation today.

The first chapter in the collection, "Plato's Book of Images," is devoted to what is arguably Plato's greatest work, the *Republic*. In this chapter, Nicholas Smith endeavors to reconcile the powerful critique of images and imitation (mimesis) that Socrates levies in book 10 of the *Republic* with the poignant and beautiful images that Plato himself provides in the same dialogue. From the image of the ship of state to the three central images that Plato has Socrates use to flesh out what Socrates refers to as the "offspring" of the Good (the sun/good analogy, the Divided Line, and the simile of the Cave), Smith argues that Plato's work is intended neither as humor nor as a straightforward blueprint for political reform, but as an educational work whose educational methodology is best understood in the light of the discussion of mathematical methodology that we find in the work itself. In brief, the essay argues that the *Republic* presents the reader with a series of images that are not at all intended in the imitative way Plato has Socrates disparage in book 10, but are rather to be used *as images* that provoke thought. "Plato's Book of Images" concludes by distinguishing this more philosophical use of images from the kind of images that comes in for criticism in the *Republic* itself.

In chapter 2, "'To Say What Is Most Necessary': Expositional and Philosophical Practice in Thucydides and Plato," Phil Hopkins argues that the intransigent, even careworn questions often asked about the range of rhetorical and discursive practices depicted in Plato's dialogues almost perfectly mirror the questions that historians and classicists ask about the role of the speeches in Thucydides' *History*. This fact suggests that a comparative reading of these two authors may have a great deal to teach us about both of them. The essay argues that both Plato and Thucydides exploit "expositional strategies" that are intended to "draw readers into a process of carefully balancing opposing accounts, which makes of the reader a peculiar kind of witness." These practices and their goals, Hopkins argues, exhibit interesting epistemological and ethical commitments.

Plato's dialogues contain many references to Greek medical practice and medical tradition. Some scholars have even supposed that Plato portrayed Socrates in many of the dialogues as extending and reinterpreting Greek medicine in such a way as to create a kind of practical philosophy rooted in questions about the nature of human life and human health. On this supposition, Socrates aims to engender or facilitate in his interlocutors a virtue comparable to health, and to free them from vices comparable to illnesses, while his conversational practice is comparable to the interaction of an astute physician with his ailing client. In "Medicine, Philosophy, and Socrates' Proposals to Glaucon About Γυμναστική in *Republic* 403c–412b," Mark Moes attempts to show the initial plausibility of this supposition and then to test it by putting it to work in reading an intriguing passage from the *Republic*. The first section of chapter 3 briefly brings into focus some medical themes in three passages from the dialogues. These are Socrates' discussion of dialectical rhetoric in the *Phaedrus*, Socrates' discussion of *gumnastikē* and *iatrikē* in the *Gorgias*, and Phaedo's account of the way in which Socrates behaved and spoke toward him and Simmias and Cebes when he warned them against *misologia* in the *Phaedo*. The second section draws out some of the implications of the supposition. The third offers a reading of *Republic* 403c–412b, where Socrates makes a series of proposals to Glaucon concerning *gumnastikē* in the polis. The essay argues that Socrates intends these proposals to provide Glaucon with opportunities for what Moes calls "diagnostic self-recognition." The essay's cogent interpretation provides confirmation for the supposition. The fourth and final section briefly discusses parallels between Plato and Thucydides in a way that dovetails nicely with the essay in chapter 2, and assesses the plausibility of a medical model of Platonic philosophizing, corresponding to the model of Socratic philosophizing discussed in the earlier sections.

Plato had an important older contemporary who made influential use of medical ideas. It may be conjectured with some plausibility (but not argued in a clinching way) that Plato concerns himself in at least some dialogues with issues raised by Thucydides, who adapted the principles and methods of Hippocratic medicine to the interpretation of the economic and political history of Athens. The Hippocratics had divided the work of the physician into three parts: semeiology, prognosis, and therapeutics, seeking general formulations that would enable doctors to read symptoms in such a way as to arrive at true classifications and prognoses of diseases. Thucydides held that the knowledge of the nature of political crises is like the knowledge of the nature of diseases, and endeavored to make history into a semeiology and prognosis of human life, enabling men of future ages to recognize recurrent ethico-political maladies by their symptoms. He treated political ways of life, such as Spartan authoritarianism and Athenian liberalism, under the medical rubric of regimens, and left to the political philosopher the task of constructing, on the basis of prognoses, more adequate systems of social therapeutics. He composed the speeches for his *History* as part of an attempt to do semeiology and prognosis on the political practices of his day. He wanted to determine such classifications or formulations (*ta eidē*) as would raise history from mere chronicle to something more "scientific," as many doctors wanted to transform medicine from a mere empirical knack into a *technē*.

In chapter 4, "Know Thyself: Socrates as Storyteller," Anne-Marie Bowery examines Socrates' role as a narrator in the five Platonic dialogues he narrates: *Charmides, Euthydemus, Protagoras, Lysis,* and *Republic.* Bowery argues that a complete portrait of Socrates must include his role as a narrator in these five dialogues. In focusing on Socrates' narrative commentary, Plato's portrayal of Socrates is cast in a new light. For example, Socrates is often taken to be the paradigm of the rational philosopher, the philosopher who chastises Apollodorus and his other friends for weeping and lamenting like women on the day Socrates will die (*Phaedo* 117d). Martha Nussbaum typifies this view. Simply put, she and many other scholars overemphasize the aspects of his philosophical search, which involves rational certainty and discounts his interest in emotional and spiritual experience. The essay makes clear how careful attention to the philosopher's narrative commentary reveals that Socrates is acutely aware of his psychological state and is quite swayed by his emotions in many instances (*Charmides* 154b, *Republic* 336d, *Euthydemus* 283d–e). When viewed through the lens of his narrative commentaries, Socrates emerges as a model of how a philosopher should employ all the dimensions of the human psyche—the emotional, the physical, the spiritual, and the rational—in the service of philosophy. By attending to the ways in which Plato presents Socrates as a narrator in the dialogues, we come to see Socratic self-examination as an ongoing interplay of ethos, pathos, and *logos*.

Chapter 5 might be subtitled "Plato's Use and Abuse of the Poets" because the essay focuses on Plato's use of Homer, a "use" that sometimes quotes Homer accurately and sometimes not. In "Homeric Μέθοδος in Plato's Socratic Dialogues," Bernard Freydberg argues that this device constitutes a kind of method for Plato, if we understand the term "method" correctly as "pursuit of knowledge" or "following after knowledge." In this study he argues that Plato uses Homer as he does to inspire in his audiences the recognition of philosophical truth. Through careful analysis and comparison of a number of interesting cases, the essay shows that Plato employs a kind of method in his quotations and misquotations of Homer.

The image of Socrates as a midwife presented in the *Theaetetus* is one of the most striking and famous in the Platonic corpus. This philosopher claims to be able to do no more than help others give birth to their own ideas. But Benjamin Grazzini shows how Plato uses the image of Socrates as a psychic *maieute* (midwife) to set up a series of questions about how it is possible to account for knowledge in the face of conflicting appearances. On the one hand, on its own terms, Socrates' account of psychic maieutics assumes that he is the "measure" of the soul and its conceptions. The ensuing conversation, however, appears to deny the possibility of attaining measured knowledge at all. "Of Psychic Maieutics and Dialogical Bondage in Plato's *Theaetetus*" goes on to argue that the account of psychic maieutics sets up the more explicitly epistemological problems with which the *Theaetetus* is concerned. On the other hand, insofar as Socrates is so easily recognized in the image of the psychic *maieute*, the essay claims that Plato uses the caricature to show how easy it was for the Athenians to recognize Socrates in the charges brought against him, and that it would have been extremely difficult for Socrates to define himself or his practice of philosophy in such a way as to distinguish himself from that public image. Grazzini concludes that the account of psychic maieutics also bears on the more explicitly political problems surrounding Socrates' trial and death.

In the *Philebus*, Plato's Socrates says he will need "a different device, different armament," while also noting that some of the previous methods will still serve (23b–c). As Martha Woodruff argues in chapter 7, the "different device" (*alles mechanes*) of the fourfold division of all that is (the limited, the non-limited, the mixture, and the cause) revives and reinterprets the other methodological contribution of the *Philebus*, the "heavenly gift" of division and classification, thus uniting two crucial parts of the dialogue. By enacting a mode of differentiating, revising, and reconciling apparent opposites, the *Philebus* practices what it preaches, exemplifying the Doric harmony of *logos* and *ergon*. Put otherwise, we might say that the *Philebus* "shows us something" at the same time as it "tells us something." The "one/many" problem plays itself out in the language we use: the identification of the one and the many proves to be "'an immortal and ageless' condition that comes to us with discourse" (15d–e). By both distinguishing and connecting terms, the essay shows how the language of the *Philebus* allows for a differentiated oneness, a unity that includes plurality. The more the dialogue makes things many—distinctions, classifications, repetitions—the more in the end it makes things one. Woodruff concludes that just as the best life belongs to the mixed category of thought with pleasure, pleasure in thought, the method of the *Philebus* itself belongs to the mixed category of reconciliation. The initial stark oppositions between hedonism and intellectualism, the non-limited and the limited, must be tested and refined by the method of classification and reconciliation. Furthermore, the essay contrasts the method of the *Philebus* with that of the *Parmenides,* in which the dramatically different language of addressing the one and the many leads to (apparently) insurmountable paradoxes.

In chapter 8, entitled "Is There Method in This Madness?" Christopher Long argues that for modern philosophy, method is designed to set forth objective rules of procedure so as to establish philosophy as a rigorous science. For Plato, however, method cannot be divorced from the contingent contexts in which philosophy is always practiced. While modern method permits no madness, there is madness in Plato's method. Long traces three strategies that constitute the method of madness that operates in the *Symposium* and *Republic*. The first is a distancing strategy in which Plato systematically distances himself from the content of the ideas expressed in the dialogues in order to provoke the sort of critical self-reflection required for philosophy. The second is a grounding strategy whereby Plato embeds philosophical debate in determinate social and political contexts so as to anchor philosophy in the concrete world of human community. The third is a demonstrative strategy in which Plato models philosophy as an activity intent on weaving a vision of the good, the beautiful, and the just into the contingent world of human politics. Together these three strategies function methodologically to show the powerful conception of philosophy embodied in the dialogues.

In chapter 9, "Traveling with Socrates: Dialectic in the *Phaedo* and *Protagoras,*" Gerard Kuperus explores Plato's method by following out two different metaphors: navigation and the labyrinth. In the *Protagoras,* the interlocutors use the metaphor of sailing or navigation in their discussion about which method to use. Kuperus analyzes this metaphor by examining some other appearances of navigation and sailing in the Socratic dialogues. He argues that with the image of navigation, Plato depicts the dialectician as a philosophical navigator who is in search of the right course in the dialogue. Similarly, in the *Phaedo,* the labyrinth is (implicitly) used as a metaphor for the way in which the dialectician must follow the thread of the argument, and so the dialogues can be understood as labyrinths of argument, of possible ways and non-ways.

The author concludes by showing that Socrates is a curious Theseus who often changes ways into non-ways, and non-ways into ways.

Plato's vivid use of images—whether through myth, metaphor, simile, or allegory—has traditionally been thought to belie a contempt for images and vision which is typically imputed to him. Contrary to a traditional view that for Plato, philosophy comprises pure reason which transcends the realm of human sense perception and denigrates vision and image, Jill Gordon returns in the concluding chapter of the volume to the theme with which the collection began. Arguing in chapter 10, "In Plato's Image," that philosophy is a distinctly human enterprise that works with and through images, Gordon examines several dialogues, including those that seem to contain critiques of vision and image, in order to demonstrate that images are consistently shown to be a part of philosophical discourse and vision a part of philosophical activity, and that human limitation necessitates this. Plato's method, his masterful use of images and appeals to vision, is therefore a necessary constituent of philosophy and serves protreptically to cast his audience's vision toward the Forms and toward the philosophical life.

Notes

1. For a historical analysis of the distinction between philosophy and literature, see Louis Mackey, "The Philosophy of Genre and the Genre of Philosophy," in *An Ancient Quarrel Continued* (Lanham: University Press of America, 2000); and Jill Gordon, *Turning Toward Philosophy* (University Park: Pennsylvania State University Press, 1999).

2. One need only consider the way in which Homer's *Odyssey* is reprised and refashioned by later authors, from Virgil's *Aeneid* to Dante's *Inferno,* Milton's *Paradise Lost,* and Joyce's *Ulysses.*

3. For the most sensible recent discussion of Platonic method, see Ruby Blondell, *The Play of Character in Plato's Dialogues* (Cambridge: Cambridge University Press, 2002), 1–52. For the claim that Plato "invents" philosophy, see Andrea Nightingale, *Genres in Dialogue: Plato and the Construct of Philosophy* (Cambridge: Cambridge University Press, 1996), 14; see also 67, 73, 133. See also Alexander Nehamas, "Eristic, Antilogic, Sophistic, Dialectic: Plato's Demarcation of Philosophy from Sophistry," *History of Philosophy Quarterly* 7 (1990): 3–16; and Gerald A. Press, "Plato's Dialogues as Enactments," in *The Third Way: New Directions in Platonic Studies,* ed. Francisco J. Gonzalez (Lanham: Rowman and Littlefield, 1995), 133–52.

4. The list of topics broached includes several key places where Socrates reflects on his or another's method. For an argument against Vlastos' claim that Socrates is an ethical philosopher pure and simple who is concerned only with moral matters, see Michelle Carpenter and Ronald M. Polansky, "Variety of

Socratic Elenchi," in *Does Socrates Have a Method? Rethinking the Elenchus in Plato's Dialogues and Beyond,* ed. Gary Alan Scott (University Park: Pennsylvania State University Press, 2002), 89–100.

5. For what is known about the characters in Plato's dialogues, see Debra Nails, *The People of Plato: A Prosography of Plato and Other Socratics* (Indianapolis: Hackett, 2002).

6. See the appendix for a chronology of the dramatic dates of Plato's dialogues.

7. John J. Mulhern showed in a 1971 paper that such an argument is required, but one still finds this sloppy turn of phrase in many works on Plato. See John J. Mulhern, "Two Interpretive Fallacies," *Systematics* 9 (1971): 168–72. Lacking an argument which proves that a particular character is presenting Plato's view, commentators could argue from the premise that Phaedrus or Pausanias in the *Symposium,* for example, are presenting Plato's views of eros. This is just what Elizabeth V. Spelman does in her essay "Woman as Body," which appears in the popular textbook *Twenty Questions,* 4th ed., edited by Lee Bowie, Emily Michaels, and Robert Solomon (New York: Harcourt, 2000), 209–14.

8. See chapter 3 in the present volume for illustrative examples.

9. Alexander Nehamas, *The Art of Living: Socratic Reflections from Plato to Foucault* (Berkeley: University of California Press, 1998), 26. This is the theme of the chapter "Socratic Irony: Character and Interlocutors."

10. Nehamas, *Art of Living,* 48. We should recall in this connection Kierkegaard's infamous suggestion that Socratic irony "can deceive a person *into the truth.*" Quoted by Nehamas, *Art of Living,* 52 without reference/citation.

11. For an analysis of the merits of the arguments of Socrates' interlocutors, see John Beversluis, *Cross-Examining Socrates: A Defense of Socrates' Interlocutors in Plato's Early Dialogues* (Cambridge: Cambridge University Press, 1999).

12. The *Symposium* depicts a Socrates who stays out all night drinking and talking with his friends before going back to his usual haunts in the city for a day of discussion. The *Crito* raises the issue of Socrates' duty to his family and friends, but Socrates of course remains true to his principles. In the *Phaedo,* we see Socrates asking Crito to have some of his men take Xanthippe and their baby home, leaving Socrates to talk with his friends in his final hours. And in the *Apology,* Socrates mentions his wife and three sons only to make the point that he is not going to go for the sympathy vote.

13. See, for example, *Statesman* 277d; *Timaeus* 29b–d; *Laws* 641d, 732a–b, 799c–e, and 859c; and the aporetic ending of the *Parmenides.*

14. Don Adams and Mark McPherran have both made this point. See Don Adams, "*Elenchos* and Evidence," *Ancient Philosophy* 18, no. 2 (Fall 1998): 287–307. Mark McPherran has developed this as the method of induction. See his "Elenctic Interpretation and the Delphic Oracle" in Scott, ed., *Does Socrates Have a Method?* 114–44.

15. The sole exception to this statement is Socrates' claim in the *Symposium* that the one thing he understands is the art of love (*ta erotika*). But insofar as eros, in Socrates' view, is a desire for what we lack, his knowledge of eros comes

down to the very same knowledge entailed in Socratic ignorance, namely, that he knows what he doesn't know.

16. This list could include Cephalus, Polemarchus, Lysis, Agathon, Meno, Meletus, and many more. Perhaps most prominently, Socrates uses the play on Meletus' name (which means "blockhead" and is cognate with the word for "care" or "concern") as the fulcrum for his counteroffensive against his accuser's carelessness respecting the charges, the truth, and the youth whom he accuses Socrates of corrupting.

17. For an excellent example of Plato's use of the prologue, see Francisco J. Gonzalez, "How to Read a Platonic Prologue: *Lysis* 203a–207d," in *Plato as Author: The Rhetoric of Philosophy*, ed. Ann N. Michelini (Cincinnati: E. J. Brill, 2002), 15–44.

18. In this connection, see, for example, Holger Thesleff, "Looking for Clues: An Interpretation of Some Literary Aspects of Plato's 'Two-Level' Model," in *Plato's Dialogues: New Studies and Interpretations*, ed. Gerald A. Press (Lanham: Rowman and Littlefield, 1993).

19. See Thomas M. Robinson, "The *Dissoi Logoi* and Early Greek Skepticism," in *Essays in Ancient Greek Philosophy VI: Before Plato*, ed. Anthony Preus (Albany: State University of New York Press, 2001), 159. Robinson suggests that the possibility exists that the *Dissoi Logoi* or one of many similar manuals of sophistical refutation in circulation at the time were read by Socrates and Plato.

20. Charles Kahn details what we know of eight authors of *sokratikoi logoi* in his *Plato and the Socratic Dialogue: The Philosophical Use of a Literary Form* (Cambridge: Cambridge University Press, 1996). Kahn examines what is known about Antisthines, Phaedo, Eucleides, Aristippus, Aeschines, and Xenophon, in addition to Plato.

21. See especially the last few pages of chapter 2, "Missing Socrates," in Jay Farness, *Missing Socrates: Problems of Plato's Writing* (University Park: Pennsylvania State University Press, 1991).

22. Pierre Hadot, *What Is Ancient Philosophy?* trans. Michael Chase (Cambridge: Belknap Press of Harvard University, 2002), 24.

23. Diskin Clay reminds us that the second edition (1970) of the *Oxford Classical Dictionary* contains an entry on "Plato" authored by two different Oxford philosophers, one of whom (J. D. Denniston) writes one numbered section on Plato's "style," while the other (Richard Robinson) writes fifteen numbered sections on Plato's arguments. In the third edition (1996) of the *Oxford Classical Dictionary*, however, the article on "Plato" makes no mention of his style or form, and it is telling that this article was written by Julia Annas, the past president of the Pacific Division of the American Philosophical Association. Thus is the state of the question today. See Diskin Clay, *Platonic Questions: Dialogues with the Silent Philosopher* (University Park: Pennsylvania State University Press, 2000), xi.

24. Cited in Hadot, *What Is Ancient Philosophy?* 65. This seems overstated or oversimplified. It is not that one must choose either to form oneself or else to learn the teachings of the school, but rather that the teachings of the various schools underwrite the school's practices or spiritual exercises.

25. Hadot, *What Is Ancient Philosophy?*, 73, quoting Goldschmidt, *Les Dialogues de Platon* (Paris, 1947), 3.

26. See Hadot, *What Is Ancient Philosophy?* The six schools are Platonism, Aristotelianism, Cynicism, Pyrrhonism (Skepticism), Stoicism, and Epicureanism.

27. Hadot puts the matter this way:

> This ethics of the dialogue explains the freedom of thought which, as we have seen, reigned in the Academy. Speusippus, Xenocrates, Eudoxus, and Aristotle professed theories which were by no means in accord with those of Plato, especially on the subject of Ideas. They even disagreed about the definition of the good, since we know that Eudoxus thought the supreme good was pleasure. Such intense controversies among the members of the school left traces not only within Plato's dialogues and in Aristotle, but throughout Hellenistic philosophy, if not throughout the entire history of philosophy. In any event, we may conclude that the Academy was a place for free discussion, and that within it there was neither scholastic orthodoxy nor dogmatism. (Hadot, *What Is Ancient Philosophy?* 64–65)

If this is true, we may wonder what the school's unity could be based upon. I think we can say that although Plato and the other teachers at the Academy disagreed on points of doctrine, they nevertheless all accepted, to various degrees, the choice of the way or form of life which Plato had proposed. It seems that this choice of life consisted, first, in adhering to the ethics of dialogue of which we have just spoken. This was a "form of life" (to use J. Mittelstrass's expression) which was practiced by the interlocutors; for insofar as, in the act of dialoguing, they posited themselves as subjects but also transcended themselves, they experienced the *logos* which transcends them. Moreover, they also experienced that love of the good which is presupposed by every attempt at dialogue. From this perspective, the object of the discussion and its doctrinal content are of secondary importance. What counts is the practice of dialogue and the transformation which it brings. Sometimes the function of dialogue can even be to run into aporia, and thus to reveal the limits of language—its occasional inability to communicate moral and existential experience.

28. Paul Rabbow, *Paidagogia: Die Grundlegung der abendlandischen Erziehungeskunst in der Sokratik* (Göttingen Vandenhoeck and Ruprecht, 1960), 102.

PHILOSOPHY IN DIALOGUE

Plato's Book of Images

Nicholas D. Smith

> The things they mould and draw, which have shadows and im-
> ages of themselves in water, these they treat in turn as images,
> seeking those Forms which can be conceived only in thought.
> *Republic* 510e1–511a1

Plato's *Republic* is a book of images. Its most famous image, perhaps, is the image in which he has Socrates compare all human beings to prisoners in a cave. But the *Republic* is also the locus classicus of that most famous image of the ship of state, whose brave ruler is compared to the ship's captain (488a1–489c7; see also 389c4–d5). The book itself begins with a somewhat spooky image reminiscent of the heroic *katabasis* or descent.[1] And indeed, considerably more imagery of various kinds can be found throughout the *Republic*.[2]

There is, however, something at least a bit unnerving about all of this imagery. Plato's own most famous view of image-makers is notoriously negative:

> Neither will the imitator know, nor opine rightly concerning the nobil-
> ity or vulgarity of his imitations. . . . On this issue, then, as it seems,
> we clearly agree that the imitator knows nothing worth mentioning of
> what he imitates, and that imitation is not serious. (602a8–9, 602b6–8)

Does Plato's own condemnation of image-makers amount to a self-condemnation? In book 5, the reader is warned that those who trade in images rather than the realities they image may be likened to those who sleep and merely dream (476c2–8). Is it, then, that Plato intended his *Republic* simply to lull us to sleep and false dreams, like Descartes' *malin genie*?

It will not come as news to hear that the *Republic* has been read in many, sometimes radically, different ways. On the basis of worries such as those I have already expressed, some interpreters have argued that we should understand the *Republic* as a kind of self-deconstructing comedy,[3] whose arguments and specific prescriptions should not be understood as σπουδαῖος. This very radical understanding of the work, however, confounds the way the work has been read since antiquity—book 2 of Aristotle's *Politics* plainly suggests that if Plato had intended his *Republic* as a joke, his best student didn't "get it." Throughout most of the history of interpretation of this text, as far as we know of it,[4] the *Republic* has been understood as a serious work of political philosophy.[5]

In this essay, I suggest a somewhat different way of understanding Plato's greatest work. In the view I propose, Plato's work is intended neither as humor (though it is sometimes funny) nor as a straightforward blueprint for political reform, but as an educational work, whose educational methodology is best understood in the light of the discussion of mathematical methodology that we find in the work itself. In brief, the *Republic* presents the reader with a series of images that are not at all intended in the imitative way Plato disparages in book 10, but to be used *as images* that provoke thought (διάνοια), in much the same way as Plato describes the proper use of images in the quotation with which I began.[6]

The Uses and Abuses of Images

As I said in the introduction, Plato compares cognitive contact with images with dreaming, and for the most part the comparison is not at all intended to be favorable. But not all dreams are mere phantasms (see 599a2): in book 7, he has Socrates credit those engaged in mathematical studies with "dreaming about what is" (533b8–c1), for although their reliance on assumptions and images prevents them from achieving the "clear waking vision" of the Forms only dialecticians can achieve, their method does allow them to make some contact with the really real (533b6–7). In fact, we sometimes find that Plato prefers to compare this use of images not to being asleep and dreaming, but to the process of awakening from doxastic slumbers:

> This, then, is just what I was trying to explain just now, about things that are provocative of thought and those that are not, where provocative things are those that lead to perceptions that are at the same time

opposites, while those that do not do this do not tend to awaken the intellect [ἐγερτικὰ τῆς νοήσεως]. (524d2–5; see also 523e1)

Plato's gripe with the imitators is not simply that they make images, then, for the geometers also do this, and Plato regards the latter's uses of images as extremely important in the process of education. The problem with the imitators is that their images are *not* intellectually provocative; instead, Plato complains, they do nothing good themselves, for they neither know the Good nor even have correct belief, and thus do not create images that are conducive to truth:

> [The poets and other such] are imitators of images of virtue and of the other things they make and do not grasp the truth. . . . The creator of the phantom [εἰδώλον], the imitator, we say, knows nothing of what is, but only the appearance. (600e4–6, 601b9–10)

But why does the same argument not also apply to the geometers, who, we may suppose, because of the defects of their methods relative to that of the dialectician, also do not know what they imitate when they shape their images? More importantly, since Plato puts all of these words into the mouth of Socrates, who repeats his well-known disclaimer of knowledge in several places in the dialogue (see, for example, at 368b4–8, 506c203), why does the same criticism not also apply to Socrates himself?

It might be tempting to answer these questions by talking about the different motivations of the geometers and Socrates, on the one hand, and the poets or visual artists whose work Plato deplores. The former, it might be insisted, are at least seekers after truth, whereas the latter seek only to flatter and to gratify their audience. Plato certainly has Socrates make this claim ("his appeal is to the inferior part of the soul" [605a10–b1]), but it is not one of Plato's most impressive arguments. After all, as defenders of literature and the arts always insist when they read this critique, why must we suppose that one simply cannot create visual or literary art that aims at revealing (however imagistically) some semblance of the truth?

Happily, however, the motivational argument does not provide Plato's only grounds for distinguishing the imitators he deplores from the image-makers he praises—including especially the one whose image he creates as the main speaker in the *Republic* itself. But to see this more clearly, we must look more closely at the epistemic condition Plato assigns to the mathematicians.

NICHOLAS D. SMITH

Mathematicians and Knowledge

The problem we encountered in the last section was that Plato criticizes the imitators as engaging in image-making without knowledge. And yet it would appear that the same objection can be made against those whose creation of images Plato seems to endorse. In this section, however, I deny this comparison. The imitators, I claim, do what they do without knowledge, whereas the mathematicians (and Socrates) do what they do with knowledge. I recognize that in saying this, I appear to contradict the very passages in which Plato has Socrates compare the cognitive states of the mathematicians unfavorably with the dialecticians, on the one hand, and also those in which Socrates himself disclaims knowledge, on the other. So in order to secure my claim, I must explain how my reading actually does not violate the sense of these texts.

Given the way contemporary philosophers approach epistemology, it might seem as if the only question we must settle here is whether or not the mathematicians generate warranted true beliefs in regard to the subjects they pursue by their use of images, or perhaps alternatively, whether their use of images is conditioned upon or derives from such cognitive states. But just to put the question this way already creates a difficulty for the Plato scholar, for the epistemology of the *Republic*, especially as it is most carefully articulated in book 5, makes it plain that unlike contemporary epistemologists, Plato does not provide an analysis of knowledge as a species of belief. In contemporary epistemology, knowledge is generally treated as a species of belief, of course—as justified or warranted true belief. Justification or warrant, we are often told, is that additional feature of knowledge that is lacking in *other* sorts of true belief.[7] But in Plato's account, not only is knowledge not some special kind of belief, but in fact it is not any kind of belief at all, but is instead an entirely different cognitive power altogether. So if we are going to make much headway in discovering how Plato makes assessments of knowledge, we will need to leave our modern epistemological presuppositions "at the door," as it were.

Plato introduces his notion of cognitive powers by likening them to our sensory capacities, such as sight and hearing. Such powers, he says, are to be distinguished by what they are naturally related to as object, and by what they produce from their activity. Knowledge (ἐπιστήμη), Plato argues, is a distinct cognitive power from belief (or opinion—δόξα) because knowledge is naturally related to what is, whereas belief is naturally related to particular sensible things.

Plato's epistemic complaint about the imitators—and his qualified epistemic approval of the mathematicians—must be understood in the light of his conception of the cognitive powers. Notice how the dreamer is distinguished from the non-dreamer in book 5:

> One who recognizes beautiful things, but does not recognize The Beautiful Itself and cannot be led to the knowledge of it—do you believe he is living in a dreaming or a waking state? Consider: Isn't dreaming, whether asleep or awake, taking the likeness not as a likeness, but as the thing itself that it is like?
> I most certainly take such a one to be dreaming.
> Well, then; to take up the opposite of this: someone who recognizes The Beautiful Itself and is able to distinguish both it and the things that participate in it, and does not take the participants to be it, or take it to be the participants—is such a one living in a waking or a dreaming state?
> Very much, he said, a waking state. (476c2–d4)

The distinction Plato has Socrates make here is not made between those who recognize only images and those who recognize *only* their originals; rather, the difference between the believer and the knower is that the knower recognizes both sorts of entities, whereas the believer recognizes only images. It would obviously appear to follow that one who understands that images actually are only images of higher realities employs images in a way that engages the cognitive power of knowledge, rather than mere belief. Precisely because this use of images characterizes the mathematician, I count the distinction in book 5 between the dreamer and the non-dreamer as support for my earlier claim that the mathematicians use images with knowledge. Their cognitive disadvantage relative to the dialecticians must not, accordingly, be understood as the disadvantage of those who do not engage the power of knowledge relative to those who do.

The actual disadvantage between these two groups is explored and described in the famous Divided Line passage of book 6. The proper interpretation of this passage is anything but uncontroversial,[8] but happily my argument here does not have to make any significant effort to interpret this image in detail. Instead, the way in which Plato characterizes the relationship between the top two subsections of the line and the lower two is sufficient for my present purposes. After first dividing the line into two unequal segments, and then subdividing each segment in the same proportion as the segments of original division, Socrates then associates the lowest subsection with shadows and reflections, and the subsection above that one with the originals of these images. He then offers his first explanation of the significance of the image/original relation between these two subsections:

> Would you, then, be willing to say that in respect of truth and untruth, the division is in this proportion: As the believable is to the knowable, so the likeness is to what it is like? (510a8–10)

Now, the relationship between the believables and the knowables Plato makes in this passage, which is said to correspond to the relationship between the images and originals in the two lower subsections of the line, can only refer to the contents of the entire lower main segment (both of the two lowest subsections, that is), and those of the entire upper segment (both subsections), respectively. "Believables" (identified in book 5 with the sensibles) surely do not belong (under this description, at any rate) above the main division of the line, initially said to divide the intelligible from the sensible domains. Hence, the "believable/knowable" distinction cannot be a way to characterize the relationship between the lower and upper subsections of the upper segment of the line. Similarly, Plato should not here be understood as comparing one of the lower with one of the upper subsections of the line, for he has yet to explicate anything about either of the upper subsections. The "believable/knowable" distinction, accordingly, must be understood as a way to characterize the first proportion of the two main segments of the line, which the proportion between the two lowest subsections, which Socrates had just explained, is supposed to replicate.[9]

If I am right about what the "believable/knowable" distinction is supposed to show, however, it follows that even though the mathematicians are contrasted negatively with the dialecticians, they are included from the very beginning of the line simile in the section associated with the "knowables." So on this ground, too, it seems clear enough that Plato regards the mathematicians as employing the cognitive power of knowledge (the power naturally related to the "knowables"). There may be some cognitive deficiency in such studies, accordingly, but that deficiency is not to be characterized as a lack of—so much as a deficient employment of—knowledge.

What, then, is the deficiency of mathematical method relative to the dialectical method? Plato answers this question explicitly, and the explanation in no way denies the possession or use of the power of knowledge to the mathematicians. Instead, their deficiency, relative to the dialecticians, is just that they continue to rely on the use of images, of which the dialecticians have no further need, and they also continue to rely on hypothesized entities for which they can offer no overarching explanation, whereas the dialecticians can explain all of their earlier hypotheses in the light of the "unhypothesized starting point of all," which is generally understood as the Good.

Socrates as Image-Maker

If my argument thus far is correct, there is a use of images that employs the cognitive power of knowledge: the use in which images are created and employed that recognizes them as mere images, and where their proper use is designed to allow the thinker who uses them to gain a better grasp of the originals they image. It is this use, then, that Plato has Socrates associate with the mathematicians.

But what about the many images that Plato has Socrates evoke? Are Socrates' images introduced as images of higher things . . . and are they employed in such a way as to expedite achieving a better grasp of those higher things? I doubt that it requires much argument to establish an affirmative answer to this question. I assume it will be more than adequate simply to remind ourselves of the way that Socrates goes about answering the challenges with which he is confronted in book 2. Insisting that the discussion of book 1 was a "glutton's feast" (see 354b1–2) because the discussants had not troubled to obtain a clear understanding of justice before taking on the subsidiary question of its preferability to injustice, Socrates elects in book 2 to postpone the actual defense of justice until a suitable understanding of justice can be obtained (see 369a5–b1). And the way in which Socrates proposes to approach the prior question, in this case, is by way of the image of large and small letters. And this image turns out to be an image of a relationship between image and original: the larger letters are used as an image of the smaller; so too the state will be used, in the discussants' search for a workable understanding of justice, as an image of the individual person (see 369a2–3). And a given individual's instantiation of justice, we find out soon after this, is itself but an image of the Form (445c5–6, 479e3). So the construction of the main argument of the *Republic* (and plainly, the most famous images of lights in the middle books) give clear instances of a use of images that has the same general feature that characterizes the use of images within the mathematical studies: these images were explicitly identified as images, and were used in order to gain a better grasp of higher things. This use of images, recall, employs the cognitive power of knowledge,[10] even though it does not yield the same degree of clarity as one capable of dialectic could achieve. Plato's Socrates is not doing mathematics, of course; but he is using images in a way that engages knowledge.

But why, then, does Socrates disclaim knowledge, if I am right in claiming that the way in which he constructs his arguments employs it? The answer to this question, I contend, may be found in the same distinction that we find Socrates making in regard to the mathematicians, who employ the cognitive power of knowledge, but whose method fails to realize the most significant effects of that power, because of its reliance on images and on unexplained hypotheses. Let us see exactly how Socrates characterizes his own epistemic condition. At 506b2, Glaucon and Socrates have reached an agreement that the rulers of the city they are imagining must know the Good. Now Glaucon presses Socrates to give his own view of what the Good is, but Socrates demurs:

> "What then," I said, "do you think it is just to speak as having knowledge about things one does not know?"
>
> "Not at all," he said, "as having knowledge, but one should be willing to speak as his conception what he conceives."
>
> "What? Haven't you observed that beliefs without knowledge are all ugly? The best of these are blind; or do you believe that those who have some true belief without intelligence are much different from blind people who go the right way?"
>
> "Not at all."
>
> "Do you wish, then, to witness ugly, blind, and crooked things, when you might hear from others what is luminous and fine?" (506c2–d1)

But of course, Socrates is here presenting Glaucon with a false alternative, and the young man seems to sense as much, for despite Socrates' very negative characterization of the products of mere belief, Glaucon urges Socrates nonetheless to continue his discussion "just as you did with justice, self-control, and the other virtues" (506d3–5). Glaucon, in other words, is not merely asking Socrates for his opinion; Glaucon takes Socrates all along *not* to have been stating "beliefs without knowledge," while also accepting that Socrates has not been speaking as "having knowledge" or even as proposing "some true beliefs without intelligence." Glaucon takes Socrates to be somewhere between these two conditions, and because Socrates responds to Glaucon's plea by continuing (with the image of the sun), we may assume that Socrates also regards himself as not merely serving up beliefs that are "ugly, blind, and crooked." His own epistemic condition, then, is one in which the power of knowledge has been engaged, but—as he employs images and makes assumptions in his attempt to gain a better grasp of truth—his own use of the power of knowledge does not produce in him (or presumably in those who listen to him) the condition he would be willing to call "having knowledge." In this passage, then, we find Socrates and Glaucon acknowledging the limitations of their method of inquiry, while continuing to insist that it is not a method that leaves them simply blind, or only lucky to happen upon the right path.

Plato as Image-Maker

By now, it will come as no surprise that I intend to claim that Plato's own use of images also reveals the same general method that he attributes to the mathematicians and that he portrays Socrates as employing with his interlocutors. Plato's own use of images, however, begins even before the use he gives to Socrates, for as I mentioned at the beginning of this essay, from the opening pages of the *Republic* the reader is bombarded with images. It is worth noticing that Plato's first images are not limited to the heroic *katabasis* imagery I mentioned earlier, however. As soon as the topic of justice is introduced, Plato offers a series of images of the conception of justice he will have Socrates defend later in the *Republic*.

Plato first has Cephalus characterize justice as consisting in telling the truth and paying back debts. Although this characterization is plainly inadequate, as Socrates quickly shows, its likeness to the conception Plato later defends—according to which a *kallipolis* will be ruled by truth-loving and lie-hating philosopher-rulers (see 382a4–c1) whose psychic harmony would make them the least likely to fail to repay a debt (442e4–443a1)—is unmistakable. After Polemarchus "inherits" the discussion from his father, he attempts to characterize justice as helping friends and harming enemies. Socrates soon reveals the inadequacies of this account, though later we may recall how it resembles Socrates' own conception, according to which everyone in the state is a friend to everyone else, whose happiness is to be maximized without unfair or special advantage to anyone (420b4–8, 465e4–466a6), and in which all Greeks should regard one another as friends, reserving the most devastating acts of war for use only against non-Greeks (469b5–471c1)—the barbarians who are "enemies by nature" to the Greeks (470c6). These same later prescriptions allow us to recall their likeness in Polemarchus' revision of his view, according to which we must help all good people and harm only the bad ones. And when Thrasymachus comes in, we are told that justice is the advantage of the stronger—a claim that remains true in Socrates' own account, for the reasons I have just stated, except that unlike Thrasymachus, Socrates does not regard the advantage, once justice is correctly understood, as belonging exclusively to the stronger, for it goes to everyone, strong and weak, in the *kallipolis*. Only Thrasymachus' claim that injustice is more advantageous than justice fails to provide a likeness of Socrates' later hypotheses.

So we also find that Plato uses images, whose inadequacies are noted, so that we can move from them to those better conceptions, of which the former turn out to be mere images. These, too, come to be revealed as only images as we climb Plato's ladder of images so as to approach those realities that are originals only, and not themselves images. But the *Republic* never takes us entirely to this point—it is, instead, a book of images.

This understanding of the *Republic* has important consequences for how we are to understand not only Plato's methodology in presenting his ideas to his readers, but also what we should conceive as his overall purpose for the work. As I noted at the outset, two of the most widely shared conceptions of the *Republic* either dismiss its seriousness altogether or else take its recommendations quite literalistically for proposed political practice. In the view I have presented, neither of these conceptions is correct. The non-serious reading of the *Republic* may be credited at least on some issues with noticing that Plato's images are disturbingly flawed. Far from showing that Plato was not serious about his images, however, we can now see that such flaws are inherent to images, and that the kind of critique of these images we get from such scholars (and later, in Aristotle's own critique) is actually an essential part of the correct use of images—for it is only because such images present both the characteristic they are intended to present (such as justice) *and the opposite characteristic* that they serve well to "awaken thought" as the kind of provocative images this method requires (523b9–524d5). But this does not mean that the presentation of the image is mere play or humor, for the project of using the image to move to the original of that image is entirely a serious one.

The flaw in the standard interpretation of the *Republic* is one that is equal but the opposite of the one that infects the non-serious view. For as a book of images, Plato certainly did not intend us to take those images in the sort of wooden or literalistic way that would harden their contours into moral or political dogma. The images of justice that Plato presents, I claim, are intended to serve as methodological "provocatives" whose proper use takes them seriously *as images,* which is to say as provocatively flawed approximations of our real intellectual goals, rather than as flawless guides to action in and of themselves. The failure of the traditional interpretation of the *Republic* is that it takes Plato's images *too* seriously: like Plato's mere dreamers, traditionalists mistake the likeness for what it is like.

In my view, readers of the *Republic* are supposed to find it, and all of its contents, *provocative*. It is intended to stimulate thought—to raise questions much more than to settle any of them. Plato offers us something like a vast "thought-experiment" under various hypotheses—the assumptions upon which his arguments are founded, assumptions that could only be finally secured if they could be linked directly to the Good itself, which plainly Plato does not do in the *Republic,* and which he almost certainly could not do with words in any case, for words are but images of thought. With the aid of many images, which we are to take seriously, but not so seriously that we forget the distortion inherent to them, we are drawn up toward those realities accessible only in thought, and we are drawn down from our hypotheses to conclusions that often trouble us and provoke us into further dispute. That Plato's book of images has impressively succeeded as a "provocative" is amply demonstrated by the extent to which we continue to debate its meaning—and its merits—even today.

Notes

1. See Charles Segal, "'The Myth Was Saved': Reflections on Homer and the Mythology of Plato's *Republic,*" *Hermes* 106 (1978): 330; Eva Brann, "The Music of the *Republic,*" *Agon* 1 (1967): i–vi, 1–117; Bruce Rosenstock, "Rereading the *Republic,*" *Arethusa* 16 (1983): 25–46.

2. See Helen Bacon, "Plato and the Greek Literary Tradition," presidential address of the American Philological Association, December 1990; George Olaf Berg, *Metaphor and Comparison in the Dialogues of Plato* (Berlin: Mayer and Mueller, 1906); Pierre Louis, *Les Metaphores de Platon* (Paris: Société d'Édition "Les Belles Lettres," 1946); Jean-François Mattéi, "The Theater of Myth in Plato," in *Platonic Writings, Platonic Readings,* ed. Charles L. Griswold Jr. (New York and London: Routledge, 1988): 66–83; Richard Patterson, "*Philosophos Agonistes:* Imagery and Moral Psychology in Plato's *Republic,*" *Journal of the History of Philosophy* 35 (1997): 327–54; D. Tarrant, "Imagery in Plato's *Republic,*" *Classical Quarterly* 40 (1946): 27–34.

3. See Plato, *The Republic of Plato,* trans. Allan Bloom (New York and London: Basic Books, 1968), 380–81; Diskin Clay, "Reading the *Republic,*" in Griswold, *Platonic Writings,* 19–33; John H. Randall, *Plato: Dramatist of the Life of Reason* (New York: Columbia University Press, 1970), 167–70; Leo Strauss, *The City and Man* (Chicago and London: University of Chicago Press, 1964), 50–62. Such interpretations have, of course, met with heavy resistance. See, for example, George Klosko, "Implementing the Ideal State," *Journal of Politics* 43 (1981): 365–89; M. F. Burnyeat, "Sphinx Without a Secret," *New York Review of*

Books 32 (May 30, 1985): 30–36, reprinted in *Plato: Critical Assessments,* vol. 1, ed. Nicholas D. Smith (London and New York: Routledge, 1998), 333–48.

4. The *Republic* was, like most of Plato's works, lost to the West until medieval times. But if Averroes is any indication, the early Muslims also did not regard the *Republic* as jest.

5. Not always as a political work we should admire, however. Plainly, the *Republic* is taken very seriously as political philosophy in Karl Popper's famous polemical attack (in *The Open Society and Its Enemies,* vol. 1, 5th ed. [Princeton: Princeton University Press, 1966]).

6. I am not the first to propose a connection between the images Plato disparages and those whose usefulness he recognizes. See, for example, H. J. Paton, "Plato's Theory of *Eikasia,*" *Proceedings of the Aristotelian Society* 22 (1921–22): 69–104; S. Ringbom, "Plato on Images," *Theoria* 31 (1965): 95–96; and J.-P. Vernant, "Image et apparence dans la théorie platonicienne de la mimesis," *Journal de Psychologie* 72 (1975): 136. My own understanding of this connection, however, is (as far as I know) original. One who disputes this connection is Elizabeth Belfiore ("A Theory of Imitation," *Transactions of the American Philological Association* 114 [1984]: 121–46), who argues her case on the basis of the differences in the terminology Plato uses to talk about images, his criticisms of image-makers in book 10 of the *Republic,* and the sorts of images he discusses in the other books. But Plato compares the philosopher-rulers to visual artists earlier in the *Republic* (at 500e2–501c3) in a way that invites the sort of concern I address here, so I am disinclined to make too much of shifts in the terminology of images from the earlier books to book 10.

7. For a particularly clear statement of this sort, see Alvin Plantinga, *Warrant: The Current Debate* (New York and Oxford: Oxford University Press, 1993), vi.

8. I survey the many different approaches to this famous image and offer my own account of it in "Plato's Divided Line," *Ancient Philosophy* 16 (1996): 25–46.

9. I provide a far more detailed objection to other interpretations of this passage in "Plato's Divided Line," 29–31.

10. For a complete discussion of Plato's discussion of knowledge as a *power,* see my "Plato on Knowledge as a Power," *Journal of the History of Philosophy* 38 (2000): 145–68.

2

"To Say What Is Most Necessary": Expositional and Philosophical Practice in Thucydides and Plato

Phil Hopkins

> He who would explain to us when men like Plato spoke in earnest, when in jest or half-jest, what they wrote from conviction and what merely for the sake of argument, would certainly render to us an extraordinary service and contribute greatly to our education.
>   Goethe

Comparative Readings, Complementary Methods

Recent scholarship has explored the purposes of the aporetic dimensions of Plato's dialogues, and this focus on "method" has opened the dialogues to subtle and productive readings. Much of it also recalls a set of careworn and intransigent hermeneutic questions. Should readers assume that Socrates' practices—the "techniques" of inquiry he employs in the dialogues—are historically accurate, or rather that they represent the development of Plato's philosophical practice? Are they a model for others to follow, in the manner of deictic oratory? Is Plato trying to communicate some truth about things and to direct judgment? Is he inviting his readers to become involved in the complexity of the issues engaged, offering conversations designed primarily to awaken the reader's own philosophical and critical faculties? Are readers to find these conversations compelling, or confusing, or protreptic, or something else?

Do Plato's characters argue against positions he himself finds cogent or support positions Plato finds problematic? Are these tensions meant to engage the reader in an inquiry that may lead to conclusions not explicitly provided in the dramatic conversations he depicts? For that matter, is what Plato's characters say most important, or their process of inquiry?[1]

Wherever one stands with respect to these interpretive questions, it is worth noting that they almost perfectly mirror the questions that historians and classicists ask about Thucydides' *History*.[2] Comparative readings of these two authors should therefore illuminate these methodological inquiries in both. This essay hopes to prompt fuller comparative readings by turning to the expositional and historiographical practices of Plato's near contemporary, the author of one of the most important literary productions of the fifth century.

When one asks about the causes of events, or the nature of human motivations and fears, or the nature of justice and the best practices for the soul, one finds oneself in the predicament Socrates formulates in the *Meno* (86e) and Thucydides advances (1.20–23) as the problem of history generally: that one must inquire into matters the natures of which are not yet or fully known, but that stand as a goal for understanding nonetheless. Thucydides and Plato not only recognized this problem; both of them developed expositional strategies aimed at overcoming it, in which the reader is not merely a passive recipient of propositions or narrative depictions, but an agent in constructing and completing the texts' historical, moral, metaphysical, and epistemological insights.

Protagoras claims that "on every subject there are two *logoi* opposed to one another."[3] Plato echoes this claim in the *Phaedrus* where Socrates concludes: "We can therefore find the practice of speaking on opposite sides not only in the law courts and in the Assembly. Rather, it seems that one single art . . . governs all speaking" (*Phaedrus* 261e).[4] The practice of antilogy, of "speaking on opposite sides," is powerfully employed in Thucydides and thoroughly investigated in the scholarship on him.[5] I will juxtapose that practice against another famous aspect of Thucydides' text: its vividness. Plutarch voices the general consensus: "In his writing, [Thucydides] is constantly striving for this vividness, wanting to turn his readers into spectators, as it were, and to reproduce in their minds the feelings of shock and disorientation which were experienced by those who actually viewed the events."[6] I bring these two aspects of Thucydides into closer relation and offer them as bearing, in a general way, on the question of Plato's expositional practices. I suggest that the "vividness" that many find at work in Thucydides involves, in part, the use of a broader antilogy than has been recognized, an oppositional art importantly related to Platonic practice and the vividness that practice also accomplishes.

In both authors, the vividness their works achieve is not primarily the result of conventional dramatic techniques. Not all of Plato's dialogues are expressed with the staging detail of the *Phaedrus* or the *Symposium.* Thucydides himself warns his readers at 1.22 that they will be disappointed if they expect dramatic storytelling (μυθῶδης) from him. The vividness in both authors results primarily from the way their expositional strategies draw readers into a process of carefully balancing opposed accounts, but not merely those accounts explicitly formulated as opposing. This process makes of the reader a peculiar kind of witness. The reader is invited to inhabit each alternative account to see the world from its perspective, but is hindered from selecting one explanation over another by a careful balancing of the compelling force of each account. The dissonance created by this strategy plagues the reader as she inhabits each account in turn such that, even while grasping the manner in which each in turn serves to explain and make sense of the world, she is called back into the balancing and is reengaged with the complexities that prevent any one account from being sufficient and complete. Socrates frequently cautions his audience explicitly in this regard: one must continually investigate the matter and previous agreements, lest one unwittingly fall into the error of believing oneself to know something one does not.

In this essay I build upon the foundation provided by scholars of Thucydides by focusing on the anticipation of Athenian victory in book 1 as an example of antilogy beyond the paired speeches, in which speech and narrative account taken together "speak on both sides of the argument" in ways that echo the pedagogical and epistemic trajectories of the Platonic dialogues.[7] In book 1 of the *History,* as in Platonic dialogue, there are many voices at work, each presenting an opinion or perspective, at times dogmatically, that other voices take up and render problematic. In both authors, the interplay of voices, balanced against each other, brings the reader to a sharp crisis of judgment where new understanding of the matter in question can begin. In both, some of the most important voices are not explicitly present. They are the ἐνδόξα, to borrow a term from Aristotle: what people say or think about the matter, the biases and prejudices of the reader. My reading involves thinking through a particular tension not explicitly voiced, as so often is the case in Plato, around which almost all of the explicit elements of book 1 can be seen to revolve.

Speaking on Both Sides of the Argument:
The Relation of Speech and Narrative

Donald Kagan noted several decades ago that "there are few arguments of longer standing in the scholarship on Thucydides than the one concerning the speeches in his *History,* and none is more important for understanding it and its author."[8] Very good work has been done examining the role of the speeches and their relation, which is generally recognized to exhibit, as M. I. Finley put it, "diametrical opposition."[9] In short, many of the speeches are antilogically paired. In these speeches, Thucydides seeks to see "both" sides and to tell both tales. Indeed, to accept one account as an explanation of the real cause or best course of action, and dismiss the other as serving only to indicate mistaken advice or an erroneous assessment of events, amounts to a very partial sort of reading.[10] To do so is to intentionally abandon the perspective made possible from hearing both sides, to ignore the careful composition of the whole, and to place oneself on one side or the other in the conflict and at that level, thus curtailing the wisdom sought and made possible by the historian.[11]

W. R. Connor has led the way in viewing the speeches as paired to accomplish larger pedagogical and epistemological goals. In the tension expressed and created both by the speeches and Thucydides' narrations, Connor believes something very important about Thucydides' text comes to the fore. While aiming at an audience that values cleverness, intellect, and self-interest, Thucydides' text does not simply affirm and reinforce those values, but rather exploits uncertainties and ambiguities in the attitudes and values of his readers to challenge and even subvert their expectations and certainties. Connor concludes: "Ultimately, I believe, the work leads the sympathetic reader—ancient or modern—far beyond the views it seems initially to utilize and affirm."[12] Thinkers in the latter part of the fifth century were deeply engaged in a complex and sophisticated investigation into the nature and use of persuasion, and of the strategies best calculated to bring about the desired convictions in their auditors. As Connor has noted, Thucydides applied the fruits of this investigation not to achieve a single response or specific evaluation of events, but to draw the reader into the attempt to *construct* sense, to awaken critical and evaluative faculties to be exercised on the matter itself of which the text is an account in a particular and even peculiar way.[13]

Thucydides offers this much remarked-upon qualification early in book 1 concerning the speeches that constitute so much of his history:

What particular people said in their speeches, either just before or during the war, was hard to recall exactly, whether they were speeches I heard myself or those that were reported to me at second hand. I have made each speaker say what I thought his situation demanded, keeping as near as possible to the general sense of what was actually said. (1.22.1)

And as for the real action of the war, I did not think it right to set down either what I heard from people I happened to meet or what I merely believed to be true. Even for events at which I was present myself, I tracked down detailed information from other sources as far as I could. It was hard work to find out what happened, because those who were present at each event gave different reports, depending on which side they favored and how well they remembered. (1.22.2)

Here Thucydides offers a claim of objectivity that some historians have latched on to, but elements of it undercut that claim. The passage calls direct attention to the fact of selection and to the difficulties involved in selection. It calls attention to the biases and error of witness accounts. It acknowledges that interpretation occurs at every level in the process of observation and in the reporting of events. Thucydides includes himself within the compass of his characterization, at least implicitly, when he assures his audience that he did not rely upon even his own eyewitness. Rather, he sought detailed confirmation or refutation as far as possible from as many sources as possible, despite the fact that the multiplication of sources meant always, whatever else, the multiplication of difficulties due to the inevitable discordance between accounts. He calls attention to ultimate reliance upon judgment. His claim that the determination of accounts was unceasingly hard work suggests a criterion for judgment more complex than consensus. He specifically denies the propriety of trusting what he merely believed to be true, but does not directly offer any other selection criteria for sifting through competing accounts. One should not miss the irony in a passage which, while seeking to reassure its audience concerning the reliability and objectivity of its account, calls attention to the unreliability of both beliefs and accounts in general while also raising questions concerning the immediate credibility of the author's own beliefs.

This tension is compounded by Thucydides' very next words, which claim that in writing his history, he intends to enable those who read his text to grasp the clear truth (τό σαφές σκοπεῖν) about both the past *and the future*.[14] To accept this bold claim, especially in light of his recent apology, requires that one accept that the words he records, spoken in isolated, context-embedded situations, provide such insight into human nature that in similar circumstances, regardless of what the people involved actually say upon those occasions, those who have encountered these words reported in the *History* would already understand the real issues and the reasons for what will come to be. The question of the accuracy of the reporting only serves to seriously complicate this claim. If one grants that any words could achieve such remarkable results, then one still needs very good reasons why *these* words provide such insight, and not, for instance, those heard in the marketplace or in the courts or in private discussion as well. What entitles the *History* alone to such a claim? I believe that its method, the way Thucydides presents his accounts so as to invite the reader into an antilogical practice of inquiry remarkably similar to what is found in Plato's dialogues, and not the words themselves, grounds Thucydides' claim.

Thucydides offers, at 1.23.6, one last claim that troubles the reading of the speeches:

> I believe the truest reason for the quarrel, though least evident in what was said at the time, was the growth of Athenian power, which put fear into the Lacedaemonians and so compelled them into war, while the explanations both sides gave in public for breaking the Peace and starting the war are as follows.

Here Thucydides distinguishes between the "truest reason" and what was said at the time. In what follows, Thucydides offers a version of what each side said in public in the dispute over Corcyra (1.31–45) and the debate at Sparta (1.66–88). The fear of the growth of Athenian power as the "true cause" that Thucydides proffers is indeed an important part of the content of several of the speeches that follow, most notably the speeches of the Corinthians, who are quick to raise the specter of Athenian imperialism. Sthenelaidas makes the threat of the growth of Athenian power the climax of his speech. At one point (1.124) the Corinthian embassy advises the Spartan League to simply make up its mind that Athens desires to rule all of Hellas, despite the fact that nothing in the details their speech presents leads to such a conclusion except the evocation of Athenian power and the fear that such power could result in imperialism. The fear of imperialism is the common attitude of the participants, coloring all discussion of the actual growth of power.

In this way, the Corinthian embassy is of a piece with the important narrative elements of book 1: the "Archaeology," which immediately precedes the programmatic statement, and the "Pentecontaetia," which follows the paired speeches. The tale of the growth of power that is the "true cause" of the war begins at the very beginning of the *History* in the section known as the "Archaeology." This section, while purporting to be as careful a recovery of ancient Greek history as is possible, given its remoteness in time, is largely a discussion of the nature of naval power and the advantage such power bequeaths.[15] This discussion begins with a description of Minos of Crete, including his efforts to build and exploit the first naval power (1.4), continues through an essay on naval power in general (1.13–15), and ends with a discussion of the emergence of Athens as a "people of sailors" (1.18). Many have noted the inordinate focus in the "Archaeology" on the nature and distribution of power available to a seafaring people and the potential for imperialism in those peoples who possess such power. While such a focus may support the idea of Athenian imperialism, it may do so only upon the application of a generalized stereotype to a particular situation. The question of whether Athens' particular circumstance aptly falls under the general category is not explicitly addressed. We will see that this invitation to perform a kind of reasoning labeled by the Greeks as εἰκός is quite important to the larger strategy that concerns us.

With respect to this description of naval power, Thucydides' early attention to Minos is both startling and telling. Minos is one of the few to be named in this section, and someone to whom the majority of Thucydides' audience would not be pleased to trace the roots of their power, since, as Herodotus reports, Minos had a well-established reputation for ruthless imperialism in the Aegean.[16] Here, as he often does, Thucydides weaves into his analysis elements that cause cognitive dissonance in the informed reader. Reference to Minos does indeed serve to raise the specter of imperialism, and does so in a manner hardly flattering to Athens, but the allusion is implicit and subversive. With a deft touch, while ostensibly relating "remote history" in a self-professed objective fashion, Thucydides plays on his readers' deeply rooted prejudices.

The "Pentecontaetia" continues the theme, but it does not portray the growth of Athenian power as explicitly imperial. It speaks of Athens fortifying herself; of Themistocles urging the defensive wisdom of making Athens' navy as strong as possible; of Ionians seeking Athenian help against the threat of dictatorship on the part of the treacherous Spartan general, Pausanias; of Sparta willingly and intentionally turning over command of the anti-Persian efforts to Athens; of Sparta advancing *her* conquests with Athenian help; of Athens putting down revolts within its alliance; and finally, in a brief account lacking any real detail, of Athens forming new alliances with Sparta's enemies.[17] In all of the above, the growth of Athenian power is described, but no detail indicates any clear imperial intentions on the part of Athens. Such intentions may have indeed been very much present, but nothing in the narrative account offered in the *History* directly indicates that they were. Again, Thucydides plays upon the prejudices of his audience, both ancient and modern, in precisely the way that the Corinthian embassy does in its speeches to Sparta—inviting the reader to simply recognize Athens as an imperial power because he suspects, or fears, or even "knows" that she was.

In the middle of these two narrative accounts is a section (1.24–88) that sets out the war's two main causes discussed at the time: the Corcyrean dispute and the Potidaean revolt. The Potidaean revolt is treated succinctly in a narrative of comparative brevity. The Corcyrean embassy, the first treated, is portrayed largely through paired speeches, one of the main elements of which is the Corcyrean offer to Athens of an alliance with their navy. Athens finds herself, after accepting the offer of alliance, capable of wielding the strongest contemporary naval force in the world, if only, according to her agreement, defensively. However, if this detail is intended to further evoke fear of imperial intentions of the sort that have been implied as typically accompanying such power, then it must do so, once again, solely by εἰκός reasoning.

After the brief discussion of these two factors leading to the war, Thucydides turns to Sparta and to the convention of her allies to which she has also invited any other states with grievances against Athens. Of the many embassies to that convention, and out of the many debates and grievances submitted, Thucydides focuses on the Corinthian embassy and the Athenian response. In the Athenian response, the importance and preeminence of Athenian naval power is again emphasized, this time as a good reason for avoiding war. This section is offered in the form of speeches given in direct discourse between Corinthian and Athenian envoys and between two of the leaders of Sparta, Archidamus and Sthenelaidas, over the wisdom of going to war. Sthenelaidas' speech urges the immediate inauguration of hostilities. Archidamus, in contrast, warns Sparta that Athens holds the upper hand in almost every respect. He reminds the Spartans that they have been taught that there is not a great deal of difference between the way they think and the way others think, and warns that it is impossible to calculate accurately events determined by chance: "Instead, we think the plans of our neighbors are as good as our own, and we can't work out whose chances at war are better in a speech" (1.84). The Spartans ignore this very Thucydidean advice, and Sthenelaidas carries the day.

The antilogy of this section is not completed, however, in the speeches of Archidamus and Sthenelaidas. For the reader of the *History*, there is a deeper antilogy that becomes apparent a few pages later, and builds upon the complex assessment of character and naval power already begun in the narratives. As book 1 closes, Pericles addresses the Athenians, counseling them concerning the war and the impending embassy from Sparta. Where Archidamus' speech is not in the least matched by Sthenelaidas, it is quite carefully balanced against that of Pericles.[18] The overall assessment of both agrees almost completely in substance and displays a remarkable symmetry. Pericles virtually restates Archidamus' claims concerning the unpredictability of war, the likelihood that the war will be long, the fact that Sparta is ill-equipped to accommodate distant engagements, the disparities of wealth and naval power, the tactical imbalance, the lethargy of Spartan deliberation (although the two differ markedly on the implications of that sluggishness), the pressing need for Sparta to delay the war to build resources, and the imperative to rely upon sound planning rather than luck. Again, the likelihood of Athenian victory is stressed, and the agreement upon this likelihood by the two most respected figures in book 1 further develops the larger antilogy that is our focus.

Perhaps the most striking of the paired speeches in book 1, however, are the speeches made before the Spartan assembly by the Corinthian and Athenian envoys. These speeches do not primarily address grievances, but instead contrast the national characters of Sparta and Athens (1.70–71 in particular). In the course of this assessment, the point is driven home that Athens has all the qualities that would tend to ensure success in war, regardless of whether those qualities are particularly admirable, and Sparta exhibits but the shell of its former self, clinging to outmoded traditions and a no longer effective national character.[19]

Making the Weaker Argument
the Stronger: The Play of Analysis
and Fact, Bad Faith and Judgment

As Connor has noted, the end effect of these speeches in conjunction with the narrative and analytic sections enjoins a consistent judgment: Athens should win the war. This judgment conflicts, of course, with fact.[20] That Athens does not win the war is not mentioned until late in book 2, but all readers of the *History* come to the text aware of the fact. The reader is led by the sum force of these sections to ask the question, "What went wrong?"[21] This reaction is both called forth by and enters again into the antilogy of analysis and fact presented by the text, inviting and fashioning an ever more complex relation between reader and author.

The speeches by themselves place the reader in complex relation to the author. Thucydides presents at length obviously biased, openly manipulative accounts without authorial comment, after chastising most people for accepting reports without testing them (1.20). There are necessarily falsities in these speeches, but Thucydides allows them to stand "untested" except by each other, the larger narrative frame, and the reader's own judgment. A further, and Platonic, complexity is brought about by the fact that the assessment which so favors Athenian victory is placed, in large part, into the mouth of the clever and persuasive embassy from Corinth, providing some distance between it and the authoritative voice of the historian. It also invites skepticism on the part of the reader, due to the fact that Corinth is a biased participant in the conflict with designs upon Spartan intentions and a long history of enmity with Athens.

In assigning such a prominent role to the interaction between Corinth and Athens, and to the Corinthian speeches, Thucydides displays fairly straightforwardly the grievances and hostilities between Corinth and Athens as a primary reason for the war.[22] Thus, another level of antilogy develops between this dramatic depiction of the long-standing hostility between Corinth and Athens as a major cause of the war and Thucydides' own offer of the "truest reason." Thucydides' selection and arrangement accomplishes this complexity, which prompts the reader to question not only the assessment of the Corinthians, but also the larger assessment we have noted building in book 1; if only because the Corinthian argument is echoed by the analysis of the two most trustworthy speakers of book 1, Pericles and Archidamus, as well as the analysis of the "Archaeology" and the "Pentecontaetia," and even Thucydides' own conclusions, presented as the result of careful and difficult investigation.

The conclusions of these analyses are also played against the narrative unfolding of events reported not long after these various assessments, which refute the Corinthian generalizations and call attention to their partial nature. One of the first characterizations of Athens, offered by the Corinthian embassy as evidence of the need for quick action, is that she is "quick to invent a plan and then to carry it out in action" (1.70). However, Athenian deliberations concerning the war are presented as hesitant.[23] Many of Pericles' assessments are also soon shown to be mistaken, such as the manner in which the relative wealth of Athens and Sparta would affect the outcome of the war, and which side would find themselves resorting to forced contributions—one of the first points in his argument for war and largely overturned as early as the siege of Mytilene. In addition, the *History* in sum serves as a balancing counterargument to the high appraisal of naval power in the analysis of book 1.

Thucydides places the analyses he offers in tension with the events that he relates in a deceptively simple fashion. In recounting events, Thucydides as author most recedes from view, but in doing so he allows the "events" to "speak against" his own analytic authority. The attentive reader, here as in Plato, is brought into some tension with the narrative, such that *as* the author recedes from view while the tensions mount, the question of authority is brought to the fore. In many of Plato's dialogues, the reader encounters a similar subtle engagement with bias, a similar ironic construction through which, if he is attentive to what Mitchell Miller calls the mimetic mirror that the dialogues are crafted to present, he is led to perform a critical reflection upon his own commitments that results in a similar complex displacement of authority on to the reader.[24]

One of the most impressive aspects of this construction, however, is that even if a reader does not attend to these complexities, he still confronts a nagging question that leads to much the same outcome. Why does the examination of the origins of the conflict in book 1, in both its narrative analysis and in the carefully crafted and paired speeches, so favor the probability of Athenian victory against the almost unanimous conviction of the time?[25] A ready and simple answer is that Thucydides thought that Athens *should* have won the war, but her own foolishness undid her. Armed with this conclusion and facing similar circumstances, a state finding itself similarly fortunate in a balance of power might suppose that were it only to avoid the same mistakes, it could not help but have every confidence of victory. Such an attitude would be reckless in precisely the way the *History* seeks to educate. Furthermore, observing in great detail how a powerful state fritters away its resources is of quite limited value for the ages, unless one supposes that general lessons serve all or most particular cases. Not only do many voices in the *History* explicitly caution that the outcome of war cannot be determined by the best and most careful divination, but such a supposition exhibits the εἰκός reasoning that ultimately ranks as the main cause for both parties' decision to go to war.[26]

Many times in the *History* this kind of supposition leads to disastrous results, and Plato clearly and repeatedly demonstrates its problems in the dialogues. Both authors depict εἰκός reasoning as problematic when those exercising it make inadequate attempts to assess the particular context and to carefully weigh all considerations, or more particularly, when what is merely εἰκός is taken for the truth. Bad faith is often the motivation for such mistakes. In Thucydides and in Plato, εἰκός reasoning involves inferences of what is likely, reasonable, plausible, or, as Socrates says in the *Phaedrus*, of what is *like* (ὅμοιος) the truth (273d). One must resort to such inferences in those cases where the truth itself is unavailable, when the issue to be decided, as is often the case in Thucydides, concerns a future event or future outcome of present strategy, deliberation, or action. The sophists often appealed to εἰκός reasoning, believing, it seems, that such reasoning is often more persuasive than the simple truth.[27] Socrates reproves the sophists for this practice in several places.[28]

There are similarities worth noting between the invitation to participate in bad faith in the use of εἰκός reasoning in Thucydides and a kind of bad faith exercised by some of the interlocutors and many of the readers of the dialogues. The very effort to come to a definition in the "Socratic" dialogues, the effort to give an "account" that would allow the possessor to recognize some part of the world for what it is, exhibits, and tempts the reader to join, a search for determinate formulas, general definitions covering all cases. In Thucydides' *History*, the bad faith prompted in the reader is ultimately educated and rehabilitated by the tensions created between the elements of the text in relation. In Platonic dialogue, the tensions that develop in the conversations of the interlocutors demonstrate that the mere possession of a "formula" or "definition" does not lead to understanding.

A telling example of how knowing a formula does not ensure understanding the matter the formula describes is found in the *Euthyphro* (8c–e), where Socrates offers Euthyphro's own formula of piety to him in several versions, the last almost verbatim, to force Euthyphro to abandon his position. After securing Euthyphro's agreement to several versions of his own formula that "no one among gods or men ventures to say that the wrongdoer must not be punished" (8e), Socrates uses that formula against Euthyphro's claim that he is acting piously in his present situation, despite the fact that Euthyphro explicitly offers the formula as a defense of his actions, since Socrates wouldn't allow the example of his actions to stand as a general definition of piety.

As is often the case in Socratic elenchus, the holder of a particular formula concerning justice or beauty or courage or some other virtue is shown not to fully understand his own formula and all it entails. And lest one think that if one could only avoid the errors of the interlocutors and approach the question more intelligently, one could succeed in coming up with the desired determinate formula where the interlocutors fail, the dialogues constantly warn otherwise. Indeed, in the *Theaetetus* (191c), Socrates suggests to his young friend that *when* the account they have settled upon seems good and true, *then* they must be most vigilant, torturing (βασανίζω) their discourse so that they may test it from all sides.[29] The *Cratylus* suggests that to avoid the grave danger of self-deception one must continuously turn back again to what has been said and test it by examining it "forwards and backwards simultaneously" (428d).

The *Cratylus* offers a nice example of the way in which Socratic elenchus insists on testing all sides of a hypothesis. In it Socrates attempts to determine whether names are natural or conventional. Socrates first posits that names are natural and then argues against that conclusion, or, we might say, stipulates an assumption in order to uncover its problems, as is his practice. Then he posits the contrary assumption, that names are conventional, and proceeds to uncover the problems with that assumption. However, his treatment of these two alternatives does not allow names to be some mix of natural and conventional elements either. His examination backwards and forwards demonstrates the incompleteness of two opposing yet plausible explanations, suggesting that one must move beyond either or both to get closer to understanding the nature of the matter.

This is precisely how the refutation of Charmides' position on σωφροσύνη works. Socrates' argument shows Charmides' account of the nature of σωφροσύνη to be flawed primarily in its partiality. To suggest that σωφροσύνη is calmness is to be obviously incomplete. Socrates does not need to demonstrate what σωφροσύνη *is* to refute that partiality. Indeed, if he is honest in his claims, he does not know. Rather, Socrates offers another definition, equally partial and equally obvious in its partiality, but opposed to the definition offered by Charmides, as an invitation for Charmides to see the flaw in his own position, and the partiality of such accounts.[30]

Socrates never finds an unassailable account for any matter he investigates, and those that come closest are consistently undercut. In the *Parmenides* (133b and 135b) a clear distinction is drawn between a correct *logos* and an irrefutable *logos* in such a manner as to suggest that Socrates is rather uninterested in the latter. The *Euthydemus* presents the possibility of an irrefutable *logos* in unflattering light in the answer the eponymous character proffers to any question: "Neither and both!" (300d). In the *Phaedo* (90c–d), Socrates claims that right or wrong *logoi* are extremely rare because most *logoi* are at times true and at times untrue. In many dialogues, interlocutors remark that a position that seemed sound to them but a few minutes ago now seems flawed. Socrates says the same about his own thinking in places, such as in the *Theaetetus* (162d), where he remarks that what they discussed earlier seemed good and true then, but now has suddenly changed to its opposite.

Socrates often works carefully to produce this outcome. When someone offers fairly reasonable opinions (such as when Critias suggests that σωφϱοσύνη is doing what is fine and beneficial, or when Theaetetus suggests that knowledge is some sort of perception), Socrates often takes up some earlier and often weaker assertion and brings it into conflict with the opinion just stated, even when the earlier position has been or clearly should be abandoned. The results of these arguments demonstrate that even the more reasonable positions are partial at best. What Socrates may indeed teach, by his practice, is how *and why* to make the weaker argument the stronger, but not in the sophistic sense. Rather, insofar as each *logos* is already weak and strong at the same time, one must weaken that *logos* which seems strong, that is, which is too compelling and persuasive, and also, at times, even quite eristically if Socrates is to serve as an example, strengthen the one which is weak so as to maintain the aporetic balance which can lead to deeper understanding.

Socrates assumes knowledge, as he says in several places, to be a whole, but accounts, by their very nature, to be partial.[31] In the *Parmenides,* the source of young Socrates' error concerning the Forms is that a *single* Form cannot be known at all. All knowledge involves a web of ideas, a συμπλοκή of Forms. Inquiry, then, in its most proper form is inquiry into the organization and structure of this weaving and not of its individual elements in isolation. Thus, what is perhaps most important is the way accounts relate to each other, building a larger picture; not only where they agree and cohere, but just as much where they contradict and refute.[32]

In both Thucydides and in Plato, readers are provided with means to the deepest possible understanding when they are invited to join in the bad faith of the participants, whether deliberating about the causes for war or about an account of piety or courage or knowledge. This invitation is as much at the heart of book 1 of the *History* as it is a central feature of almost every dialogue. Just as the dialogues invite their readers to participate in the search for an account along with the interlocutors, the *History* invites its readers to entertain the same fears as the participants, and to come to the same conclusion: that the growth in power of neighboring states must be feared a danger to self-determination and *requires* preemptive war. Indeed, if Thucydides' intention were merely to show that, regardless of what others thought, he believed the advantage did indeed lie with Athens in a war with Sparta, but that somehow that advantage was squandered until the unforeseen and unexpected happened, he could have related as much in briefer compass and more direct fashion. Instead, he draws the reader toward this interpretation despite the likelihood that the reader comes to the text thinking just the opposite.

Both authors' methods invite the reader to inhabit the perspectives and prejudices of the participants—to "see" at first hand the *fear* of imperialism as the "true cause" of the hostilities or the perplexity the interlocutors experience as they seek to understand the matter they question. The reader of the *History* is invited to discover the conception of power the participants in the conflict perceived; and is invited to witness, as it were, the complex motivations bound up in those perceptions, to live inside them and explore their impact. Thucydides makes it clear that it was power as it existed not only in fact, but in the perceptions of the participants, that was the power that compelled Sparta to war.

Such power is not readily apprehended in propositions concerning either its nature or its component elements, any more than the nature of justice or piety is apprehended in universal definitions. Thucydides could have stated straightforwardly that Sparta and Corinth held certain perceptions of Athens and her abilities, and that these induced them to fear her power and imperialistic tendencies; but such an account would fall far short of the kind of illuminating and compelling insight into the war and into human nature that most commentators have depicted as the remarkable power of Thucydides' *History,* and which he states as its aim. No amount of supporting detail or argument provided to augment those straightforward propositions would suffice to accomplish the vividness which Plutarch remarks upon, let alone the value for the ages that Thucydides promises.

Antilogical Insight

One might suggest that drama in general offers these benefits, and that the similarities between Thucydides and Plato are similarities in dramatic style; but the dramatic similarities are limited, and much more than drama connects these authors. The vividness of the *History*, as of Plato's dialogues, is primarily created by means of antilogy, accounts opposed and presented as exclusive but which, when engaged carefully, lead, like Platonic dialectic, beyond the antitheses of the original pairing into deeper understanding. The paired speeches call on us to think carefully about the details of the growth of Athenian power offered by one side of the discussion and then refuted or reinterpreted by the other side. The further balancing of analysis in the "Archaeology" with speeches that serve to reinforce that analysis, as well as those speeches that call it into question, moves the reader beyond simple affirmation or rejection of propositions, and offers him the opportunity to see and interpret the motivations of the actors in his attempt to make sense of events. Indeed, Thucydides' readers are carefully invited to balance not only the speeches, nor even merely the speeches and analyses, nor even analyses and fact, but also to balance an exercise of bad faith with the exercise of careful judgment. This latter balancing particularly characterizes Platonic dialogue.

Thucydides crafts levels of antilogy within and between all the elements of his text such that his readers are invited, as a kind of witness both to the war and to human nature, to remain within the antilogy, to learn what that balancing itself can teach. This is also in part the work of ἀπορία in the dialogues.[33] In the larger antilogy of the *History,* and in Platonic dialogues, the reader is hindered from deciding which side is right or should prevail. The placement and balancing of elements serves to call each position into question and keeps the reader engaged in the process of judgment rather than being swayed to one side or the other and so brought, untimely, to a decision or conclusion. Thucydides asks his readers to carefully investigate what lies behind analysis and speech. In sifting through the alternative accounts such as he himself encountered, his readers are encouraged to recognize that, as he warned in his programmatic statement, judgment is difficult, requires a sensitive touch, and is never final, univocal, or partisan.

This craft is all the more remarkable for being produced by someone who *is* biased and who recognizes that fact, as his caution at 1.22 makes clear.[34] One of the most important elements of the larger antilogy of the *History* is that precisely because his readers know the outcome of the war, and because this knowledge is skillfully woven into the complex antilogy of the text, one is led to question the force of the words of all the speakers, and not only those whose judgment Thucydides has openly called into question. One is forced to question the words spoken by Archidamus and Pericles, and those offered by Thucydides himself.[35]

In both Thucydides and Plato the reader is heavily coached, certainly. Much of the work has been done for him, so to speak. But the tensions the texts produce are as much a part of the coaching as any of the propositions used to produce them. As Socrates tells Polus in the *Gorgias* (472c), only one witness matters, and for Plato and Thucydides that witness is the reader, whom they bring into inquiry and judgment by means of their expositional strategies. The *reader's* assumptions, biases, and commitments are made to stand as antilogical elements in balance with the text. Neither Thucydides nor Plato offers the banal lesson that judgments differ as to events or the nature of things. They offer a lesson in the value those different judgments offer to philosophical, ethical, and historical inquiry. One might fear that if one abandons the hope that the best account will emerge as true and subdue all rivals, one relegates all accounts to the status of exercises in persuasion. Such a fear forgets that we have no other way to recognize an account as "true" except it persuade us. Both Thucydides and Plato offer important and subtle lessons about the ultimate use and frailty of persuasion, and unfold potent critical possibilities for competing accounts.

Like Thucydides, Socrates most often insists on inquiring by means of at least two, and two opposed, accounts. Socrates, like Thucydides, recognizes that even the most careful inquiry into the way things are will be inevitably incomplete and unceasingly hard work. To understand as fully as is humanly possible is to do so partially, provisionally, contingently, and repeatedly. Both insist that inhabiting more than one account in no way hinders, but rather enriches, understanding; whereas the decision *for* one exclusive account necessarily curtails understanding. The *Sophist* offers a particularly interesting example since it sets up its inquiry into the nature of the sophist as a rather mechanical διαίρεσις, a division of the matter into a branching oppositional structure. In each of the several attempts, a different branch is followed, and in each case the result is incomplete and fails to "hunt down" the entity sought for. It becomes clear that what is sought will never be found *if* it is sought exclusively within one or the other of the opposed pairs. But it is also clear that the repeated effort has helped them to more richly understand their quarry.

The *Symposium* makes much the same point, both in whole and in Diotima's speech explaining the inability of simple oppositions to tell the whole story. Rather than merely present an argument against Agathon, as those who preceded him in the conversation did with their predecessors, Socrates crafts an antilogy between himself and his fictional character, Diotima. Socrates frequently invents interlocutors and places arguments into their mouths designed to engage and mirror his auditors in complex ways, and his practice in this regard is a strong echo of Thucydides' practice in the *History*. In this case, Agathon and the other guests are encouraged by his technique to encounter both his and their own positions in a more balanced way through the ironic distance that at the same time brings them into a more direct relation to their own words. The dialogue between Diotima and Socrates engages and opposes the *logoi* of the other speakers who have preceded him in ways that, much like the speeches in the *History,* play upon and subvert the auditors' prejudices, expectations, and values.[36]

To accomplish the subtler and richer understanding that both Di-

32

otima and the *Symposium* as a whole commend, and that Thucydides desires for his readers, a certain oppositional tension must be fostered.[37] In the *Sophist*, the Eleatic Stranger prompts Theaetetus to see that though they began their inquiry into Being deeply confused about not-Being, they have come to the point where they finally recognize that they are equally confused about Being. At this point, and not before, the Eleatic Stranger claims that there is hope "precisely because both *that which is* and *that which is not* are involved in equal confusion" (250e). Now they can push through their inquiry as far as possible toward deeper understanding. This tension, both Thucydides and Plato teach, is the basis for good deliberation and good judgment, judgment which aims to accomplish a real understanding of the complexities of the world.

Thucydides makes it clear in the "Archaeology" that he is adept at constructing straightforwardly propositional accounts of events.[38] Since he is able, when he wishes, to give an argued, discursive interpretation from evidence in terms that historians still find compelling and sophisticated, regardless of their points of contention with this or that element of the account, the fact that he does not do so in the vast majority of his work should prompt his readers to ponder why. Plato makes it clear that should he have desired to render a more direct and didactic account of *his* positions, he certainly could have done so. Both authors choose instead to offer their readers the opportunity to participate in a kind of vivid antilogical drama, where the text requires their effort to complete its work.

Thucydides, like Plato, offers many alternative, even diametrically opposed, accounts to prompt his readers to enter along with him into the hard work of coming to understanding that he describes at 1.22, a work that could not be accomplished if one of the two or several accounts was simply selected as the "correct" explanation, the "truest reason" for the events and their outcomes. In crafting his antilogy, Thucydides, like Plato, demonstrates that even the ability to assess and judge the equality and the appropriateness of the considerations to each circumstance, as is required for εἰκός reasoning to be productive, is never provided once and for all, and certainly not as propositions, but is instead a matter of the ability to remain engaged within balancing and balanced antilogy, carefully selected to assist one in seeing the matter from as many sides as possible, such that one is thereby able to develop a deeper sense of the structure of the world, of its particular circumstances, and of the beliefs and motivations of the people engaged in living their lives within it.

As Socrates says in the *Republic* (537c), the one who is συνοπτικός is a dialectician, and the one who is not, is not. Both Thucydides and Plato suggest that synoptic ability will be found and gained, if at all, in an ongoing practice, an always underway quite evocative of Diotima's description of philosophy in the *Symposium* that, far from calling for final decisions upon each individual matter of investigation or upon the nature and structure of the world, instead calls for an understanding that always approaches and then reapproaches its judgment concerning the world. The richness of arguing both sides is revealed when all participate in the inquiry, carefully examining what each thinks he understands of the terms involved and their relations and then testing those understandings, and in so doing, revealing heretofore unrecognized complexities in their relations. Both Thucydides and Plato select exempla exhibiting the particular problems necessary for them to address δόξα, to witness or stand as evidence in the Greek sense for and against our biases and prejudices. In that sense, "evidence" (τεκμήριον) is prominently derived from *logos* that contradicts itself or is contradicted by actions—precisely what is offered in both the speeches in their relation to the narrative, and so often in Socratic elenchus.[39] Both authors gloss over problems that would controvert these efforts, but magnify problems when doing so furthers such aims. In neither case is the goal valid generalizations from induction, but rather a process of seeking through the problemata of the *logoi* what those tensions themselves can show.

In this way, the expositional strategies of both Thucydides and Plato reveal a harmonious vision of the nature and process of human understanding. One of the most remarkable aspects of his programmatic statement is that Thucydides, who is a witness to the events he seeks to witness to his readers, sets aside his status as eyewitness and seeks *logoi* that will help *his readers become* the spectators/witnesses Plutarch conjures. Like Thucydides, Plato, as a similar and similarly strange witness to both Socrates and the beginnings of philosophy, seeks to show his readers primarily themselves, by means of *logoi* that call upon them to witness, as participants, their own search for wisdom and judgment, striving for virtue, and the nature of understanding.

Notes

1. In the past decade, scholarship that attends to Plato's use of the literary and dramatic as critically important to understanding the dialogues has multiplied in both quantity and quality. Indeed, it is now too voluminous to cite in anything like an exhaustive fashion. However, the following represent interesting and influential works in this new genre: Charles L. Griswold Jr., ed., *Platonic Writings, Platonic Readings* (New York and London: Routledge, 1988); J. A. Ariei, *Interpreting Plato: The Dialogues as Drama* (Lanham: Rowman and Littlefield, 1991); Gerald Press, ed., *Plato's Dialogues: New Studies and Interpreta-*

tions (Lanham: Rowman and Littlefield, 1993); Kenneth Sayre, *Plato's Literary Garden: How to Read a Platonic Dialogue* (Notre Dame: University of Notre Dame Press, 1995); R. B. Rutherford, *The Art of Plato* (Cambridge: Harvard University Press, 1995); Francisco Gonzalez, ed., *The Third Way: New Directions in Platonic Studies* (Lanham: Rowman and Littlefield, 1995); Charles Kahn, *Plato and the Socratic Dialogue: The Philosophical Use of a Literary Form* (Cambridge: Cambridge University Press, 1996); Thomas Szlezák, *Reading Plato* (New York: Routledge, 1999); Jill Gordon, *Turning Toward Philosophy: Literary Device and Dramatic Structure in Plato's Dialogues* (University Park: Pennsylvania State University Press, 1999); Gerald Press, ed., *Who Speaks for Plato? Studies in Platonic Anonymity* (Lanham: Rowman and Littlefield, 2000); Harold Tarrant, *Plato's First Interpreters* (Ithaca: Cornell University Press, 2000); Diskin Clay, *Platonic Questions: Dialogues with the Silent Philosopher* (University Park: Pennsylvania State University Press, 2000); Ann N. Michelini, ed., *Plato as Author: The Rhetoric of Philosophy* (Cincinnati: E. J. Brill, 2002); and Ruby Blondell, *The Play of Character in Plato's Dialogue* (Cambridge: Cambridge University Press, 2002).

2. W. R. Connor, *Thucydides* (Princeton: Princeton University Press, 1984), opened the door to more philosophical engagement with Thucydides in recent years. Peter Kosso's conceptual analysis, "Historical Evidence and Epistemic Justification: Thucydides as a Case Study," *History and Theory* 32 (1993): 1–12, argues that historical evidence in general serves as an appeal to coherence and uses Thucydides to make the point that the most credible historical evidence is that evidence which has passed a number of potentially eliminative tests— a claim about evidence that strongly evokes Socratic elenchus. Cynthia Farrar, *The Origins of Democratic Thinking* (Cambridge: Cambridge University Press, 1988), offers a thorough treatment of Thucydides as a political philosopher. Touching on the philosophical questions of the relation of form and content, see J. L. Moles, "Truth and Untruth in Herodotus and Thucydides," in *Lies and Fiction in the Ancient World,* ed. C. Gill and T. P. Wiseman (Austin: University of Texas Press, 1993), 88–121; and Michael C. Leff, "Agency, Performance, and Interpretation in Thucydides' Account of the Mytilene Debate," in *Theory, Text, Context* (Albany: State University of New York Press, 1996), 87–96. Leff, following Gomme, finds the Mytilene debate to be in part a subtle and critically reflective commentary on the very process of rhetorical debate (89). Indeed, quite interestingly for our purposes here, his analysis, following Andrewes and Farrar and contrary to Kagan, interprets Cleon's speech as directly violating its own maxims and advice, thus serving Thucydides' larger didactic purposes. See also Gregory Crane, *Thucydides and the Ancient Simplicity* (Berkeley: University of California Press, 1998); Mary F. Williams, *Ethics in Thucydides* (Lanham: University Press of America, 1998); and especially Timothy Rood, *Thucydides: Narrative and Explanation* (Oxford: Oxford University Press, 1999). However, questions concerning the philosophical influence and import of Thucydides' text predate Connor's work. See W. K. C. Guthrie, *History of Greek Philosophy,* vol. 3 (Cambridge: Cambridge University Press, 1969), on the *phusis-nomos* controversy; Friedrich Solmsen, *Intellectual Experiments of the Greek Enlightenment* (Princeton: Princeton University Press, 1975), on the import of the "new learning"; and J. H.

Finley, *Three Essays on Thucydides* (Cambridge: Harvard University Press, 1967); the works of Jacqueline de Romilly generally; and H. P. Stahl, *Thukydides: Die Stellung des Menschen im geschichtlichen Prozess* (Munich: Beck, 1966), on the *History* as an attempt to understand human nature.

3. Diogenes Laertius, *Lives of Eminent Philosophers*, 9.51.

4. Socrates most often uses the term ἀντιλογικός in its sophistic and technical sense as a kind of eristic, a merely semantic verbal opposition, as in *Republic* 454, *Euthydemus* 278a and 301b, *Lysis* 216a, and *Theaetetus* 164c. Other problems arising in the use of oppositional speech noted by Socrates include the failure to distinguish the hypothesis from its consequences, as in *Phaedo* 101e and *Parmenides* 135–36, and the failure to properly perform διαιρέσις, as in *Philebus* 17a and *Phaedrus* 265e and 266a–b. I use the term in its more general sense of opposing arguments or accounts. Socrates recognized the value of such opposing accounts. His concern was not with contradiction per se, but with the eristic use to which contradiction may be put.

5. Many scholars have noted that both Thucydides and his audience were clearly influenced by the sophists and by other developments of the fifth century's "new learning." Thucydides was variously reputed to be the student of Antiphon, Anaxagoras, or Protagoras. He makes clear himself how much he admired Antiphon at 8.68, and he seems to hold Pericles in unusually high regard in the early part of the *History*, taking special care to assess and justify his character and actions. Pericles, as a student of Protagoras, was himself deeply engaged in the "new learning." There is a significant amount of literature remarking the similarities of rhetorical technique in prose writers of the fifth century, particularly writers of epideictic and dicanic oratory; but for a solid introduction to that discussion, see Thomas Cole, *The Origins of Rhetoric in Ancient Greece* (Baltimore: Johns Hopkins University Press, 1991); and, earlier, J. H. Finley, *Three Essays on Thucydides*. More recent studies include Philip Stadter, "The Form and Content of Thucydides' Pentecontaetia (1.89–117)," *Greek, Roman and Byzantine Studies* 34, no. 1 (1993): 35–72; and Ian Plant, "The Influence of Forensic Oratory on Thucydides' Principles of Method," *Classical Quarterly* 49 (1999): 62–73.

6. Plutarch, *De gloria Atheniensium*, 3.346–47.

7. Connor, *Thucydides*, in particular, notes and explores this expositional tension; see 41ff.

8. Donald Kagan, "The Speeches in Thucydides and the Mytilene Debate," in *Studies in the Greek Historians*, Yale Classical Studies 24 (Cambridge: Cambridge University Press, 1975), 71. Kagan reviews the controversy between scholars on whether Thucydides reports speeches accurately or makes them up for his own purposes. There are a number of scholars who take the speeches in the *History* to represent either what the speakers actually said, for example, Finley, Kagan, and Marc Cogan, *The Human Thing: The Speeches and Principles of Thucydides' History* (Chicago: University of Chicago Press, 1981); what they needed to say to get their point across and persuade an audience, for example, A. W. Gomme, A. Andrewes, and K. J. Dover, *A Historical Commentary on Thucydides* (Oxford: Oxford University Press, 1981); or models for orators on what should

be argued and how in given situations, for example, Thomas Cole and George Kennedy, *The Art of Persuasion in Greece* (Princeton: Princeton University Press, 1963). For a more recent contribution to the debate along similar lines and one armed with an admirable, if not fully persuasive, philological analysis of the difficult language of 1.22, see Thomas Garrity, "Thucydides 1.22.1: Content and Form in the Speeches," *American Journal of Philology* 119 (1998): 361–84. A. J. Woodman, *Rhetoric in Classical Historiography* (Portland: Areopagitica, 1988), 11–14, following closely the arguments of G. E. M. De Ste. Croix, *The Origins of the Peloponnesian War* (Ithaca: Cornell University Press, 1972), argues with impressive evidence that verbatim speeches in classical history were not only not a general practice (only Cato includes verbatim speeches and they are *his own*), but not even an expectation. His interpretation of the programmatic statement at 1.22 is that Thucydides claims only to capture the "general gist" of what was actually said at the time, the equivalent of a thesis statement or summary. His interesting and unusual conclusion for the presence of so many long speeches in the *History* is that they are there to perfect Thucydides' intentional rivalry with Homer, since speeches play a significant role in the *Iliad*. As regards the paired speeches in particular, there are those who take the speeches to represent what Thucydides himself thought, in each pair, to be a correct and an incorrect response to the situation; and those who take the speeches to show, in the speech of the winning side, what the losing side overlooks or refuses to see, acting out a kind of bad faith. But there are others, notably Connor, who find in the mechanism of the paired speeches something more complex that disallows a clear verdict for one over the other.

9. M. I. Finley, in the introduction to Rex Warner's translation of the *History of the Peloponnesian War* (New York: Penguin Classics, 1972), 25.

10. See Paul Woodruff, *On Justice, Power and Human Nature* (Indianapolis: Hackett, 1993).

11. Indeed, the speeches through which these "sides" are related rarely seem to convince those listening. Thucydides is careful to show that, most often, the decisions made after speeches urging a given action have already been determined by the needs, desires, or fears of the actors. I am indebted on this point and more broadly to Paul Woodruff, both from conversation and from his paper "*Eikos* and Bad Faith in the Paired Speeches of Thucydides," *Proceedings of the Boston Area Colloquium in Ancient Philosophy* 10 (1994): 115–45.

12. Connor, *Thucydides*, 15. This is an apt observation with respect to Platonic dialogue as well. Thomas Szlezák in *Reading Plato* has likened the dialogues to a ladder that must eventually be discarded.

13. Connor, *Thucydides*, 17.

14. The term σαφής is commonly used to denote the plain, manifest, distinct reality. See Liddell and Scott's *Greek-English Lexicon*, s.v. One finds it used in this way in a number of the fragments of the pre-Socratic philosophers.

15. Connor, *Thucydides*, emphasizes this aspect of the "Archaeology"; see 24ff.

16. Herodotus, *The Histories*, 1.171, 173; 3.122; 7.169–71.

17. Thucydides expected his audience to be familiar with the growth of the

Delian League, but it is remarkable that the text omits many of the details of this growth. The only alliance noted is with Corcyra.

18. Thucydides, in his characterizations of these two, notes especially Archidamus' ἔμπειρος, or wisdom derived from ample experience (1.80), and the constancy of Pericles' γνώμη, his opinions and judgments (1.140). See Connor, *Thucydides*, 50. Plato also frequently completes the balancing of *logoi* between interlocutors through discussion with other interlocutors, or with characters Socrates seems to invent precisely for that purpose.

19. The appeal to Athenian character and disposition is only part of the account developed in this section, however. The narrative also emphasizes the role of luck and of the intrigues of other states in bringing Athens to her place upon the Hellenic stage, for which, therefore, she cannot take sole credit or blame. Ironically, there is very little in book 1 that depicts Sparta's historical importance. Were the reader not familiar with the growth of the Peloponnesian League and Sparta's formidable and famous land forces, he might be quite surprised at the suggestion of 1.18 that Sparta stood alongside Athens as the two preeminent powers at the time of the Persian War.

20. Athens was the winner of what is called the Archidamian War, the first phase of the war before the peace of Nicias. However, Thucydides portrays that peace as badly needed by both sides. Furthermore, the peace is related near the beginning of book 5, after the dark investigation of book 3, which includes the detailed analysis of the moral failure connected to the civil dispute at Corcyra, and book 4's telling depiction of Athenian folly (flirting with disaster in its rejection of peace) and the puzzling decline of Spartan military power. Athens' eventual defeat is mentioned as early as book 2. Such early success throws her later defeat into sharper relief, even without Thucydides' depiction of the largely fortuitous and puzzling character of the early victory.

21. The common wisdom at the time of the outbreak of the war was that Athens would not be able to last long against Sparta, which Thucydides acknowledges at 7.28.

22. In book 1, Corinth speaks approximately as much as the rest of the speakers combined.

23. On several occasions the Athenians' second-guessing, as in the case of who to send to Syracuse to lead the war effort there, causes them a great deal of trouble. Of course, some of the Corinthian description is so hyperbolic as hardly to be credited.

24. See Mitchell Miller, *Plato's Parmenides: The Conversion of the Soul* (University Park: Pennsylvania State University Press, 1986), 4–5.

25. Not all of book 1 invokes Athenian victory so straightforwardly. An alternative, if equivocal, prediction is offered by the Oracle at Delphi who, when consulted (1.118), pronounces Sparta the ultimate victor if she will "fight with all her might," a fact to which Corinth later calls attention at the vote for war.

26. That war is unpredictable is put forward by the participants themselves upon no less than four major occasions in book 1: Athens, in her address to Sparta in response to the grievances presented against her (1.78); Archidamus, in his speech to the Spartans following (1.82); Corinth, in her final address to

Sparta at the vote to go to war (1.122); and Pericles, in his speech to the Athenians after the Spartan embassy (1.140). Thucydides foreshadows the mistakes that do indeed contribute to the Athenian loss fairly early in book 1 (1.69), where, in the first Corinthian address to Sparta, Corinth maintains that it was Persian mistakes that cost Persia the war and that their own success with Athens thus far was due mainly to Athenian blunders. That Corinth does so in the very speech that lays out the Athenian strength of character serves also to call into question the value of the Corinthian assessment for a prognosis of victory. Pericles also augurs the outcome when he states that he is much more afraid of Athenian mistakes than of Spartan schemes and plans (1.144), but he does so in the very speech in which he eloquently calls the Athenians to prepare for and welcome war.

27. See, for example, Gorgias, *The Apology of Palamedes;* Aristotle, *Rhetoric* 2.24.11; and Aristophanes, *Clouds* 889–1104. Thucydides' sophistic training would have included recognizing and utilizing εἰκός reasoning.

28. See, for example, *Euthydemus* 305–7, *Phaedrus* 272–74, and *Gorgias* 462–66. However, in those cases where the matter being investigated is so abstract or complex as to make the truth difficult or even impossible to attain, or pertains to divine matters, even Socrates resorts to εἰκός reasoning, and does so explicitly as the best method available under the circumstances. See *Phaedrus* 246a, *Republic* 506ff, and *Timaeus* (in particular 29b–d, 44c–d, 48d, and 72d).

29. *Phaedo* 85d.

30. The failure also in this case allows the reader to see that Charmides does not in fact possess σωφροσύνη, given the relation of σωφροσύνη with knowledge established later in the dialogue. If σωφροσύνη is related to knowledge, and knowledge is knowledge of opposites, as is suggested at the end of the dialogue, then the very partiality of Charmides' answer is an indictment against his possession of the virtue.

31. Perhaps the clearest expression of this insight is to be found in the *Phaedrus* (270c), where Socrates asks, "Do you think one would be able to understand worthily the nature of the soul from the *logos* without understanding the nature of the whole?" Also in the *Phaedrus* (249b–c; see also 259e and 260e), Socrates remarks that "human souls must understand a *logos* according to a Form, moving from many perceptions to a unity which has been brought together by means of reason [λογισμός]." See also *Laws* 965c.

32. In the *Meno*, Socrates is careful to argue *both* for the hypothesis and against the hypothesis that virtue is teachable, even though the positive argument appears convincing to Meno. In the *Phaedo* as well, Simmias and Cebes participate both negatively and positively in the examination of the hypotheses. Socrates, although arguing for the positive position for the most part with respect to the Forms, and also for the immortality of the soul which is connected to the hypothesis of the Forms, reminds us at the end that his *logos* has not convinced him of the truth of his hypotheses. In the *Parmenides* (135b–c), after suggesting that the power of dialectic depends upon distinguishing Forms for each of the things that are, Socrates is led on a journey through possible hypotheses concerning ideas that turn up again in the *Sophist* as the "Great Kinds." There

is a balanced opposition stressed even in the names of these Forms, but also in the process of the journey. It is expressly stated that Zeno's thesis must be tested so as to examine the consequences for the Many and the One *both if* there are many things, and also if there are *not* many things.

33. As Protarchus puts it in *Philebus* 20a: "Let us not imagine that the end of our discussion is a mere puzzling of us all."

34. Thucydides' very selection of material reveals bias. Although he details the Melian affair with care, he only briefly mentions the other Athenian massacres. It is striking, for instance, that he omits all mention of religious reasons for the war, such as the conflict over the control of Delphi. It is interesting to compare Herodotus 7.151 on the Athenians' relation to the Persians to Thucydides' account at 1.97. This contrast is important, since Thucydides explicitly criticizes all previous writers for not covering this period accurately, adequately, or with chronological precision. He then proceeds to give even briefer compass, with occasional chronological lapses, to several elements—the relation of Athens to Persia, and her relation to Peloponnesus, particularly for the period known as the "First Peloponnesian War," among the foremost. For instance, the background to the truce mentioned in 1.112 is not explained, nor is the Spartan treaty with Argos noted until 5.14. Hornblower called attention to Thucydides' selectivity and posited that Thucydides often explains in detail one particular event, such as the Melian massacre, or the civil dispute at Corcyra, while omitting other civil conflicts or massacres, in order to set the chosen event up as paradigmatic, and in so doing, betrays his concern to explain larger issues rather than individual events. Finley suggests, in his introduction to *Portable Greek Historians* (New York: Penguin, 1977), 13: "One good example was sufficient for his purpose; the rest would be useless repetition."

Thucydides is less concerned, I would admit, to hinder us from accepting his moral judgment as that is made apparent in his selection and relation of particular events. However, he does construct his text so as to call upon us to re-examine any final conclusions on our part. The Melian Dialogue (5.84–116) is sharply illuminating in this regard for the very reason that although both sides could point to good reasons for what they asked, even to claim right on their side, both sides make decisions that result in disaster. Thucydides' discussion of this event is closely followed by his narration of the Sicilian expedition, and like the juxtaposition of many of the details of his narrative, this suggests that Thucydides has a judgment himself concerning these events. He does not often state that judgment explicitly, however; and the fact that his judgment is often clear is no argument against the equally present fact that he arranges his narrative not only to highlight the failures in justice or moderation that he believes contribute to disaster, but also in such a manner that the readers are allowed, if not forced, to judge these matters for themselves. See Connor, *Thucydides,* 236–37, for a detailed discussion of several instances of the balancing between the narrative and the speeches surrounding individual characters.

35. Kosso states: "The style of point-counterpoint is indeed an epistemically informative feature of the text, but it subverts rather than reinforces our confidence" ("Historical Evidence," 8).

36. Plato then has a new character break into the conversation and present a *logos* that engages Socrates and Diotima, as well as all the other speakers, in a stunning disquisition on opposition itself, and which offers Socrates as the quintessential "in-between" character who combines in himself almost all the extremes opposed to each other throughout the dialogue.

37. Along these lines, Connor, *Thucydides*, 233, has this comment to offer:

> We can even suspect that Thucydides was sometimes inviting challenge and reassessment, a historical rereading of his text in which details and reactions postponed or minimized in his narrative are given a second look and then seen in a new relationship, with a new weighting. Certainly he knew that his treatment of almost every major figure, Pericles, Cleon, Demosthenes, Nicias, Alcibiades, would in his own day be controversial and would cut against conventional wisdom and judgments. His is sometimes a revisionist, often a polemical work, designed to provoke rather than suppress dissent.

38. Ironically, in the same passage Thucydides also claims that the truth of what happened in the past beyond immediate recall is impossible, or at least very difficult, to determine.

39. Aristotle, *Rhetorica ad Alexandrum*, 9.1. See also Plant, "Influence of Forensic Oratory," 67–71.

3

Medicine, Philosophy, and Socrates' Proposals to Glaucon About Γυμναστική in *Republic* 403c–412b

Mark Moes

Plato's dialogues contain many references to Greek medical practice and medical tradition. Some scholars have even supposed that Plato portrayed Socrates in many of the dialogues as extending and reinterpreting Greek medicine in such a way as to create a kind of practical philosophy rooted in questions about the nature of human life and human health.[1] On this supposition, Socrates aims to engender or facilitate in his interlocutors a virtue comparable to health, and to free them from vices comparable to illnesses, while his conversational practice is comparable to the interaction of an astute physician with his ailing client. The following essay attempts to show the initial plausibility of this supposition and to test it by putting it to work in reading an intriguing passage from the *Republic*. This essay also maintains that Plato's own practice in writing the dialogues is in many ways similar to Socrates' practice as depicted in the dialogues. The first section briefly brings into focus three passages from the dialogues that might be construed as evidence for the supposition. The second draws out some of its implications. The third offers a reading of *Republic* 403c–412b, where Socrates makes a series of proposals to Glaucon concerning γυμναστική in the πόλις. A fourth and concluding section addresses the plausibility of a medical model of *Platonic* philosophy, corresponding to the model of Socratic philosophy discussed in the earlier sections.

Medicine and Philosophy in the
Phaedrus, Gorgias, and *Phaedo*

Three of the most extensive and most potentially illuminating discussions of medicine in relation to Socratic practice are found in the
Phaedrus, Gorgias, and *Phaedo.* Consider first Socrates' comparison in
Phaedrus 259e–274b between the practice of medicine and the skillful
use of truthful rhetoric. There Socrates redefines rhetoric to mean not
mere persuasion but rather leading souls (ψῡχᾰγωγία) by means of discourses, not only in the law courts and on other public occasions but
also in private (261a). He divides truthful uses of rhetoric into non-
dialectical and dialectical kinds. When at 268a he begins to examine
the limitations of non-dialectical rhetorical techniques, Socrates compares the skill of the good rhetorician to that of the good doctor. He
says that a qualified doctor not only possesses basic healing skills but
also knows *on whom* to exercise them, *when* to exercise them, and precisely *how* to apply them in this or that concrete case. Likewise, a good
rhetorician not only possesses skill in basic non-dialectical rhetorical
techniques but also in dialectical ones.[2]

Socrates contends that the rhetorician must possess the latter
skills in order to be able to learn when and how to exercise this or that
rhetorical technique in the presence of a particular auditor or audience.
The method of rhetoric is similar to the method of medicine, according
to Socrates, in the following way:

> In both cases there is a nature that we have to determine, the nature
> of the body in medicine, and of the soul in rhetoric, if we mean to
> be scientific and not content with mere empirical routine when we
> apply medicine and diet to induce health and strength, or words and
> rules of conduct to implant such convictions and virtues as we desire.
> (270b3–9; trans. Hackforth)

In succeeding passages Socrates insists that the soul must be studied as a whole, grounding this strategy on the authority of Hippocrates,
who insisted that the body be studied as a whole. The truthful rhetorician, he urges, must use dialectic to determine what components the
soul has and what active and passive powers the components possess,
and also what kinds of discourse there are and what communicative
powers they possess.[3] The truthful rhetorician, Socrates says at 271b–c,

> classifies the types of discourse and the types of soul, and the various
> ways in which souls are affected, suggesting the type of speech appro-

priate to each type of soul, and showing what kind of speech can be
relied on to create belief in one soul and disbelief in another, and why.
(Hackforth)

The truthful rhetorician develops the "ability to discern each kind of
ψῡχή as it occurs in the actions of real life" (271e) and "to make clear to
himself that the person actually standing in front of him is of just this
particular sort of character" (272a). Only then can he "apply speeches of
such and such a kind in this particular way in order to secure conviction
about such and such an issue."

It is striking that in the discussion to this point Socrates has treated
dialectic as an instrument of rhetoric, and has redefined rhetoric as a
ψῡχᾱγωγία that, since it is not confined to public contexts, can be exercised in any conversational context. Any reader familiar with the whole
corpus of dialogues is familiar with Socrates' way of exemplifying his
teachings in his own practice. If we assume that Socrates the philosopher is ipso facto a truthful rhetorician, then his remarks here suggest
that in his own conversational practice he models himself on the physician, able to *diagnose* the condition of an interlocutor before trying to
bring him back to health.

A passage in the *Gorgias* also makes conspicuous use of medicine
as a model for the use of knowledge in the practice of helping others to
become virtuous. In 461b–465e Socrates gets Gorgias to admit that it
is possible for both bodies and souls to be in conditions such that they
appear to be healthy though they are actually unhealthy.[4] He maintains
that the treatment of diseases of the soul requires the practice of a craft
which works on ψυχαι in a way analogous to the way in which the crafts of
medicine, gymnastic, pharmacology, dietetics, and the like work on bodies.[5] He speaks of two crafts concerned with the treatment (θεράπεία)
of the body, gymnastic (γυμνάστικη) and medicine (ιατρική), and two
concerned with the treatment of the ψῡχή, legislation (νομοθετική)
and an art of justice (δῑκαιοσύνη). Each pair includes one art of disease prevention and health maintenance (γυμνάστικη for the body and
νομοθετική for the soul) and one art for restoring health after disease
has taken hold (ιατρική for the body and δῑκαιοσύνη for the soul).

A third illuminating reference to medicine in relation to Socratic
practice is found in the *Phaedo*, in Phaedo's account of the way in which
Socrates behaves toward him and Simmias and Cebes when he warns
them against the hatred of arguments (88c–91c). The three have become depressed over the inconclusive nature of the discussion about
survival. Socrates behaves in a way strikingly similar to the way one
would describe the manner of a good physician:

> What impressed me was, first, the *pleasant, kindly, appreciative* way in which he received the two boys' objections, then *his quick recognition of how the turn of the discussion had affected us,* and lastly the *skill with which he healed* our wounds, rallied our scattered forces, and encouraged us to join him in pursuing the inquiry. (89a; trans. Tredennick, emphases mine)

Socrates tells Phaedo that there is no greater evil one can suffer than to hate λόγος.[6] A person who hates λόγος (ὁ μισόλογος) is like a person who hates other people (ὁ μῖσάνθρωπος). The misanthrope is someone who lacks skill (ἄνευ τέχνης) in human affairs and so, betrayed by persons he naively held to be completely truthful, trustworthy, and healthy (ὑγιῆ), comes to hate all men and to believe that no one is healthy (ὑγιὲς) in any way at all. The μισόλογος is someone who lacks skill in discourses (ἄνευ τῆς περὶ τοὺς λόγους τέχνης) and so, disappointed when many discourses that initially seemed promising and convincing turn out to be unsatisfactory, comes to believe there is no health (οὐδὲν ὑγιὲς) or reliability in any object or argument. Socrates says it is pitiable when such a person does not blame himself or his own lack of skill but rather, because of his distress, shifts the blame away from himself to λόγος and spends the rest of his life deprived of knowledge and truth. The belief that no *logoi* are healthy is a dangerous one. More correct is to believe that *we* are not healthy (ὑγιῶς ἔχομεν) and must take courage and be eager to achieve soundness (ὑγιῶς ἔχειν).

According to this Socratic account, both the hatred of arguments and the hatred of persons arise from false hopes based on unrealistic standards of what human nature and human λόγος can accomplish. The best remedy for such hatreds is to gain a more realistic understanding of the capacities of the human soul and of the functions, strengths, and weaknesses of various kinds of λόγος. It is to develop a skill for judging character so as to withhold complete trust from less than healthy persons, and to develop an ability for conducting discourse with dialectical skill.[7] We find here clear echoes of Socrates' account of true "medicinal" dialectical rhetoric at *Phaedrus* 268a–272b and of his introduction of a medical model for the care of the soul at *Gorgias* 462b–465e. In all three accounts Socrates calls for a skillful understanding of human nature and a skillful use of λόγος, and characterizes both persons and λόγοι as sometimes healthy and sometimes unhealthy.[8] He implies that the skilled practitioner *diagnoses* situations very carefully and makes use of λόγοι accordingly. From the three accounts it is possible to construct a view that we might call the medical model of Socratic philosophizing. The following section further explores some potentially illuminating implications of this view.

Implications of the Medical Model

A first interesting implication of the medical model is that virtue, like bodily health, is not a constraining disposition that *limits* an agent's activity, but a state of proper functioning that is necessary for the performance of a host of higher activities.[9] Vice, on the contrary, like disease, is an inward condition that *does* limit or prevent the actualization and operation of uniquely human activities. This idea is explicit in Socrates' suggestion in book 4 of the *Republic* (444d–e) that the virtue of righteousness is a sort of health of soul, a proper relationship among the powers of a soul and a proper functioning of the powers in union. It implies that an important area of moral concern is the development of the self, and that self-control and self-perception are of great moral importance.[10] And since virtue in this view enables persons to perform well the crafts and practices of benefit to the community, it supports not only the individual's own good but also that of the community. A second implication is that both health and virtue are conditions that can be apparently but not really present. One may believe oneself or someone else to be healthy when he is not; so one may believe someone to be virtuous when he is not. One may have unfulfilled needs that are being frustrated by the wrong satisfaction of current desires, and one may be ignorant of this, or one may deliberately avoid attending to it. There are forms of pseudo-health and pseudo-virtue that only become manifest when body and soul are tested in challenging conditions (see *Gorgias* 464a).

The point about challenging conditions carries us to a third interesting implication of the model. A virtuous person lives well, in part, because he is strongly resistant to vice. He is more or less invulnerable to strong temptations to exchange higher for lesser values or to give in to powerful corruptive influences in his social, cultural, and spiritual environment, just as the healthy body is highly resistant to potentially powerful corruptive influences from the bodily environment.[11] One way in which one might be resistant to corruption is that one might know in advance what bad influences one must be on guard against. And this truth points to a fourth implication of the model. For just as there are forms of disease whose symptoms, courses, and causes are common knowledge to doctors and to health-minded persons, so there are forms of vice whose symptoms, courses, and causes are common knowledge to the wise, who learn them from literature or from experience. Socrates explicitly mentions that vice has forms (εἴδη ἔχει ἡ κακία) at *Republic* 445c1–2, forms which he goes on to discuss in book 8 after being interrupted at the end of book 4.

A fifth implication of the model is that the Socratic practitioner accommodates his questions and suggestions to the prejudices, interests, and level of knowledge of his interlocutor, so that the interlocutor might come to recognize not merely his own intellectual errors and inconsistencies, but also his own character flaws generally.[12] Thus there is an important disanalogy between medical diagnosis and cure on the one hand and Socratic conversational practice on the other. In an ordinary physician-patient relationship, a physician is often able to achieve a successful diagnosis without the patient understanding the nature of the disease diagnosed or the principles in accord with which the diagnosis is carried out. But when a Socratic moral guide diagnoses a twist or flaw in character, it is all-important that his interlocutor come to recognize the flaw in himself; otherwise he will be unable to return to flourishing self-consciously, responsibly, and freely on the basis of his own deliberate choices.[13] The diagnosis must be achieved by the interlocutor and not only by the guide. The interlocutor must recognize and acknowledge his own real deficiencies, and a guide must help him to do this without being insulting or threatening, without violating his trust. Therefore, the sage employing medicinal rhetoric often must work by indirection. This is one aspect of Socrates' use of irony in conducting his conversations.[14] The practitioner will often say less than he knows, dissemble, and hide himself.[15] Furthermore, just as the ailing person must be actively engaged in his own diagnosis, so he must be actively engaged in his own therapy.[16] This is a sixth implication of the model. To model virtue and vice on health and illness need not commit one to a view that vicious persons are exempt from (some degree of) responsibility for their own conditions.[17]

A seventh implication of the view we have been discussing comes to light when one thinks about the role that Socrates thinks ἔρως plays in bringing persons back to health. The human body possesses an urge for self-construction, self-repair, and self-maintenance. It can heal its own wounds, it is attracted to things that will sustain it and satisfy it as an individual body, and it is disposed toward sexual reproduction in order to sustain family, race, and species. A main work of the good doctor is to remove obstacles to the right functioning of this urge.[18] Socrates seems to suggest in various contexts that this urge functions in a special way on the level of mind and intellect, so that if it is released and properly directed by a philosophic guide, it leads to the gestation of true virtue at the core of the personality. There is in a man a structure of desire and interest that directs the attention of his intellect to some things and aspects of things and away from others that he does not wish to see. Consequently, a man's capacity for apprehending the truth depends upon his having right order in the structure of his desires and interests.[19] And the philosophic guide must help him to achieve this right order so as to

release and to properly guide the erotic urge. Socrates calls attention to
this urge when in the *Symposium* he narrates the account of the ascent
of ἔρως to the vision of Beauty itself. He alludes to it when he speaks of
a power of learning present in everyone that is like an eye that does not
work properly until the whole soul is turned in the right direction (in
the story of the Cave at *Republic* 518c). He thinks the urge can go awry
when internal or external conditions are unsuitable for its proper functioning. For example, in his account of the false philosophers at *Republic*
491a–493d, he suggests that the more vigorous the nature the more corrupt it can become when it lives badly or lives in a bad society.

Socrates in various contexts also suggests that the state of health
at which this urge aims makes possible a certain insight into or *vision*
of an absolute beauty and goodness.[20] We can count this as an eighth
implication of the model. At *Symposium* 210e–212a, for example, he describes the experience of the initiate who completes the healing "ascent
of Eros." The initiate "catches sight of something wonderfully beautiful
in its nature" (210e) and thereupon becomes able "to give birth not to
images of virtue but to true virtue, because he is in touch with true
beauty" (212a). And at *Republic* 475d–480a, Socrates contrasts the "lover
of sights and sounds" with the philosopher who "sees both the beautiful itself and the things that participate in it and doesn't believe that
the participants are it or that it itself is the participants." Socrates is
showing Glaucon that virtue is the kind of good that Glaucon himself
characterized at 357b–c as "good for its own sake and also for the sake
of what comes from it, such as knowing [φρονεῖν], for example, and
seeing [ὁρᾶν] and being healthy [ὑγιαίνειν]." The interchangeability of
health, knowledge, and vision suggested by these passages is convergent
with what scholars have noted about the relationship between knowledge and vision in the Platonic dialogues.[21] It also dovetails with the
medieval Scholastic commonplace that intellectual vision (*intellectus*) is
a higher and healthier activity than that of abstracting forms and making laborious inferences (*ratio*),[22] and that love gives one the means of
seeing.[23] A host of Socratic utterances testify to his visionary model of
knowledge and health.[24]

The connections drawn by Socrates among health and knowledge
and vision suggest a ninth implication of the model. No formal rule-
governed method by itself will be sufficient for imparting right vision to
those who lack it. A Socratic guide will have to exhibit the convergence
of many different sorts of consideration into a coherent pattern in a way
that makes sense for his interlocutor. Λόγοι of many and various kinds
will be instrumental to this exhibition. The Socratic guide will have to
take into account fine differences among persons and situations that

defy reduction to an algorithm, in order to enable any given interlocutor to achieve insights of his own in his own way. The guide will sometimes have to exhort his interlocutor to engage in complex and strenuous intellectual activities, sometimes involving formal or informal inference, sometimes involving the careful consideration of jokes, stories, myths, or whatever. Often he will have trouble getting the interlocutor to think for himself at all.[25] In these respects, the Socratic "method" differs importantly from that of Descartes and the Continental Rationalists, from that of the British Empiricists, and from that of Kant. Seeing things rightly, according to Socrates, does not require the having of perfectly clear and distinct self-evident intellectual intuitions available to any rational person, or the discernment of the rules of association of incorrigible sense data, or the discovery of necessary conditions for human experience in general. John Henry Newman was in unwitting agreement with Socrates when he worked out his conception of an *illative sense* to denote the perfection or virtue of reason, the right operation of a complex of intellectual powers. Newman called this sense

> a *living organon.* . . . [It] is not mere common sense, but the *true healthy action of our ratiocinative powers,* an action more subtle and more comprehensive than the mere application of a syllogistic argument. (emphases mine)[26]

Let us turn now to a passage in the *Republic* in which a surprising number of the themes we have been discussing come into play.

An Application of the Model: Socrates' Proposals to Glaucon About Gymnastic Education in *Republic* 403c–412b

From the point of view of the medical model, many of Socrates' conversations with Glaucon in the *Republic* seem to be attempts to provide him with opportunities for diagnostic self-recognition. Xenophon's remarks in the *Memorabilia* about Socrates checking a twenty-year-old Glaucon from acting on his naive political ambitions seem to agree with such a reading.[27] The connection drawn in the *Charmides* between lack of temperance and the misguided political careers of Charmides and Critias also points in the same direction. For the future tyrannical oligarch Critias in that dialogue defines justice as "minding one's own business," the phrase used to define justice for Glaucon in book 4 of the *Republic*. We shall now explore a reading of *Republic* 403c–412b whose cogency will hopefully provide some further confirmation that the model we have been discussing is really at work in the dialogue.

In this passage Socrates elicits Glaucon's consent to four proposals concerning the γυμνάστικη to be practiced by the guardians of the imaginary πόλις. To understand the force of the proposals, we must keep in mind Socrates' characterization in the *Gorgias* of lawmaking (νομοθετική) as γυμνάστικη for the πόλις and ψυχή.[28] Socrates' purpose in making the proposals comes into focus when one refers back to *Republic* 368e–372e, where Socrates and the others originally decided to examine the founding of a πόλις. Their guiding idea was that if they could watch a city coming to be in theory, they could also see justice and injustice come to be in it (369a). This in turn would facilitate insight into how justice and injustice come to be in a *soul* (368e). But at 372e it was *Glaucon's* dissatisfaction with the simple diet and lifestyle of the inhabitants of the healthy city that prompted a decision to focus their examinations upon the origins of a luxurious and *diseased* πόλις, and so, by analogy, upon the origins of a diseased and vicious soul. Hence it is significant that Socrates directs his questioning concerning gymnastic training to Glaucon and not (directly) to Adeimantus. Glaucon's lack of justice, not to mention his inability to recognize his own bad dispositions, was earlier manifested in his overly eager assent to the project of building a fevered πόλις ruled by military guardians and enforcing strict forms of censorship of μουσική. Now Socrates is attempting to prevent the twenty-year-old Glaucon from acting on his naive and exaggerated political ambitions. How then do Socrates' proposals concerning gymnastic education constitute a Socratic strategy for providing Glaucon with opportunities for diagnostic self-understanding?

The First Proposal

Socrates' first proposal (403d–404e) is that the diet, regimen, and lifestyle of the guardians of the imaginary πόλις be kept simple and non-luxurious. Glaucon's athleticism and political ambitions doubtless dispose him to imagine himself as one of the guardians, and Socrates' language here plays to Glaucon's elitist self-conception. Socrates says it would be inappropriate and absurd for a guardian to need a guardian to keep him from drunkenness and gluttony. He calls the guardians "athletes in the greatest contest" (403e) and says they need a more sophisticated kind of training than other athletes (404a). Any would-be warrior who reads Homer, Socrates lectures, learns that a non-luxurious way of life constitutes a "simple and decent γυμναστική" and that Homer never mentions the heroes as eating sweet desserts (404b). Glaucon agrees to Socrates' suggestion that a lifestyle centered upon such luxuries makes one's body unhealthy. Then Socrates teases Glaucon with gentle comic irony: "If you think that is right, my friend, then you must not really approve, as you seem to [ὡς ἔοικας], of the Syracusan's table or of the Sicilian's subtly seasoned dishes [404d1–3] . . . or of Corinthian call-girls [d5] . . . or of Attic pastries." Glaucon says he disapproves of all of them.

Of course there is a dramatic irony expressed in this exchange, which becomes apparent when it is read in light of that earlier exchange between Socrates and Glaucon in book 2, at 372a–373a.[29] There Socrates describes the healthy πόλις whose members meet one another's basic needs, feast (εὐωχήσανται, 372b6) with their children, hymn the gods, and live happily without a life of constant luxury and sybaritic pleasure.[30] In that πόλις neither ἔρως nor θυμός operates in the unruly and dysfunctional way in which it operates in Socrates' account of the divided soul in book 4. But no sooner does Socrates finish his account of the healthy πόλις than Glaucon shows his distaste for it and emphatically calls it a "city of pigs." From that point on, the conversation turns into a discussion of how to constitute and preserve a *sick* πόλις more to Glaucon's liking. Glaucon misses the significance of the turn, and Socrates' task becomes that of showing him a way out of his dimly understood predicament. An important move in carrying out that task is made when Socrates conducts the discussion of his first gymnastic proposal.

The Second Proposal

Let us turn to Socrates' second proposal, articulated and defended at 404e–408c and 409e–410b. The proposal is that doctors in the πόλις imitate the Asclepiads before Herodicus by not practicing "this sort of modern medicine that plays nursemaid to diseases" (τῇ παιδαγωγικῇ τῶν νοσημάτων ταύτῃ τῇ νῦν ἰατρικῇ, 406a5–6), which wears people out treating the symptoms of diseases that it will not cure.[31] Herodicus, the physician who introduced this modern sort of medicine, was a physical trainer who "mixed gymnastic with medicine" (μείξας γυμναστικὴν ἰατρικῇ, 406a8–9). In line with what he said in the *Gorgias* passage mentioned above, Socrates is proposing that γυμναστική should map out and promote a virtuous and healthy way of life or πολιτεία for citizens that prevents diseases from taking hold in the first place. It should not be concerned with the regulation and treatment of diseases in either πόλις or ψυχή or σῶμα. He is thereby implicitly reproaching Glaucon again for those attitudes that motivated him to agree to train a political elite to guard and preserve a luxurious and enflamed (φλεγμαίνουσαν, 372e8) πόλις. (Socrates in the earlier context drew attention to how the customary lifestyle in the enflamed πόλις involves "prostitutes and pastries" [373a3–4] and a great need for doctors [373d1].)

On the political level, confusing γυμναστική with ιατρική has devastating consequences. It results in mapping out a way of life in which diseases are allowed to proliferate but in which their symptoms are so controlled that their energy-draining and potentially deadly character is hidden from consciousness. Instead of legislating for the maintenance of virtue and prevention of vice, legislators attempt to keep social disorders within manageable limits by means of complex legislation. They communicate the message that vice is to be regulated but not prevented, and fail to educate for virtue by laying down a regimen of sound laws. They provide elaborate and ongoing treatments of the symptoms of vices in such a way that the vices themselves are never diagnosed as such or acknowledged. Judges or jurors (δικάσται) [32] (or attorneys), on the other hand, try to remake long-standing and well-tested laws by reinterpreting them in strained and radical ways, becoming themselves legislators instead of working to restore social health by making wise applications of good laws. Wrongdoers become their own advocates and "take pride in being clever at doing injustice and then exploiting every loophole and trick, writhing and twisting their way through every escape hatch, in order to escape conviction" (405b5–c3).

Socrates comes back to his point about the bad results of mixing γυμναστική with ιατρική in a conversation with Adeimantus at 423d–427a. One of the primary motifs of that conversation is that the most important function of statutes is to provide for good education and upbringing (παιδείαν . . . καὶ τροφήν, 423e5). Properly reared children, maintains Socrates, become μέτριοι who easily see (διόψονται) for themselves the right ways to behave (423e5–7). It isn't appropriate to impose orders upon persons who are fine and good, because such persons will easily find out for themselves whatever needs to be legislated (425a7–e2). Vicious men, on the other hand, will "spend their lives enacting a lot of laws, and then amending them, believing that in this way they will attain the best" (425e5–7). Adeimantus agrees with the point, at least in a verbal way, saying that such men

> live like those sick people who, through licentiousness, aren't willing to abandon their harmful way of life . . . their medical treatment achieves nothing, except that their illness becomes worse and more complicated, and they're always hoping that someone will recommend some new medicine to cure them. (425e8–426a4; trans. Grube)

At 403d8–9 Socrates got Glaucon to strongly agree to a related idea: that if we devote sufficient care to the mind (εἰ τὴν διάνοιαν ἱκανῶς θεραπεύσαντες παραδοῖμεν) we can entrust it to take care of the details of bodily regimen, while we indicate only the general patterns to be followed (403d7–e2). In the conversation with Adeimantus, Socrates reaffirms his teaching that misguided legislation, operating outside of its proper sphere, fails to serve some of the most important *educative* purposes of legislation. It legislates not with the aim of educating for virtue but with the aim of treating symptoms of diseases whose real roots lie in vice and in the seedbed of vice—bad family life, bad upbringing, bad education, and bad personal choices. Far from preventing these things, misguided legislation can in some instances even encourage and sustain them. We might understand Socrates as offering an object lesson to this effect when he provokes his fellow imaginary lawmakers in book 5 to legislate for the abolition of the family and for eugenic programs among the guardians.[33] At 405a1–4, Socrates elicits Glaucon's enthusiastic, but not truly insightful, assent to the following thesis:[34]

> And as licentiousness and disease breed in the city, aren't many
> law courts and hospitals opened, and don't medicine and law exalt
> themselves [σεμνύνονται] when even large numbers of free men
> are extremely [or violently, σφόδρα] zealous about them?

Perhaps this passage is best read as an ominous foreshadowing of the radical proposals of book 5.

Having discussed the meaning of "mixing γυμναστική with ἰατρική" in its political application, let us turn back briefly to its physical and psychological applications. On the level of the care of one's body, confusing the two results in an all-absorbing regimen of treatments for the amelioration of the symptoms of one's unhealthy living. It also results in an equally all-absorbing regimen of behavior aimed at avoiding the often more painful (in the short run) treatments required for a real return to health, and at hiding from the real causes of physical problems. In consequence, as Socrates points out in 406a–e, one squanders one's resources, time, and energy on expensive palliative treatments, so that one is prevented from exercising those abilities that the πόλις needs and that are made possible by a healthy physical constitution. Such misguided practice prolongs one's life but disables one from "doing his own work" (the slogan of the oligarchs, and a phrase familiar from the *Charmides*). Not only does it prevent slaves and craftsmen from doing their physical and manual work, but it also prevents those who do not need to do manual work from becoming truly *virtuous*, whether in respect to household management, military service, or public office. The most important thing (Τὸ μέγιστον, 407b8) about the excessive treatment of illness, says Socrates, is that it works against intellectual virtue, against forms of learning (μαθήσεις) or of thought (ἐννοήσεις), and against *attentions to oneself* (μελέτας πρὸς ἑαυτὸν, 407b8–c1).

At this juncture, it is helpful to recall that Socrates earlier told Glaucon: "A fit body doesn't by its own virtue make the soul good, but instead the opposite is true, a good soul by its own virtue makes the body as good as possible" (403d; see also 408e; *Charmides* 155–57). In a very telling way, Socrates said to Glaucon of this thesis: "You should look into it" (403d1). At this later point in the conversation Socrates tries to drive the earlier point home by getting Glaucon to see that his own youthful intemperance and preoccupation with physical athleticism is in danger of preventing him from the achievement of that higher health that is virtue of soul. Socrates' present proposal concerning proper γυμναστική in the πόλις is meant, like the first one, to give Glaucon himself another opportunity for insight into the state of his own ψυχή, another chance for diagnostic self-recognition. All along, he has been condoning bad γυμναστική for a sick πόλις and, by implication, for the sick soul, his own soul. Socrates intends to get Glaucon to see that it is imperative to avoid "playing nursemaid to disease" both in legislating for the πόλις and in governing his own life as a free citizen. For it is as easy to confuse γυμναστική with ιατρική where the care of the soul is concerned as where the care of the body is concerned. In both cases, the confusion motivates one to pursue an all-absorbing and debilitating regimen of behavior that is aimed at avoiding what is required for a real approach toward health of soul, and at hiding from the real causes of one's behavioral-psychological problems.[35] Socrates attributes to Asclepius the clear perception that no one has the leisure to be ill and under treatment all his life, and insists that this is a truth as much about rich people who seem to be happy (εὐδαιμόνων δοκούντων) as about manual laborers (406c7–8).[36]

We are now in position to grasp a new aspect of the significance of Socrates' original inspiration to take the πόλις as a model for the ψυχή, and not vice versa. It was not only because the "letters" of justice are written larger in the πόλις than in the soul that he considered the idea to be a godsend (368d). For a πόλις is by definition a self-governing and independent thing. Socrates thinks of the individual ψυχή as self-governing, and so thinks any polity that encroaches too much on individual self-governance and independence is an unhealthy polity. Had he chosen to model the πόλις upon the ψυχή, he would have come out with an organic theory of the πόλις. And there is danger that the analogy between the relations of cells/humors/organs to larger organisms, on the one hand, and the relations of citizens to the body politic, on the other, will bias the theorist of the organic πόλις toward devaluing individual liberty and self-governance. Instead, he comes out with a vision of the self-governing and free individual citizen.[37] So at 405b1–3 Socrates suggests to Glaucon that it is shameful and a great sign of vulgarity "to be forced to use a justice imposed by others, as masters and judges."[38] Plato's Socrates seems to be, then, a "non-libertarian liberal" concerned about the (conceptual and not just practical) impossibility of imposing virtue upon other souls through legislation and police enforcement.[39]

The Third Proposal

Glaucon's political ambition and unrealistic estimate of his own virtuousness dispose him to think of himself not only as a capable legislator but also as a capable judge or interpreter of the law. He suggests to Socrates that the best judges (δικάσται) are those who are "streetwise," those who have associated with people whose natures are of every kind, just as the best doctors are those who have handled the greatest number of cases of persons sick and healthy (408c5–d3). Socrates responds with his third proposal (408d4–409e2). It is that judges in the πόλις ought to be persons of good character with unsullied backgrounds, persons who have lived righteous lives. It may be true that being a good physician does not depend upon good physical health, and the cleverest doctors may be those who from youth have had most experience with sickness in themselves and others. Nevertheless, the best judges are those who from youth have had least association and experience with bad characters and have avoided indulgence in any injustice and so kept their souls healthy. It isn't possible for a soul that has been nurtured (τεθράφθαι) among vicious souls from childhood on and has committed every kind of injustice to come through this as an astute (ὀξέως) judge of other people's injustices (409a1–5). If someone is to be able to judge soundly (κρινεῖν ὑγιῶς) concerning justice and injustice, he must himself be inexperienced and guileless (ἄπειρόν καὶ ἀκέραιον) while he is young (409a5–7). It is true that decent and fair people (ἐπιεικεῖς), when they are young, appear simple and guileless (εὐήθεις) and are easily deceived by the unjust, because they have in themselves no experiences like those of the vicious to serve as models (παραδείγματα) to guide their judgments. In the long run this is no disadvantage, however, for they turn out to be the best judges of character. They learn about injustice late in life after having trained themselves (μεμελετηκότα) over a long period to recognize (διαισθάνεσθαι) what sort of thing evil is by nature, making use not of their own experiences (οὐκ ἐμπειρίᾳ οἰκείᾳ) but of knowledge (ἐπιστήμη, 409b8).

The streetwise person who has committed many injustices, on the other hand, remains ignorant of sound character (ἀγνοῶν ὑγιὲς ἦθος, 409d1) because he has no paradigm (παράδειγμα) of it in himself. Yet because he usually meets other vicious people, he *seems* to be very clever, to have a healthy mind and sound judgment, both to himself and to others, just as many people carry diseases in their bodies of which they are unaware. Vice never comes to know anything about itself or about virtue (πονηρία μὲν γὰρ ἀρετήν τε καὶ αὐτὴν οὔποτ᾽ ἂν γνοίη, 409d7–8).[40] Socrates twice mentions mental παραδείγματα in this section in order to bring to light the important effects of one's own experiences upon one's intellectual capacities. He says that guileless people are easily deceived at first because they have *in themselves* (ἐν ἑαυτοῖς, 409b1) no experiences of doing injustice to serve as παραδείγματα to guide their dealings with the unjust. And he says that the unjust person is condemned to ignorance of healthy character (ὑγιὲς ἦθος) because he has no παράδειγμα of this healthy character in himself. Then too, he says that whereas the guileless person can eventually get an ἐπιστήμη that will enable him to recognize what sort of thing evil is by nature (409b8), and will also get επιστήμη of himself (409d9), the vicious person will never know anything about virtue or about himself. "Virtue will in the course of time," he says, "if natural endowments are improved by education, get hold of knowledge [ἐπιστήμην, 409d9] both of herself and of vice." Why does Socrates think this?

The key to understanding Socrates here is provided in the passage in the *Phaedo* that we discussed in the first section of this paper. In that passage Socrates drew for Phaedo a connection between the misanthrope and the hater of λόγος. The misanthrope, lacking skill in human affairs and often betrayed by people, comes to hate and mistrust everyone, just as the hater of λόγος, lacking skill in λόγος and disappointed by λόγος, comes to hate and distrust it. The hater of λόγος does not blame himself or his own lack of skill, but rather shifts the blame to the λόγος and spends the rest of his life deprived of knowledge and truth. Unable to understand his own lack of health, he deprives himself of the means to become sound again. According to Socrates, the remedy for misanthropy is to develop a skill for judging character so as to withhold complete trust from less than healthy persons, and the remedy for hatred of λόγος is to develop an ability to use it with rhetorical and dialectical skill. But here in the *Republic*, Socrates is teaching Glaucon that a life of injustice bars one from availing oneself of either of these remedies. Doing injustice and experiencing it in oneself makes one distrustful of good older people at the wrong time (ἀπιστῶν παρὰ καιρὸν, 409c7–d1; recall that the καιρός is the appropriate time for medical intervention) and thereby unable ever to trust a teacher or friend enough to learn from him. One's personal interactions become tainted by one's own injustice, and one is barred from the kind of trustful intimacy that only a pure soul can experience. Just as the state of one's body conditions the way one responds to foods and other stimuli, so the state of one's mind and will conditions the way one responds to proposals and exhortations of one's teachers and friends. Socrates is bringing home to a young and ambitious Glaucon that virtue is not a constraining disposition that *limits* an agent's flourishing, but the proper functioning that is necessary, among other things, for the activity essential to human nature of *learning from one's teachers and friends.*[41]

Another clue to a sound understanding of Socrates' strategy in this passage was discussed in the second section of this paper—that it is a part of the concept of virtue that a virtuous person lives well because he is strongly resistant to vice. As we mentioned earlier, one way in which one might be resistant to vice is that one might know in advance what bad influences one must be on guard against. Wise men know the symptoms, courses, and causes of the forms of vice. Young people who trust their elders and their literary traditions can learn these from them without having to live through debilitating periods of vice that, even in the fortunate cases, at least greatly hinder and slow down their intellectual and moral development.[42] Such seems to be a main lesson of the Myth of Er.[43] This is why Socrates says that "virtue, if *natural endowments are improved by education* [ἀρετὴ δὲ φύσεως παιδευομένης], will in time get hold of knowledge both of itself and of vice" (409d8–10).

People are not born virtuous. So what could Socrates mean by the natural endowments that need to be educated? He must be referring, among other things, to that ἔρως or will to truth and goodness mentioned earlier, that ἔρως that when properly guided leads to the gestation of true virtue at the core of the personality, but that often goes awry when internal or external conditions are unsuitable for its proper formation and expression. We noted earlier that Socrates draws connections among ἔρως and health, knowledge, and vision. These connections are also relevant to understanding Socrates' way with Glaucon in the passage now under consideration. For there is in a man a structure of desire and interest that directs the attention of his intellect to some aspects of things and away from other aspects of things which he does not wish to see or is unable to see. Both intellectual and moral virtues involve right apprehension of value or the good, and this apprehension is only possible for someone with well-formed desires and interests. Mere argument by itself is not necessarily sufficient for imparting vision of value to those who lack the right dispositions. But these dispositions are formed to a significant degree by one's customary behavior. Hence, no one can become a good judge of good and evil, justice and injustice, unless he lives in a certain way. And this is precisely the point Socrates is making in this section.

The third proposal is meant to provide Glaucon with another opportunity for self-recognition and self-diagnosis and another opportunity to recognize the errors in the project to which he has been assenting since 372c. Socrates wants him to question himself as to whether he may not be a poor judge of character, his own and that of others, and this not only because of his own character defects and his own lifestyle, but also simply because of his *youth*. Yet he apparently has not yet lost all capacity to learn from Socrates. Later on, after Socrates has described the development and nature of the various degenerate character types (571a–576b), Glaucon takes over from Adeimantus the role of chief interlocutor. Socrates says to him: "Come, then, and like the judge [*krites*] who makes the final decision, tell me who among the five—the king, the timocrat, the oligarch, the democrat, and the tyrant—is the first in happiness, who the second, and so on in order" (580a). And Glaucon answers: "The best, the most just and happy, is the one who rules like a king over himself" (580b). And in 582d Socrates gets Glaucon to admit that the lover of wisdom judges (κρίνει) best concerning the value of various types of life.

The Fourth Proposal

Socrates' fourth proposal (410b5–412b5) is that γυμναστική and μουσική be instituted together not with the intention that the former train the body (τὸ σῶμα θεραπεύοιντο, 410c2) and the latter train the ψυχή. Rather, they should be instituted together in order to complement one another in providing a coordinated training for the whole ψυχή. Γυμναστική—the use of physical training, dance, athletic contests, horse races, and the like (412b)—has as its primary purpose not the acquisition of physical strength but rather the "awakening" (ἐγείρων, 410b6) and "right nurture" (ὀρθῶς τραφὲν, 410d7) of the spirited part of the soul, and the harmonizing of the spirited part of the soul with the wisdom-loving part (411e5–412a1). It also has an intellectual expression.[44] Μουσική, on the other hand, is intended to nurture and arouse the wisdom-loving part of the soul (410e3, 411d1–5), to soften, tame, and temper the spirited part of the soul without suppressing it, and to make it useful for learning and philosophy (411a9–11; 411d1–5). The two practices have been instituted *together* for the sake of attuning and coordinating the spirited and wisdom-loving powers of the soul (μουσικήν

MARK MOES

τε καὶ γυμναστικὴν ἐπὶ τὸ θυμοειδὲς καὶ τὸ φιλόσοφον, 411e5–6). They make it possible for these powers to be blended (412a4–5) into harmony with one another, each being stretched and relaxed to the appropriate degree (411e4–412a2), as the strings of a lyre must be stretched or relaxed if they are to be attuned to each other. Only the soul that has harmonized the love of wisdom with the aggressive instincts becomes at once both healthy-minded and courageous (σώφρων τε καὶ ἀνδρεία, 411a1). Its aggressive instincts are moderated and guided by wisdom,[45] and its other pursuits (including its *intellectual* pursuits and not only its athletic and gymnastic pursuits) are strenuously disciplined, tough-minded, and fueled by spiritedness in their execution.[46] The overseer (ἐπιστάτος, 412b1) of a πόλις must have a soul of this kind, if the way of life of the πόλις (its πολιτεία) is to be preserved.

A corollary of this view of the coordinate roles of μουσική and γυμναστική, and of the correlative unity of various virtues, is that either discipline practiced excessively and to the exclusion of the other can produce an unbalanced and unhealthy personality. A person who practices lifelong γυμναστική unaccompanied by training in μουσική disposes his mind toward savagery and toughness, toward raw physical courage not moderated by wisdom. Any love of learning there might have been in his soul becomes feeble and deaf and blind.[47] One reason Socrates gives for this enfeeblement of the philosophic power in the athlete who is "unmusical" is that he never tastes of any learning or inquiry or partakes in any discussion (λόγου) or in any of the rest of μουσική (411d2–3). Another is that his spirited power is neither awakened nor cultivated (ἐγειρόμενον, 411d4) nor nurtured (τρεφόμενον, 411d5) properly, because his perceptions are never cleansed (διακαθαιρομένων τῶν αἰσθήσεων αὐτοῦ, 411d5).[48] Socrates even says that the person who practices γυμναστική without μουσική becomes a μισόλογος (411d7), a hater of λόγος, and unmusical (ἄμουσος, 411d7). Such a person never makes use of persuasion by means of discourses but always savagely bulls his way through life like an animal, living in ignorance and stupidity without either rhythm or grace.[49]

On the other hand, a person who practices lifelong μουσική without γυμναστική disposes his mind toward softness and tameness. Even the *philosophic* part of his nature, instead of becoming well nurtured, rightly cultivated, and orderly, is relaxed too far and becomes softer than it should (410e1–3). He exercises his wisdom-loving capacities in too relaxed, soft-minded, and undisciplined a way, without the aggressiveness which prevents him from being too easily persuaded, too easily intellectually satisfied, too mindlessly a partisan or ideologue, or too obsequious a student or disciple.[50] He separates his mind from his aggressive emotions and even represses, forgets, and hides from them, so that they express themselves in more or less pathological forms of irascibility and irritability instead of in healthy aggressiveness and hard intellectual work. He melts away and cuts out of his soul his spiritedness (ἐκτήξῃ τὸν θυμὸν καὶ ἐκτέμῃ . . . ἐκ τῆς ψυχῆς, 411b3) and becomes a "faint-hearted warrior" (or "limp spearman"; μαλθακὸν αἰχμητήν, 411b4).[51] If by nature the person had a weak spirit, he does this quickly. If he had a strongly spirited nature, he makes his spirit weak and unstable, flaring up at trifles and extinguished just as easily, becoming not only irascible and irritable but also filled with discontent, rather than spirited (411b7–10).[52]

Let us notice that Socrates' explications of the fourth proposal show Glaucon that there was something wrong with his assent to proposals Socrates had earlier made concerning musical education. Earlier Glaucon had agreed to ban from the πόλις the use of dirges and lamentations and of any but the Dorian and Phrygian musical modes in educating the guardians, and to exclude from use the multi-stringed instruments (accompaniment to epic recitations) and flutes (accompaniment to tragic performances) (398d–399e). But in 411a Socrates says that the music of the flute and of the sorrowful modes is capable, when used properly, of softening θυμός and making it useful:

> When someone gives music an opportunity to charm his soul with the flute and to pour those sweet, soft, and plaintive tunes *which we were just discussing* [ἃς νυνδὴ ἡμεῖς ἐλέγομεν] through his ear, as through a funnel, when he spends his whole life humming them and delighting in them, then, at first, whatever spirit he has is softened, just as iron is tempered, and from being hard and useless, it is made useful. (411a5–11)

It is only when someone listens to such music unrelentingly, holding out and not letting up (ἐπιχέων μὴ ἀνιῇ, 411b1), and without balancing this behavior with some pursuit of γυμναστική (perhaps of intellectual as well as physical kinds), that he melts away and cuts out of his soul his spiritedness, becomes irascible and irritable, is filled with discontent, and perhaps loses hope and courage. Socrates' lesson for Glaucon is that he is ignorant of the importance and proper function of a great deal of good music, and that epic and tragedy contain lessons for him that he can ill afford to ignore. Unless he avails himself in the right way of their healing power, his θυμός will never be properly cultivated or nurtured, because his perceptions will never be cleansed (411d4–5).

The fourth proposal attempts to show the spirited and aggressive Glaucon how he might achieve the kind of knowledge that he needs in order to become a truly good statesman and a truly wise and coura-geous person. Socrates implies that in order to become a true guardian of himself and of others, Glaucon will have to pursue literature and philosophy with the kind of aggressive eagerness with which he is now tempted to pursue coercive political power. When Socrates articulated for Adeimantus the program of censoring scandalous and offensive passages from Homer and Hesiod, Glaucon raised no objection. His apparently premature assent to this program manifested his extreme crassness and superficiality as an interpreter of myths, his lack of appre-ciation of their edifying power. For cutting out from the myths all depic-tions of unjust deeds and characters would deprive would-be guardians with unjust characters of manifold opportunities for self-diagnosis and self-recognition. It would constitute a highly questionable form of both political and psychological repression or censorship, perhaps an expres-sion of the sort of self-censorship and self-deception that, according to some Freudian and post-Freudian theorists, is intrinsic to or symptom-atic of a variety of psychopathologies.[53] Glaucon's assent to the program was another expression of what Socrates had warned him against ear-lier—the mixing of γυμναστική with ιατρική. Socrates has already sug-gested that such practice makes one pursue an exhausting project of avoiding what is required for a real approach toward health of soul, and of hiding from the real causes of one's behavioral-psychological problems.

There is a natural tendency to presume that what is philosophical or rational is either painless or at least minimizes pain. But especially painful is the process of thinking about shameful aspects of oneself or about painful experiences. What we find "unthinkable" may often be only what we find too painful to contemplate, and the world comes with no assurance that the truth is always pretty and pleasant. Gain-ing the capacity to think painful thoughts may be among the prerequi-sites for becoming a wise person. Recall Er's vision of the souls making bad choices because they had participated in virtue through habit but without philosophy and had been "untrained in suffering" (619c–d).[54] Socrates is showing Glaucon that gymnastic of the body trains one to endure and even despise physical suffering, and that this carries over to other kinds of pain as well, such as the pain of grasping truths hid-den in products of μουσική. Later in the dialogue Glaucon shows his disdain for those persons he calls the "lovers of sights and hearing," who although they are unwilling to attend a discussion "run around to every chorus at the Dionysia, just as though they had hired out their ears for hearing" (475d). Glaucon apparently dislikes tragedy and does not run to every chorus at the Dionysia. Tragedy reveals men's weakness, their inability to control their situation, and their vulnerability.[55]

When Socrates reopens the discussion of imitation in book 10 at 595a–b, he initially allies himself with Glaucon's anti-tragic point of view. But then Socrates conducts a *dialectical* examination of the pedagogical value of tragic and comic poetry. After articulating a long case *against* poetry (595a–606d) that presumably corresponds to Glaucon's views on the matter, he moves to a higher standpoint at 606e and following, calling for a *defense* of the value of poetry.[56] For Glaucon poetic works are just tales whose surface features may be imitated or aped in a slavish way, not objects for inquiry and interpretation. Since Socrates knows about Glaucon's anti-tragic views and character, he tries in the fourth proposal to exhort him to mental toughness and to a more strenuous and philosophical study of the products of poetic craft.[57]

Earlier Socrates had suggested to Glaucon, as we have seen, that the virtuous person is able to acquire knowledge of both virtue and vice, knowledge of the truth both about his own character and that of others. Virtuous people have the power to recognize in advance and to disable tendencies in themselves that could lead to vice. A main purpose of the serious study of edifying literature is to impart this power. Vicious people often lack it, remaining utterly ignorant of the power of such tendencies in themselves and even protecting themselves against recognizing their ignorance. They are, in the language of *Phaedo* 89d–e, the μισόλογοι who have succumbed to the greatest of evils, the hatred of λόγος, of literature and of reasonable discourse. Socrates does not want Glaucon to succumb to it, any more than he wanted Phaedo to do so.

Later on, at 586c and following, Socrates makes a number of therapeutic suggestions to Glaucon about the harmful potentials of bodily ἔρως and of θυμός when they are disconnected from the love of wisdom. Indeed, the entire discussion between Socrates and Glaucon from 576b to the end of the *Republic* seems to be an extended therapeutic lesson for Glaucon about the need for the unification of bodily ἔρως and θυμός with wisdom.[58] The purpose of book 10 in particular seems to be, as suggested previously, to reveal the power of literature to contribute to this unification.[59]

Plato's Dialogues as Medicinal Rhetoric

The Socrates who makes the four proposals is a character in a Platonic dialogue. The question that now confronts us is whether his strategies with Glaucon cast any light upon *Plato's* philosophic method, and particularly upon Plato's reasons for writing in dialogue form.[60] Does a medical model of Socratic philosophy cast any light on *Plato's* philosophic practice? This section articulates an answer to this question, one that may need to be refuted in whole or in part, or at least more or less qualified in whole or in part, by scholars more learned in Greek history and philology than the author.

We can recall that in the *Phaedrus* Socrates treated dialectic as an instrument of rhetoric along with other non-dialectical instruments, and redefined rhetoric as a ψυχαγωγία that, since it is not confined to public contexts, can be exercised in any conversational context. Plato's written dialogues conspicuously depict long stretches of dialectical argumentation, but they also depict interlocutors employing non- dialectical discourses and techniques—stories, tropes of all kinds, myths, allusions to religious mysteries, experiences, rituals, and so on.[61] And since Plato *wrote* the dialogues, he doubtless envisioned that at least some of the time his readers would "listen in" on them and "converse" with them or engage in συνουσία with them, in *private* contexts of study and silent reading.[62] Again, there is evidence that Plato's aim in writing dialogues was not to work out and defend a system of philosophic doctrine but rather to perform ψυχαγωγία in relation to his readers.[63] This is especially so if the *Seventh Letter* is taken to be either a genuine Platonic letter or a letter written in accordance with things known about Plato's attitudes.[64] So there are some obvious analogies between Socrates' truthful rhetorician interacting with interlocutors, on the one hand, and Plato's interaction with his readers, on the other.

But Socrates in the *Phaedrus* also modeled the rhetorician-leading-his-audience-to-truthful-understanding upon the physician-diagnosing-an-interlocutor-and-leading-him-to-health. And this medical model of philosophizing, as we saw, also appeared in the *Phaedo* in Socrates' remedy for μισολογία and μισανθρωπία. The remedy consisted in the skillful employment of λόγοι (presumably both dialectical and non-dialectical), the skillful study of human nature, the skillful judging of character, and the skillful withholding of complete trust from less than healthy persons. Again there seem to be analogies between the person applying Socrates' remedy and the Plato who wrote the dialogues with such literary and logical skill yet refrained from speaking his own mind directly and didactically. Are there any other indications that Plato might have conceived of himself as a "philosophical physician" while composing the dialogues?

Plato had an important older contemporary who made influential use of medical ideas. It may be conjectured with some plausibility (but not argued in a clinching way) that Plato concerns himself in at least some of the dialogues with issues raised by Thucydides,[65] who adapted the principles and methods of Hippocratic medicine to the interpretation of the economic and political history of Athens.[66] The Hippocratics had divided the work of the physician into three parts: semeiology, prognosis, and therapeutics, seeking general formulations that would enable doctors to read symptoms in such a way as to arrive at true classifications and prognoses of diseases. Thucydides held that the knowledge of the nature of political crises is like the knowledge of the nature of diseases, and endeavored to make history into a semeiology and prognosis of human life, enabling men of future ages to recognize recurrent ethical-political maladies by their symptoms.[67] He treated political ways of life, such as Spartan authoritarianism and Athenian liberalism, under the medical rubric of regimens, and left to the political philosopher the task of constructing, on the basis of prognoses, more adequate systems of social therapeutics.[68] He composed the speeches for his *History* as part of an attempt to do semeiology and prognosis on the political practices of his day. He wanted to determine such classifications or formulations (εἴδη) as would raise history from mere chronicle to something more "scientific," as many doctors wanted to transform medicine from a mere empirical knack into a τέχνη.

In taking seriously the possibility that Plato's project is in important ways and on some level similar to Thucydides' project so understood, we are led to raise certain intriguing questions. One is whether Plato might not have depicted Socrates' philosophic practice with the aim of provoking and initiating readers into doing semeiology, prognosis, and therapeutics on cultural practices of their own time. Another is whether the depictions of apparent espousals by philosophers of antiliberal political programs in certain dialogues are not really Platonic invitations to *readers* to do semeiology and prognostics on the anti-liberal practices of their own day. Critics such as Cochrane and Popper take Plato to be making detestable *therapeutic* proposals.[69] But reading him alongside Thucydides suggests a different picture. Plato may be burying his own therapeutic suggestions beneath the surface of the dialogues, or he may be doing diagnostics in some parts of dialogues while making therapeutic suggestions elsewhere in the same dialogues, or simply leaving social therapeutics as a homework problem for the ages. The Hippocratic doctor, after all, exercised great discretion and believed that therapy is initiated mainly by abetting and removing obstacles to the natural urge to self-healing.[70] It may be that in remaining silent by writing mimetic dialogues, Plato is employing the remedy for μισολογία and μισανθρωπία that he put into the mouth of Socrates in the *Phaedo*, withholding complete trust from less than healthy persons.[71] Must we take for granted that the proposals for an "ideal πόλις" in the *Republic*, or even the legal proposals of the Athenian Stranger in the (unfinished)

Laws, constitute actual Platonic therapeutic recommendations? Might not these proposals only be speech acts whose illocutionary force depends upon the role they play in *diagnoses* and *prognoses*? We must not forget that Socrates in the *Republic,* after "building in speech" an "ideal πόλις," works out in books 8 and 9 the ways in which this "ideal πόλις" is the starting point for an inevitable decline into various pathological conditions.

Some salient and recurrent features of Plato's dialogue form are at least compatible with the possibility that Plato is following Thucydides in attempting to train his readers in an interesting kind of ethical-political pathology, or to invite them to a serious examination of conscience. Many of the dialogues depict conversations between either Socrates or some other philosophic master and one or more non-philosophers or philosophic neophytes. The non-philosophers are mostly real characters from Athenian history notorious for their personal failings or known to have been implicated in some way in the decline of Athens in the late fifth century.[72] The masters often say it is essential to their purposes that they use the question-and-answer method.[73] Plato depicts the masters as first attempting to refute or examine the non-philosophical interlocutors by posing questions to them, or eliciting opinions from them, and then as posing further questions or making further suggestions on the basis of their responses. There are indications in the texts of many dialogues that there are silent auditors listening to the conversations, as if Plato were inviting the reader to count himself among them. Many of the dialogues appear to end inconclusively, and even if they seem to contain a good deal of positive doctrine, careful scrutiny of the text often reveals implicit Platonic critiques or qualifications of that doctrine.[74] Plato never directly addresses the reader or appears as a participant in any of his dialogues. As author he hides himself and implicitly withholds complete commitment to any positive theses.[75] He often declines to supply even his philosophic characters with the best case they might have available for a thesis. Instead he puts bad arguments into their mouths or has them miss opportunities to produce better arguments or fuller expositions of their views, as if he wanted readers to try out for themselves better arguments or fuller expositions.[76] Often the masters ask the interlocutors to announce the results of the conversations; rarely do they commit themselves in an unqualified way to any positive theses produced during the conversations.

A medical model of *Platonic* philosophy is able to go some distance in making these features intelligible. The model can be summarized like this. Plato depicts Socrates (or other philosophic "physicians") as working to engender health in the πόλις of Athens, in the only way possible, by practicing the "true politics" that Socrates mentions in the *Gorgias* (or the ψυχαγωγία that Socrates mentions in the *Phaedrus*) so as to transform individual lives. He shows them trying to do this by attempting to restore to health[77] (or by offering means of preserving or improving the health of)[78] the souls of persons of influence on the body politic—poets, rhetoricians, sophists and other teachers, citizen-politicians, aspiring citizen-politicians like Glaucon, military men, and so on. Readers know in retrospect that many of the interlocutors of the dialogues were more or less directly implicated in the decline of Athens at the end of the fifth century.[79] According to this model, Plato carries on something very like Thucydides' project in his own very different and inimitable way.

Furthermore, many of the depicted conversations are in important ways like interactions between physicians and their clients. On the level of Plato's relation to his readers, therefore, they constitute quasi-medical or quasi-psychiatric *case histories* that set forth records of diagnoses of typical deformities of soul that contributed to Athens' decline, and of attempted cures of those maladies. Or at least they suggest therapeutic regimens for such maladies. They urge readers to recognize similar maladies in themselves and others, and to learn methods and to assimilate conceptual resources useful for curing them. The historical and personal failures of many of the interlocutors, some known to readers and some dramatized and made thematic in the dialogues themselves, serve to motivate readers to strive to avoid a similar fate. On healthier readers the dialogues at least urge the necessity of the kind of gymnastic training, as it were, that might help them avoid falling into disease. Because of their intricacy and the philosophic cunning with which they are composed, studying the dialogues can be itself a health-conducive and health-sustaining regimen.[80] Depending upon the maturity, talent, and interests of the reader, Plato's relationship to this reader might be conceived either as a physician-client relationship or as a medical professor–medical student relationship. Furthermore, the non-systematic character and lack of closure to the corpus of dialogues as a whole might be explained with the aid of the medical model. An adequate set of case studies needs only to be a fairly representative and pedagogically useful set of examples of common types of disease, or of the types of cases a person is apt to confront.

In closing, we return to Plato's depiction of Socrates' interaction with Glaucon in the *Republic*. Taking Plato to have written dialogues in the role of a therapist helps us to understand that depiction. As I maintained in the previous section of this paper, Socrates seems in many stretches of his conversation with Plato's brother Glaucon[81] to be attempting to provide him with opportunities for recognizing the dangerous potentials of his naive political ambitions and of his own ignorance about ψυχή and πόλις. Plato depicts Socrates as pretending to agree with Glaucon's opinions and attitudes about an ideal πόλις in order to lure him into a diagnostic self-examination that he would otherwise resist.

We might compare Socrates' interaction with Thrasymachus and Glaucon in the *Republic* with Socrates' interaction with Critias and Charmides in the *Charmides*. In the *Charmides,* Plato's purpose in depicting Socrates' examination first of Charmides (158e–162b) and then of Critias (162c–175d) is to depict a diagnosis (and prognosis) of the negative potentials of the influence that Critias exerts upon Charmides. In the *Republic,* Plato's purpose in depicting Socrates' examination first of Thrasymachus and then of Glaucon is to depict a diagnosis of the negative potentials of the influence that Thrasymachus exerts upon Glaucon. But whereas readers know that Critias and Charmides became members of the murderous Thirty Tyrants,[82] Glaucon is perhaps best remembered for what he did not do: he did not follow the example of Critias and Charmides and share in their notoriety. Socrates, who took an interest in Glaucon for the sake of Plato, managed to check his political ambitions.[83]

To put things in this way is to dissent from certain readings of the *Republic* that presuppose a "developmentalist" view of the Platonic corpus.[84] These take Plato's dramatization of Socrates' relation with Glaucon as indicating Plato's giving up his earlier practice of depicting a purely elenctic Socrates in order to begin to use Socrates as a mouthpiece for the expression of positive philosophical-political doctrines of his own. According to one such reading, Socrates' three interlocutors in book 1 are either too non-philosophical (Cephalus), too obsequious (Polemarchus), or too hostile (Thrasymachus) to elicit from Socrates a well-defended positive account of justice. Plato brings in Glaucon because he can provide Socrates with a real challenge and wrest from him such an account. Glaucon is more "rational" than Thrasymachus because he is willing to engage in real dialectic. Plato puts his own ethical-political views into the mouth of Socrates conversing with Glaucon.[85] An apparently serious problem with such an interpretation is that it commits one to thinking that Plato endorses those political features of the "ideal πόλις" which many readers find scandalous.[86] And it makes no sense of the diagnostic dimension of Socrates' conversation with Glaucon.

A view more in keeping with the reading expressed in the previous section of this paper would take Glaucon as sharing some of the mistaken attitudes of Socrates' interlocutors in book 1. In particular, Glaucon shares with them the belief that justice is anti-erotic. They all think that eros must be suppressed if justice is to be realized in πόλις and ψυχή. Though Glaucon pays lip service to the desirability of justice by *saying* he does not accept Thrasymachus' view of it, he nevertheless *shows* that he too thinks justice can only be gotten by restraining ἔρως, rather than by redirecting and transforming it. For in book 4 he endorses both the moral psychology and the conception of social justice articulated there. But it is no exaggeration to say that the "just" city of book 4 is simply a disguised tyranny justifying itself in terms of the language of virtue, the very thing that Thrasymachus unmasked in book 1. Thrasymachus' account of justice may be a de facto true account of many polities, but it is difficult not to share Socrates' sense that Thrasymachus' account does not tell the whole story about justice. The "just" soul of book 4 is the mirror image of a Thrasymachean polity. It represents indeed that unjust life, disguised as a just life, that the naive and ambitious Glaucon finds tempting. Or at best it is a model of what Aristotle will call the merely continent but non-virtuous soul. For it maintains its unity by means of strict control of ἔρως and θυμός by a passionless and calculating utilitarian rationality.

But in later passages Socrates tries to get Glaucon to see that the moral psychology of book 4 is *mistaken*. The paradoxical proposal at the midpoint of the dialogue, from 471c to 474a, initiates Socrates' movement from diagnosis to cure. The new proposal is that if a truly ideal πόλις were to be realized, it would have to be ruled by philosophers, the most erotic souls of all. In them ἔρως is being redirected and transformed and desires are becoming properly organized and aimed. In them, strife between reason and desire is resolved by an awareness of the Good, which makes it possible for ἔρως to become rational and for reason to become erotic. Whereas kings rule *over* cities, enshrining their false opinions and worshiping their desires, philosophers order and rank their desires in accordance with their knowledge (however partial) of true goodness, and help their followers (not subjects) to do the same. But the just πόλις is meant to be a model for the just ψυχή, with the philosopher-ruler playing the role of reason and the other citizens playing the roles of the passions. So Socrates' lesson for Glaucon is that both the three-part πόλις and the three-part ψυχή are diseased. In the just ψυχή there is no need for the passions to be *controlled* by any other part of the soul. Nor in the completely just πόλις is there any need for certain classes of citizens to be controlled by a ruling class. This *new* model of πόλις and ψυχή suggested by the discussion after 471c is meant to elicit Glaucon's recognition of the distortions in the sick πόλις and ψυχή of books 2–5.

Socrates goes to great pains in the latter parts of the dialogue to get Glaucon to see that the philosopher is in love with truth, and will not tolerate the edifice of lies that constitutes the "just" city elaborated up to

471c. In the section running from 471c to the end of book 7, philosophic rule is contrasted with the delusory order of the totalitarian, coercive, and cavelike πόλις of books 2–5. Books 8 and 9 show how the supposedly just "aristocratic" regime will anyway self-destruct and transform from a hidden tyranny into a manifest one; by implication an "aristocratic" soul, in which reason, split off from passion, has failed to bring desires into harmonious relation, will self-destruct as well. Socrates' objective all along is to show the impossibility of conserving and hiding forever the deceptions and self-deceptions in sick "aristocracies" or in falsely "aristocratic" souls.[87]

If this is Socrates' strategy with Glaucon, Thrasymachus comes off as having more integrity than Glaucon, not less. For whereas he acts consistently with his views, Glaucon is torn between the life of Thrasymachus and the life of Socrates. If he is to get anywhere with Glaucon, Socrates must not merely *argue* that the just life is superior to other lives.[88] He must bring Glaucon to a deeper self-encounter. Failing this, Glaucon will accept the argument on the level of notional apprehension, but then go on to rationalize his own grabs for coercive power over others in the name of justice, because his subterranean desires will not have been exposed and transformed. Socrates cannot just bluntly accuse Glaucon of being an ignorant young idealist with "impractical expectations." (See Socrates' questions to Adeimantus at 494c–d.) Socrates must proceed by indirection, not for logical reasons, but for psychological and pedagogical reasons. He must use not only dialectical, but also non-dialectical, techniques of rhetoric.[89] Glaucon *says* that he does not espouse Thrasymachus' accounts of justice and excellence, and he is no doubt sincere. But sincerely to avow adherence to certain values is one thing, and to live in a way consistent with such an avowal is another. For there can be an apprehension of value that is merely verbal or notional but which falls short of a real and effectual apprehension. In the early parts of the *Republic*, Plato diagnoses for us the divided condition of Glaucon's soul. Then he shows us how Socrates healed him, or at least set him on the path toward healing.

Notes

1. See, for example, Werner Jaeger, "Greek Medicine as Paideia," in *Paideia: The Ideals of Greek Culture*, trans. Gilbert Highet, 3 vols. (New York: Oxford University Press, 1944), 3:3. See also Werner Jaeger, "Aristotle's Use of Medicine as Model of Method in His Ethics," *Journal of Hellenic Studies* 77, pt. 1 (1957): 54–61. See also John Haldane, "Medical Ethics—An Alternative Approach," *Journal of Medical Ethics* 12 (1986): 145–50. See my *Plato's Dialogue Form and the Care of the*

Soul (New York: Peter Lang, 2000), especially chap. 2. Two scholars who have
worked on the role of medical ideas in Plato's dialogues are Joel Warren Lidz
and Mario Vegetti. See Joel Warren Lidz, "Medicine as Metaphor in Plato," *Journal of Medicine and Philosophy* 20 (1995): 527–41. Lidz discusses some of the relevant historical antecedents to medical themes in Plato as well as the ethical and
philosophical significance of some of the medical terms and metaphors employed in the dialogues. See also Mario Vegetti, *La Medicina en Platone* (Venice:
Il Cardo Editore, 1995). Vegetti examines the role of medical ideas in the "Socratic dialogues," and also in the *Gorgias, Symposium, Phaedo, Republic,* and *Phaedrus.* See also the references listed at the end of my article "Plato's Conception
of the Relations Between Moral Philosophy and Medicine," *Perspectives in Biology
and Medicine* 44 (Summer 2001): 3. G. E. R. Lloyd's *In the Grip of Disease: Studies
in the Greek Imagination* (Oxford: Oxford University Press, 2003) surveys some
interactions among philosophy, religion, and medicine from the Archaic to the
Hellenistic period, focusing especially upon views of selfhood, causality and
responsibility, authority, catharsis, evil, and diseases of the soul and of society.

2. If non-dialectical rhetorical techniques (for example, those employed
in poetry) work to transform an auditor's emotions, and if emotions possess
some cognitive potential, then the use of non-dialectical techniques may be as
important as the use of dialectical ones in the project of communicating truths.
On the other hand, if emotions have a cognitive component, then the use of
dialectical techniques may have an important influence upon the emotions.

3. At *Phaedrus* 270c and again at 273e Socrates maintains that one cannot
achieve serious understanding of the nature of the soul without understanding
the nature of the *kosmos* as a whole (270c), without dividing *everything* according
to kinds (273e). In the discourse of the Divided Line in the *Republic,* Socrates
provides a schematic division of (1) kinds of being in the κόσμος, (2) active and
passive powers of the ψυχή, and (3) kinds of λόγος. It would be interesting to
explore in greater depth the interrelations between Socrates' image of the Divided Line and his discussion of dialectical rhetoric in the *Phaedrus* and of the
τεχνη of λόγος in the *Phaedo.* See notes 58 and 59.

4. We need not impute to Plato any crude dualistic metaphysical conception of the nature of soul and body. See Paul Stern, "Socrates' Final Teaching,"
chap. 5 of *Socratic Rationalism and Political Philosophy: An Interpretation of Plato's
Phaedo* (Albany: State University of New York Press, 1993).

5. It is worth emphasizing here that a craft, though it can explain its own
procedure, is to an important extent a non-propositional and non-theoretical
sort of *knowledge how.* Craft knowledge is more than knowledge of the truth of
propositions and more than observational knowledge. It is akin to an agent's
non-observational "feel" for his own skilled performances. Jaeger says that a
τεχνη is "that knowledge of the nature of an object, which aims at benefiting
man, and which is therefore incomplete as knowledge until it is put in practice."
See Jaeger, *Paideia,* 3:21.

6. It ought to be kept in mind while reading this passage that λόγος in
Greek can denote words, sentences, stories, myths, discussions, arguments, relations, proportions, and even the power of reason itself.

7. Here one should remember that in the *Phaedrus dialectical* rhetoric is connected with *Hippocratic medicine*. Charles Kahn discusses the meaning of "dialectic" in "The Emergence of Dialectic," chap. 10 of *Plato and the Socratic Dialogue* (Cambridge: Cambridge University Press, 1996). An interesting suggestion on this can be found in Mitchell Miller, *The Philosopher in Plato's Statesman* (The Hague: Martinus Nijhoff, 1980), ix–xix. Socrates often criticizes a thesis in such a way as to preserve its partial truth while at the same time showing how and in what respects it is erroneous.

8. In its application to persons "health" denotes good order in body and soul. In its application to λόγοι it is used analogously or paronymously to mean "causing or inducing health in a soul," or "produced or caused by a healthy soul."

9. I have discussed many of the points made in this section in more detail in "Plato's Conception of the Relations Between Moral Philosophy and Medicine." Joel Lidz's discussion of what he calls "medical metaphors in Plato's ethics" in his "Medicine as Metaphor in Plato" treats from a different perspective some of the issues I am concerned with in this section.

10. See Lidz, "Medicine as Metaphor," 531.

11. Lidz writes: "A successful moral upbringing produces a character which is resistant to bad influences (*Rep* 367a), just as 'a man in health and strength can drink any water that is at hand without distinction' (*Airs, Waters, and Places*, ch. 7). In short, our moral sense . . . requires constant attention from childhood. No moral theory offered to adults can substitute for that ongoing attention." See Lidz, "Medicine as Metaphor," 530.

12. See R. B. Rutherford, *The Art of Plato* (Cambridge: Harvard University Press, 1995), 11–12. Rutherford says that a Platonic portrayal of an exchange between Socrates and an interlocutor captures "both the delicacy of tactful exploration of another's painful thoughts or experiences, and the rapidity of an interrogator's reactions when seeking out weakness, pursuing guilt, or hunting down error." It would be interesting to explore the relation between Socrates' conversational strategies, on the one hand, and the theories concerning *conversational implicature* explored by Paul Grice and his students. See Kenneth Taylor, "Language and Action," chap. 6 of *Truth and Meaning: An Introduction to the Philosophy of Language* (Oxford: Blackwell, 1998).

13. Lidz discusses how difficult it may be to call a corrupt person toward moral change. He writes: "Such a state of corruption is produced by training and practice which result in an inferior character and is difficult to correct, since it is a corruption of the very faculties which would be needed to correct it" (Lidz, "Medicine as Metaphor," 535).

14. From our twentieth-century perspective, it seems as if Socrates foreshadows the practice of psychoanalysts such as Heinz Kohut, who purposely cultivated transference relationships with interlocutors in such a way as to mirror back to them, and so give them an opportunity for recognizing, their own psychological conditions. Another perspective on the theme of helping an auditor achieve self-recognition is offered by H. W. Rankin in "A Modest Proposal About the *Republic*," *Apeiron* 2, no. 1 (November 1967): 20–22. Rankin defends

the view that Plato was a writer of mime and should be read like a satirist trying to get his audience to see its own foibles and flaws. Jokes are not merely expressions of the unconscious, but also ways of influencing and bringing unconscious factors to light.

15. One might in this connection think of Socrates covering himself with a veil while delivering his first speech in the *Phaedrus*. One thinks in this connection of the way in which, according to Socrates at *Republic* 393d, the poet-author of "narrative with imitation" hides himself.

16. In the *Republic* there are many passages in which either Glaucon or Adeimantus asks Socrates for a quick answer to some deep philosophical question which he does not want to think through for himself. Socrates always exhorts him to think for himself. See 358d, 367a–e, 427d–e, 434d–435a, 435c–d, 449c–450c, 451a–b, 457c–e, 472a, 506b–d. An excellent discussion of this aspect of the philosopher-interlocutor relationship as depicted in the Platonic dialogues can be found in Miller, *Philosopher in Plato's Statesman*, ix–xix. On page xiii Miller says that there is an important sense in which each man must "make the philosophic ascent for himself." See also Mitchell Miller, *Plato's Parmenides: The Conversion of the Soul* (Princeton: Princeton University Press, 1986), 3–12.

17. The Athenian Stranger in *Laws* 720b–e seems to indicate this when he says that the free medical practitioner does not give prescriptions until he has won the patient's support. Lidz, "Medicine as Metaphor," 530, cites P. Carrick in support of the view that "for Plato the responsibility for carrying out a program of mental and physical hygiene rests squarely with each person." See P. Carrick, *Medical Ethics in Antiquity* (Boston: D. Reidel, 1985), 27ff.

18. Jaeger says that the principal axiom in Hippocrates' doctrine of sickness is that healing is initiated by the body itself, and all the doctor need do is to watch for the point where he can step in to help the natural urge to self-healing. See Jaeger, *Paideia*, 3:28.

19. An interesting discussion of the interrelation of cognitive and affective factors in what Socrates considers to be the highest kind of knowledge can be found in Emile de Strycker, "The Unity of Knowledge and Love in Socrates' Conception of Virtue," *International Philosophical Quarterly* 6 (1966): 428–44.

20. According to Strycker, good vision of the whole is like good vision of the material world to the extent that there is always more observation to be done. Good vision of value expresses itself in more appropriate and consistent deeds and utterances, just as good physical vision enables one to function better in the physical environment.

21. See, for example, Gerald Press, "Knowledge as Vision in Plato's Dialogues," *Journal of Neoplatonic Studies* 3, no. 2 (Spring 1995): 61–89. Kenneth Sayre attempts to show that one never knows propositions but always *states of affairs*. Knowledge for Sayre is a cognitive access to a state of affairs, whereas belief and many other cognitive states are intentional attitudes to propositions. See Kenneth Sayre, "A Surface Map of Cognitive Attitudes," chap. 1 of *Belief and Knowledge: Mapping the Cognitive Landscape* (Lanham: Rowman and Littlefield, 1997).

22. See the brief summary of the Thomistic theory of knowledge in Fulton Sheen, "Critical Appreciation of the Modern Objections Against Intelligence,"

pt. 2, chap. 3 of *God and Intelligence in Modern Philosophy: A Critical Study in the Light of the Philosophy of Saint Thomas* (New York: Longman's, Green, 1938).

23. The dictum of Richard of St. Victor is "ubi amor, ibi oculus." Quoted in Thomas Aquinas, *Commentary on the Sentences*, 3.d.35.1.21.

24. For example, there is Socrates' reference to "keen eyesight" at *Republic* 368c–d and his description at *Phaedrus* 247a of the soul's journey at the edge of the universe in terms suggestive of viewing a theatrical spectacle (θεωρία can mean being a spectator at the games or theater). Then there is his mention of the descent from divine θεωρία to that of human beings at *Republic* 517d, and his mention of the contemplation (θεωρία) of all time and existence at *Republic* 486a (see also 500b–c). See Press, "Knowledge as Vision." This understanding of knowledge as vision does not necessarily fall prey to Heidegger's objection that it is bound up with the "metaphysics of presence." For the soul in *Phaedrus* 247 is moving around the rim of the inner universe, and seeing the Forms therefore from different "angles" and "distances." This soul will have to synthesize its apprehensions, retentions, and protentions of the Forms, and this will be an endless task.

25. See note 16 above.

26. John Henry Newman, *An Essay in Aid of a Grammar of Assent* (Garden City, N. Y.: Image Books, 1955), 251. See all of chaps. 8 and 9. On p. 268 Newman quotes Aristotle's mention of an "eye of experience" in a discussion of φρόνησις at *Nichomachean Ethics*, bk. 6, chap. 11 (1143b13).

27. Xenophon's brief depiction of a conversation between Socrates and Glaucon indicates that Glaucon was as a youth highly ambitious and quite ignorant. See Xenophon, "Memoirs of Socrates," 3.6 in Xenophon, *Conversations of Socrates* (London: Penguin, 1990), 152–56. See also Nalin Ranasinghe, *The Soul of Socrates* (Ithaca: Cornell University Press, 2000), 2–3, 4–6, 15–16. On Ranasinghe's reading, Glaucon believes that injustice is natural and that he, a member of the natural aristocracy, is born to rule. He is driven by a fierce ambition to wield power, and thinks one must reform first the city and only then the soul. Socrates thinks that a desire to rule others is indicative of a disordered soul that does not know itself, and is trying to make Glaucon aware of the absurdity of his political ambitions without publicly shaming him.

28. Perhaps the *Laws* may be read as a depiction of the Athenian Stranger's prescribing a gymnastic *regimen* for a particular πόλις, intended to maintain it in health once it is founded. (There is a poem by the great Attic legislator Solon, the kinsman of Plato's maternal great-great grandfather, in which Solon speaks of the πόλις as an organism susceptible to disease, whose health is maintained by following a regimen contained in a good code of laws.) But it does not go without saying that Plato endorses the regimen in every respect. See note 39.

29. See note 14. Socrates hides, so to speak, his deepest communicative intentions beneath the surface of the conversation. Mark Gifford has a good discussion of the difference between the dramatic irony "internal" to a Platonic dialogue and "external" dramatic irony that refers to a character's behavior outside a dialogue but known to Plato's audience. See Mark Gifford, "Dramatic Dialectic in *Republic* Book 1," in *Oxford Studies in Ancient Philosophy* 20 (2001):

37–52. For attempts at classifying types of irony, see Wayne Booth, *Rhetoric of Irony* (Chicago: University of Chicago Press, 1974), especially chaps. 8 and 9. See also D. C. Muecke, *The Compass of Irony* (London: Methuen, 1969).

30. Perhaps the contrast lies not in that the members of the healthy society never feast or enjoy luxuries, but that they do so on special occasions and for the enhancement of family life, whereas the guardian class of the aristocracy pursues a decadent lifestyle of constant feasting and luxuriousness. Rankin (see note 14) draws attention to the parallel between the *Republic* and Cynic-Stoic πολιτεῖαι. He says that these were modeled on comedy and mime, and that family life was a favorite subject. He says the Cynic-Stoic works were satirical sermons striking at the basic assumptions of contemporary society in favor of something that they claimed was more simple and natural. We need to keep in mind the distinction between the picture of felicitous family relations in the paradise and the proposals for abolishing the family in book 5 of the *Republic*.

31. See also the phrase used in 407b1: νοσοτροφία τεκτονικῇ.

32. The term δικάσται refers mainly to members of a jury. Athenian juries decided questions of guilt and of penalty, combining functions we divide between jury and judge.

33. The radical program outlined in book 5 calls for the abolition among the guardians of natural family relations and parenthood, for the recruitment of sufficiently "spirited" women as guardians, and for the eugenic breeding of men and women guardians. This program can be read, on one level at least, as both a parody of Aristophanes' *Ecclesiazusae* and a parody of the ὕβρις of idealistic political reformers drunk on power. See Ranasinghe, *Soul of Socrates*, 15–18. Yet on another level, the inclusion of both men and women in the guardian class of the πόλις might symbolize the marriage of "masculine" political ability with "feminine" philosophy in the perfectly actualized *soul*. This view suggests interesting relationships between the early parts of book 5 and Socrates' characterization of philosophy as "spiritual pregnancy" in the Diotima speech in the *Symposium* and at *Republic* 490a–b (see also *Republic* 495b–496a). See Leon Harold Craig, "The Portrait of a Lady," chap. 6 of *The War Lover: A Study of Plato's Republic* (Toronto: University of Toronto Press, 1994).

34. In terms made familiar by John Henry Newman, Glaucon's assent is "notional" but not "real."

35. The censorship of literature and music can play a role in avoidance behavior and self-deception, as we shall suggest below.

36. Asclepius was of course a mortal who was deified as a god of healing. He brought the art to perfection and is said to have raised Hippolytus from the dead, the only one ever to raise a mortal from death. In this passage he is invoked as the healer showing the way toward the revivification of Athens.

37. My remarks here on the soul-state analogy in the *Republic* dovetail nicely with those of Diskin Clay, "Reading the *Republic*," in *Platonic Writings, Platonic Readings,* ed. Charles L. Griswold Jr. (New York and London: Routledge, 1988), 24–33.

38. The rhetoric of this whole section is, like that of the previous section, accommodated to Glaucon's elitist self-conception, appealing frequently to his

sense of shame, for example, at 405a6, 405b1, 405b6, and 405d4. At 410b1–3 Socrates appeals to Glaucon's self-conception as someone who is already well educated when he says that the μουσικός will make no use of ιατρική that is not absolutely necessary.

39. Even if Plato's Socrates (or Plato) endorsed the radical political policies of book 5, he would not necessarily endorse that they be implemented and required by law. The feminist policies aired by the Athenian Stranger in the *Laws* do not clinch the matter of Plato's view on this, for their status is also unclear. Clay points out that the status of the utopian proposals in the *Republic* and *Laws* is connected, in his "Reading the *Republic*," 29 and n24. Also see Clay on the way "the closure of positions taken by the speakers within the dialogue is challenged by a dialogue that refuses to conclude," 21–24. Myles Burnyeat, in an emotional discussion of Leo Strauss's view of the *Republic*, writes that Strauss's "crowning insult to the critical intellect" is his insinuation that "the just city is against nature because the equality of the sexes and absolute communism is against nature." Burnyeat says this insinuation is completely opposed to "what Plato wrote and Aristotle criticized." See Burnyeat, "Sphinx Without a Secret," in *Plato: Critical Assessments,* vol. 1, ed. Nicholas D. Smith (New York and London: Routledge, 1998), 341–43. Burnyeat has also argued that Plato presents his "best city in speech" as a practical political teaching in "The Practicability of Plato's Ideally Just City," in *On Justice,* ed. K. Boudouris (Athens: Hellēnikē Philosophikē Hetaireia, 1989), 94–105. Burnyeat, to my mind, not only wrongly assumes that Aristotle's cursory allusions to Plato must always be taken as good evidence for Plato's authorial intentions in the dialogues, but reads the *Republic* in such a way as to miss frequent indications in the text that practical realization is not Socrates' concern. There is also a need to interpret the significance of the Athenian Stranger's repeated indications in the *Laws* (for example, 739c, 740a, 773b) that radical communism is contrary to human nature.

40. So the vicious person is unable to take his own prejudices or conflicts of interest into account and to compensate for them in his judgments.

41. In Thrasymachus we see an example of a man who has become totally incapable of granting that anyone might be truly virtuous, and has come to believe that human goodness lies in manipulative and coercive power alone. He is unable to benefit from Socrates' refutations of his views, even though Socrates treats him as a friend (see 498c–d). In the moral scheme of Thomas Aquinas there are two virtues that perfect the will, justice and friendship (*Summa theologica* 1–2.ae.57.1).

42. There seems to be a critical backward reference here to the earlier proposal to censor out of the literary education of guardians any depictions of unjust deeds and characters. If ἐπιστήμη is of Forms, then knowledge of injustice must involve awareness of various Forms of both virtue and vice. Compare the reference to "forms of vice" in 445c and throughout the tale of the decline of the polities in books 8–9. Note also the depictions of vice and folly in the Myth of Er. Compare Socrates' remarks at 402c. The *Republic* and the other dialogues are in great part examinations of forms of virtue and vice.

43. See the mention of the Myth of Er in note 56 below.

44. See note 46.

45. An interesting dramatic irony here: one aim of the censorship of passages from the epics was to augment spiritedness so as to produce absolutely fearless warriors (for example, 387c). Now Socrates urges a very different purpose for μουσική and γυμναστική together, to provide a tempering, guiding, and cathartic influence on innate aggressiveness.

46. An interesting study could be made of Plato's use of the notion of intellectual γυμναστική for the ψυχή in the dialogues as a whole. In dialogues such as the *Parmenides, Theaetetus, Sophist,* and *Statesman,* the philosophical protagonist's chief interlocutors—Socrates himself, Theaetetus, and "young Socrates"—are all taken through formidable "mental gymnastics" during the course of the conversations. And it is noteworthy that the conversations depicted in the *Theaetetus, Sophist,* and *Statesman* all occur in a gymnasium (as do those depicted in the *Lysis* and *Charmides*). The old master Parmenides finds flaws in the young Socrates' understanding of the Forms and participation, and decides accordingly to show him a way in which he can be "trained gymnastically" so as to better understand the relation between Forms and their instances. (In *Parmenides* 135a–137c there are at least five occurrences of "γυμναστική" and cognates in the description of the method of hypothesis.) See Jaeger, *Paideia,* 3:30–36. In book 10 of the *Republic* (613bc and 621d; also earlier at 465d, 503a, 504a, 583b) we find references to prizes the just man wins from men and gods for victory in the games. This seems to recall and "trump" the prizes of those engaged in the games at the festival of Bendis in book 1. See Rutherford, *Art of Plato,* 217.

47. At 571d–572a Socrates describes the bedtime ritual of the healthy person, who rouses his reason but soothes his θυμός every night before he goes to sleep.

48. It should not be lost on the reader that this phrase might be construed as evidence that Socrates (and Plato) held a somewhat "Aristotelian" view of the function of μουσική and ποιητική. It is also noteworthy that Socrates draws a close connection in this passage between φιλοσοφία and μουσική.

49. Compare Socrates' sketch of the timocratic personality in 548d–549c. Adeimantus is inclined to classify Glaucon as a timocratic type, the type that loves γυμναστική and hunting (549a). Socrates says the timocratic type differs from Glaucon in the following respects: he is more unmusical but a *lover of it* (φιλόμουσον) and he *loves to listen to discussions* (φιλήκοον) (548e4–5).

50. The unspirited thinker, perhaps, never makes appropriate use of, say, the methods of hypothesis or of collection and division. Socrates often pairs philosophical learning with γυμναστική in the *Republic* (410e, 441e, 498b, 503e–504a, 504a–d, 526b, 535b–d, 539d). Later in the dialogue Socrates proposes that the male and female guardians "exercise" naked together, and the "gymnastic" with which their education concludes is five years of strenuous "exercise" in dialectical arguments (539d–e). Perhaps this suggests on a symbolic level that men and women need to philosophize together. See note 33.

51. This is a phrase from *Iliad* 17.588, where Apollo tells Hektor that earlier Meneleos had been a μαλθακὸν αἰχμητήν. Plato quotes the same phrase at *Sym-*

posium 174c. Presumably Plato enjoyed the phrase's punning between cowardice and sexual impotence.

52. There may be a nod again here to Thrasymachus, and Socrates may be trying to show Glaucon that he will end up like Thrasymachus if he is not careful in the future to balance his pursuits.

53. To me it seems plausible that in the censorship discussions, Plato is indeed depicting Glaucon's eagerness to hide from the grim realities depicted in Homer and Hesiod and the tragedians, but to dress up his denial as an exercise in righteousness. Modern students of Greek culture see pervasive psychoanalytic themes in Greek theogonies and mythologies. See, for example, Richard Caldwell, "The Psychology of the Succession Myth," an interpretive essay in *Hesiod's Theogony* (Newburyport: Focus Classical Library, 1987), 87–103; and Philip Slater, *The Glory of Hera: Greek Mythology and the Greek Family* (Princeton: Princeton University Press, 1968). See also Bennett Simon, *Mind and Madness in Ancient Greece: The Classical Roots of Modern Psychiatry* (Ithaca: Cornell University Press, 1978), 215–16; Anthony Kenny, "Mental Health in Plato's Republic," in *The Anatomy of the Soul: Historical Essays in the Philosophy of Mind* (New York: Barnes and Noble, 1973); and Pedro Lain Entralgo, *The Therapy of the Word in Classical Antiquity* (New Haven: Yale University Press, 1970), especially chaps. 1–2.

54. See Craig, *The War Lover*, 74.

55. See Mary P. Nichols, "Spiritedness and Philosophy in Plato's *Republic*," in *Understanding the Political Spirit: Philosophical Investigations from Socrates to Nietzsche*, ed. Catherine Zuckert (New Haven: Yale University Press, 1988), 58. See also her remarks about Glaucon's character in "Glaucon's Adaptation of the Story of Gyges and Its Implications for Plato's Political Teaching," *Polity* 17, no. 1 (Fall 1984): 34–36.

56. See notes 2 and 6. The dialectical discussion of poetry in book 10 begins with the case against poetry's value to the πόλις, but then in the Myth of Er shows that the study of the right kind of poetry is necessary in a healthy πόλις. The *Republic* itself, while violating all the strictures against poetry in the sick πόλις, is an instance of poetry "not only pleasant but beneficial to regimes and human life" (607d). See my "Mimetic Irony and Plato's Defense of Poetry in the *Republic*," *Journal of Neoplatonic Studies* 5, no. 1 (Fall 1996): 43–74. For a discussion of a number of very different approaches to reading the *Republic* over the centuries, see Gerald Press, "Continuities and Discontinuities in the History of *Republic* Interpretation," *International Studies in Philosophy* 28, no. 4 (1996): 61–78.

57. For further remarks about Glaucon's character, see Allan Bloom, "Interpretive Essay," in Plato, *The Republic of Plato* (New York and London: Basic Books, 1968), 337–40, 342, 345–46, 401, 412, 415, 423.

58. It might be argued that one of Socrates' reasons for articulating the image of the Divided Line at the end of book 6 is a desire to emphasize the harmonious relationships among various rational powers in a healthy soul. On this reading, the line shows that a human comes to understand and exemplify goodness only when his rational powers function together harmoniously, as the segments of the line corresponding to the powers are interrelated according

to ordered mathematical ratios. It also suggests that the rational powers of the soul are both cognitive and affective (because on each level they are ordered toward images of the Good). See notes 2 and 3. The discussions in books 7–10 of the *Republic* seem aimed stepwise at the four powers of the soul distinguished in the Divided Line: book 7 at νοῦς and διάνοια, books 8–9 at πίστις, and book 10 at εἰϰασία (including the poetic power).

59. It is noteworthy that the argument about the soul's immortality at 608c–612a culminates in a portrayal of the soul in its pure state as simple and not differing from itself as the divided soul was represented as doing in book 4. "We must not think that the soul in its truest nature . . . differs with itself. . . . What we've said about the soul [in book 4] is true of it as it appears at present . . . that is why we have to look somewhere else in order to discover its true nature . . . to its love of wisdom. . . . Then we would see what its true nature is, and be able to determine whether it has many parts or just one" (611c–612a). Of course, Socrates "divided" the soul into powers in the image of the Divided Line. But the soul can be divided in two ways. First, it can become disintegrated when its powers do not work in unison as they should. Second, it can also be divided *conceptually* into its various powers by a mind trying to understand it. See note 3. When Socrates discusses conceptual division for the sake of understanding in *Phaedrus* 263b–266b and 270c–274a, he speaks of being able to cut things along their natural joints and not to splinter any part like a bad butcher might do (265e).

60. The fact that some dialogues are narrated and some are direct, and that there are nestings of direct dialogues within narrated dialogues and nestings of narrated dialogues within direct ones is of course important. See David Halperin, "Plato and the Erotics of Narrativity," in *Methods of Interpreting Plato and His Dialogues,* ed. James C. Klagge and Nicholas D. Smith, Oxford Studies in Ancient Philosophy supplementary volume (Oxford: Clarendon, 1992), 93–130.

61. See Michael Frede, "Plato's Arguments and the Dialogue Form," in Klagge and Smith, eds., *Methods of Interpreting Plato,* 201–19. See especially Frede's discussion of "gymnastic dialectic" at 213–14. See also David Roochnik, *Beautiful City: The Dialectical Character of Plato's Republic* (Ithaca: Cornell University Press, 2003).

62. I am sympathetic with some of the points Griswold makes in his ironic reading of the critique of writing in the *Phaedrus.* See Charles L. Griswold Jr., *Self-Knowledge in Plato's Phaedrus* (New Haven: Yale University Press, 1986), especially chap. 6 and the epilogue. See also Ruby Blondell, *The Play of Character in Plato's Dialogues* (Cambridge: Cambridge University Press, 2002): 110–11. Yet, in my judgment, Plato's critique of writing in the *Phaedrus* is meant to be taken seriously.

63. See the discussion of knowledge as vision in the section entitled "Implications of the Medical Model" above.

64. See Kenneth Sayre, "A Maieutic View of Five Late Dialogues," in Klagge and Smith, eds., *Methods of Interpreting Plato,* 221–43, esp. 230–37.

65. Rutherford, *Art of Plato,* 66–68. Note especially the remarkable parallel between Thucydides' *stasis* chapters (3.82–83) and *Republic* 560–61, and

the parallel analyses in the two writers of the connection between Athenian imperial expansion and political-moral decline. Note also parallel ideologies of power in Callicles and Thrasymachus, on the one hand, and the Athenians at Sparta and Melos in Thucydides, on the other. There are also parallel emphases in both on the intellectual element of statesmanship, and parallel adaptations and deepenings of the sophistic concept of the rhetorical virtuoso. An axiom of Thucydides' political thought, according to Werner Jaeger, was that human nature consists in the constant ascendance of passion and the will to power over intellect. Plato seems to want to parry this view. See Jaeger, *Paideia*, vol. 1, chap. 6, n21. David Grene compared and contrasted Plato and Thucydides in *Man in His Pride: A Study of the Political Philosophies of Thucydides and Plato* (Chicago: University of Chicago Press, 1950).

66. See Charles N. Cochrane, *Thucydides and the Science of History* (New York: Russell and Russell, 1965). This work was first published at Oxford in 1929. See also Werner Jaeger, "Thucydides: Political Philosopher," chap. 6 of vol. 1 of *Paideia;* and Jaeger, "Greek Medicine as Paideia," chap. 1 of vol. 3 of *Paideia.*

67. Fifth-century medical thinkers arrived at the conception of types (εἴδη) of human nature, of bodily structure, of disposition, of illness, and so forth. A. E. Taylor in his *Varia Socratica* studied the frequent occurrence of the terms εἶδος and ἰδέα in the Hippocratic writings. See Jaeger, *Paideia* 3:296n45. Jaeger says that Plato transferred these concepts to the realm of ethics and from there to his entire ontology. See Jaeger, *Paideia* 3:24.

68. See Cochrane, *Thucydides*, 30–31.

69. Cochrane thought Plato was doing therapeutics in a regrettable way. See Cochrane, *Thucydides*, 91, 102, 105. Popper, of course, thought that the "spell of Plato" was the partial inspiration of many enemies of the "open society."

70. See note 18 above.

71. This suggestion is in keeping with the views of Mitchell Miller about why Plato remains anonymous. See note 16. I would add that the "freeborn physician" (*Laws* 720b–e) aims to bring a client (a reader) to understand his own diseases (by seeing them mirrored in those of the interlocutors depicted). And he aims at the reader's cooperation in his own therapy (by experiencing the "kindling" of philosophic understanding through careful and persistent study of the dialogues). Plato cannot know in advance what particular needs his reader will have, and if he gives his reader some "empirical injunction with an air of finished knowledge, in the brusque fashion of a dictator," he becomes but a slave doctor treating slaves (*Laws* 720c).

72. Ruby Blondell makes the important point that Plato's choice of interlocutors for Socrates mirrors the norms of Platonic Athens, as viewed from a "public," elite male, "upper class" perspective. In my terms, Socrates diagnoses those who exhibit symptoms most typical of important contributors to Athens' problems. See Blondell, *Play of Character*, 66.

73. See, for example, Socrates' remarks at *Gorgias* 448d–e, 451d–e, 461d, 462c–d, 466b–c; *Protagoras* 334a–336b; *Theaetetus* 150c–d, 167d–168b; *Cratylus* 390c; and Parmenides' remarks at *Parmenides* 136c–137b. On the importance of paying attention to the philosophic differences among the philosophic masters

in the dialogues, see Catherine Zuckert, "Hermeneutics in Practice: Gadamer on Ancient Philosophy," in *The Cambridge Companion to Gadamer*, ed. Robert J. Dostal (Cambridge: Cambridge University Press, 2002), esp. 219–20.

74. See Halperin, "Plato and the Erotics of Narrativity," 108–20, on especially the *Symposium* and *Phaedrus*. See note 60.

75. For stimulating reflections on the silence of Socrates in the dialogues (and of Plato outside the dialogues), see Paul Plass, "Philosophic Anonymity and Irony in the Platonic Dialogues," in Smith, ed., *Plato: Critical Assessments*, 1:201–20.

76. See George Rudebusch, "Plato's Aporetic Style," in Smith, ed., *Plato: Critical Assessments*, 1:349–56.

77. Health in this context would admit of degrees and would be related (perhaps by way of "identity" and perhaps not) to moral virtue and to philosophic insight. See Sayre's reflections on the characterization of philosophic insight in the *Seventh Letter* referenced in note 64. Health would be a state of soul that expressed itself in appropriate and consistent deeds and utterances, especially in deeds consistent with one's utterances. It would fundamentally be an ongoing genuine, appropriate, and complete response to value.

78. In the "later dialogues," Theaetetus, "young Socrates," and even Socrates himself appear as interlocutors being "examined" by master philosophers. Perhaps it would be mistaken to take them as manifesting maladies of soul. But if health admits of degrees, and can be lost, we might read these dialogues as depicting more or less healthy characters being diagnosed as needing treatment pertaining to the *maintenance* or *improvement* of their soul's health. These dialogues might be characterized as concerned more with γυμναστική than with ιατρική. See note 46. See also my *Plato's Dialogue Form*, 53–56. The *Seventh Letter* characterizes philosophic wisdom as "self-sustaining."

79. For some discussion of Plato's use of "historical irony" or "emphasis" in his choice of interlocutors, see Blondell, *Play of Character*, 34–37. Blondell and other commentators suspect that there are implicit critiques in the dialogues even of Socrates himself (perhaps, for example, because he did not write anything, or was insufficiently erotic himself, or what have you). This raises important questions that I cannot address here. I am skeptical toward the view, but it would not be incompatible with the medical model. Perhaps there are different kinds of philosophizing depicted in the dialogues (see note 73), and certain limitations of Socrates' particular style are implicitly criticized in some places.

80. Halperin, "Plato and the Erotics of Narrativity," 126–29, suggests that the paradoxes and antinomies of interpretation that arise for careful readers of the texts function to arouse their "hermeneutic ἔρως." ψυχαγωγία becomes in a sense "seduction" of readers into the quest for the final "meaning" of the dialogues, the quest to grasp the source of the beauty of the dialogues. This seems right. But we need not think that the dialogues "deconstruct" all the "claims" made in and by them, or forsake realism about truth, beauty, and goodness. Sorting out differences between diagnostic and therapeutic moves made in and by the dialogues can go some way toward removing apparent antinomies of interpretation. The hermeneutical instability (or difficulty) of the dialogues

serves Plato's purpose of getting readers involved in salutary intellectual gymnastic exercises. Halperin says something like this about the *Phaedrus* and *Symposium* ("Plato and the Erotics of Narrativity," 120–29). And I make a similar point about the *Philebus* in my *Plato's Dialogue Form*, 159–60. Hermeneutical antinomies can be invitations to higher kinds of systematic thinking, or they can be pointers to mysteries—truths in which simplicity and vast complexity coincide—that must for the time being escape our full grasp. See Plass, "Philosophic Anonymity and Irony"; and Frede, "Plato's Arguments and the Dialogue Form," 214–19. In "the Good" there is a *coincidentia oppositorum:* a mutual interpenetration and unity of perfections (the interweaving of the Forms?) that are ostensibly inconsistent with one another and cannot appear on the natural plane except in mutual separation.

81. Perhaps Plato dramatizes his brothers' faults so richly in this dialogue because he understands his brothers well. Or perhaps they mirror for him his own youthful political ambitions. Perhaps he wants to show that biological kinship does not necessarily bring with it ethical kinship. Perhaps Plato wants to rejoice in the fact that they, who like Charmides and Critias were members of Plato's family, escaped a tragic fate through the intervention of Socrates. At any rate, an examination of the depictions of Plato's relatives in the dialogues shows that Plato usually puts their faults on display through these depictions. Plato's relations with his own family were fraught with many of the same kinds of problems that existed between Socrates and his motley group of adherents. In the *Charmides* Charmides and Critias, the former Plato's maternal uncle and the latter his mother's cousin, are drawn as persons on their way to becoming members of the Thirty Tyrants. Plato's brother Glaucon (or a symbolic stand-in for him) and his half brother Antiphon are both given unflattering depictions at the beginning of the *Parmenides*. See the discussion of Plato's depictions of his relatives in the dialogues in Jonathan Ketchum, "The Structure of the Plato Dialogue" (Ph.D. diss., State University of New York at Buffalo, 1981), 425–31.

82. It is important, I think, that the Thirty Tyrants were a *pro-Spartan* aristocratic junta, for the "ideal πόλις" of books 2–5 has many Spartan elements. See Rutherford, *Art of Plato*, 93–94. See also G. R. F. Ferrari, introduction to *Plato: The Republic*, Cambridge Texts in the History of Political Thought (Cambridge: Cambridge University Press, 2000), esp. xiv ff.

83. Ranasinghe, *Soul of Socrates*, 2, 5.

84. For a brief definition of developmentalist ways of interpreting Plato, see Francisco J. Gonzalez, ed., *The Third Way: New Directions in Platonic Studies* (Lanham: Rowman and Littlefield, 1995).

85. See Blondell, *Play of Character*, 165–99. For a related view, see C. D. C. Reeve, *Philosopher-Kings: The Argument of Plato's Republic* (Princeton: Princeton University Press, 1988), 33–41. On this view Socrates practices what Frede calls "didactic" dialectic with Glaucon. I do not want to deny that Plato's characters *ever* function as Plato's "mouthpieces."

86. Many ancient readers of the *Republic* did not take the political proposals of the dialogue to be endorsed by Plato. See Julia Annas, "The Inner City:

Ethics Without Politics in the *Republic*," chap. 4 of *Platonic Ethics, Old and New* (Ithaca: Cornell University Press, 1999), 72–95; see also 1–7.

87. On book 10, see notes 56 and 58. For partial readings of the *Republic* compatible with this reading, see Nalin Ranasinghe, "Glaucon's Republic," chap. 1 of *Soul of Socrates*. See also Rutherford, *Art of Plato*, 218–27; and Clay, "Reading the *Republic*," 24–33.

88. A medical model of Socratic (and Platonic) practice need not imply that Socratic or Platonic arguments found in either diagnostic or therapeutic segments of dialogue are unimportant. It need only emphasize that all four of the segments of the Divided Line, including the segments corresponding to νοῦς and to πίστις and εἰϰασία, represent aspects of human rationality. See notes 58 and 59.

89. See Frede, "Plato's Arguments and the Dialogue Form," 216–19.

4

Know Thyself:
Socrates as Storyteller

Anne-Marie Bowery

Though Plato's expertise as both a philosopher and a dramatic literary stylist is commonly acknowledged, his skillful use of narrative framing techniques has not received significant scholarly attention.[1] This omission is unfortunate because the narrative dimensions of the Platonic dialogues provide additional depth and complexity to Plato's characterization of Socrates as the paradigmatic philosopher. Narrative analysis recognizes that Plato writes his dialogues in different ways.[2] He constructs enacted dialogues and reported dialogues. In an enacted dialogue, like the *Gorgias, Euthyphro, Crito,* or *Laches,* the dramatic action is unmediated by a narrator's voice. The audience receives the dramatic action of the dialogue directly. In reported or narrated dialogues, on the other hand, a narrator relates the central dramatic action to the audience. The audience receives the dramatic action through the narrator's filter. Plato creates two types of reported dialogues. Either Socrates narrates the dramatic action or a Socratic disciple narrates the events.[3]

When reflecting on why Plato may have crafted the dialogues in this way, it is helpful to consider the reading practices of Plato's original audience. To understand ancient reading practices, the contemporary reader must be mindful of several things. First, ancient texts were generally regarded as records of oral speech.[4] It is not surprising, then, that "texts were mostly read aloud."[5] Second, ancient texts did not have spaces between their words. As a result, the reading process was slower and more laborious. Jocelyn Small explains: "Reading words that are all run together dramatically affects the way a reader processes those words. . . . You read much more slowly."[6] Third, for the ancient reader, reading was a communal activity. H. Gregory Snyder explains: "To be brought to life, a text required a performer and almost always presumed the presence of an audience. This audience may have partaken in the performance to a greater or lesser degree."[7] While certain evidence suggests that at least some ancient Greeks read silently, the general point about ancient textual oral performance still obtains.[8]

Scholars actively debate the textual practices surrounding the creation and dissemination of the Platonic dialogues. In Harold Tarrant's view, the dialogues were generally performed inside the Academy. Typically, Plato or another teacher would read or "narrate" the dialogue to the students. The narrator might supply additional information as the "text" was performed. Tarrant suggests that Plato allowed the dialogues with narrative frames to be disseminated publicly. In this more public context, the narrator/author could not always be present. As a result, the narrative frame serves the narrator/author function. The narrative frame gives the new audience necessary information about how to enact and interpret the dialogues.[9] Borrowing Umberto Eco's terminology, Victorino Tejera suggests that the narrative dimensions of the dialogues function as "self-focusing devices" that allow the text itself to guide its own interpretation.[10] They reveal philosophically important dimensions of the dialogue to the audience.

How exactly do these narrative markers function? Consider the opening of the *Phaedo*. The outer frame is set in Phlius. Some Pythagoreans took refuge there after the uprisings in Croton. By setting the dialogue in this Pythagorean enclave, Plato places the entire dialogue in a Pythagorean context. Furthermore, there are numerous references to words and images associated with Pythagoreanism.[11] Simply put, the Pythagorean setting of the narrative frame and the repetition of words and images associated with Pythagoreanism tell the audience to attend to other Pythagorean allusions that occur throughout the dialogue. If these narrative frames and markers do indeed function as self-focusing devices that guide the dialogic audience, then once that preliminary attunement is accomplished, the audience has been provided with what Thomas Szlezák sees as a hermeneutic key to unlock the philosophical meaning of the dialogue.[12] Because of these "narrative precautions" that "guide the audience," the audience has learned what to listen and look for as the dialogue progresses.[13] While these narrative markers may have originally helped an audience hear the philosophical complexity in an oral performance, they can still function in a similar manner in our age of silent, private, rapid reading if we take time to consider them.

Many important philosophical themes emerge when we consider the narrative dimensions of dialogues. Elsewhere, I offer a comprehensive analysis of these themes.[14] Here, I examine Socrates' role as a narrator in the five dialogues he narrates: *Lysis, Republic, Charmides, Protagoras,* and *Euthydemus*.[15] In these dialogues, Plato presents a dual depiction of

Socrates. He creates a character named Socrates and a narrator named Socrates. "Socrates the narrator" narrates events in which "Socrates the character" takes part.[16] In an enacted dialogue like the *Gorgias* or the *Euthyphro*, the audience only sees Socrates as a character in the dialogue. As a result, we primarily see Socrates in action and not in reflection. We must infer his thoughts from his actions. At times, this may be easy to do. For example, it is clear that Socrates thinks Euthyphro is wrong-headed in his understanding of piety. At other times, Socrates' opinions and motivations are less clear. Why does he allow Chaerephon to detain them in the agora and arrive late to the feast of speeches in the *Gorgias* (447a)? Why does Socrates seem so eager to leave at the end of the *Philebus* (67b)? While these enacted dialogues contain many dramatic clues that help the audience infer this information about Socrates, when Socrates the narrator reflects on situations such as these, the audience's ability to understand Socrates' views increases dramatically. This examination will suggest that a richer, deeper portrait of Socrates' commitment to the philosophical life emerges when we attend to this dual aspect of Plato's presentation of Socrates. By attending to how Plato presents Socrates both as a narrator and as a character, we see Socratic self-examination as an ongoing interplay of ethos, pathos, and *logos*.

The Dialogues Socrates Narrates: *Lysis, Republic, Charmides, Protagoras*, and *Euthydemus*

Working in order of narrative complexity, I summarize the content of these five dialogues. I also describe their narrative structure, the narrative setting, Socrates' narrative presence, and his relationship with his narrative audience.

The *Lysis* begins with Socrates speaking to an unknown audience at an unknown place and an unknown time. Socrates tells his unnamed audience, "I was on my way from the Academy straight to the Lyceum, following the road just outside and beneath the wall; and when I got to the little gate by Panops spring, I happened to meet Hippothales, Hieronymus' son, and with them some other young men standing together in a group" (203a). Hippothales asks if Socrates will join them at "this new wrestling school" (204a).[17] Initially Socrates hesitates, but after some conversation, he follows them. He seems particularly interested in meeting Lysis, the object of Hippothales' intense erotic fascination

(206d). Hippothales suggests that Socrates converse with Ctesippus and "his closest companions [Lysis or Menexenus] will be sure to join them" (206d).

With this goal in mind, Socrates enters the wrestling room. He describes the physical setting (206e–207b). Socrates then tells his audience that Menexenus "came to take a seat beside us" (207b). Menexenus soon leaves (207b). Socrates and Lysis discuss the nature of love and friendship. They focus on familial love and obligation and its relationship with self-improvement. (207c–210a). After Socrates reduces Lysis to aporia (210d), Socrates almost reveals his real purpose. But he realizes Hippothales wishes to keep his interest in Lysis secret (210e). Lysis now asks Socrates to repeat the conversation with Menexenus, who has returned to them (211a). Socrates encourages Lysis to do so instead. Eventually Socrates, Lysis, and Menexenus all converse. Lysis' aptitude for philosophy impresses Socrates (213e). They explore the nature of friendship but reach no final conclusion. The dialogue ends aporetically. Socrates tells his audience about the guardians and older brothers of Menexenus and Lysis breaking up the conversation, but "they still have been unable to find out what a friend is" (223a).

Socrates narrates this dialogue in a straightforward manner. The level of his narrative description is consistent throughout. He does not comment on the narrative process itself anywhere in the dialogue. He does not interrupt the story with any direct conversation with his audience and his audience asks no questions of him. As a result, the dialogue remains entirely within the temporality of the narrated events. As a narrator, Socrates appears trustworthy.[18] He does not qualify his narrative with any claims about not remembering clearly.[19] There are no obvious lacunae in his account and he does not simply summarize the events. Socrates provides useful background information for his audience (203a, 206e–207b, 207d, 223a). He describes the emotional responses of his interlocutors (204b, 204c, 213d, 222b) and assesses their philosophical ability (213d–e, 218c, 222b). He offers insight into the motivations of the other characters (207b, 211a, 213d). Socrates also describes his state of mind and emotional responses to these narrated events (203a, 210e, 218c, 223a). By providing insight into his state of mind, Socrates' reliability as a narrator increases. For example, when Socrates admits to his audience that he almost revealed Hippothales' interest in Lysis to Lysis himself (210e), the audience's ability to trust Socrates the narrator increases. Socrates the narrator did not have to include that aspect of his behavior in the narrative. That Socrates tells his present audience about his social duplicity and offers an explanation for it assumes a level of honesty and trust in the relationship between himself and his narrative audience that was not present between the characters in the narrated events.

The *Republic* also begins with Socrates speaking: "I went down yesterday to the Piraeus with Glaucon" (327a). We do not know where he retells the story, nor to whom he speaks. We do not know Socrates' motivation for narrating this lengthy conversation about justice. We do know slightly more about the narrative setting than we do in the *Lysis.* Socrates says that the events of the dialogue took place the day before. Given that the dramatic date of the journey to Piraeus occurs in 411 B.C.E., we can set the retelling at a fixed time as well.[20] As in the *Lysis,* Socrates is headed from a particular place, Piraeus, to a particular place, the city of Athens, but is sidetracked from his intended destination. As in the *Lysis,* Socrates narrates the circumstances leading to the shift in destination: "Catching sight of us from afar as we were pressing homewards, Polemarchus, son of Cephalus, ordered his slave boy to run after us and order us to wait for him. The boy took hold of my cloak from behind and said, 'Polemarchus orders you to wait'" (327b). Seeing that he cannot convince Polemarchus to let them continue to Athens, Socrates agrees to visit Cephalus' home (328b).

There Socrates converses with Cephalus (328e–331d), Polemarchus (331e–336e), Thrasymachus (337a–354c), and Glaucon and Adeimantus long into the night. They examine the nature of justice in the soul by looking at the nature of justice in the city. Socrates recounts their conversation. He tells the audience about the ring of Gyges (359d), the nature of Homeric narrative and the ancient quarrel between philosophy and poetry, the tripartite division of the soul and the corresponding division of classes in the feverish city, the education of the guardian, the communal sharing of women and raising of children, the necessity of philosopher-kings, the sun as the offspring of the Good, the Divided Line, the allegory of the Cave, the degeneration of political regimes, the return of the poets to the city, and the Myth of Er.[21] Socrates presents himself as a trustworthy narrator. He does not qualify his narrative with claims about not remembering clearly. Again, there are no obvious lacunae in the account and he appears willing to retell this lengthy account to his audience. Also, Socrates' inclusion of his own observations about the events that he narrates increases the level of trust that the narrative audience has in Socrates as a narrator.

In the first two books of the *Republic,* Socrates actively narrates. He provides detailed commentary and insight into the motivations of the characters (336b, 337a, 338a, 342d, 344d, 350d, 357a, 368c). In book 3

Socrates, Glaucon, Adeimantus, and the others discuss simple, imitative, and mixed narrative styles (392e following). Here the philosophical
content leads the audience to reflect upon the narrative structure of the
Republic itself.[22] Additionally, as a character within the story, Socrates
tells narrative stories to his dramatic audience at pedagogically significant moments, for example, the allegory of the Cave (book 7) and the
Myth of Er (book 10), and other characters, such as Glaucon, also tell
stories (359d following). In all these ways, the structure and theme of
the *Republic* call attention to the narrative process in a way that the *Lysis*
does not. However, perhaps due to the dialogue's length, Socrates' narrative commentary largely disappears after 449a.[23] As a narrator, Socrates
moves into the temporality of the narrated events. On this point, Jacob
Howland notes that "the *Republic* ends in direct discourse even though it
began in indirect discourse. The effect is to make the reader forget that
Socrates is narrating the dialogue."[24]

The *Charmides* also begins with Socrates narrating: "Yesterday evening we returned from the army at Potidaea and having been a good
while away, I thought that I should like to go and look at my old haunts"
(153a).[25] Again, we do not know to whom Socrates speaks or exactly
where he is when he recounts these events to his friend. While Socrates
considers his narrative audience a "friend" (154c, 155c), his identity is
otherwise indiscernible. As in the *Lysis* and the *Republic*, his audience
does not interrupt the narrative. As in the *Republic*, we can assign an approximate dramatic date to the story that Socrates chooses to narrate,
either 432 or 429 B.C.E.[26] However, we do not know how much time has
elapsed between the narrated events and the subsequent narration.[27]

Socrates amply describes the setting. The encounter took place "at
the Palaestra of *Taureas,* which is over against the temple of Basile, and
there I found a number of persons, most of whom I knew, but not all.
My visit was unexpected, and no sooner did they see me entering than
they saluted me from afar on all sides" (153a). Socrates also explains the
dramatic context. Chaerephon hails him from behind (153b). Chaerephon immediately refers to another report about the battle that they
have heard but only incompletely (153c). Socrates is asked to recount
episodes from the battle. Socrates then asks "about the state of affairs in
the city and about the present state of philosophy and about the young
men, whether there were any who had become distinguished for wisdom or beauty or both" (153d). These references to previous narrative
activity call attention to the fact that Socrates is telling a narrative. This
specificity of the narrative setting starkly contrasts the indeterminacy
of its retelling. This movement from aporia to knowledge in these nar-

rative dialogues demands further consideration. Here, I simply suggest that it symbolizes the philosophical power of narrative to move us from ignorance to wisdom.

The narrative focus shifts when Charmides enters the Palaestra (154b). Socrates agrees to pretend that he has the cure for Charmides' early morning headaches (155b). Socrates is mesmerized by his brief glances beneath Charmides' cloak (155d), but once he regains composure, he tells the story of King Zalmoxis and the headache charm (156d–157d). Socrates then recounts the conversation between himself, Critias, and Charmides about the nature of *sophrosune* and how one gains control of tyrannical desire. The dialogue ends without any clear indication that Charmides has benefited from the discussion about this "great good," and with a strong suggestion that Charmides would choose force over the persuasive capability of genuine philosophical conversation.

In addition to these many structural similarities between the *Charmides*, *Lysis*, and *Republic*, Socrates' narrative style in the *Charmides* resembles his narrative style in the preceding dialogues. Socrates provides details about the setting and perceptive comments about his interlocutors. Socrates also assesses his own emotional state and intellectual attitudes (153b, 153c–d, 155c–e, 156d, 162c, 170c). Socrates' narrative voice remains a consistent presence throughout the dialogue, and the dialogue remains in the temporality of the narrated events. Throughout the dialogue, Socrates presents himself as a reliable narrator. He does not qualify his narrative with any claims about not remembering clearly. One might think that Socrates' admission of his willingness to mislead Charmides about having a cure for his headache would detract from Socrates' narrative reliability. However, as was the case in the *Lysis*, Socrates' willingness to reveal his subterfuge to the audience demonstrates a level of trust and honesty between himself and his friend that was clearly not present in his encounter with Charmides and Critias. As with the preceding dialogues, Socrates' willingness to narrate the conversation implies an amiable relationship between himself and his narrative audience, a relationship where he can speak freely in a way that he could not during the narrated events.

The *Protagoras'* narrative structure differs from the preceding three dialogues.[28] It starts with a brief enacted exchange between Socrates and a friend (309a–310a). A friend questions Socrates: "Where have you just come from, Socrates?" The friend apparently knows Socrates well, as his answer to his initial query evidences: "It's pretty obvious that you've been hunting the ripe and ready Alcibiades" (309a). This enacted beginning increases the dialogue's narrative complexity because it creates a dramatic context in which Socrates the character becomes Socrates the narrator. The enacted beginning calls the audience's attention to the fact that Socrates will narrate the subsequent events. Though this beginning is enacted and not reported, the dialogue contains many structural similarities and thematic parallels with the other dialogues Socrates narrates. We do not know exactly where or when this conversation occurs.[29] It takes place almost immediately after the events that Socrates will soon narrate. Again, this indeterminacy is even more apparent when compared to the detail that Socrates' narrative provides. This extended enacted conversation between Socrates and his friend may suggest something about the narrative audience of the other narrated dialogues. For example, though we do not see the request for Socrates' narrative in the other three dialogues, we can assume that Socrates is narrating in response to a request, as he does here. Also, the friend indicates that other people are present in the narrative audience (310a). It is likely that a group of people listen to the other narratives that Socrates tells.[30] We can also assume that Socrates willingly narrates to people he considers friends and to people interested in the story.

After the initial conversation between Socrates and his friend, Socrates tells the story in an uninterrupted fashion. The narration begins in Socrates' bedroom: "Just before daybreak, while it was still dark, Hippocrates, son of Apollodoros and Phason's brother, banged on my door with his stick, and when it was opened for him he barged right in and yelled in that voice of his, 'Socrates, are you awake or asleep?'" (310b). As he does in most of the preceding dialogues, Socrates reports a change in physical location. Actually, two location shifts occur. Hippocrates and Socrates move from the bedroom and walk in the courtyard of Socrates' house (311b) as they discuss Hippocrates' motivation for seeking out instruction from a sophist (311b–314c). Once they arrive at Callias' house, Socrates recounts their encounter with the doorman (314d) and he describes the numerous sophists in attendance (314c–317e). Socrates narrates his initial conversation with Protagoras about the possibility of teaching political virtue (317e–320c) and recounts the narrative that Protagoras tells of Prometheus (320c–328d). Socrates also relates their conversation about the unity of the virtues (329d–331b). Socrates reports his desire to stop the conversation and he explains how Alcibiades intercedes on his behalf (335c–338e). After being "persuaded to stay" (335d), Socrates recounts Protagoras' interpretations of Simonides' poem and his own (338e–347a) and how he asks Prodicus for help. Socrates then narrates the final conversation about the interrelationship of virtues like courage and wisdom and their relationship to pleasure and the good (348c–362a). Unlike the *Euthydemus,* the *Protagoras* has no enacted conversation at its end. As a result, the audience cannot see the effect that Socrates' narrative has on his friend.

Socrates presents himself as a trustworthy narrator.[31] Though Socrates' narrative commentary tapers off after 348c, prior to that point, he offers even more narrative commentary than he has offered in the preceding dialogues. He describes the setting of the narrated events and the characters within the dialogue. Socrates reports on his state of mind as he does in the preceding dialogues (328d, 331e, 335d–e, 339e). He also tells how Protagoras responds to him and how the people present at Callias' house respond to each speaker.[32] As a narrator, Socrates calls attention to the interactive dimensions of listening to an oral performance like a sophistic speech or a philosophical narrative. He implicitly asks his narrative audience to become conscious of their responses to his narrative. In this way, Plato uses Socrates' role as a narrator to call our attention to the narrative process itself. This increased commentary on the performative dimensions of the characters' speeches within the dialogue adds to the *Protagoras*' narrative complexity.

The *Euthydemus*' narrative structure is elaborately crafted. The dialogue begins with an enacted conversation between Socrates and a friend. This time, the friend is named; he is Crito.[33] As in the *Protagoras,* the dialogue begins with the friend asking Socrates a question about a recent encounter (271a–272d). Though we do not know where or when their conversation takes place, we know it occurs the day after the events he will soon narrate (271a). We also know that the narrated events take place in the Lyceum in Athens, probably in the 430s. Socrates' narrative commentary remains a consistent presence throughout the dialogue. Socrates appears confident in his narrative ability. He tells Crito, "I can't pretend that I did not pay attention for I certainly did" (272d), and he underscores his confidence soon after: "I remember it well and will try to tell you the whole story from the beginning" (283a).[34] The dialogue's intricately nested structure, the fact that it shifts between the temporality of the conversation between Crito and Socrates and the temporality of Socrates' narrative, calls continuous attention to Socrates' narrative activity.

Socrates begins: "I was sitting by myself in the undressing room just where you saw me and was already thinking of leaving. But when I got up, my customary divine sign put in an appearance, so I sat down again" (272e). He then narrates his encounter with Euthydemus, Dionysodorus, Clinias, and Ctesippus: "The entire company of men present in the Lyceum besought the pair to demonstrate the power of their wisdom" (274d). Socrates carefully recounts the sophistic exchange. He enumerates each argumentative turn and describes the rhetorical effect of their strategies. Socrates uses a variety of metaphors to describe their wordplay: being struck by a ball (277b), a heavy blow (303a), a skillful dance (276d), a wrestling match (271c, 277d), and even a wild boar attack (294d). He carefully chronicles his response to their argument (271d, 282c, 282d, 283d, 286c, 288b, 294d–e, 295e, 301a, 301b, 302b, 303a).

The dramatic context in which Socrates tells this narrative may suggest something about the overall purpose of the other dialogues Socrates narrates. Here the pedagogical dimension of Socratic narrative is clear. Crito wants to hear the story because the apparent health and flourishing of Euthydemus, particularly when compared to his own son, Critobulus, appeals to him (271b). Socrates tells him, though not without irony, that they have much to learn from Euthydemus and Dionysodorus. He tells Crito that their performance was an "incitement to virtue" (283b). Crito appears willing to hear what he will learn from them (272b–d).

Socrates frequently addresses Crito directly (275c, 283a, 303a, 303b, 304c). These direct references underscore the fact that Socrates tells the story for his benefit, to elicit a philosophical response from Crito. Crito's interruption of the narrative (290e–293b) also reinforces his particular presence as the narrative audience. Additionally, the dialogue ends with Socrates and Crito in conversation (304c–307b). This enacted ending, which parallels the enacted beginning, is the only such occurrence in the entire Platonic corpus.[35] This enacted conversation allows the audience of the entire dialogue to see how Crito, a character within the enacted frame, responds to Socrates' narrative provocation. We see that Crito affirms his love of listening and his willingness to learn (304c). We also see that Crito is able to separate himself from Socrates' ironic enthusiasm for Euthydemus' teaching. He "would rather be refuted by arguments of this kind than use them to refute" (304d). We also see that Crito responds to Socrates' narrative about his encounter with Euthydemus and Dionysodorus by telling a brief narrative about a conversation with "one of those clever people who writes speeches for the law courts" (304d). In fact, Crito imitates many Socratic narrative techniques in his mini-narrative. The person comes up to him as he was walking. Crito asks many questions of him and leads their conversation to philosophy (304e). Crito also uses the narrative as an attempt to show Socrates how he might be perceived by others who see no distinction between the sophistic display he just witnessed and genuine philosophy (305a–305b). The behavior of Crito, as audience to Socrates' narrative within the dialogue, models an appropriate response to the narrative

Socrates tells. Though Crito still does not know how to educate his sons, his behavior in the enacted frame helps the dialogic audience recognize the pedagogical motivation of Socrates' narrative performance.

Seeing Socrates Differently

In recent years, the concept of rationality has undergone a radical reassessment. In fields ranging from neuroscience to economics and biology to psychology, it is becoming increasingly clear that human choice is motivated by a wide range of factors.[36] Even within philosophical circles, the primacy of Cartesian rationalism is under revision.[37] Unfortunately, some scholars still regard Plato and Socrates as philosophers who are deeply suspicious of emotional experience and the role it plays in philosophy. Martha Nussbaum's portrait of Socrates in *Cultivating Humanity* typifies this view.[38] She regards Socrates as a beneficial pedagogical model precisely because he exemplifies a rigorous commitment to rational self-examination.[39] Many other scholars of ancient thought either tacitly or explicitly share Nussbaum's characterization of Socratic philosophy.[40] Careful attention to Socrates' narrative remarks cautions us against holding this narrow view of Socratic rationality, however, because it is clear that Socrates the narrator focuses on the emotional states of the interlocutors as well as on their logical argumentation. In this section, I analyze three dramatic markers of intense emotional responses that Socrates includes in his narratives: the eroticism of these narrated dialogues, numerous instances of blushing, and several examples of laughter.[41]

The erotic dimensions of these narrative dialogues give one obvious indication of the importance of emotion in Socrates' narrative portrayal of his philosophical practice. Here I will simply focus on the instances in which Socrates describes the lover-beloved relationship to provide insight into the emotions and motivations of the characters whose activities he reports in the narratives that he tells.

Throughout the *Lysis,* Socrates' interest in the erotic emerges. Socrates changes his original plan of action once the erotic interest of Hippothales manifests itself.[42] This strong interest in eros continues. For example, he tells Hippothales "that there is no longer any need for you to tell me whether you are in love or not, since I am sure you are not only in love, but pretty far gone in it too by this time. For though in most matters I am a poor useless creature, yet by some means or other I have received from heaven the gift of being able to detect at a glance both a lover and a beloved" (204c). Socrates also includes many details about Lysis' beauty and how he and the characters respond to it in his narrative (207a–b).

Socrates' narrative in the *Charmides* also focuses the audience's attention on the appearance of a beautiful youth and the intense erotic response to that beauty. He tells his friend: "All the company seemed to be enamored of him. Amazement and confusion reigned when he entered, and a second troop of lovers followed behind him. That grown men like ourselves should have been affected in this way was not surprising, but I observed the boys and saw that all of them, down to the very smallest, turned and looked at him as if he had been a statue" (154b).

The entire narrative of the *Protagoras* occurs in response to the friend's relentless query about Socrates' and Alcibiades' relationship (309a–c). Socrates the narrator reinforces that interest by mentioning the erotic relationship between Pausanias and Agathon (315e) and referring to how Alcibiades intercedes on his behalf (336c–e). The appearance of Hippocrates in Socrates' bedroom early in the dialogue also adds to the erotic framing of his narrative (310b). Indeed, when Hippocrates bursts into Socrates' bedroom and asks, "Socrates, are you asleep or awake" (310b), he asks the very same question that Alcibiades claims to have asked Socrates in his attempt to seduce him (*Symposium* 218c).

The *Euthydemus* is also filled with erotic overtones. For example, Socrates mentions the lovers of Clinias (273b, 274d) and Ctesippus' desire to look at Clinias (274c) at the very beginning of his narrative and Ctesippus' anger on his behalf later (283e). While not absent from the dramatic context of the *Republic*, eros is considered in more general philosophic and political terms in that dialogue. Nonetheless, Socrates does mention Glaucon's lover (368a), sexual relations between the citizens (372a and throughout book 5), and all the kisses awarded to the valorous guardians (468c).

As a narrator, Socrates interlaces his narratives with these erotic details. He wants his audience to hear about the philosophical conversations that occur with the erotic allegiances of the characters in mind. These references to eros give an emotional shading to Socrates' narrative portrayal of his practice of philosophy. What philosophical purpose might their inclusion serve? Perhaps Plato wishes to suggest that Socrates sees an emotion, like eros, as key to understanding both his own sense of self-knowledge and the importance that emotions play in human interaction. At the very least, the prevalence of erotic themes in his narrative frame should direct our attention to the other emotional responses that Socrates includes in his narratives: blushing and laughter.

In each of these dialogues narrated by Socrates, an interlocutor blushes.[43] These blushes are physical indications of various emotional responses ranging from modesty to embarrassment to erotic affection. For example, Socrates tells his friend that "Charmides blushed and the blush heightened his beauty, for modesty is becoming in youth" (*Charmides* 158d), and the narrative audience learns that Hippothales blushes when Socrates calls attention to his erotic interest in Lysis (*Lysis* 204b and 204c). Characters also blush when they must admit some morally ambiguous aspect of their desires. For example, Hippocrates blushes when he admits Protagoras is a sophist (*Protagoras* 312a). An interlocutor's blush might also indicate that some hidden personal allegiance has been brought to light, as Charmides' smile indicates at *Charmides,* 161c.

On other occasions, a character's blush signifies his shame or frustration over his inability to answer the question put before him. For example, in the *Euthydemus,* Socrates tells us, "the boy [Clinias] blushed and looked at me in doubt" (275d). Similarly, in the *Republic,* Socrates "saw what I had not yet seen before—Thrasymachus blushing" (350d). This shaming of Thrasymachus parallels the interaction between Protagoras and Alcibiades in the *Protagoras:* "It looked to me that Protagoras was embarrassed by Alcibiades' words, not to mention the insistence of Callias and practically the whole company. In the end, he reluctantly brought himself to resume our dialogue and indicated he was ready to be asked questions" (348b). In these instances, the interlocutors' blushing embarrassment indicates their admission of aporia, the point of philosophical perplexity, where the characters admit the inadequacy of their previous assumptions. Socratic cross-examination depends upon the admission of aporia. When an interlocutor recognizes the conceptual limitation of an intellectual position, the argument transcends the impasse of thought. Socrates' narrative uses an emotional response, the blush, to signal this philosophical turning point, where the possibility of continued conversation emerges.[44]

Laughter also appears in each of these dialogues. Laughter can indicate a range of emotional responses. Laughter can reveal personal allegiance between interlocutors: "Whereupon he [Charmides] laughed slyly, and looked at Critias" (*Charmides* 162b). It can indicate personal desire: "He [Hippocrates] laughed and said, 'You bet he has, Socrates. He has a monopoly on wisdom and won't give me any'" (*Protagoras* 310d). It can reveal a character's attitude toward Socrates: "He [Thrasymachus] listened, burst out laughing very scornfully, and said, 'Heracles! Here is that habitual irony of Socrates'" (*Republic* 337a). Laughter can also indicate a character's aporia. For example, "Glaucon laughed and said . . . 'for I don't have a good enough idea at the moment of what we're to say'" (*Republic* 398c).

Laughter is quite prevalent in the *Euthydemus;* Socrates notes the laughter of the speakers and the surrounding crowd in the Lyceum on four occasions (273d, 276d, 298e, 303b). His narrative links laughter with aporia. For example: "Then indeed the two men's admirers laughed loud and long, applauding their wisdom, but all the rest of us were dumb-struck and had nothing to say. Euthydemus noticed our aporia and wanted us to admire him more; so he would not let the boy alone, but went on asking, and doubling and twisting around the same question like a clever dancer" (276d). Similarly, Socrates' remarks to Crito at 303b underscore this relationship between laughter, aporia, and the audience's response: "Whereupon, my dear Crito, there was no one there who did not praise to the skies the argument and the two men, laughing and applauding and exulting until they were nearly exhausted." Here Socrates mentions the interlocutors' laughter to call attention to this deeply aporetic moment. In this dialogue, however, the admission of aporia occurs with such frequency that it seems to be the real point of their conversation. These abundant references to laughter suggest the futility Socrates feels when conversing with these sophists. Any encounter with them ends in aporia or an untenable contradiction of thought. Unlike Socratic philosophical conversation, it offers no "reorientating insight that shows a path through the aporia."[45] Indeed, Socrates describes the effect of their rhetoric as enchanting captivation: "But now it almost seemed as if the pillars of the Lyceum applauded the pair and took pleasure in their success. Even I myself was so affected by it as to declare that I had never in my life seen such wise men; and I was so absolutely captivated by their wisdom that I began to praise and extol them" (303c). Socrates' ironic remarks to Crito make clear that he does not believe genuine philosophical pedagogy occurred. These instances occur in enacted dialogues as well. For example, Euthyphro's admission of aporia is clear from both his words and his deeds (*Euthyphro* 11b–e). However, because this dialogue is enacted, the audience does not hear Socrates' own reflections on the process of elenchus. Without this narrative observation, the focus of Socrates' and Euthyphro's exchange remains on the process of elenchus itself rather than on its effect.

In contrast, these narrated dialogues offer insight into why Socrates the character acts as he does. These insights into Socrates' motivation for action reveal how he uses his emotional acuity to guide the philosophical conversation. To explain further, as a character within the narrative, Socrates adeptly recognizes the emotional responses that people have toward him. He recognizes that Cephalus greets him warmly (*Republic* 328b) and that Charmides seems reticent with him (*Charmides* 159b). Socrates' motivation for philosophical conversation arises from his attunement with the emotions and motivations of his interlocutors and not simply from his commitment to finding truth through philosophical refutation. Consider the following passages in this regard:

> Critias heard me say this, and saw that I was in a difficulty, and as one person when another yawns in his presence catches the infection of yawning from him, so did he seem to be driven into a difficulty by my difficulty. But as he had a reputation to maintain, he was ashamed to admit before the company that he could not answer my challenge or determine the question at issue, and he made an unintelligible attempt to hide his perplexity. In order that the argument might proceed, I said to him, "Well then Critias." (*Charmides* 169c)

Another example occurs in the *Lysis*. "I then, wishing to relieve Menexenus, and charmed with the other's intelligence, turned to Lysis and directing my discourse to him, observed, 'Yes Lysis you are quite right'" (213e). The *Protagoras* also provides insight into how Socrates uses these emotional responses to further the philosophical discussion. Socrates tells his friend, "I could see that Protagoras was really worked up and struggling by now and that he was dead set against answering any more. Accordingly, I carefully modified the tone of my questions" (333e).[46] By examining these narrative passages more carefully, we see that Socrates uses these emotional observations to direct his philosophical inquiries. His compassion for others shapes his philosophical conversations with them.

How Socrates Sees Himself

By attending to the role that Socrates plays as a narrator in the dialogues, the careful reader sees how Socrates the narrator provides insight into the thoughts, emotions, and experiences of Socrates the character. Examination of these passages will reveal that Plato uses this narrative presentation to help the audience understand the process of acquiring self-knowledge. This narrative portrait of Socratic self-knowledge should stimulate our own process of philosophical self-discovery by providing a model of a philosopher engaged in the ongoing process of self-discovery through thoughtful reflection on experience.[47] In this section, I examine the passages where Socrates describes his thoughts, his philosophical process or procedure, his emotional states, and the passages where he reports on the attitude he takes toward his emotions. It will become clear that Socratic self-knowledge is not simply a rational process of examination turned inward but one infused with a remarkable degree of passion, sensitivity to feeling, and reflection on the emotional dimensions of human experience.

A Socratic State of Mind

Though Socrates the narrator could simply narrate these dialogues as a reported factual account of events, he includes descriptions of Socrates the character's state of mind. Consider the opening passages of these narrated dialogues again. Socrates begins the *Charmides:* "Yesterday evening we returned from the army at Potidaea and having been a good while away, I thought that I should like to go and look at my old haunts. So I went into the Palaestra" (153a). A similar self-observation begins the *Republic:* "I went down to the Piraeus yesterday with Glaucon, son of Ariston, to pray to the goddess; and, at the same time, I wanted to observe how they would put on the festival, since they were now holding it for the first time." Socrates also assesses his experience: "Now, in my opinion, the procession of the native inhabitants was fine; but the one the Thracians conducted was no less fitting a show" (327a). This passage suggests that Socrates can judge fairly and impartially, that he does not immediately prefer the Athenian performance simply because he is Athenian. The *Protagoras* begins with a brief exchange between Socrates and his friend. In this initial conversation, Socrates recounts his thoughts about his encounter with Alcibiades and Protagoras (309a–310). Once Socrates begins narrating, he includes numerous indications of his thoughts and perceptions. For example, Socrates "recognizes [Hippocrates] and his fighting spirit (310a, 310c). Socrates wants to "see what Hippocrates was made of and begins to question him" (311b). In this way, Socrates the narrator focuses the audience's attention on both the narrated events and the mind-set of Socrates the character.

The enacted conversation that begins the *Euthydemus* also emphasizes Socrates' state of mind. Though not without ironic undertones, Socrates tells Crito that he thought the brothers were "amazing" and that he has "a mind to hand myself over to these men" (272a) were it not for the "anxiety he would feel at disgracing them" (272c). Once Socrates begins his narration, he immediately describes his state of mind: "I was sitting by myself in the undressing room just where you saw me and was already thinking of leaving. But when I got up, my customary divine sign put in an appearance. So I sat down again" (272e).[48]

By beginning his narratives in this way, Socrates the narrator gives the audience a window into Socrates the character's thoughts. While these beginning observations that Socrates makes about his state of mind are often fairly mundane, it is still important for the audience to see that Socrates does begin his narratives by reporting his thoughts. By constructing these Socratic narratives in this manner, Plato may be suggesting to the audience of the dialogue that they should notice other indications of Socrates describing his patterns of thought. For example, in the *Lysis*, Socrates relates the nuances of a complicated social situation:

> On receiving this reply from Lysis, I turned my eyes on Hippothales, and was on the point of making a great blunder. For it came into my head to say, "This is the way, Hippothales, that you should talk to your favorite, humbling and checking, instead of puffing him up and pampering him, as you do now do." However, on seeing him writhing with agitation at the turn the conversation was taking, I recollected that though standing so near, he didn't wish to be seen by Lysis. So I recovered myself in time, and forbore to address him. (*Lysis* 210e)

Since Socrates also includes his own response to the social situation in his narrative, the audience can see how he responds to the situation in a way that the other dramatic characters in the dialogue do not. Socrates' narrative commentary provides information to the auditors that none of the characters receive.

Another example occurs in the *Charmides:* "I am convinced of the truth of the suspicion which I entertained at the time, that it was from Critias that Charmides had heard this answer about temperance (162c). Consider the *Protagoras* as well:

> Protagoras ended his virtuoso performance here and stopped speaking. I was entranced and just looked at him for a long time as if he were going to say more. I was still eager to listen, but when I perceived that he had really stopped I pulled myself together and looking at Hippocrates, merely managed to say, "Son of Apollodorus, how grateful I am to you for suggesting that I come here." (328d–e)

This remark is directed to Socrates' friend, not to the characters within the dramatic action of the narrative. Socrates' narrative audience and the audience of the dialogue receive this information about his state of mind, but the characters that Socrates the character interacts with do not have access to Socrates' thoughts about his experience. Similarly, Socrates' narrative remarks in the *Euthydemus* are for Crito's benefit. The audience of the dialogue is privy to remarks such as, "This made me suppose that they thought we were jesting before, when we asked them to converse with the young man, and that this was the reason why they jested and did not take it seriously. So I told them still more earnestly that we were really serious about it" (283c). Crito and the audience of the dialogue might sense the irony in Socrates' remark, but the characters within the reported action of the *Euthydemus* do not. And consider the *Republic,* where Socrates addresses his narrative audience: "I too was at a loss, and looking back over what had gone before, I said, 'It is just, my friend, that we're at a loss, for we've abandoned the image we proposed'" (375d). These examples of Socrates' narrative commentary let the audience of the dialogue follow Socrates' thought processes throughout the entire dialogue.[49] The audience understands more of Socrates' thoughts and experiences than do the characters in the dialogues.

The enacted dialogues contain numerous moments where Socrates the character becomes a narrator. In these instances, the audience can see Socrates' thoughts quite clearly, just as they do in the dialogues narrated by Socrates. For example, in the *Apology* the character Socrates, on trial for his life, narrates how he received his reputation for human wisdom; he tells of Chaerephon's trip to the Delphic oracle (21a–23a). Similarly, in the *Crito,* an enacted dialogue, Socrates the character narrates an imagined conversation between himself and the Athenian laws that gives Crito, his immediate audience, and the dialogic audience deeper insight into Socrates' acceptance of the punishment of the Athenian court (50c–54c). Socrates the character also becomes a narrator in the dialogues narrated by other narrators. In the *Phaedo,* Socrates the character narrates his intellectual autobiography to give his dramatic audience insight into why he distrusts natural philosophy and comes "to take refuge in discussion and investigate the truth of things by means of words" (97c–99e). Similarly, in the *Symposium,* Socrates the character narrates his encounters with Diotima to his fellow symposiasts (201d–202c).

These passages reveal that Socrates does not present himself as the all-knowing philosopher with complete knowledge of the narrated events. Rather, he struggles through an arduous process of finding knowledge through human interaction. Furthermore, he regularly admits his aporetic moments of thought and displays an ongoing commitment to move beyond them. He continually reassesses what he thought to be the case. In doing so, he reassesses his previously held values, beliefs, and assumptions. By describing his pattern of thinking as he narrates, Socrates the narrator teaches his narrative audience to regard these impasses as part of philosophy. The narrative dimensions of these texts show Socrates in the process of thinking. As a result, the thoughts and words and deeds of Socrates the character are easier to emulate.

The audience sees the necessity of reassessing knowledge and admitting aporia. They are crucial components of the philosophic life. It is important to note that though Socrates' modes of thinking are more apparent in these dialogues, it also becomes increasingly apparent that Socrates does not follow a single philosophical method in any of these dialogues. Indeed, as Gary Scott suggests, "The more one pays attention to Socrates' larger objectives with the characters he encounters, the less uniform and generic his method appears to be in the various 'case studies' Plato has dramatized for posterity."[50] Though Socrates' actions may be easier for the audience to understand and emulate when they have access to his thoughts about his actions, it is not because Socrates' actions are part of a single methodological approach. Rather, it is because, as Brickhouse and Smith suggest, "Like the prisoners in Plato's cave, Socrates was and is only 'like us' (see *Rep.* VII. 515a) in what he could bring to the task of overcoming ignorance."[51]

Socrates' Emotional Responses

Throughout these dialogues, Socrates the narrator describes the emotional responses of Socrates the character. Consider these examples from the *Protagoras*. Socrates recalls that "we were all overjoyed at the prospect of listening to wise men, and we laid hold of the benches and couches ourselves and arranged them over by Hippias" (317e). Here an emotional state, being overjoyed, hastens the beginning of a philosophical exchange. Later Socrates recalls, "I was taken aback, and said to him, 'Do you consider the relationship between justice and piety really only one of some slight similarity?" (331e). Again, Socrates' narrative describes how an emotional state, being taken aback, furthers the philosophical conversation. Socrates also describes the emotional effect of Protagoras' words in starkly physical terms: "Protagoras got a noisy round of applause for this speech. At first I felt as if I had been hit by a good boxer. Everything went black and I was reeling from Protagoras' oratory and the others' clamor. Then, to tell you the truth, to stall for time to consider what the poet meant, I turned to Prodicus and call[ed] on him" (339e). Again, a nonrational state, "reeling from the oratory and noise," turns the philosophical conversation in a new direction. Socrates calls on Prodicus to help him interpret Simonides' poem. Similarly, in the *Lysis*, Socrates recalls that "I was rejoicing, with all a hunter's delight, at just grasping the prey I had been so long in chase of, when presently there came into my mind, from what quarter I cannot tell, the strangest sort of suspicion. It was that the conclusions at which we had arrived were not true" (218c). Here too an emotion, "rejoicing," coupled with a "strange suspicion," helps Socrates realize that their argument about friendship is leading them astray (218c).

Indeed, Socrates mentions his emotional response to sophistical arguments throughout the *Euthydemus*. They provide a running commentary on the sophistic exchange, much like Aristophanes' hiccups punctuate Eryximachus' pedantic oration in the *Symposium*. Consider these examples: "I was surprised by this" (273d), "I was delighted and replied" (282c), "I was glad to hear it" (282d), "I was troubled when I heard this" (283d), "I was astonished at the argument" (286c), "I was so eager to have the wisdom of the pair that I was already trying to copy it" (301b), "Then I, Crito, lay speechless, just as if the argument had struck me a blow" (303a), "I was so absolutely captivated by their wisdom that I began to praise and extol them" (303c). After hearing these emotional responses to philosophical argument, Socrates' narrative audience should recognize his emotional investment in the philosophical life. They should recognize an ongoing interplay between Socratic philosophical practice and emotional awareness.

Socratic State of Character

In the *Nicomachean Ethics*, Aristotle makes a useful distinction between passions, faculties, and states of character (2.5). He says, "Passions are feelings like anger, fear, confidence, envy, joy, friendly feeling, hatred, longing, emulation, and pity" (2.5.1105b).[52] According to Aristotle, faculties enable us to feel these passions, and states of character are revealed in how we respond with reference to the passions, "the things by which we stand well or badly with respect to the passions" (2.5.1105b). For Aristotle, virtue is a state of character both affected by deliberate thought and action and eventuating in deliberate thought and action. In the preceding sections, I have shown that Socrates the narrator assesses the passions and faculties of both himself and his interlocutors. In this section, I show how Socrates the narrator conveys a sense of what Aristotle means by state of character. Socrates the narrator describes the attitude that Socrates the character takes with respect to his emotions. At times, Socrates the character struggles to find an appropriate response to his emotional response; at other times, he exhibits remarkable self-acceptance. Since Socrates' narratives include this added dimension of what Aristotle terms "states of character," the narrative audience can observe how Socrates responds to his emotions and integrates them into his self-knowing character.

In each dialogue he narrates, Socrates recounts a moment when his emotions overwhelm him. Consider the *Euthydemus:* "As far as I was concerned, Crito, when I had fallen into this difficulty, I began to exclaim at the top of my lungs and to call upon the two strangers as though they were the Heavenly Twins" (293a). Also, consider the *Charmides:* "I caught a sight of the inside of his garment, and took flame. Then I could no longer contain myself. I thought how well Cydias understood the nature of love, when in speaking of a fair youth, he warns someone 'not to bring the fawn in the sight of the lion to be devoured by him,' for I felt that I had been overcome by a sort of wild-beast appetite" (155c). And consider another example previously mentioned from the *Protagoras:* Socrates is overwhelmed when "Protagoras got a noisy round of applause for this speech. At first I felt as if I had been hit by a good boxer. Everything went black and I was reeling from Protagoras' oratory and the others' clamor" (339e). Similarly, in the *Republic,* "I was astounded when I heard him, and looking at him, I was frightened. I think that if I had not seen him before he saw me, I would have been speechless" (336d). An example from the *Lysis* differs somewhat in that Socrates has an initially positive emotional response to their philosophical argument, followed by a sudden reassessment. Socrates comments, "[I had] the satisfied feeling of a successful hunter and was basking in it, when a very strange suspicion, from where I don't know, came over me" (218c).

In these instances, Socrates the narrator describes his extreme emotional response and how quickly it overcame him. But Socrates does not simply report his emotions: his fear, astonishment, satisfaction, desire. After each instance, he reports how he responds to these emotions. Immediately after gazing beneath Charmides' cloak, Socrates reports, "When he asked me if I knew the cure for the headache, I answered, though with an effort, that I did know" (*Charmides* 155c) and explains how "his approving answers reassured me, and I began by degrees to regain confidence and my natural heat returned to me" (156d). Similarly, though astounded by Dionysodorus' sophistic display, Socrates tells Crito, "The result was that even I myself, Crito, was finally compelled, out of sheer disbelief, to ask whether Dionysodorus even knew how to dance, to which he replied that he certainly did" (*Euthydemus* 294d). Though astonished by Protagoras' account, Socrates manages to respond, "Then, to tell you the truth, to stall for time to consider what the poet meant, I turned to Prodicus" (*Protagoras* 339e). Though frightened by Thrasymachus, Socrates can respond calmly: "I had looked at him first, so that I was able to answer him; and with just a trace of a tremor, I said, 'Thrasymachus don't be too hard on us.'" Yet Socrates does not stop there. He appeals to his "friend" Thrasymachus not to give up the pursuit of their argument (*Republic* 336d). Though stunned by the strange suspicion that overcomes him in the *Lysis,* Socrates can still think clearly: "Maybe what we had all agreed to wasn't true after all." This calm reflection about the "awful thought" leads to another emotional response where he exclaims, "Lysis and Menexenus, our wealth has all been a dream!" (*Lysis* 218c). Each reassessment reveals that Socrates uses his emotional reactions as an opportunity to explore himself more fully. He uses his emotions to aid his philosophical inquiry into himself.

These passages make it difficult to continue regarding Socrates as Nietzsche's "tyrant of reason." But they also raise a larger issue about Plato's philosophical motivation for presenting Socrates as both a character and a narrator. Many of the moments where Socrates reflects on his mood, his emotional state, and his state of mind are ironic. Sometimes this irony carries over into what Socrates the character says out loud in the dramatic context of the dialogue, but more often than not, Socrates the narrator gives the information to his narrative audience. Of course, the audience of the dialogue receives this information as well. Indeed, they can distinguish between the comments Socrates makes as a character and the comments he makes as a narrator. Plato's audience also sees how the characters within the narrative frame respond to Socrates' remarks. As a result, his audience has, at least potentially, a pedagogic and hermeneutic advantage over both the characters within the dramatic action of the dialogue and the characters in the narrative frame. Theoretically this external, or dialogic, audience may be better prepared to apply the philosophical insights of the dialogues to the dilemmas and difficulties of their own lives. However, if as Alexander Nehamas suggests, Plato constructed his dialogues with precisely this possibility in mind, the audience of the dialogues might well be led astray by their privileged hermeneutical stance.[53] Platonic irony "uses Socratic irony as a means for lulling the dialogues' readers into the very self-complacency it makes them denounce. It is deep, dark, and disdainful. It is at least as arrogant a challenge to Plato's readers as Socrates' irony was to his interlocutors and perhaps even more so."[54] At the same time, the reflective, self-corrective model of Socrates the narrator remains present for us. By imitating this model, we create the possibility of overcoming our own ignorance and self-deceptive tendencies. In this way, the narrated dialogues continually exhort us to know ourselves more fully, more deeply, and more completely.

Notes

I would like to thank the Baylor University College of Arts and Sciences for sabbatical leave, which supported my work on this chapter. I also thank Gary Scott and Phil Hopkins for their careful reading of early versions of this essay, the Baylor University Philosophy Colloquium members for helpful comments on the penultimate draft, and the students in my 2004 and 2005 Plato seminars for their individual insights and collective philosophical eros.

1. There are some exceptions. See Leo Strauss, *On Plato's Symposium*, ed. Seth Benardete (Chicago: University of Chicago Press, 2001); Ruby Blondell, *The Play of Character in Plato's Dialogues* (Cambridge: Cambridge University Press, 2002); Thomas Szlezák, *Reading Plato* (New York: Routledge, 1999); Harold Tarrant, "Chronology and Narrative Apparatus in Plato's Dialogues," *Electronic Antiquity* 1, no. 8 (1994), and "Orality and Plato's Narrative Dialogues," in *Voice into Text*, ed. I. Worthington (Leiden: Brill, 1996), 129–47. Some scholars have explored the importance of narrative with respect to individual dialogues. See David Halperin, "Plato and the Erotics of Narrativity," in *Methods of Interpreting Plato and His Dialogues*, ed. James C. Klagge and Nicholas D. Smith, Oxford Studies in Ancient Philosophy supplementary volume (Oxford: Clarendon, 1992), 93–129; Kenneth Dorter, *Plato's Phaedo: An Interpretation* (Toronto: University of Toronto Press, 1982); Patrick Coby, *Socrates and the Sophistic Enlightenment: A Commentary on Plato's Protagoras* (Lewisburg: Bucknell University Press, 1987); Mitchell Miller, *Plato's Parmenides: The Conversion of the Soul* (University Park: Pennsylvania State University Press, 1991); Catherine Zuckert, "Plato's Parmenides: A Dramatic Reading," *Review of Metaphysics* 51 (1998): 875–906; Alfred Geier, *Plato's Erotic Thought: The Tree of the Unknown* (Rochester: University of Rochester Press, 2002); Allan Bloom, *Love and Friendship* (New York: Simon and Schuster, 1993); Thomas Chance, *Plato's Euthydemus: An Analysis of What Is and What Is Not Philosophy* (Berkeley: University of California Press, 1992); Claudia Baracchi, *Of Myth and Life and War in Plato's Republic* (Bloomington and Indianapolis: Indiana University Press, 2002); and Jacob Howland, *The Republic: The Odyssey of Philosophy* (New York: Twayne, 1993). However, there is no full-scale study of Plato's use of narrative techniques.

2. Harold Tarrant tells us that "an introduction to Plato known to us from a papyrus, Oxyrhynchus Papyrus no. 3219 . . . apparently distinguishes 'narrated' from 'dramatic' dialogues, and investigates origins of the 'purely dramatic' dialogue in fr. 1, accepting that Sophron the mimographer was a literary model, but denying that Alexamenos was" (Harold Tarrant, *Plato's First Interpreters* [Ithaca: Cornell University Press, 2000], 6).

3. "Of the thirty-five Platonic dialogues, twenty-five are performed. We can say that is the normal case. There is one intermediate case in which we almost see a narrated dialogue transformed into a performed one, and that is the *Theaetetus*. Nine are simply narrated" (Strauss, *On Plato's Symposium*, 13).

4. According to Malcolm Parkes, "Isidore of Seville (c. 560–636) could state a preference for silent reading which subsequently became established as the norm" (Malcolm Parkes, *Pause and Effect: An Introduction to the History of Punctuation in the West* [Berkeley: University of California Press, 1993], 1).

5. Paul Saenger, *Spaces Between Words* (Stanford: Stanford University Press, 1997), 9.

6. Jocelyn Small, *Wax Tablets of the Mind* (London and New York: Routledge, 1997), 19.

7. H. Gregory Snyder, *Teachers and Texts in the Ancient World: Philosophers, Jews, Christians* (London and New York: Routledge, 2000), 2.

8. William Harris, *Ancient Literacy* (Cambridge: Cambridge University Press, 1989); J. Waugh, "Neither Published nor Perished: The Dialogues as Speech Not Text," in *The Third Way: New Directions in Platonic Studies,* ed. Francisco J. Gonzalez (Lanham: Rowman and Littlefield, 1995), 61–80; Elinor West, "Plato's Audiences, or How Plato Replies to the Fifth-Century Intellectual Mistrust of Letters," in Gonzalez, ed., *The Third Way,* 41–60; Kevin Robb, *Literacy and Paideia in Ancient Greece* (Oxford: Oxford University Press, 1994); Jesper Svenbro, "The Interior Voice: On the Invention of Silent Reading," in *Nothing to Do with Dionysus? Athenian Drama in Its Social Context,* ed. John Winkler and Froma Zeitlin (Princeton: Princeton University Press, 1990), 366–84; K. Robb, "Orality, Literacy and the Dialogue Form," in *Plato's Dialogues: The Dialogical Approach,* ed. Richard Hart and Victorino Tejera (Lewiston: Edwin Mellen, 1997), 29–64; Yun Lee Too, *The Pedagogical Contract: The Economies of Teaching and Learning in the Ancient World* (Ann Arbor: University of Michigan Press, 2000).

9. Holger Theslef, *Studies in Platonic Chronology,* Commentationes Humanarum Litterarum 70 (Helsinki: Societas Scientiarum Fennica, 1982); Eric Havelock, *A Prologue to Greek Literacy* (Cincinnati: University of Cincinnati Press, 1971); and Gilbert Ryle, *Plato's Progress* (Cambridge: Cambridge University Press, 1966).

10. According to Victorino Tejera: "Plato's dialogues do contain overt or covert hints—self-focusing devices as Umberto Eco calls them—about how the reader or interlocutor is to take what will be said. Such hints, if they are to be reliable pointers to the design of the work, must be internal (endogenic) to it. They will override externally generated instructions about the work or its interpretation offered by unreliable or partisan secondary sources like Diogenes Laertius and the Hellenistic Pythagoreans" (Victorino Tejera, *Rewriting the History of Ancient Greek Philosophy* [Westport: Greenwood, 1997], 96).

11. Numerous references to hearing provide an obvious, though often overlooked, indication of the particular orientation of this Pythagorean audience. For a full exposition of how these narrative markers can guide a philosophical interpretation of the *Phaedo,* see Anne-Marie Bowery, "Recovering and Recollecting the Soul," in *Plato's Forms: Varieties of Interpretation,* ed. William Welton (Lanham: Lexington Books, 2003), 111–36.

12. Szlezák, *Reading Plato,* 28–29.

13. Gary Scott, *Plato's Socrates as Educator* (Albany: State University of New York Press, 2000), 193n6.

14. For example, these dialogues emphasize Socrates and his pedagogical relationships, the sophists and their students, and the lover-beloved relationship. Homeric allusions and the presentation of philosophy as an intellectual and spiritual journey all figure prominently in the dialogues. Epistemological problems associated with the dissemination of knowledge and the limitations of human wisdom also make a prominent appearance, as do metaphysical considerations of space and physical location, time, and temporality. I am currently at work on two books, *A Philosophic Muse: Plato's Socrates as Narrator* and *The Socratic Epics: Telling Tales of Socrates,* that explore these dimensions of the Platonic dialogues.

15. I use the following translations: *Lysis*, trans. Stanley Lombardo, in *Plato: Complete Works*, ed. John M. Cooper (Indianapolis: Hackett, 1997), 687–707; *Charmides*, ed. Rosamond Kent Sprague, in *Plato: Complete Works*, 639–63; *The Republic of Plato*, 2nd ed., trans. Allan Bloom (New York: Basic Books, 1991); *Protagoras*, trans. Stanley Lombardo and Karen Bell, in *Plato: Complete Works*, 746–90; *Euthydemus*, trans. Rosamond Kent Sprague, in *Plato: Complete Works*, 708–45. I leave out a consideration of the *Menexenus* and the *Rival Lovers* due to space considerations and to the contested authenticity of these dialogues.

16. Anne-Marie Frosolono makes a similar distinction with respect to Augustine's dual role in the *Confessions*, "Thus Spoke Augustine: An Analysis of the Relationship Between Language and Spirituality in the *Confessions*," *Contemporary Philosophy* 15, no. 1 (1993): 4–7. My sense of "Socrates the character" includes the various Socratic characters, the elenctic Socrates and the constructive Socrates, that Ruby Blondell (2002) masterfully analyzes. In the narrated dialogues, each of these Socratic characters is filtered through the lens of "Socrates the narrator."

17. On Plato's *Lysis*, see Hans-Georg Gadamer, "Logos and Ergon in Plato's *Lysis*," in *Dialogue and Dialectic: Eight Hermeneutical Studies on Plato*, trans. P. Christopher Smith (New Haven and London: Yale University Press, 1980), 1–20; James Haden, "Friendship in Plato's *Lysis*," *Review of Metaphysics* 37 (1983): 327–56; Aristide Tessitore, "Plato's *Lysis:* An Introduction to Philosophic Friendship," *Southern Journal of Philosophy* 28 (1990): 115–32; Francisco Gonzalez, "Plato's *Lysis:* An Enactment of Philosophical Kinship," *Ancient Philosophy* 15 (1995): 69–90; G. Scott, *Plato's Socrates as Educator* (Albany: State University of New York Press, 2000); Geier, *Plato's Erotic Thought*.

18. Ronna Burger writes: "There can be in principle, it seems, no such thing as a reliable narrator: a reliable narrator, like a perfect image, would become so superfluous that his narrative report would be indistinguishable from the original event and therefore no reconstruction at all" (Ronna Burger, "Plato's Non-Socratic Narrations of Socratic Conversation," in Hart and Tejera, eds., *Plato's Dialogues: The Dialogical Approach*, 127). See also Wayne Booth, *The Rhetoric of Fiction*, 2nd ed. (Chicago: University of Chicago Press, 1983).

19. See, in contrast, Apollodorus' characterization of Aristodemus' narrative ability (*Symposium* 173b and 223d).

20. Kenneth Moors, "The Argument Against a Dramatic Date for Plato's *Republic*," *Polis* 7 (1987): 6–31.

21. On Plato's *Republic*, see Ruby Blondell, "Letting Plato Speak for Himself," in *Who Speaks for Plato? Studies in Platonic Anonymity*, ed. Gerald Press (Lanham: Rowman and Littlefield, 2000); Allan Bloom, "Interpretive Essay," in *The Republic of Plato*, 2nd ed., trans. Allan Bloom (New York: Basic Books, 1991); Leon Craig, *The War Lover* (Toronto: University of Toronto Press, 1996); Howland, *The Republic;* and Claudia Baracchi, *Of Myth and Life and War in Plato's Republic* (Bloomington and Indianapolis: Indiana University Press, 2002).

22. See Dorrit Cohn, "The Poetics of Plato's *Republic:* A Modern Perspective," *Philosophy and Literature* 24 (2000): 34–48; and David Roochnik, *Beautiful City: The Dialectical Character of Plato's Republic* (Ithaca: Cornell University Press, 2003).

23. The narrative dimensions of the *Republic* may help ascertain whether or not there was an early proto-*Republic* and if book 1 were originally an independent dialogue, the "Thrasymachus." See, for example, Holger Thesleff, "The Early Version of Plato's *Republic*," *Arctos* 31 (1997): 149–74.

24. Howland, *The Republic*, 4.

25. On Plato's *Charmides*, see Drew Hyland, *The Virtue of Philosophy: An Interpretation of Plato's Charmides* (Athens: Ohio University Press, 1981); Thomas Schmid, *Plato's Charmides and the Socratic Ideal of Rationality* (Albany: State University of New York Press, 1998); and Christopher Planeaux, "Socrates, Alcibiades, and Plato's *Ta Poteideia*: Does the *Charmides* Have an Historical Setting?" *Mnemosyne* 52 (1998): 72–77.

26. See Schmid, *Plato's Charmides*, 171n2; and Hyland, *Virtue of Philosophy*, 27.

27. N. Van Der Ben suggests that a good deal of time has elapsed between the dramatic events and the narrative retelling. See N. Van Der Ben, *The Charmides of Plato: Problems and Interpretations* (Amsterdam: B. R. Grüner, 1985), 84.

28. On Plato's *Protagoras*, see David Roochnick, *Of Art and Wisdom: Plato's Understanding of Techne* (University Park: Pennsylvania State University Press, 1996); and Coby, *Socrates and the Sophistic Enlightenment*.

29. Though most scholars assign a dramatic date somewhere in the late 430s.

30. An audience of more than one is also clearly indicated at *Phaedo* 58d and *Protagoras* 310a.

31. Socrates does make two very minor qualifications about his narrative memory. He "thinks" it was Critias who spoke after Alcibiades (336e), and he begins to ask questions "something like this" (338e), but these brief remarks do not detract from his overall display of narrative prowess.

32. See *Protagoras* 317d, 317e, 320c, 333d, 333e, 334d, 335b, 337c, 338b, 338e, 339e, 340d, 348c.

33. Throughout the dialogues, Crito's emotional allegiance to Socrates is unrivaled by any other character. Indeed, aside from Socrates, Crito appears in more dialogues than any other character. In the *Apology*, Crito offers to pay a fine on Socrates' behalf (38c). In the dialogue named after him, we learn that Crito visits Socrates in prison each day, content to sit quietly by his side and watch him sleep (43b). Crito attempts to arrange for his escape from prison (*Crito* 45b). Crito attends to the details associated with Socrates' last day and death sentence (*Phaedo* 60b, 63d, 115b–118a). Socrates even directs his last words to Crito, asking him to pay the debt he owes to Asclepius and not to forget it. Crito closes Socrates' mouth and eyes the moment after he dies (*Phaedo* 118a). In this dialogue, Socrates' ongoing discussion of his emotional state and thought process suggests that the intimacy between them is reciprocal.

34. Despite this display of narrative confidence, Socrates does allude to his inability to remember (*Euthydemus* 290e). On this point, Szlezák remarks: "In order to highlight the importance of recognizing that mathematics is subordinate to dialectic, Plato interrupts the narrative of the dialogue and makes Crito ask whether the young Clinias said such a clever thing (290e). . . . To our

amazement Socrates is not willing to guarantee that it was Clinias; it might also have been Ctesippus" (Szlezák, *Reading Plato*, 88).

35. The *Phaedo* ends with Echecrates making a summation (118a). The last line of the *Protagoras* has elements of a summation: "Our conversation was over so we left" (362a). However, there is no extended final conversation in the external frame of any other dialogue.

36. Steven Dubner, "Calculating the Irrational in Economics," *New York Times* (online), June 28, 2003. See also Antonio Damasio, *Descartes' Error: Emotion, Reason, and the Human Brain* (New York: Avon Books, 1994).

37. See Robert Solomon, "The Joy of Philosophy: Thinking Thin Versus the Passionate Life," *Review of Metaphysics* 55 (2002): 876–78; and "Reasons for Love," *Journal for the Theory of Social Behavior* 32 (2002): 115–44; Robert Roberts, *The Schooled Heart* (Cambridge: Cambridge University Press, 2003); Martha Nussbaum, "Upheavals of Thought: The Intelligence of Emotions," *Graduate Faculty Philosophy Journal* 23 (2002): 235–38; *Poetic Justice: The Literary Imagination and Public Life* (Boston: Beacon Hill, 1995); and *Love's Knowledge: Essays on Philosophy and Literature* (New York: Oxford University Press, 1990); Steven Toulmin, *Return to Reason* (Cambridge: Harvard University Press, 2001); and Genevieve Lloyd, *Man of Reason: Male and Female in Western Philosophy* (Minneapolis: University of Minnesota Press, 1984).

38. Despite the fact that she argues strongly for the affective dimension of human experience throughout her now extensive corpus, Nussbaum's view of Socrates remains problematic. For a critique of her view of Socrates, see Michael Beaty and Anne-Marie Bowery, "Cultivating Christian Citizenship: Martha Nussbaum's Socrates, Augustine's *Confessions*, and the Modern University," *Christian Scholar's Review* 31 (2003): 21–52; and also Bruce S. Thornton, "Cultivating Sophistry," *Arion* 6, no. 2 (1998): 180–204.

39. In what does the Socratic ideal consist? According to Nussbaum in *Cultivating Humanity*, it

> means a life that accepts no belief as authoritative simply because it has been handed down by tradition or become familiar through habit, a life that questions all beliefs and accepts only those that survive reason's demand for consistency and for justification. Training this capacity requires developing the capacity to reason logically, to test what one reads or says for consistency of reasoning, correctness of fact, and accuracy of judgment. (Martha Nussbaum, *Cultivating Humanity* [Cambridge: Harvard University Press, 1997], 17–18)

40. This interpretation of Socrates is famously presented by Friedrich Nietzsche. I mention only one example:

> If one needs to make a tyrant of reason, as Socrates did, then there must exist no little danger of something else playing the tyrant. Rationality was at that time divined as a saviour; neither Socrates nor his "invalids" were free to be rational or not, as they wished—it was *de rigueur*, it was their last expedient. The fanaticism with which the whole of Greek thought throws itself at

rationality betrays a state of emergency: one was in peril, one had only one choice: either to perish or—be absurdly rational. . . . The moralism of the Greek philosophers from Plato downwards is pathologically conditioned: likewise their estimation of dialectics. Reason = virtue = happiness means merely: one must imitate Socrates and counter the dark desires by producing a permanent daylight—the daylight of reason. One must be prudent, clear, bright at any cost: every yielding to the instincts, to the unconscious, leads downwards. (Friedrich Nietzsche, *Twilight of the Idols and The Anti-Christ,* trans. R. J. Hollingdale [London: Penguin Books, 1990], 43)

41. There are also numerous references to wildness, anger, and agitation throughout these dialogues. See *Euthydemus* 272e–273c, 294d, 295d–e; *Republic* 336b–c; *Charmides* 153b, 162c; *Protagoras* 310b, 314c, 333e.

42. Geier, *Plato's Erotic Thought,* 74–75.

43. Burger, *Plato's Dialogues,* 140n10.

44. See *Charmides* 169d.

45. Miller, *Plato's Parmenides,* 6. The Eleatic Stranger offers an excellent articulation of the positive dimensions of aporia: "Then we've now given a complete statement of our confusion. But there's now hope, precisely because both that which is and that which is not are involved in equal confusion. That is, in so far as one of them is clarified, either brightly or dimly, the other will be too. And if we can't see either of them, then anyway we'll push our account of both of them forward as well as we can" (*Sophist* 251a).

46. See also *Protagoras* 335b.

47. Howland, *The Republic,* 33–34, makes this point quite forcefully with respect to the *Republic.*

48. In the *Lysis,* Socrates simply begins by reporting on his actions, rather than his state of mind: "I was walking straight from the Academy to the Lyceum, by the road which skirts the outside of the walls, and had reached the little gate where is the source of the Panops, when I fell in with Hippothales, the son of Hieronymus, Ctesippus the Paeanian, and some more young men, standing together in a group" (203a). He soon turns toward a reflection of his own state of mind: "He answered only with a blush. So I added, Hippothales, son of Hieronymus, there is no longer any need for you to tell me whether you are in love or not, since I am sure you are not only in love, but pretty far gone in it too by this time. For though in most matters I am a poor useless creature, yet by some means or other I have received from heaven the gift of being able to detect at a glance both a lover and a beloved" (204b).

49. See also *Euthydemus* 295e; *Republic* 329e and 357a.

50. See Gary Scott, *Does Socrates Have a Method? Rethinking the Elenchus in Plato's Dialogues and Beyond* (University Park: Pennsylvania State University Press, 2002), 6.

51. Tom Brickhouse and Nicholas Smith, "The Socratic Elenchos?" in Scott, *Does Socrates Have a Method?* 145–57.

52. Aristotle, *Nicomachean Ethics,* trans. David Ross, rev. J. L. Ackrill and J. O. Urmson (Oxford: Oxford University Press, 1998), 35.

53. Alexander Nehamas explains how such a seduction might well occur. "For in the process of producing in us a disdain for Socrates' interlocutors, the dialogues turn us into characters just like them. In observing Euthyphro deceive himself in Plato's fiction, we deceive ourselves in our own life" (Alexander Nehamas, *The Art of Living: Socratic Reflections from Plato to Foucault* [Berkeley: University of California Press, 1998], 44). Nehamas's distinction between Platonic and Socratic irony does not take into account the distinction between Socrates the character and Socrates the narrator, but when this distinction is taken into account, Platonic irony becomes even more complex.

54. Nehamas, *Art of Living*, 44.

5

Homeric Μέθοδος in Plato's Socratic Dialogues

Bernard Freydberg

Does Socrates have a method? Does Plato have a method in the deployment of his "Socrates become beautiful and new"?[1] These are urgent questions not only to those of us who are concerned about how the names of these founders of our philosophical enterprise have become misapplied, used in a context they clearly would have found appalling—in training lawyers, for instance. "The Socratic method" has become a cliché that refers to hard-hitting question-and-answer exchanges quite apart from the concerns with truth and justice that animated Socrates. Further, even the elenctic activity of Socrates comprised only one of the ways he practiced philosophy, and often not the predominant one. For example, the *Republic,* although it recounts a conversation in which there occurred much question and answer, is a very long narration culminating in a great myth. For another, the *Theaetetus* includes many long speeches. Further, the *Parmenides* finds Socrates on the *other* end of the exchanges. Surely not least, the *Timaeus* and the *Sophist* find Socrates making significant remarks at the beginning, then falling silent.

Can any of these properly be called "methods" in the modern sense of the word? In other words, does the very word "method" do violence to both the letter and the spirit of the dialogues? Indeed, Socrates uses the word μέθοδος on very few occasions and never, or perhaps only obliquely, in reference to his own practice. Ἔλεγχος is never called a μέθοδος. There are, however, many casual references: at *Phaedrus* 269d6– 8 Socrates says, "But insofar as there is an art of rhetoric, it does seems apparent to me that the μέθοδος for acquiring it is not to be found in the manner that Lysias and Thrasymachus have pursued it." The only μέθοδος by which the art of rhetoric can be genuinely acquired is that by which one comes to know "the nature of the whole" (270c2), whereby both the souls and the bodies of others would be known.[2] This knowledge is impressive indeed:

BERNARD FREYDBERG

Isn't this the way to think [διανοεῖσθαι] about the nature of anything?
First, it is necessary for us to consider whether the object regarding
which we would become experts [τεχνιϰοὶ] and capable of transmit-
ting our expertise is simple [ἁπλουν] or complex [πολθειδές]. Then,
if it is simple, we must investigate its power: What things does it have
what natural power of acting upon? By what things does it have what
natural disposition to be acted upon? If, on the other hand, it has
many forms [εἴδη], we must enumerate them all and, as we did in the
simple case, investigate how each is naturally able to act upon what
and how it has a natural disposition to be acted on by what. (*Phaedrus*
270c10–d7)

But no one, of course, is in possession of either this knowledge of the
whole of the world or of the μέθοδος by which one could acquire it. If
one were to claim that this method of determining the nature of things
is a scientific or systematic ideal of some kind, it is nevertheless clear
that Socrates makes no claim that he possesses it. Such a method yielding such knowledge would surely be worth having, but this contradicts
Socratic ignorance. In the case of rhetoric, Socrates ridicules it in the
Gorgias, calling that so-called art that persuades by λόγος—rhetoric—
not an art (τέχνη) but a "knack" (ἐμπειρία) and a "massage" (τριβή).[3]
Thus, the conversation in the *Phaedrus,* which takes place under the
false supposition that there is such an art, has a striking effect upon
the μέθοδος spoken of in its aforementioned context: this μέθοδος lo-
cates itself on the outside of philosophy. This "only proper method," a
method that would enable one to know the souls of others, would make
its possessor wise.

Examples of other casual uses of the word μέθοδος can be found
at *Phaedo* 79d2–e5 and *Theaetetus* 183c2. In the former, Socrates asks
Cebes a question concerning the comparison of the soul and the body
with respect to their orientation toward "things that are of the same
kind." By virtue of this orientation, "its experience then is what is called
wisdom." Cebes answers, "I think, Socrates . . . that on this μέθοδος,
even the dullest would agree that the soul is altogether more like that
which always exists in the same state rather than like that which does
not." In the latter, after a lengthy ἔλεγχος Socrates tells Theaetetus,
"We are not going to grant that knowledge is perception, not at any
rate on the *methodos* that supposes that all things are in motion" (*Phaedo*
183b9–c2). In both the more robust of the casual uses above and the
more modest ones cited here, the Greek μέθοδος and our word "procedure" seem synonymous, or at least close to being so.[4] But perhaps
this almost reflexive association is made too quickly. Perhaps there

is much more to think about in connection with the Greek word μέθοδος.

Μέθοδος is never employed in connection with Homeric imagery in the Platonic dialogues. Yet I will argue that in addition to the more prosaic understanding spoken of above, there resides a more thorough-going and deeper sense of μέθοδος that echoes in its original Greek association. This original sense of μέθοδεία, of which μέθοδος in the sense of a way of inquiry or a systematic procedure is an indirect etymological offshoot, finds it associated with "craftiness" or "wiliness." As is the case with many of our philosophical words that come from Greek, the earlier openness of μέθοδεία gradually became rendered more technical. The gain in precision comes at the cost, in my view, of not being able to read the Platonic dialogues in the manner that they present themselves to us. That is to say, the image of Socrates presents neither a harbinger nor an exemplar of a more rational philosophical method, but rather that of a wily friend who invites us to enter into the aporetic activity of philoso-phy, who insinuates a need in us to submit ourselves to its ever-surprising rigors and pleasures. Nowhere, perhaps, is this confusion and seduction more evident and more fruitful than in Plato's attachment of Homeric language to the voice of this image. Socrates speaking Homer: What about it?

In this paper, I will suggest that Plato has at least this one philo-sophical μέθοδος in connection with Homeric imagery: he treats many of the key images in very much the way he has Socrates praise poetry in the *Ion* (as will be discussed more fully below). Genuine poets like Homer produce works that bring great goods to humankind. These works are the products not of intellect, but of inspiration. The proper *philosophical* approach to these works can therefore not be a *literal* treat-ment of their content, such as the disparity in the exchange of armor be-tween Diomedes and Glaucus, but must treat the images as opening out into these underlying great goods, such as friendship (φιλία) and the clash between family and political (tribal) identity.[5] One major task of the poet is to sing of these great goods through poetic images inspired by the Muses. One major task of the philosopher is to interpret these images for the sake of the human search for wisdom.

Two Going Together

The Homeric citation beginning "σύν τε δύ'" (two together) will serve as the paradigm for my treatment of the Plato-Homer philosophical relation. The entire line declares, in the dialogues, that two going together can see better than one alone. This "seeing together," I will strive to show, applies not only to the dialogical interplay between interlocutors; it applies also to the mutually nurturing relation between philosophy and poetry.

In the *Iliad*, the passage "σύν τε δύ' ἐϱχομένω, καί τε πϱὸ ὃ τοῦ ἐνόησεν" ("when two go together, one perceives before the other") occurs in the context of the nocturnal deliberations of the demoralized Achaians, who were beaten back by Hector and the Trojans on the previous day.[6] Upon Nestor's entreaty for someone to sneak into the camp of the Trojans, either to capture one or to overhear their plans, "Diomedes of the great war cry" volunteers at once, but adds:

> But if some other man would go along with me
> there would be more comfort in it, and greater confidence.
> When two go together, one of them at least looks forward
> to see what is best; a man, by himself, though he be careful,
> still has less mind [νόος] in him than two, and his wits [μῆτις]
> have less weight. (*Iliad* 10.222–26)

In Homer, then, "two going together" shows forth two virtues simultaneously: greater courage (that is, greater comfort and confidence) and greater insight. Interestingly, unlike εἶδος, which refers in Homer only to outward appearance, νοῦς can suggest the perceived look of something or can suggest the deliberating intellect.[7] The warriors' journey turns out to be successful: Diomedes and Odysseus capture the Trojan Dolon who, after supplying a wealth of information out of fear for his life, is beheaded. Socrates will, of course, adapt this traditional (and brutal) image for its philosophical yield.

Symposium 174d2–3 reads: "Σύν τε δύ', ἔφη, 'ἐϱχομένω πϱὸ ὁδοῦ' βουλευσόμεθα ὅτι ἐϱοῦμεν." ("'When two,' he said, 'going on the path together, we can deliberate about what to say.'")

Protagoras 348c7–9 reads: "ἡγοῦμαι γὰϱ πάνυ λέγειν τι τὸν Ὅμηϱον τὸ—σύν τε δύ' ἐϱχομένω, καὶ τε πϱὸ ὃ ἐνόησεν." ("I think that Homer said it all in the line—when two go together, one perceives before the other.")

In the *Protagoras*, the citation is an exact reproduction of book 10, line 224, of the *Iliad*. The setting in the *Protagoras* in which the Homeric passage occurs could not, it seems, be more different. The interplay between Socrates and Protagoras is tense. Protagoras neither wishes to be the questioner nor the respondent in a question-and-answer exchange on virtue with Socrates. Only when shamed by Alcibiades does he reluctantly agree to be the respondent. Socrates declares his own confusion on this topic, and quotes Homer approvingly on the need of a partner in searching out and testing what one believes to have discovered. Although subsequent praise of Protagoras may seem merely ironic ("You are not only good yourself, but also able to make others good"; 348e), his urging of a joint philosophical search could not be more sincere.

The enemy here is not Troy nor is the battle with Hector and the Trojans. Rather, Socrates has relocated the poetic figure into the activity of philosophy, where "two going together" are dialogical partners (whether friendly or not) and the enemy in the darkness is blind ignorance and falsehood concerning the most important matters for human life. Socratic sincerity in this search with Protagoras is proven in the outcome of the dialogue: although Socrates has clearly "won" the argument, the two men have switched positions on the teachability of virtue, so the matter must be left as unsettled despite the victory. Here, the Homeric exploration by which two go together yields ἀπορία, that great philosophical gain whereby one is divested of confidence in formerly held opinions that do not stand up to scrutiny. Such "beheading" is a benefit!

I will treat the *Symposium* quotation at much greater length, because the employment of "two going together" is much subtler here and because that analysis opens the way to the further methodological concerns that will be elaborated in the next section of this paper. These concerns, adumbrated in this analysis, address the "underlying meaning" (ὑπόνοια) of the Homeric images. Unlike in *Protagoras*, Plato has Socrates take only part of the line, and he further alters it by adding a "path." In so doing he seems merely to be making the quotation more fitting to its context. But looking more critically, one can make another observation. The Homeric line in the *Symposium* occurs in a *comic* context. In Apollodorus' recollection that is many times removed from the event of the symposium, Socrates has gone to the baths "so that beauty might match beauty" (174a). But Socrates' famously misshapen face could be no match for Agathon's youthful beauty—although the seriousness to which Platonic comedy is always given over is this: to the beauty of poetry, Socrates will match the beauty of philosophy.

Further, Socrates encounters the uninvited Aristodemus, who agrees to accompany Socrates on the understanding that Socrates has invited him along—but the latter arrives at Agathon's without Socrates, who "drew his thoughts [νοῦν] into himself" (174d5) and stands still on the porch of his neighbor. Nothing whatsoever was discussed on the topic agreed upon, namely what the two would say to Agathon upon their arrival. In other words, the two did not literally "go together" to Agathon's. Nor did their pathways at the symposium seem to intersect. On account of the large quantities of wine he consumed, Aristodemus remembered some of the speeches on ἔρως entirely, some partially, and forgot others—including his own, presumably—completely. Yet Aristodemus deserves κῦδος for his recollection of the speeches and his relating them to Apollodorus.

Much has been made of the ending of the *Symposium,* where we find Socrates challenging Agathon and Aristophanes, the two (drunk and exhausted) poets present, to admit that the same person could write comedy and tragedy. As the poets fall asleep, Socrates goes off to spend the next day "as he did the others" (223d11). This is taken to bear witness to the superiority of the philosopher to the poet, at least as a disciple of Dionysus, as well as one who answers the call of Apollo. However, even a brief overview of the speeches as recorded reveals a more complex relation.

The speech of Aristophanes is a tragic speech given by a comedian. The original spherical, four-armed, four-legged human beings committed ὕβρις, and so were sliced in half by Zeus for their insolence. Ἔρως is the search for one's other half. A human being, by himself or herself, is incomplete. Ἔρως is the search for one's other half, so as to make oneself whole as far as possible in this, our realm of fated finitude. Aristophanes' speech presents ἔρως as concerned with completeness, but does not give an account of its orientation toward goodness.

Agathon's speech, by contrast, presents a direct leap of ἔρως to goodness, without stopping at all for consideration of human finitude with its struggles and its errors. In other words, Agathon, the tragedian, presents a comic speech, in the sense that the limits to which humanity is given over present no obstacle to such a leap.[8] Ἔρως is everything good, nothing bad, "ornament of all gods and men together, most beautiful and virtuous leader whom all men must follow, singing beautifully and sweetly and partaking of the music he sings as he enchants the mind of every god and man" (197e1–5). To readers of English only it may seem mysterious that this speech, so transparently superficial in content, would receive such enthusiastic applause. Even Agathon's position as host and recent victor could not justify it. However, in Greek Agathon's speech is a tour de force of spontaneous rhythm and rhyme, a showpiece of a talented poet. As is well known, Socrates immediately sets out to chide his friends for applauding Agathon's false and sophist-like praise of ἔρως, then performs an ἔλεγχος upon Agathon's view that reveals ἔρως lack of beauty and goodness.

However, Socrates' own speech has three features that bind it to that of his poetic predecessors. (1) The speech is presented as inspired by a Muse-like figure, Diotima of Mantinea. Further, although this figure is original with Plato, Mantinea was associated with the mythical Arcadian region upon which pastoral poetry called.[9] (2) The presentation of ἔρως as finite coheres with Aristophanes' speech (as the latter was quick to note; 212c5). And (3) the orientation of ἔρως toward goodness coheres with the speech of Agathon. The incorporation of the key elements of both poetic speeches in that of Socrates, together with the distancing of himself from the source of his inspiration just as do Homer, Aristophanes, and Agathon, suggests that the two—poetry and philosophy—go together and feed one another. One might say that the comic traveling along the pathway by Aristodemus and Socrates that led to the house of Agathon imaged the kindred and more fundamental "going together" of philosophy and poetry that issued from the *Symposium*.

The Philosopher Splits the Poetic in Two

In one of the most telling but seldom cited passages in the *Republic*, Socrates alludes significantly to the "underlying sense" (ὑπόνοια) belonging to poetry, a deeper sense that will play a major role in the life of the philosopher. This ὑπόνοια respects the *divine inspiration* of the poet praised so unconditionally by Socrates in the *Ion*. There, he affirms that the poet in his "sane" state is quite ordinary, but under the sway of divine madness has many true and useful things to convey to humankind.[10] The censorship of the poets spoken of in the building of the "city in speech" issues from precisely such "sanity," precisely such calculation. The inspired person, in fact, is banned from this city, however wonderful his or her inspiration proved to be.[11] Let us consider a discussion of censorship and ὑπόνοια in the *Republic*:

> But Hera's binding by her son, and Hephaestus' being cast out by his father who was being beaten, and all the battles of the gods Homer made, must not be accepted in the city, whether they are made with an underlying sense or without an underlying sense. A young thing cannot judge what is an underlying sense and what is not. (378d3–8)[12]

The principle guiding the censorship of poetry in the city has only to do with the shaping of the young souls of its guardians. As I have argued elsewhere, this "principle" leads to features from the questionable to the absurd.[13]

For one, the young guardians-in-training are selected for their capacity to be vicious to others yet gentle to their own, a paraphrase of Polemarchus' earlier refuted notion of justice as helping one's friends and harming one's enemies. For another, these most spirited youths are to be fed poetic pabulum, and in the course of this feeding to have virtually every human emotion with any taint of darkness purged from their souls.[14] Finally, the good, for these guardians, is equated with the opinion of the rulers of what is good for the city. On the way to securing this opinion in their souls, they would have to be told many lies—including the ultimate whopper known as the "noble lie," from which they are supposed to believe that this rigorous education was like a dream, when in reality they were being fashioned under the earth.

However one interprets the Platonic city in speech, it is incontrovertible that the education of the guardians has little in common with the education of the philosopher as the latter is imaged in the *Republic*. So too will poetry play a vastly different role. Most convincingly, while the guardians are educated to regard *goodness* as the opinion of what is best for the city, for the philosopher the Good is far beyond the reach of opinion, even (Socrates says) "beyond being." In an equally incontrovertible manner, the first poetic line that occurs to the one who has been liberated from the realm of the shadows of the cave and into the light (516d5–7) is the very same first line *banned* first of all from the education of the guardians—the famous Achilles in Hades passage, where the dead hero says:

> I would rather be on the soil, a serf to another,
> To a man without lot whose means of life are not great
> Than to rule over all the dead who have perished. (*Odyssey* 11.489–91)

In book 7 of the *Republic*, Socrates confidently claims that the liberated one would rather " 'be on the soil, a serf to another man, to a portionless man' than to opine those things and live that way" (516d5–6).

The "underlying sense" of the Achilles in Hades passage may seem like a preference for a meager life and a picturing of death as the most undesirable fate for a human being. However, its ὑπόνοια could not be more different. It is a song of praise for a life oriented toward truth and being (the light), since such a life is superior to one given over to shadows, superior to lives like the ones of the men in the cave to whom the discerning of shadows (opinions) constitutes the limits of their questioning.

There are many other instances where Socrates splits the poetic in two, as evidenced by the same passage cited approvingly in one context and disapprovingly in another. A pattern will clearly emerge, according to which the non-hyponoetic (that is, literal) meaning of the passage will be denounced in a non-philosophical context while the underlying sense receives praise. For example, for the training of the guardians, Socrates would ban *Odyssey* 10.444–45:

> [Tiresias] alone has intelligence even after death,
> but the rest of them are flittering shadows.

Socrates calls this passage and others like it "neither true nor beneficial *to the men who are to be fighters*" (386c7; emphasis mine). Since these men are the ones to be reared so as to help friends and harm enemies, to be inculcated with the opinion of what is best for the city and to do battle fearlessly, *any* passage that would present death as miserable would seem to harm this rearing. But even this view, according to which the young souls are shaped entirely by the non-hyponoetic, literal meaning of the poems they hear, and according to which their natural concern with death could be completely excised along with the excising of a few selected passages from Homer and other poets, presupposes a malleability of the spirited human soul that is highly questionable at best.

Nevertheless, even granting this malleability and granting the efficacy as well as the (however remote) possibility of training soldiers by means of such censorship, an affirmative philosophical use of this same passage is found at the conclusion of another dialogue, the *Meno*. After demonstrating to his obtuse interlocutor that there are no teachers of virtue of the kind Meno supposed (since the wisest statesmen could not pass their virtue on to their sons), Socrates concludes that virtue comes from divine dispensation to the virtuous, but without their understanding it. That is why there are no teachers nor will any be found "unless there is someone among our statesmen who can make another into a statesman. If there were one, he could be said to be among the living what Tiresias was said to be among the dead, namely that 'he alone retained his intelligence while the others are flitting shadows.' In the same manner such a man would, as far as virtue is concerned, here also be the only true thing compared with shadows" (100a1–7).

Here the philosophical ὑπόνοια is exposed precisely through the Homeric image. No longer at war, Odysseus has just left the house of Circe after many swinelike years with her directions to an encounter with the prophet Tiresias. After making the required sacrifices and entering Hades, the encounter begins. Tiresias knows that Odysseus is seeking his return to Ithaca and informs him that this journey will be most difficult, will cost him all of his men, but that it can be accomplished if he takes certain precautions and adheres to them rigorously. He must "contain his own spirit [θυμός]" (*Odyssey* 11.105) and that of his companions, especially from the slaughter of forbidden cattle, and to accomplish this he must "keep [his] mind on homecoming [νόστος]" (11.110). Odysseus, of course, follows the prophet's directives, which are fulfilled.

In the *Meno*, the image of the mythical prophet directing Odysseus is likened to the one who knows what virtue is, and so can instruct others by means of this knowledge. But Tiresias' prophetic talent comes to him only after he has been blinded by Athena, whom he glimpsed (quite by accident) bathing naked, and who compensates him for the blindness she has caused by giving him this gift and also a staff by which to walk about.

Tiresias' sight is always accompanied by the self-recognition that *he cannot see*. It also belongs to Tiresias' sight that no one else in Hades has it—it was "acquired" by him alone, through the entreaties of his mother, as a result of his own deed. In the dialogue, Plato has the Homeric image function as a paradigm for a search that each *living* human being must take up for himself or herself alone. Since it is not given to us to see originals (such as virtue καθ' αὐτό) whole and pure, just as Tiresias was barred upon penalty of his sight from seeing a goddess naked, it is our task to keep our spirit in check and to be mindful of those matters that matter most to human habitation on earth and in our πόλεις, that is, in our homes.[15] This means for us to be mindful of our ignorance about these matters, and to continue the questioning that will bring us ever nearer to virtue in the very search for it.

Thus, Plato uses the Homeric image Socrates would ban from the education of young soldiers in another dialogue as a vicarious image for the one who would seek virtue sincerely. In the mouth of Socrates speaking it to the uncomprehending Meno, we are given an oblique but unmistakable glimpse of how this image should function in our philosophical lives.

Another such cross-dialogical instance occurs with *Odyssey* 17.485:

> For the gods take on all sorts of transformations, appearing as strangers from elsewhere, and thus they range at large through the cities, watching to see which men keep the laws, and which are violent.

The suitor Antinoös has just struck the "vagabond" who he and his colleagues do not know is Odysseus, and the suitors scold Antinoös, since the vagabond may turn out to be a god in disguise and so wreak vengeance upon them.

This passage would be expunged from the poetry intended for the education of the young soldiers, because it is useful to the city for them to believe that the gods, as well as being always good, are constant and always the same.[16] But at the beginning of the *Sophist* Socrates uses this same passage, where it functions both as his introductory, playful challenge to Theodorus and to the Eleatic Stranger, and as his bridge to the central philosophical issue that will drive the dialogue. When Theodorus and the Stranger, who is "a companion of the people around Parmenides and Zeno" (216a3), arrive for their appointment, Socrates asks Theodorus whether he realizes that he has brought some god (τινα θεὸν): "Beside the other gods the god of strangers especially becomes a companion to those men who participate in just reverence," and he "looks down on both outrages and lawful conduct" (216b1–2).

The ironic play consists of Socrates' denigrating his own skill in λόγος without having heard a word from the Stranger. Here the previously banned passage is readmitted as a philosophical provocation, a stimulant to the activity of λόγος and the determination of its measure. Theodorus' answer, that the Stranger is not a god (θεὸς) but godlike (θεῖος) as all philosophers are, meets with Socrates' approval. The genuine ὑπόνοια of the poetic image, however, is the matter of the self-concealment of the true being of a human being, in this case the *appearance* of the philosopher and of the sophist in the city. In the case of the *philosopher* in the city, his or her true being appears in three guises, stated a bit differently on two early occasions: statesman, sophist, and madman; statesman, sophist, and philosopher.

Thus, just as one must take great care not to abuse a god who might be appearing in a transformed human shape lest one be the object of divine retribution, one must also be most mindful if one wishes to distinguish a genuine philosopher from one of the misleading appearances of philosophy in the city and in order to protect one's soul from bad rearing. Since "philosopher" is one of the appearances, but there are also "artificial [πλαστῶς] . . . philosophers" (216c6) (just as there are madmen who are entirely non-philosophical), the task of distinguishing "being" from "appearance" can be a daunting one.

This paper clearly does not call for an extended interpretation of the *Sophist*. My opinion is that despite many epochal insights, many blind alleys, and many suggestive pathways that deserve further exploration on their own, the effort to distinguish the philosopher from the sophist fails ultimately because the silence of Socrates after the dialogue's opening leaves the Stranger and young Theaetetus not as "two going together" so that two minds are better than one, as the Homeric image sings. Rather, the terms dictated by the Stranger—either an uninterrupted long speech or, best of all, a conversation with someone "unirritating and compliant" (ἀλύπως τε καὶ εὐηνίως), restrict the outcome to the limits of the Stranger's vision. In light of the Homeric image, one wonders: What sort of being is the Stranger an appearance of?

In all three cases treated in this section, the inspired Homeric image is used to open up a philosophical vista, a vista that is explored in questioning λόγος.

῞Υβϱις and Its Aftermath: Giants (and Horses)

The exploits of giants who are capable of inflicting grievous pain upon gods and also, in the case of Ephialtes and Otos, of killing them and ascending to the throne of Olympos, are sung in both the *Iliad* and the *Odyssey*.[17] These images can be examined for their philosophical use in the Platonic dialogues, just as the prior cases of a twofold split in the use of the images could. Treating the Ephialtes and Otos myth first, we find that it is told somewhat differently across the two epics. The context of the passage in the *Iliad* (5.381–92) is Diomedes' painful wounding of Aphrodite with his spear as the latter was carrying out the wounded body of her beloved son Aineias. As she cried of her wound to her mother Dione, Dione reminded her that immortals often suffer pains at the hands of mortals when immortals fight one another. Indeed, Aphrodite's own brother Ares had been chained by Ephialtes and Otos who were too strong for the god of war, and Ares would have perished had it not been for the intervention of Hermes (who was tipped off by their stepmother Eëriboia). The *Odyssey* presents a version that varies slightly. Ephialtes and Otos were fathered by Poseidon and Iphimedeia (wife of Aloeus); they grew at a young age to magnificent heights and were strikingly handsome; they threatened to pile up mountains so as to reach and challenge the gods on Olympos. On his visit to Hades, Iphimedeia recounts these details to Odysseus, and concludes the tale with the following:

> They would have carried it out if they had come to their primes,
> but the son of Zeus whom Leto with ordered hair had borne him,
> Apollo, killed them both, before the down gathered
> below their temples, or on their chins the beard had blossomed.
> (11.317–20)

In the *Symposium*, Plato places this mythical account in a Homeric epic within another mythical speech, Aristophanes' λόγος on the origin and meaning of ἔϱως, but has Aristophanes use it for his own purposes. In Aristophanes' version, Ephialtes and Otos were struck dead by lightning—suggesting that Zeus was their slayer, perhaps offering a third myth of these giants.[18] As recounted earlier, the original four-legged, four-armed human beings challenged the gods. Zeus called a council of the gods, and decided to punish this ὕβρις of the original human beings by slicing them in two, a procedure that would both weaken them and increase the number of sacrifices they would offer. Apollo takes on the task of healing their wounds.

Here the original human beings are contrasted with these giants most unmistakably. In the Homeric myth, Ephialtes and Otos would have been successful in their quest to conquer Olympos had they been permitted to grow to their youthful prime (ἥβα). No doubt their paternal lineage gave them more power than other children of gods and mortal women, but no account is given for this exceptional strength. Further, as Dione explains to Aphrodite,

> Many of us who have our home on Olympos endure things from men
> when ourselves we inflict hard pain on each other. (*Iliad* 5.383–84)

On the other hand, the original human beings in Aristophanes' myth had no such divine lineage and no such divine squabbling to influence their behavior. Therefore, they had no possibility of inflicting any pain at all on the gods. The humans simply assumed that, by virtue of their strength and speed, they were far more powerful than they really were. Further, and far more important to the Aristophanic presentation, unlike Ephialtes and Otos who could be killed and represented no loss, the Olympian gods *needed* human beings for what they had to offer them, just as human beings needed the gods in order to be mindful of the due measure appropriate to their status.

The subtle adaptation of the Homeric tale within Aristophanes' speech reveals a philosophical opening in yet another way. Unlike Ephialtes and Otos, human beings "as they are now" are weak and needy of another for wholeness and completeness. This is the definition of ἔρως at which this speech arrives. Further still, they require *reminders* lest they commit ὕβρις again and so must be halved again. In Aristophanes' myth, the wrinkles Apollo leaves around the stomach serve precisely as these reminders (μνήμαι) of past sufferings. Their philosophical analogue is the recollection of the way our desires (our stomach) may lead us beyond what is proper to a human being, but that when we are so mindful even our weakness, our flaws, and our needfulness do not preclude a life of love and happiness.

Another giant who inflicted pain on the gods was "the strong son of Amphitryon" (*Iliad* 5.392), namely Heracles. The giant's "actual" father was Zeus, his mother was Alcmene, whose mortal husband was Amphitryon. He struck [Hera] beside her right breast with a tri-barbed arrow, so that the pain (ἄλγος) he gave her could not be quieted (5.393–94). He also struck [Hades] among the dead men at Pylos, and gave him to agony (ὀδύνῃσιν) (5.397).

At *Odyssey* 17.566–67, after commenting on the ὕβρις of the suitors, his fear of their large numbers and of their hostility, Odysseus laments the beating he endured from Antinoös, saying:[19]

> For even now, as I went through the house, doing
> no harm, and this man struck me and gave me over to suffering
> [ὀδύνῃσιν].

Socrates calls his great myth in the *Phaedrus* an ἀπόδειξις that the clever (δεινοῖς) will not trust (ἄπιστος), but that the wise (σοφοῖς) will trust (πιστή) (245c1–2; emphasis mine). Ἀπόδειξις is usually translated straightforwardly as "proof," both in general and in translations of Plato.[20] However, as John Sallis has observed in a matter of highest importance for the reading of Plato, "Ἀπόδειξις means a showing forth, an exhibiting of something about something, a making manifest of something so that it can be seen in its manifestness. Thus, for the Greeks a proof was anything but a technique of a sort that could be employed in almost total detachment from the content and that could serve as an appropriate insight into the matter itself in its manifestness."[21] In the conclusion of this paper I will venture my own translation, inspired by that of Sallis, and suggested by Plato's use of Homeric imagery.

During the great myth, Socrates speaks of the charioteer's bringing the hubristic, unruly horse to order:

> He violently yanks the bit back out of the teeth of the insolent
> [ὑβριστοῦ horse, only harder this time, so that he bloodies its foul-
> speaking tongue and jaws, sets its legs and haunches firmly on the
> earth [πρὸς τὴν γῆν] and gives it over to pain [ὀδύναις]. (*Phaedrus*
> 254e2–5)

The literal poetic connection, clearly, is between ὕβρις and pain. The pain inflicted by mortals upon immortals, and upon those mortals like Odysseus who are under special divine guidance, has enormous punishment or death to the perpetrator as its consequence.[22] Plato's use of this allusion in the *Phaedrus* is of particular interest for several reasons. First of all, the Platonic-Socratic mythical charioteer directing two horses, one "beautiful and good and from stock of the same sort" (246b), while the other is the opposite and has the opposite sort of bloodline (246b), functions as an image of a human soul having many lives (an immortal soul and a mortal body). The Platonic-Socratic mythical notion of a region beyond the heavens in which the divine banquet occurs and toward which the human souls long to ascend after their bodily lives have ended and whose heights are proportional to the quality of their prior embodied lives seems to be a far cry from the Homeric Hades.

Great pain in return for pain hubristically visited is poetically presented in Homer through physical wounding or killing. But in the great myth of the *Phaedrus* the emphasis is upon the pleasure a human soul can enjoy by mastering the hubristic horse that dwells within each of us. The pain to which the bad horse is subjected leads directly to the greatest delight. In controlling the bad horse ("a companion to ὕβρις and boastfulness"; *Phaedrus* 253e2) and through the philosophical ἔρως that such restraint makes possible, the Platonic myth emphasizes the almost inexpressible happiness the just human soul feels in recollecting a glimpse of the divine banquet through the beholding of the beauty of one's beloved. The emphasis on justice shows that this image is designed for *this* life.

There is, however, one quasi-similarity in content between the Homeric and the Platonic imagery. In Plato, the souls do journey through Hades, with the better ones actually enjoying the journey. But some other souls are deposited into Hades, namely the ones that encouraged others to indulge their bad horse, like the seductive and false "non-lover." The non-lover (that is, the soul that has no genuine ἔρως) "tosses the soul around for nine thousand years on the earth and leads it, mindless, beneath it" (*Phaedrus* 257a1–2). At this point, it is worth noting from the previous passage that the violent yanking of the bad horse is done, in large part, to anchor it properly *on the earth*. This, the "steering" of our earthbound nature, determines the fate of our souls—in language that at least seems less mythical, it determines the quality of our lives *here*.

This is what the dialogue wants us to see as Socrates demonstrates it to Phaedrus in a manner that is in its own way as magnificently poetic (and more concentrated, albeit less oblique) than the work of Homer. The references in the great myth of Plato to the Homeric images of "giving over to pain" open out in Plato to the possibility of a happiness that belongs to human beings alone.

Conclusion: Platonic-Socratic Ἀπόδειξις

Neither ἀποδείκνῦμι nor its noun form, ἀπόδειξις, are Homeric words. Both occur first of all in the classical age of Greece.[23] Literally, ἀποδείκνῦμι means "show from." Lexical definitions include "exhibit," "point out," "demonstrate," and also "prove." However, as we have seen in the *Phaedrus*, the great myth has been called an ἀπόδειξις that would gain the trust of the wise (σοφοῖς) but not of the clever (δεινοῖς); and citing yet another quality of the myth that may sound paradoxical to our modern ears, there are a number of claims to its *truth* within it (for example, 245c4, 247c5–6).[24]

How can we understand this peculiar notion of ἀπόδειξις? I suggest that we understand it as *showing forth the ὑπόνοια of the poetic inspiration by means of showing forth the inspiration that belongs to philosophy with its own ὑπόνοια*. Philosophical ἀπόδειξις, then, is an interpretive doubling, not a formal proof at all. Its way is the way of inspired questioning exploration. Truth is, in the great Heideggerian interpretation of the Greek word ἀ-λήθεια, un-forgottenness, un-hiddenness.

The Myth of Er, which ends the *Republic*, recalls two other Homeric images. Er, who is not Ἀλκίνου (literally "strong of mind," a pun on the name of king Alkinoös in the *Odyssey*) but rather ἀλκίμου (strong), is the only human who returns to earth after dying, that is, crossing the river Λήθη (forgetfulness) and descending into Hades. In the course of his journey he sees Odysseus, who renounces his former life governed by the love of honor, choosing instead the life of "a private man who minds his own business" (*Republic* 620c6–7). I suggest that this "myth within the myth" exemplifies one key method—inspired hyponoetic doubling, or, if that formulation sounds too technical, "two going together"—that Plato has Socrates use in order to glean the genuine philosophical content for his readers. The ὑπόνοια of Odysseus' mindful homecoming is precisely the choice in this life of a person who, like Socrates, minds his own business. This is one key feature of the "wily" μέθοδος with which Plato, with the poetry he loves, draws us into philosophy.

Notes

1. For translations I generally consulted *Plato: Complete Works*, ed. John M. Cooper (Indianapolis: Hackett, 1997) as my initial contact; and *Platonis Opera*, ed. John Burnet (Oxford: Oxford University Press, 1968) to supply the Greek in accordance with which I made my revisions. On occasion I consulted other translations as well, as indicated in the notes. For my Homer translations, Lattimore served as my only first contact, and *Homeri Opera*, ed. David B. Monro and Thomas W. Allen (Oxford: Oxford University Press, 1966) supplied the Greek. Thanks to all of the above. Responsibility is mine alone.

This particular phrase (Σωκράτους . . . καλοῦ καὶ νέου γεγονότος) is from the *Second Letter* (314c2–4), the authenticity of which is disputed by some. I employ it for two reasons: (1) because of the eloquent way it speaks to the issue of

Platonic writing; and (2) because it places the Socrates of the dialogues first of all as a philosophical creation, rather than as primarily a historical personage. The argument does not depend on its authenticity at all.

2. The Greek is "τῆς τοῦ ὅλου φύσεως"; Cobb has "the nature of the whole in a general sense." Both readings are possible, but the one I gave, which more resembles Nehamas' and Woodruff's, seems more in accord with the Platonic text.

3. *Gorgias* 463b4. Donald Zeyl translates τριβή as "routine," but it seems clear to me that Socrates intends the more biting meaning as primary.

4. The Cooper edition seems to prefer "way of inquiry," which preserves the ὁδός but suggests more than one Greek word. It's a difficult call. I've decided to leave μέθοδος untranslated.

5. Diomedes the Achaian and Glaukos the Trojan confront each other on the battlefield, but discover that they were the very best of friends in childhood. Enthralled by their accidental reunion, they exchange their armor as a sign of their mutual delight (*Iliad* 6.119–233), "but Zeus stole away the wits of Glaukos / whom exchanged with Diomedes the son of Tydeus armor / of gold for bronze, for nine oxen's worth the worth of a hundred" (6.234–36).

6. *Iliad* 10.224.

7. As I demonstrated in *The Play of the Platonic Dialogues*, εἶδος always occurs not merely as a visible quality but as belonging first and foremost to the *self-presentation* of what shows itself. And what shows itself in the manner of *eidos* in the Homeric epics is always a human being or a god. The only exception is a trivial one, occurring in book 18 where Odysseus uses a derivative of εἶδος to describe Argos, Eumaios' dog.

8. Aristophanic comedy presents many such leaps. The best known to philosophers is in *Clouds,* which finds Socrates swinging in a basket from the sky. *Peace* has its hero, the farmer Trugaios, ascend to Mount Olympos on a dung beetle. *Birds* has its "heroes" Euelpides and Peisetairos build a city called Νεφελοκοκκυγίαν ("Cloudcuckooland" in Jeffrey Henderson's translation) and also has them grow wings. But Aristophanes' comedies are inspired and rich, unlike Agathon's encomium to ἔρως.

9. See the *Oxford Classical Dictionary,* ed. Simon Hornblower and Antony Spawforth (Oxford and New York: Oxford University Press, 1996), 919, 1119.

10. See especially *Ion* 533c9–535a2, and in particular 533c7–d4: "That is why the god takes [the poets'] intellect [νοῦς] away from them when he uses them as his servants, as he does prophets and holy diviners, so that we who hear should know that *they* are not the ones who speak those verses that are of such high value, for their intellect is not in them."

11. Before such a gifted person, Socrates says, we would fall on our knees, but "we would say that there is no such man among us in our city, nor is it lawful for such a man to be born there" (!) (*Republic* 368a5–6).

12. I translate the ὑπό- as "underlying" because it suggests that the genuine sense of Homeric poetry in Plato, as will be shown, is its underlying or "deeper" sense.

13. In "*Mythos* and *Logos* in Platonic *Politeiai*," in *History of European Ideas*

16, nos. 4–6: 607–12, I attempt to show that the excision of the exploits of epic heroes would both alienate the souls of the young who need to be educated and would also "carve whole pieces out of the Greek soul" (608). This matter is treated more generally in chapter 7 of *The Play of the Platonic Dialogues* (New York: Peter Lang, 1997).

14. Among the passions and emotions to be purged are the following: (1) strife (among the gods and elsewhere; *Republic* 378b8ff.); (2) violation of oaths (379e2–3); (3) causing evil (380a2–4); (4) lying (382a1ff., 389b2ff.); (5) fear of death (386a7ff.); (6) crying and lamenting (in general, and for lost loved ones; 387d4ff.); (7) and laughing (388e5ff.). There are many others, including—albeit obliquely—ἔρως! (396d2).

15. In chapter 3 of *The Play of the Platonic Dialogues*, I attempt to show that there is never any claim in *any* of the dialogues that an original, an εἶδος, has been noetically sighted, despite the many gestures in that direction that the text makes. Rather, every time it appears that such an ascent to such a sighting might occur, Socrates either breaks off the discourse, either with some words of disclaimer (for example, "as it seems to me," or "a god knows if it happens to be so") or else with a remark on the need for a longer path, another method, a more well-prepared interlocutor. I interpret these dodges as playful in the highest sense, that is, as reminding us of what we *cannot* see in order that we hold ourselves within the limits of what we *can*.

16. Book 2 of the *Republic*, 380d1ff.

17. The Homeric images I treat in this section were all gleaned from suggestions in Cooper's notes.

18. I have not been able to determine why there are three different myths of the lineage of Otos and Ephialtes. All three have their hubristic challenge to the gods as their theme, but I have not been able to discover, either in the literature or through my own study, why Poseidon, Apollo, and Zeus are called their father in three different contexts. I would welcome any insight on this matter.

19. See note 15 above.

20. Regarding the *Phaedrus* in particular, this is the translation of Nehamas and Woodruff in the Cooper volume. Helmbold and Rabinowitz also have "proof," as do Hackforth (in the Hamilton and Cairns volume) and Jowett. There are exceptions, but while they are better, they are not particularly expansive. On page 50 of her *Plato's Phaedrus: A Defense of Philosophical Writing* (Birmingham: University of Alabama Press, 1980), Burger renders it as the less loaded "demonstration," as does Cobb in *The Symposium and the Phaedrus: Plato's Erotic Dialogues* (Albany: State University of New York Press, 1993).

21. John Sallis, *Being and Logos: Reading the Platonic Dialogues*, 3rd ed. (Bloomington: Indiana University Press, 1996), 135–36.

22. "Enormous punishment"; for example, Diomedes' wounding by "limp spearman" Paris after his earlier attack on Aphrodite. Once Odysseus removed Paris' arrow from Diomedes' foot, the latter experienced "hard pain" and had his charioteer "drive him back to the hollow ships, since his heart was heavy" (*Iliad* 11.368–400).

23. H. Liddell and R. Scott, *Greek-English Lexicon*, rev. H. S. Jones (Oxford: Clarendon, 1989), 195.

24. "Now we must first understand the truth about the human soul" (*Phaedrus* 245c4). "I must dare to speak the truth, especially since the truth is my subject" (247c5–6). A word on Socrates' apparent placing of the poets as sixth from the top in the great myth (248e1–2): the Greek, literally translated, says that the soul that is sixth from the great vision will be granted "the life of a poet or some *other* mimetic artist." However, given that Homer is a divinely inspired poet, the passage does not at all claim that he (or Hesiod) were *mimetic* poets. Further, if Socrates did mean to place all poetry sixth, this would undermine not only his frequent appeals to it, but also his own poetical passages, including the great myth!

6

Of Psychic Maieutics
and Dialogical Bondage
in Plato's *Theaetetus*

Benjamin J. Grazzini

> Knowledge differs from right opinion by a bond.
> *Meno* 98a8

The conversation recounted in Plato's *Theaetetus,* it seems, almost did not happen. Indeed, one might say that the conversation among Socrates, Theodorus, and Theaetetus about what knowledge itself is almost miscarried. Despite the fact that he understands the sort of answer Socrates is looking for—even despite the fact that he "cannot get rid of a feeling of concern" (148e5–6) about it—Theaetetus claims that he is not able to say what knowledge is.[1] Socrates, however, does not give up so easily: "You are in labor, my dear Theaetetus, not on account of being empty, but pregnant" (148e7–8). Socrates then accounts for his peculiar practice of philosophy in terms of psychic maieutics, that is, the midwifery of the soul.[2] Theaetetus is pregnant with some conception concerning knowledge; Socrates has the skills to bring Theaetetus' offspring to light, and to determine whether it is viable or an empty wind-egg. This account suffices to reassure and encourage Theaetetus, who comes out with: "As it now appears, knowledge is nothing other than perception" (151e2–3).

Socrates' account of psychic maieutics initiates two overlapping lines of thought. One is more limited to the *Theaetetus* and concerns the relationship between the knowledge implied or assumed by Socrates' claims to be a midwife of the soul, and the ensuing discussion of what knowledge is. The other extends from the *Theaetetus* through the *Soph-*

ist and *Statesman* toward the *Apology,* and concerns the relationship between the image of Socrates, psychic *maieute,* and his trial. I will only be
able to gesture toward how the issues that arise in the *Theaetetus* inform
the latter. My aim here is to show how it makes sense, in this particular
conversation, for the image of Socrates as a midwife of the soul to be
at issue. To that end, I will follow as closely as possible the implications
of how psychic maieutics appears in the *Theaetetus,* the extent to which
Socrates' account of psychic maieutics appears to be at odds with itself,
and how psychic maieutics relates to the conversation it makes possible.
Throughout, I will be primarily concerned with the tension between
the apparent familiarity of Socrates, psychic *maieute,* and the extent to
which that familiarity is called into question by the *Theaetetus.*[3]

* * *

Perhaps the most striking thing about Socrates' account of psychic maieutics is how familiar it appears. Socrates introduces psychic maieutics in order to explain certain things that Theaetetus has heard about
Socrates, namely, that Socrates is "very strange" and makes people perplexed (149a8–10). These facts are not disputed, only that those who
assert them know why Socrates is so strange. That is, Socrates does not
offer to correct a misunderstanding, but to explain the cause or reason (*aition;* 149b2) for an apparently common understanding. Indeed,
Socrates later affirms that those who say that he questions others but gives
no answers of his own because he has no wisdom speak truly (150c4–7).
Throughout his conversation with Theaetetus and Theodorus, Socrates
denies that he has any wisdom of his own, that he is contributing anything to the conversation other than helping to bring to light and test
Theaetetus' offspring, and that he has any more than the little knowledge needed to "take a speech" (161b4) from another.[4] This denial of
wisdom is perhaps the most recognizable aspect of Socrates' character,
calling to mind the "human wisdom" Socrates admits in the *Apology,*
namely, that he does not think that he knows when he does not know.[5]

Another familiar aspect of Socrates' account of psychic maieutics
is that Socrates denies that his interlocutors learn anything from him.
Rather, "they have found many beautiful things within themselves, and
given birth to them" (150d6–8). As in the *Apology,* on this basis Socrates
denies responsibility for the subsequent actions of his patients. Some
leave too soon, either because they think that they are the cause of their
success, or because they are persuaded by others (150e1–4). And it is
not Socrates, but his daimon, that determines which of those who want
to return to Socrates are allowed to do so. The link between Socrates'

denial of being a teacher and his denial of being responsible for the subsequent actions of his associates closely echoes *Apology* 33b3–6: "And whether one of these becomes an upright man or not, I would not be justly held responsible, since I have never promised or taught any instruction to any of them."[6]

The emphasis on his interlocutors bringing forth from within themselves also seems to invoke the notion of recollection as it is developed in the *Meno* and *Phaedo:* that learning is a matter of recollecting knowledge attained by the soul prior to a human being's birth. Here, too, Socrates' patients are said not to gain knowledge from him, but—if at all—from their own experience of conceiving and giving birth to psychic offspring.[7] The other point I want to highlight is what Socrates marks out as "the greatest part" of his art of psychic maieutics: his capacity to test the psychic offspring of others and distinguish between the true and the false, between fruitful offspring and images (150b9–c3). Although Socrates does not tell Theaetetus just how this testing is accomplished, the invocation of the elenchus, the process of examination and refutation by questioning that is the hallmark of "Socratic" method, seems unmistakable.[8] That is, the picture of Socrates, psychic *maieute,* is a picture of Socrates as one who claims no wisdom of his own and who spends his time talking with others, questioning them and trying to show them where their opinions are at odds with one another. This is the Socrates who claims to have devoted his life to this practice in the service of the god, and who is occasionally prevented from certain actions by a daimon. It may even be the Socrates who claims that learning is really a matter of recollecting knowledge grasped by the soul prior to birth. In short, this is the Socrates we have all heard about since the time we were children (or at least undergraduates). Socrates, psychic *maieute,* appears to be as familiar to us as those facts psychic maieutics is supposed to explain are to Theaetetus. As R. G. Wengert puts it: "Everyone is familiar with the image of Socrates as a spiritual midwife."[9]

It is all the more puzzling, then, that upon further reflection the picture of Socrates that emerges from his account of psychic maieutics becomes less and less familiar. In the first place, it is Plato's Socrates who is so easily recognized therein. I do not emphasize this point in order to enter into speculation about what in Plato's texts can be marked out as historically "Socratic" and what "Platonic." It is not clear what would count as criteria for such a distinction—but even if there were grounds for making it, Socrates, psychic *maieute,* is evidently a piece of Platonic fiction. Some have suggested that a reference to the miscarriage of an idea in Aristophanes' *Clouds* (137) supports the claim that the image of midwifery was historically associated with Socrates, but as Myles Burnyeat has argued, there is no reason to think that this is the case. "It must, then, be the power of the image, its striking one as so absolutely the 'right' representation of what Socrates does, that blinds people to Plato's explicit sign-posting" to the contrary.[10] Again, it is primarily on the basis of the Platonic corpus that the image of Socrates as a midwife of the soul appears so familiar to us. I emphasize the ease with which Socrates is recognizable in that image because it seems that in the *Theaetetus* Plato deliberately engages with a caricature of Socrates.[11]

Although I focus almost exclusively on the *Theaetetus* in this essay, it is worth keeping in mind that in the *Sophist* and *Statesman*, too—which along with the *Theaetetus* constitute a sort of trilogy—Plato can be seen to draw on a picture of Socrates that Plato himself helped to create.[12] I refer to the Eleatic Stranger's definition of the noble-born sophist (*Sophist* 230b4–231b8), and his discussion of how the city cannot tolerate any transgression of its laws (*Statesman* 297d3–e6; 299b2–300c3).[13] The former reads like an entry on Socrates in an encyclopedia of philosophy, and the latter like a summary of Socrates' trial and execution. I cannot fully defend this claim here, but arguably the trilogy as a whole is informed by a concern both with the way in which Socrates appears to others and with the problem of accounting for knowledge in the face of conflicting appearances. Insofar as the trilogy is dramatically set on the day of and the day following Socrates' indictment, those concerns take shape in light of Socrates' trial and death.[14] That is, it seems that these images of Socrates both allow Plato to show how easy it is for the Athenians to recognize Socrates in the charges brought against him, and how the more explicitly epistemological and ontological problems at stake in these dialogues are intimately related to the more explicitly political problems surrounding them.[15]

* * *

Psychic maieutics appears unprecedented. The *Theaetetus* is the only Platonic text in which Socrates is explicitly linked with the figure of a midwife, and there seems to be no precedent for such an account within the *Theaetetus* itself.[16] When Socrates introduces psychic maieutics into the conversation his primary aim is to reassure and encourage Theaetetus, who is ready to abandon the attempt to say what knowledge itself is. The explanation of psychic maieutics does achieve this end. Theaetetus agrees that it would be shameful not to exert himself in every possible way, and says, "As it now appears, knowledge is nothing other than perception" (151e2–3). This is one sense in which Socrates' account of psychic maieutics makes possible the discussion of knowledge recounted in the *Theaetetus*—without it, it seems, the conversation would have miscarried. It is not clear, however, why Socrates needs to keep Theaetetus talking, nor why he offers the account of psychic maieutics in order to do so. As Scott Hemmenway puts it: "In its particular place in the dialogue . . . the very richness of the description seems at first sight to be incommensurate with the immediate needs of the conversation."[17]

Or rather, there are reasons for Socrates to keep Theaetetus involved in the conversation, and for Socrates to be concerned with his ability to account for himself. The problem is that those reasons appear to be at odds with the principles of psychic maieutics. At the beginning of the dialogue, Eucleides notes that the conversation he has recorded took place "a little before" (142c6) Socrates' death. At the end of the dialogue, Socrates says that he must go to be indicted on the charges brought against him by Meletus (210d1–3). In this light, it is no surprise that Socrates is concerned with how he appears to others. It seems that the discrepancy between Socrates' self-understanding and the Athenians' understanding of him brings Socrates to trial and ultimately convicts him. Recall the "first charges" recounted by Socrates in the *Apology:* "There is a certain Socrates, a wise man, a thinker on the things aloft, who has investigated all the things under the earth, and who makes the weaker argument the stronger."[18] Thus, it also makes sense that Socrates would be concerned with the issue of knowledge on this of all days. For, presumably, if he can account for knowledge, for the possibility of knowledge in the face of conflicting appearances, then he would be in a better position to account for himself before the jury—or at least to understand why he is bound to be condemned.[19]

It is also odd that, although Socrates' account of psychic maieutics appears to be offered with an eye toward his upcoming trial, he insists that Theaetetus "not tell on [him] to the others" (149a6–7), that is, to keep this explanation of Socratic philosophizing a secret. Why, if this is supposed to be a genuine account of what Socrates does and why, should it be kept secret? This aspect of the account of psychic maieutics also appears less than familiar in light of Socrates' claim in the *Apology* that if someone says that "he has ever learned from me or heard privately anything that everyone else did not, know well that he does not speak the truth" (33b6–8). Socrates does not tell anyone else about his career as a psychic *maieute,* and he asks Theaetetus not to tell anyone else; the account of psychic maieutics is something that is not heard by everyone.

What is more, these are Socrates' concerns, not Theaetetus'. One of the essential features of midwifery is that midwives are those who are past the age of childbearing. Midwives must once have been fertile, insofar as their ability to serve as midwives depends on that experience, "human nature being too weak to acquire art with respect to things of which it has no experience" (149c1–2). Yet midwives cannot at the same time bear children of their own, because their care for their own would interfere with their care for others. Thus, it seems that serious concerns underlie Socrates' apparently playful interest in seeing himself reflected in the less than handsome face of Theaetetus.[20] Insofar as this is the motivation for Socrates' account, however, it seems to run counter to the principles of psychic maieutics.

Yet it is not simply the case that the action and context of the dialogue contradict the account of psychic maieutics. Socrates' initial response to Theodorus' enthusiastic description of Theaetetus, and his initial attitude toward Theaetetus, set up and deepen the image of midwifery. After Theodorus speaks so highly of Theaetetus, Socrates' first question is: "Which of the citizens is his father?" (144b7). Socrates begins his conversation with Theaetetus by asking about the sorts of things the boy is learning from Theodorus. And after Theaetetus has come out with "it appears that knowledge is nothing other than perception," Socrates suggests that Protagoras used to say the same thing, only differently, when he said that a human being is the measure of all things. "You've read that?" Socrates asks Theaetetus. "Yes, many times" (152a4–5). At least initially, then, Socrates' concern for the boy takes the form of an interest in his social and intellectual background. Or, to stay with the language of conception and birth, Socrates wants to know about Theaetetus' parentage.

The issue of parentage runs throughout the discussion of Theaetetus' "knowledge is perception" and Protagoras' "a human being is the measure of all things." In part, this follows from the account of psychic maieutics. As Socrates is concerned with Theaetetus' offspring, he is also concerned with Theaetetus as the offspring of various teachers and experiences. This also leads to the language of orphaned *logoi*, which appears when Socrates asks Theodorus to take responsibility for the Protagorean hypothesis—Protagoras himself being dead and unable to defend his offspring.[21] To be sure, there is quite a bit of play in these passages, but there also seems to be something very serious at stake in the way in which psychic maieutics is bound up with concerns about how the present bears the weight of the past.

In the first place, allowing that Socrates' art of psychic maieutics proceeds on the basis of some knowledge of or familiarity with its patients makes much more sense than thinking that Socrates knows in advance which patients will need to undergo a more or less painful labor, which "drugs and incantations" (149c9–d1) to use, and so on.[22] Perhaps more significantly, however, there is a connection between this aspect of psychic maieutics and the concerns Socrates brings with him to this conversation. The charges to which Socrates responds in the *Apology*— both the "first charges" and the charges of Meletus' indictment—can be summed up as follows: Socrates does injustice by challenging the authority of the traditions of the Athenians. That is, in addition to the issue of how Socrates appears to his fellow citizens (and so how he can account for himself), there is the further issue of the authority of tradition. That authority seems to be something that Socrates must challenge insofar as he takes his task to be that of a gadfly, yet something that he can only challenge at the risk of convicting himself of being a danger to the city.

Psychic maieutics appears familiar as an account of Socrates' practice of philosophy, yet the fact that the language of midwifery is unprecedented in the Platonic corpus, and even more so the details of Socrates' account, call into question that familiarity. Insofar as the image of the psychic *maieute* appears somewhat out of place with respect to the conversation in which it appears, two further questions arise: Why should Socrates offer an account of himself at all, and why this account in particular? With respect to the latter, the language of birth and parentage can be seen to raise a set of concerns about the authority of tradition, and this, too, follows from the proximity of the conversation recounted in the *Theaetetus* to Socrates' trial and death. With respect to the former, a tension emerges between the extent to which Socrates' personal concerns can be taken to motivate his actions in this conversation, and the extent to which the account of psychic maieutics appears to rule out allowing those concerns to come into play at all.

* * *

In order to develop this line of thought, I turn to a more detailed consideration of what Socrates actually says about his art of psychic maieutics. Here again I begin with the apparent familiarity of Socrates' account. In part, that familiarity is due to the ease with which we can follow the translation of the discourse of midwifery into the discourse of psychic maieutics. Everything that belongs to the art of midwifery, Socrates says, also belongs to his art of psychic maieutics (150b6–7). Midwives practice their art on women; Socrates practices his on men. Midwives are concerned with the body; Socrates, with the soul. Midwives help to bring forth and care for children; Socrates, the thoughts and opinions of others. Midwives are most skilled at knowing who would produce the best children together; Socrates knows which youths to send to which teachers. Midwives practice their art in the service of Artemis; Socrates practices his art in the service of the god. Socrates does not name the god responsible for psychic maieutics, but in light of the other connections between the *Theaetetus* and the *Apology,* where Socrates claims to act in the service of Apollo, it is plausible to think that here, too, Socrates is acting in the service of the god of Delphi, especially insofar as Apollo is Artemis' twin brother.[23] The translation, it would seem, is complete.

Yet two features of Socrates' art remain outstanding. One Socrates himself calls "the greatest part" of psychic maieutics, namely, his capacity to determine "whether the thought of the youth gives birth to an image and a falsehood, or something fruitful and true" (150b9–c3). This critical function has no parallel among midwives. The other outstanding feature of the account is not explicitly recognized as a difference by Socrates, but has become the source of much controversy. Socrates says that as midwives are no longer capable of bearing children, he is "barren of wisdom" (*agonos sophias;* 150c4). He also says that he "has no wisdom" (150c6), that the god "prevents [him] from generating" (*gennan;* 150c8), and that he is "not completely wise" (*ou panu ti sophos;* 150d1).[24] Later in the dialogue, Socrates repeats that he is incapable of generating the wise things of which he is offering a taste to Theaetetus (157d1). How are we to understand these claims in light of the fact that midwifery depends on prior experience of conceiving and bearing offspring?

It seems that three broad interpretive strategies are possible here. The first is to take Socrates' remarks to mean that he has never given birth to any psychic offspring of his own, and that he therefore lacks the experience necessary to practice his own art. Thus, the account of psychic maieutics is contradictory, or at least paradoxical. The second is to again take Socrates to mean that his soul has never given birth, but to infer that Socrates here implicitly assimilates himself to the status of the divine. That is, Socrates, like Artemis, needs no prior experience in order to bring to light and test the psychic offspring of others. And this would be one very good reason for keeping psychic maieutics secret, on this of all days. The third possibility is to distinguish between Socrates' claims to have never brought forth any wisdom of his own, and the claim to have never given birth to psychic offspring without any further qualification, and thus avoid the conclusion that either Socrates is superhuman, or he is offering an incoherent account of himself.[25]

I take the distinction between Socrates' claims about his lack of wisdom and any claim about psychic offspring without any further qualification to be crucial. It seems that psychic maieutics is not primarily concerned with wisdom at all, but with bringing thoughts or opinions to clarity such that they can be reflected upon. More significant in this respect is that it seems that the majority of psychic offspring turn out to be wind-eggs—and insofar as this is the case, there is no reason not to include Socrates among those who have come out with various opinions only to find that they are untenable. Note, however, that this only means that one is not forced to conclude that Socrates' account is contradictory or paradoxical on its own terms. Socrates' ambiguous relationship with the divine and the political consequences of that relationship remain. Even in the *Apology*, Socrates' invocation of his daimon can only show that he does believe in some gods—not that he also believes in the gods of the city, or that he has not introduced new divinities.

More significantly, what is perhaps the greatest difficulty in understanding Socrates' denial of having brought forth any wisdom of his own still remains: insofar as he claims to be a psychic *maieute*, Socrates must claim for himself a highly specialized knowledge.[26] Socrates determines who is pregnant. Socrates determines whether and how to make a given patient's labor more or less difficult. Socrates determines who will most fruitfully associate with whom. Socrates determines whether the offspring is viable or an empty wind-egg. It is not clear how Socrates can maintain the implied claim that his knowledge of psychic maieutics is an integral part of the process, and at the same time claim that he does not make any contribution of his own.[27] Whether Socrates has no wisdom, or only a little, or even that of a god, qua psychic *maieute* he assumes the status of the measure of all things concerning the soul and its offspring. At this point in the text, that assumption appears without justification. What is more, the remainder of the *Theaetetus* seems to deny the possibility of attaining measured knowledge of things at all.

* * *

I want to suggest that Socrates' account of psychic maieutics allows for an alternative approach to the issue of knowledge. For it is not simply the case that Socrates' account of psychic maieutics reassures and encourages Theaetetus. Socrates establishes a complex series of relationships, which I will articulate in terms of dialogical bondage, among himself, Theaetetus, and the attempt to say what knowledge itself is. The language of *sunousia*, "being together," runs throughout Socrates' account of psychic maieutics.[28] Midwives are said to be the cleverest matchmakers because they know what sort of woman must be with (*sunousia*; 149d7) what sort of man so as to produce the best children. Those of Socrates' associates to whom the god is gracious, as their association (*sunousia*; 150d4) advances, make wonderful progress and bring forth many beautiful things. And it is *sunousia* with Socrates that those who come back after having left too soon beg for (151a2). *Sunousia* spans a range of meanings including conversation, association, community, and even sexual intercourse.[29] Socrates thus reasserts an erotic dimension of dialogue that Theodorus had excluded at the outset.[30]

Perhaps more significantly, Socrates shifts the terms of the discussion from what seems to be a statement of method to a description of the relations binding those who seek knowledge together. Crucially, this is not the substitution of one method or account of method for another; it is the articulation of the conditions in virtue of which philosophical inquiry can be pursued in conversation. Socrates does not account for the critical capacity he claims for himself—he does not even describe the process of testing as such—but rather describes the experiences of various patients he has encountered. Of those who submit to Socrates' art of psychic maieutics, those who follow through with their treatment, and whom the god allows, make wonderful progress, finding within themselves and giving birth to many beautiful things (150d3–8). Although Socrates claims that his patients learn nothing from him, he nevertheless says that he and the god are the cause (*aition;* 150e1) of this finding and giving birth. Those who leave Socrates' care too soon miscarry, confuse falsehoods and images with the truth, and end up appearing ignorant both to others and to themselves (150e1–8). Of those who leave Socrates' care prematurely, some want to come back. Of those who seek to resume their treatment, some are allowed to return—though they seem to be few in number. The implication is clear: in order to see your pregnancy through, you must submit to Socrates' art of psychic maieutics. This is the first strand of the dialogical bond: Theaetetus is bound to Socrates.

The second strand is twofold: Theaetetus is bound to the task of seeing his psychic offspring brought to light, and he is bound to the task of saying what knowledge itself is. These two do not coincide insofar as the attempt to say what knowledge itself is, as a matter of inquiry, neither begins nor ends with Theaetetus. Socrates warns Theaetetus that these two bonds conflict with one another. If Theaetetus' offspring turns out to be false, he must be willing to sever the "maternal" bond for the sake of pursuing the investigation of knowledge (151c2–d3).[31]

The third strand is complex as well. Theaetetus is bound to himself, but in different respects. In the first place, he is made responsible for his share of the conversation. Further, insofar as Theaetetus must be willing to give up his offspring, he appears to be bound to himself more than to anything he might bring forth. The question is whether Theaetetus is to be bound more strongly to himself or to the inquiry. One implication of Socrates' cautionary tale about those who leave prematurely seems to be that there is a danger in caring more for oneself than for the inquiry in which one engages with Socrates. On the other hand, however, it seems that Theaetetus is to share in Socrates' professed care for the boy, and, more significantly, that Theaetetus is bound to himself in the sense of what he is to become. Theaetetus will emerge from this experience wise, ignorant but aware of that ignorance, or ignorant without self-knowledge. In light of Socrates' remarks at the end of the dialogue (210b11–d4), and Eucleides' report of Socrates' remarks about Theaetetus' promising future (142d1–3), it seems that Theaetetus' care for himself (even if this does not mean pursuing philosophy) takes precedence. But this indication comes only after the conversation. When Theaetetus first hears about psychic maieutics, it is not clear where his responsibilities lie.

The dialogical bond is articulated along three axes: Socrates, the inquiry, and Theaetetus.[32] Socrates, too, is thus bound. As we have seen, Socrates brings to bear on this conversation certain issues concerning his indictment and trial, namely his ability to account for himself, and his ability to account for the discrepancy between the various ways in which he might appear to himself and others. When those issues were first brought to light, it was not clear how to understand the apparent tension between the extent to which Socrates is bound to his personal concerns, and the extent to which the terms of the conversation entail that those concerns must be set aside for the sake of Theaetetus' pregnancy.

Insofar as these two sets of concerns cannot be separated, however, it seems that they must in some way be commensurate with one another. As indicated earlier, I take it that the significance of emphasizing the physical resemblance between Socrates and Theaetetus is that on this, of all days, Socrates needs to be concerned with how he appears to others.[33] And the possibility of accounting for how there can be conflicting appearances of what would seem to be one and the same is at the heart of the problem of knowledge as it is addressed in the *Theaetetus*. The destruction of the hypothesis that a human being is the measure of all things shows how it cannot be the case that whatever someone might say about Socrates is simply the truth of Socrates. It also shows that whatever Socrates might say about himself cannot be the end of the story either. Similarly, this issue can be seen to underlie Socrates' worry about the possibility of accounting for false opinion. For, if he cannot say how false opinion is possible, how could he say that Meletus, or the jury, is wrong to think that he corrupts the young and is guilty of impiety? Socrates' concern for Theaetetus and Theaetetus' offspring is at the same time (though in a different respect) a concern for his own situation. And insofar as Socrates' primary concern seems to be with how he appears to others, he cannot address that problem except by taking it up through an engagement with others. Socrates needs to look at Theaetetus in order to see what he himself looks like. Socrates is bound to himself through Theaetetus, and the conversation they share. This, however, is only to say that the connection between Socrates' desire for self-knowledge and Theaetetus' effort to say what knowledge itself is cannot be ruled out in advance. If the two concerns are incommensurable, this cannot be determined in advance, but only on the basis of what Socrates and Theaetetus actually say and do. Just as there is no way to rule out the possibility of Socrates learning about himself by serving as psychic *maieute*, there is no way to guarantee that the relationship will not become abusive.

This point seems to be acknowledged at least twice in the text. The first is the speech Socrates makes in the voice of, and on behalf of, Protagoras (165e8–168b5). Socrates here brings against himself two charges. Insofar as Socrates seems to have been arguing against a caricature of the Protagorean position, he has not done justice to the Protagorean hypothesis. "Whenever you examine something of mine through questioning, if, answering as I would answer, the one being questioned falls, then I am refuted—but if he answers otherwise, the one being questioned is himself refuted" (166a8–b1). And insofar as Socrates appears to have taken advantage of Theaetetus' youth and impressionable character in order to frighten the boy into agreeing with him, Socrates accuses himself of corrupting this youth (166a2–6).[34]

The other moment that is crucial in this respect, and indeed, decisive for the conversation as a whole, is when Socrates defers the discussion of Parmenides that should have followed the discussion of the Protagorean-Heraclitean position (183b7–184b1). Two aspects of this moment are particularly significant. On the one hand, it is an indication of how Theaetetus understands the relationship to which he is bound. Theaetetus challenges Theodorus and Socrates to follow through on their proposal to examine first "the flowing ones," that is, those who say that everything is in motion, and then "the partisans of the whole," that is, the Eleatics (181a4–b1).[35] He thus appears to place more weight on the bond between the interlocutors and their shared inquiry than on the bond among the interlocutors themselves. Socrates defers this responsibility, however, because he is afraid that he will not understand what Parmenides said, let alone meant, and because to take seriously the words of old father Parmenides would "take so long as to do away with the discussion of knowledge" (184a8–9). For the sake of Theaetetus and Theaetetus' pregnancy, then, Socrates puts aside the issues that have been rising up like a flood since they broached the question of knowledge—issues of motion and rest, the political issues surrounding Socrates' trial, and his relationship to the philosophical tradition he inherits.

Socrates, no less than Theaetetus, is bound to the task of saying what knowledge itself is. In the first place, if Socrates is to make good on his account of psychic maieutics, he must see Theaetetus' pregnancy and birth through to the end. And if Socrates is to learn anything about himself by looking at Theaetetus, he is bound to their shared inquiry. Perhaps more significantly, despite Socrates' denials of making any contribution, his part in this drama is essential—and not only insofar as Theaetetus probably would not have thought of himself as pregnant were it not for Socrates' intervention. Recall the ways in which Theaetetus is bound to Socrates. It is Socrates' task to determine when Theaetetus' offspring has been fully brought to light; it is Socrates' task to determine whether that offspring is viable. And this is not merely an instrumental role. No matter how impartial the maieutic measure might claim to be, insofar as there can be no simply subjective nor simply objective measure, that act of determination at the heart of psychic maieutics makes an essential contribution to the process as a whole. It is Socrates' translation of Theaetetus' "knowledge is perception" into Protagoras' "a human being is the measure of all things" that seems to stand out most clearly as the sort of contribution Socrates' account would deny. It seems that the translation is justified, first insofar as it elicits Theaetetus' familiarity with Protagoras' writings, and then insofar as Socrates can show how the two are "twins"—but this is only after the fact. In showing how Protagoras said "the same things, but in a different way" (152a1–2), Socrates does bring something new to the conversation. This is just one example, but Theaetetus seems right to say, as he does at the end of the conversation, that Socrates has brought forth more from Theaetetus than was in him (210b6–7).

Socrates is bound to Theaetetus. In one sense, this is obvious. Qua psychic *maieute,* Socrates is bound to care for his patient, and when Socrates puts off the discussion of Parmenides and focuses the conversation on Theaetetus, he appears to acknowledge his responsibility to the boy. But how, then, are we to understand Socrates' denials that he is responsible for the consequences of his associations with others? Again, the denial of responsibility follows from the denial of being a teacher. Socrates claims to have no wisdom or expertise to teach, nor does he charge or receive fees commensurate with such knowledge. Insofar as Socrates does not enter into any contractual arrangement, there can be no "implied warranty of service."[36] If this is the case, however, then we again face the problem of Socrates' assumption of the status of measure. Insofar as Theaetetus is bound to Socrates, and Socrates is the measure, that is, has the power to determine pregnancy, birth, and viability, it remains a question how Socrates will act on that power. The account of psychic maieutics (indeed, the conversation as a whole) may be an elaborate ruse allowing Socrates to use Theaetetus as an occasion to learn about himself. Focusing on this aspect of psychic maieutics, Joan Harrison suggests that "Socrates' own *logos* in the *Theaetetus* becomes a tyrant; in his *ergon* so does Socrates."[37]

Now, such a conclusion seems too hastily drawn. As indicated above, Socrates' concern for Theaetetus and his interest in pursuing his own self-knowledge need not be at odds with one another. And insofar as Socrates gives more consideration to Theaetetus at crucial moments in the conversation, it seems that in this case he does make good on the promise of psychic maieutics. The more significant point, I take it, is that there is no way to guarantee this. Socrates' practice of psychic maieutics can only be defended on the basis of what he actually does in this conversation with Theaetetus. Socrates' twin denials of being a teacher and being responsible entail an ambiguity inherent in his character. On his own terms, Socrates cannot say in advance how dialogical bondage will play out in a given situation, that is, whether he will appear to be a virtuous midwife, or guilty of malpractice.[38] If Socrates insists that he is not responsible for his patients, he opens himself to the charge of being a tyrant. If Socrates accepts responsibility, then he opens himself to the charge of reneging on his obligations. This follows from the account of psychic maieutics, as well as from the indication Socrates gives at the end of the dialogue of what he might be able to provide his patients. If Theaetetus conceives again, he will conceive better things in virtue of what he has experienced with Socrates, and if he does not, at least he will be less harsh with his associates, and not suppose that he knows that which he does not. This much, and nothing more, Socrates' art of psychic maieutics can do (210b11–c5). Socrates has no exchange-value, nor can he force his interlocutors to take him seriously. That is, it seems that there is no way to say in advance whether Socrates will appear to be a philosopher, a sophist, or a tyrant—or simply foolish.

* * *

In conclusion, I would like to bring the notion of dialogical bondage more explicitly to bear on the issue of knowledge. In particular, it seems that the notion of dialogical bondage reveals another sense in which Socrates' account of psychic maieutics makes possible the conversation recounted in the *Theaetetus*. That account not only prevents the conversation from miscarrying, but also establishes the conditions for the possibility of their having a dialogue at all insofar as it binds together Socrates, Theaetetus, and their shared attempt to say what knowledge itself is. Throughout the dialogue, as a sort of undercurrent, runs an emphasis on the shared agreement or commitment necessary for the conversation to take place, and to continue. From the very beginning, when Socrates urges Theaetetus to not "back out of what has been agreed upon" (145c2–3; trans. Benardete), to the end of the dialogue, when Socrates asks, "Are *we* still pregnant and in labor" (210b4; my emphasis), the standard to which Socrates appeals is what they are able to agree upon together. This is perhaps most striking in their engagement with the Protagorean hypothesis. Socrates speaks on behalf of Protagoras and his orphaned *logos*—"for the sake of justice" (164e6–7)—because Protagoras is dead, and cannot defend himself and his offspring. It is worth quoting one of the most striking passages in the dialogue at length. Speaking of Protagoras, Socrates says to Theodorus:

> But, my friend, it is not clear if we are running past what is right. For it is likely that he, being older, is wiser than us. And if, for example, he were to pop up right here, just up to the neck, after charging me with saying a lot of nonsense and you with agreeing with me, he would, as is likely, slip down and run off. But I suppose it is necessary for us to make do ourselves, such as we are, and always say what we believe. (171c10–d5)

That is, if there were some other standard to which they could appeal, Socrates, Theaetetus, and Theodorus might be better able to say what knowledge is—but there is no other standard. They show how it cannot be simply the case that a human being is the measure of all things. On the Protagorean hypothesis, the self-identity of beings is dissolved in the flow of coming-to-be and passing-away. There is no thing that subsists about which we could speak, nor anything we could say about it. The flowing ones have, "according to their own hypothesis, no words" (183b3–4). When we say that a human being is the measure of all things, we render ourselves unable to say anything at all.

Socrates and Theaetetus also show how it cannot be simply the case that things have their own measures, to which knowledge must correspond. To adequately address this issue would take so long as to do away with the present discussion, but I take this to be the hypothesis underlying the discussions of right opinion and right opinion with *logos*. In both discussions, things are taken as being what they are independent of their being known, and knowledge as right opinion (as opposed to false opinion) would correspond to the correct belief or judgment about those things.[39] Now, the fact that I opine or judge that such and such is the case cannot determine the truth or falsity of my opinion.[40] Some other standard must be brought to bear on my opinions. Knowledge is supposed throughout these sections of the *Theaetetus* to be that which would bridge the gap between this indeterminacy of opinion and the world. But insofar as knowledge itself is being treated in terms of opinion, that gap can never be closed. And this, I take it, is why Socrates and Theaetetus are unable within this framework to say how false opinion is impossible. For if there is no way to say how my opinions relate to that which they are opinions of, that is, no way to test them, then there is no way to know that I am right. This has the striking consequence that I also cannot ever be wrong—but this is just to say that knowledge is impossible.

Thus Socrates, Theodorus, and Theaetetus must come to an agreement among themselves, such as they are. Dialogical bondage seems to allow for an alternative to the two failed hypotheses explicitly treated in the *Theaetetus*. It also allows for a dialectical or dialogical understanding of measure. Recall Socrates' interest in Theaetetus' heritage. It is on the basis of what he learns about Theaetetus through their conversation that Socrates can serve as the measure of Theaetetus' labor. The measure, then, is neither simply in Theaetetus, nor simply in Socrates—both are measured against their shared attempt to say what knowledge is, and it is the determinacy that emerges from the dynamic of dialogical bondage that allows Theaetetus' offspring to be tested.[41] This does not, however, do away with the contingency or vulnerability of that agreement. In fact, it has the crucial consequence that Socrates will not be able to define himself or his practices in such a way as to eliminate the possibility of conflicting appearances.

I have said that with the account of psychic maieutics Plato can be seen to engage with a caricature of Socrates. That caricature allows for a critical engagement with Socrates' practice of philosophy (and philosophical practice more generally). Plato thus sets in motion two distinct—though not unrelated—series of questions. On the one hand, insofar as Socrates, psychic *maieute*, must assume the status of the measure of the soul and its conceptions, that caricature lays the ground for the basic question underlying the ensuing conversation: How can we attain and account for measured knowledge? It seems that the maieutic relationship, understood in terms of what I have called dialogical bondage, provides an alternative to the assumption that the measure must lie either in the knower or in the known. But insofar as it follows from this that knowledge is a matter of a reciprocal relationship of measuring and being measured among those who participate in dialogue, this means knowledge is not something to be attained once and for all.

On the other hand, insofar as Socrates is so easily recognized in that caricature, it begins to make clear how easily the Athenians could recognize Socrates in the charges brought against him. Indeed, insofar as one of the consequences of the *Theaetetus* is that Socrates cannot define himself or his practices in advance so as to distinguish himself from that public image, it becomes unclear how Socrates could account for himself so as to refute the charges brought against him. The distinction between Socrates as one who cares for the youth of the city and Socrates as one who corrupts the youth of the city will not be a matter of method, but a matter of how particular relationships play out and are understood in light of their consequences.[42]

Notes

1. See *Theaetetus*, 147c7–d2, 148b6–c1, and 148e1–6. Unless otherwise noted, all translations are my own, following Plato, *Platonis Opera*, vol. 1, ed. E. A. Duke, W. F. Hicken, et al. (Oxford: Oxford University Press, 1995).

2. I use the language of psychic maieutics and its derivatives (for example, "psychic *maieute*" in reference to Socrates) throughout. "*Maieute*" is not one of Plato's words, but is the most straightforward English name for a practitioner of the *maieutike techne*. While I acknowledge the risk of obscurity, this is not a stubborn insistence on an idiosyncratic vocabulary. Insofar as one of the main themes of this essay is that it is the differences between Socrates' description of his mother's art of midwifery and his own art of psychic maieutics that implicitly call into question the image of Socrates as a midwife of the soul, it is necessary to avoid conflating those differences by using the language of midwifery equivocally. Moreover, given the problematic status of Socrates' claims to and simultaneous denials of knowledge, the somewhat suspect connotations that come with attaching the word "psychic" to any activity in contemporary (American) English idiom works in our favor as critical readers of Plato's texts.

3. I am by no means the first to take a more critical stance toward the issue of psychic maieutics. See, for example, Seth Benardete, *The Being of the Beautiful* (Chicago: University of Chicago Press, 1984); and "Plato's *Theaetetus*: On the Way of the Logos," *Review of Metaphysics* 51, no. 1 (1997): 25–53; and Joan C. Harrison, "Plato's Prologue: *Theaetetus* 142a–143c," *Tulane Studies in Philosophy* 27 (1978): 103–23. For a different response to the question of what Plato is doing in engaging this caricature of Socrates, see David Sedley, *The Midwife of Platonism: Text and Subtext in Plato's Theaetetus* (Oxford: Clarendon, 2004). As his title indicates, Sedley reads the *Theaetetus* as Plato's account of how Socrates made Plato's own conceptions possible, and helped bring them to light.

4. *Theaetetus* 150d6–8, 157c7–d2, 161a7–b6.

5. *Apology* 20d8, 21b1–e1. I take the fact that I could as well appeal to the so-called early or Socratic dialogues, or indeed almost any member of the Platonic corpus, to strengthen the sense of familiarity about the picture of Socrates, psychic *maieute*.

6. Translations of the *Apology* are from Plato and Aristophanes, *Four Texts on Socrates*, trans. Thomas G. West and Grace Starry West (Ithaca: Cornell University Press, 1984). For an extended analysis of this passage and Socrates' relationship with the paid professional teachers of his time, see Gary Alan Scott, *Plato's Socrates as Educator* (Albany: State University of New York Press, 2000), 13–49.

7. The relationship between psychic maieutics and recollection has been debated at least since the oldest extant commentary on the *Theaetetus,* an anonymous commentary most likely dating from the second half of the first century B.C.E. See H. Diels and W. Schubart, eds., *Anonymer Kommentar zu Platons Theaetet* (Berlin: Weidmannsche Buchhandlung, 1905). On the issue of dating the commentary, see David Sedley, "Three Platonist Interpretations of the *Theaetetus,*" in *Form and Argument in Late Plato,* ed. C. Gill and M. M. McCabe (Oxford: Oxford University Press, 1996), 79–103. Two issues appear to be at the heart of the controversy. One concerns the relationship between psychic maieutics as what appears to be a method and recollection as what appears to be a theory or doctrine. The other concerns the relationship between the possibility of false offspring in the *Theaetetus* and the way in which the notion of recollection implies that knowledge is in the soul and available for recollection. See, for example, Myles F. Burnyeat, "Socratic Midwifery, Platonic Inspiration," *Bulletin of the Institute of Classical Studies* 24 (1977): 7–16; reprinted in *Essays on the Philosophy of Socrates,* ed. Hugh H. Benson (Oxford: Oxford University Press, 1992), 53–65; F. M. Cornford, *Plato's Theory of Knowledge* (London: Routledge and Kegan Paul, 1935); and Plato, *Theaetetus,* trans. John McDowell (Oxford: Oxford University Press, 1973). For the purposes of the present discussion, there is no need to claim or seek any stronger connection between maieutics and recollection—it is enough that the echoes of or allusions to the notion of recollection add to the apparent familiarity of the picture of Socrates, psychic *maieute.* What I will have to show, however, is that that picture is presented as it is for the sake of appearing familiar.

8. See, for example, Burnyeat, "Socratic Midwifery," 55; Scott R. Hemmenway, "Philosophical Apology in the *Theaetetus,*" *Interpretation* 17, no. 3 (1990): 329; Ronald Polansky, *Philosophy and Knowledge: A Commentary on Plato's Theaetetus* (Lewisburg: Bucknell University Press, 1992), 60; McDowell, trans., *Theaetetus,* 116–17; Cornford, *Plato's Theory of Knowledge,* 27ff. See also *Sophist* 230b4–231b8. For a recent reappraisal of the elenchus and the question of Socratic method, see Gary Alan Scott, ed., *Does Socrates Have a Method? Rethinking the Elenchus in Plato's Dialogues and Beyond* (University Park: Pennsylvania State University Press, 2002).

9. R. G. Wengert, "The Paradox of the Midwife," *History of Philosophy Quarterly* 5, no. 1 (1988): 3.

10. Burnyeat, "Socratic Midwifery," 54. Burnyeat offers a list of exemplary studies at p. 62n4. Drawing on Kenneth Dover's study of Aristophanes (K. J. Dover, *Aristophanes' Clouds* [Oxford: Oxford University Press, 1968]), Burnyeat questions the viability of inferring from an otherwise unprecedented one-word reference in the *Clouds* to a historically accurate and common image associated with the figure of Socrates. See also Dover's *Aristophanic Comedy* (Berkeley and Los Angeles: University of California Press, 1972), 119: "If, however, this concept [sc. midwifery] was used by the real Socrates, it is surprising that it should not appear in Plato until a fairly late work, and certain other images with which the Aristophanic Socrates mystifies Strepsiades, 'bring machines to bear on

you' (479 f.), and 'snapping up' a problem (489 f.), are not known in the fourth century Socratic tradition." The problem is that Burnyeat appeals to the power of the image in order to argue against the association of psychic maieutics with the historical Socrates. The concern with the distinction between Plato and the historical Socrates seems to blind Burnyeat to the distinction between Plato and his characters. While Burnyeat limits the image of psychic maieutics to the *Theaetetus,* he goes on to claim that that image "signals a return to the aporetic style of those early dialogues and to the Socratic method which is the substance of that style" (55)—although he sees that "return" as being qualified by the tentative or "more modest" (57) epistemological stance of the *Theaetetus* vis-à-vis the *Meno.* It is the all-too-easy acceptance of psychic maieutics as a generalized method that I find most problematic. The singularity—emphasized by Burnyeat himself—of psychic maieutics seems to me to indicate that we cannot even take psychic maieutics as obviously Platonic, let alone as a Platonic appropriation of Socrates, without qualification.

11. See Rachel Rue, "The Philosopher in Flight: The Digression (172c–177c) in Plato's *Theaetetus,*" *Oxford Studies in Ancient Philosophy* 11 (1993): 71–100. Rue's insightful article shows how the "philosopher" of the digression is also a caricature of Socrates, or of the image of the philosopher more generally. More significantly, she articulates how Plato uses that caricature to criticize "a general tendency in philosophy—especially Platonic philosophy—to look to essences and eternal truth, to flee distraction by the senses and the accidental features of particular things and events" (91).

12. See A. A. Long, "Plato's Apologies and Socrates in the *Theaetetus,*" in *Method in Ancient Philosophy,* ed. Jyl Gentzler (Oxford: Clarendon, 1998), 113–36. While I agree with Long that there is a sense in which Plato "never stops rewriting the *Apology*" (119), I do not agree that the transition from the *Theaetetus* to the *Sophist* marks a turning point for Plato away from a more "Socratic" to a more "scientific" mode of philosophizing (let alone to what Long calls an "unambiguously elitist" philosophy, "separate from practical life" [132]). Plato's critical engagement with the practice of philosophy appears consistent throughout his writings, whether the figure of Socrates plays a primary role therein or not.

13. One might also compare the remark in Plato's *Second Letter* about the dialogues being the work of "a Socrates made young and beautiful" (314c).

14. *Theaetetus* 210d2–5; *Sophist* 216a1–2; *Statesman* 257a1–2.

15. This political dimension of the *Theaetetus,* along with the *Sophist* and *Statesman,* though still largely underexplored, has been taken up in terms of a "philosophical trial" preceding Socrates' trial before the jury court. See, for example, Mitchell H. Miller, *The Philosopher in Plato's Statesman* (The Hague: Martinus Nijhoff, 1980); Stanley Rosen, *Plato's Sophist: The Drama of Original and Image* (New Haven: Yale University Press, 1983); and *Plato's Statesman: The Web of Politics* (New Haven: Yale University Press, 1995); and Benardete, *Being of the Beautiful.*

16. Wengert, "Paradox of the Midwife," offers the following statistics: The word "midwife" (*he maia*) and cognates appear twenty-six times in the Platonic

corpus. Of those, only two do not occur in the *Theaetetus,* and neither of those (*Cratylus* 421a5 and *Statesman* 268b1) is concerned with Socrates' practice of philosophy. In addition, all but six of the twenty-four occurrences of the language of midwifery in the *Theaetetus* are found in the three Stephanus pages comprising Socrates' initial account of his art of psychic maieutics. See also Leonard Brandwood, *A Word Index to Plato* (Leeds: W. S. Maney, 1976).

17. Hemmenway, "Philosophical Apology," 326.

18. *Apology* 18b7–c1.

19. In light of Socrates' remarks in the *Apology* (for example, 31d–32a, 37b) about the impossibility of teaching a multitude in a short time, and of a multitude as such becoming philosophic—though not only in that light—there is something a little odd about thinking that a philosophical account of knowledge would really be much help in the courtroom.

20. *Theaetetus* 144d8–e1.

21. *Theaetetus* 164e2–165a3. Theodorus (who at 145b10–c2 is said not to be the sort of man to joke around) refuses to take responsibility for Protagoras' orphaned *logos,* saying that Callias the son of Hipponicus has already been appointed guardian of Protagoras' children. See also *Phaedrus* 275e4–6.

22. The issue of the knowledge implied or assumed by Socrates' account of psychic maieutics will be dealt with in more detail below.

23. *Apology* 20e6–21a9. The hesitation with which Socrates says that he undertook his examination of the oracle's pronouncement seems to be echoed by the language of force and necessity in Socrates' account of psychic maieutics, for example, 150c7–8: "The god compels me to practice maieutics" (*maieuesthai me ho theos anankazei*).

24. This phrase in particular, *ou panu ti sophos,* has been at the center of the interpretive debate surrounding Socrates' denials of being wise and the knowledge his art of psychic maieutics must presuppose. For a summary of the debate about how to translate the phrase, see Sedley, "Three Platonist Interpretations," esp. 98–101. The basic question is whether to take this as meaning that Socrates is "not at all" wise, or (as Sedley, following the anonymous commentary, renders it) "not completely" wise. The qualified sense of the latter—which Sedley argues is more grammatically accurate—allows both for the human wisdom Socrates claims for himself in the *Apology* and for an interpretation of the *Theaetetus* that does not have to conclude that Socrates' account of psychic maieutics is simply contradictory or paradoxical.

25. For example, Wengert, "Paradox of the Midwife," argues that Socrates' account leads to an unresolvable paradox. Benardete, "On the Way of the Logos," argues that Socrates does identify himself with the god in this passage, and that "there is nothing to" Socrates' art of psychic maieutics (28). The anonymous commentator is perhaps the most sympathetic reader of psychic maieutics, although insofar as he takes the *Theaetetus* as a whole to be a maieutic argument for the model of knowledge he finds in the *Meno,* he limits his ability to reckon with the *Theaetetus* on its own terms.

26. For more on the knowledge evidently presupposed in Socrates' account, see Sedley, *Midwife of Platonism,* 33–35. No less problematically, Socrates

identifies wisdom and knowledge at the very beginning of the conversation (145d11–e7). Also, one should bear in mind that Socrates does say that psychic maieutics is an art (*technē*). Just within his initial account of psychic maieutics, Socrates explicitly refers to it as such at 149a4, 149a7, 150b6, 150c1, and 151b1. This claim, too, should make one wonder about the apparent familiarity of psychic maieutics as an account of Socratic philosophizing. Socrates is most often distinguished from the sophists on the basis of his denial that he has any technical knowledge that can be taught to another, and the fact that he neither asks for nor receives any payment for his conversations. See *Apology* 19d8ff., 33a5–b8. See also Scott, *Plato's Socrates as Educator*, 13–49; David Roochnik, *Of Art and Wisdom: Plato's Understanding of Techne* (University Park: Pennsylvania State University Press, 1996), esp. chap. 1.

27. See note 3 above.

28. See Kenneth M. Sayre, *Plato's Literary Garden* (Notre Dame: University of Notre Dame Press, 1995), esp. the appendix, "How to Read a Platonic Dialogue: *Sunousia* in Plato's *Theaetetus*," 197–232.

29. *An Intermediate Greek-English Lexicon: Founded upon the Seventh Edition of Liddell and Scott's Greek-English Lexicon* (Oxford: Oxford University Press, 1889; reprinted in 1999), 779.

30. *Theaetetus* 143e6–144a1. When he first begins to tell Socrates about Theaetetus, Theodorus is grateful for Theaetetus' ugliness, lest people think that Theodorus speaks so highly of the boy out of love, and not from the apparently disinterested standpoint of a teacher.

31. This warning is repeated at 160e6–161a4 (although there it is Theodorus who accepts this condition on behalf of Theaetetus).

32. While I do not thematize Theodorus' role in the conversation, I do not mean to suggest that it is unimportant. See Rue, "Philosopher in Flight," esp. 92–100, for an account of how Socrates' interaction with Theodorus enacts the movement of drawing someone into philosophical activity.

33. For a different view on this likeness, see Ruby Blondell, "Reproducing Socrates: Dramatic Form and Pedagogy in the *Theaetetus*," *Proceedings of the Boston Area Colloquium in Ancient Philosophy* 14 (1998): 213–38.

34. At the beginning of their conversation, Theodorus praises Theaetetus for being "like a flow of olive oil" (144b4). This image captures the ease with which Theaetetus moves through his studies. At the same time, however, like any liquid, a flow of olive oil will take the shape of its container. This seems to be part of what is at stake in Socrates' interest in Theaetetus' background: the extent to which Theaetetus conforms to his environment, and the extent to which he might be able to maintain his own measure.

35. This is Fowler's translation (Plato, *Plato VII: Theaetetus and Sophist*, trans. H. N. Fowler, Loeb Classical Library [Cambridge: Harvard University Press, 1921]). There appears to be a play on words in the Greek *hoi tou holou stasiotai* between the sense of "those who stop the whole" and "those who stand for the whole." Fowler's "partisans of the whole" picks up nicely on the sense of *stasis* as civil war or factional dispute.

36. Scott, *Plato's Socrates as Educator*, 21.

37. Harrison, "Plato's Prologue," 122.

38. This not only plays into the engagement with the figure of Protagoras, but also is intimately related to their continual worry about knowledge with respect to the future. Perhaps more than anything else, it is the inability to secure judgment about what might happen that undermines the attempts to say what knowledge itself is. See *Theaetetus* 166d5–168c2, 171d9–172c1, 178a ff., and 186a10–b4.

39. This is perhaps most clearly seen in the image of the soul as an aviary, where knowing is taken up in terms of grasping what is known (197b–200d).

40. See Benardete, *Being of the Beautiful,* 1.149.

41. See Francisco J. Gonzalez, "Giving Thought to the Good Together: Virtue in Plato's *Protagoras,*" in *Retracing the Platonic Text,* ed. John Russon and John Sallis (Evanston: Northwestern University Press, 2000), 113–54, esp. 124–27. Gonzalez shows that *sunousia* establishes a dialogical standard for the discussion of virtue in the *Protagoras* as well. See also *Gorgias* 486d4–487e8 and *Phaedrus* 265d5–10.

42. An earlier version of this paper was presented in the Participants' Conference at the Collegium Phaenomenologicum, Città di Castello, Italy, July 13, 2002. My thanks to those who participated in that discussion for their comments and criticisms. I would also like to thank Eric Sanday for our ongoing conversations, which have allowed me to say more than was in me, and Gary Scott for his efforts in seeing that this volume did not turn out to be a wind-egg.

7

Plato's Different Device: Reconciling the One and the Many in the *Philebus*

Martha Kendal Woodruff

> Socrates, as you said yourself, it is difficult to follow in these matters. But if they are repeated again and again, perhaps both questioner and respondent may end up in a satisfactory state of agreement.
>
> *Philebus* 24e

So says Protarchus toward the beginning of Plato's *Philebus*. His statement may appear to be merely a passing comment, but actually, when understood broadly, it sheds light on the whole dialogue. Different kinds of repetition prove to be crucial to the reconciliation of apparent opposites, which in turn proves to be one of the main philosophical achievements of the dialogue. The method of repetition and revision shows the crucial role played by λόγος: language, in its power continually to restate and reclassify, helps to allow a reconciliation between Socrates and the other speakers, and between the opposing categories—such as constancy and change, intelligence and pleasure, determinacy and indeterminacy—with which the interlocutors wrestle. One of the most central of these polarities, "the one and the many," manifests itself in a special way through such revisions. As Socrates says at one point, the convergence of the one and the many seems to be a permanent feature of our statements (15d5–7). But only a certain sort of language, one that repeats, revises, and classifies in the right way, can find a balance between the one and the many. To the extent that the *Philebus* achieves such a balance, it indicates Plato's vision of a complex unity, a oneness that embraces a measured plurality.

The *Philebus* not only introduces new dialectical methods but *enacts* them. The dialogue incorporates both of the new methods that demand repetition and promise reconciliation: the "heavenly gift" of division and classification and the "different device" of the fourfold ontology. When I speak of method, I do not mean it in the sense of a modern, scientific method, but in the original Greek sense of "being on or along a road or pathway."[1] By retracing the pathway along which this dialogue travels, we can find the hidden unity among its diverse topics. This dialogue both analyzes and practices the two new methods through a special brand of language. As Gadamer puts it:

> The special importance of the *Philebus* lies precisely in the fact that the dialectic discussed in it becomes aware of itself in the actual conduct of the Socratic dialogue. The theory of dialectic must be grasped on the basis of the concrete situation of coming to a shared understanding.[2]

The *Philebus* contains a significant reflexivity; it *does* what it *says*.[3]

Platonic reflexivity is by no means exclusive to the *Philebus*, of course. Another example occurs in the *Parmenides*, which I will use, in this essay, as a critical foil to the *Philebus*. In the *Parmenides*, the self-reflective dialectic is problematic in that it leads only to a dichotomy between the one and the many, an unworkable "either/or" between monism and pluralism. Without excluding other readings, I shall, for the purposes of this essay, view the *Parmenides* as a *via negative*, a demonstration of the paradoxes resulting from the *absence* of the right kind of repetition which would lead to reconciliation. But while I think Plato wants his audience to take such problems seriously, the negative self-reflections of the *Parmenides* do not necessarily represent a conclusion, but rather a provocative exploration.[4] The *Philebus*, I will argue, reopens the exploration, "repeats" the *Parmenides*—with a difference.

In both dialogues, self-reflection makes philosophical language itself the object of analysis. But the role of language differs in the two dialogues and even changes within each one. In the *Parmenides*, in which the elder master challenges a young and naive Socrates, discursive classification leads to apparently insurmountable contradictions and polarities. On the one hand, we find the eternal, the constant and the knowable, all in the realm of being; on the other hand lie the temporal, the particular, the changeable, all in the realm of becoming. In this case the discursive powers of repetition serve only to distance the two sides further from each other, the ideal one from the actual many, or else to erase the distinction altogether. This situation culminates in the extraordinarily dense, difficult paradoxes enumerated at length by Parmenides.

By contrast, in the *Philebus* Plato introduces a more flexible method to navigate the middle way between extremes. The dialogue begins with some assumed polarities of its own, but through the concrete use of the classifying scheme and the fourfold ontology, they become harmonized with each other by the end. While one cannot simply collapse the distinctions between intelligence and pleasure, the determinant and the indeterminate, the one and the many, the dialogue shows us that we cannot leave them in stark opposition either. The dialogue still leaves basic ontological and linguistic problems unresolved, ending as it does on a note of indeterminacy. But it goes a long way toward reconciling the one and the many, being and becoming.

As in the *Parmenides* and other Platonic dialogues, then, style in the *Philebus* contributes to substance. Theoretical problems cannot be separated from their concrete expression: the eventual reconciliation of abstract polarities is inseparably bound up with the actual practice, by the interlocutors, of repeating, differentiating, and classifying.[5] Only through the right sort of repetition, which is not redundant, can the speakers and the subjects agree.

The resulting language of reconciliation depends upon the ontology of the mixture, which provides the basis for overcoming stark dualisms. As the best life in the end proves to be a well-harmonized mixture, so too the success of the *Philebus* itself belongs to the mixed category, in both language and thought. In the concluding discussion, Socrates speaks of discovering "a road [ὁδὸν] that leads to the Good" (61a), which resides in proportionate mixtures. If the Good dwells in such a mixture, and the dialogue is itself a kind of mixture, then the dialogue demonstrates the path toward the Good while analyzing it. As Seth Benardete claims: "The peculiarity of the *Philebus* thus seems to lie in the reconstruction of the Good within itself. It works up the Good while exhibiting the Good."[6] As I hope to show, Plato's dialectical-methodical concerns prove to be connected to the search for the Good as the mixed life. The dialogue "mixes" dialectics and ethics through the practice of repeating, revising, and reconciling; in brief, the dialogue practices what it preaches.

To anyone familiar with the dialogue or its commentators, such praise may come as a surprise. This work in particular has long received criticism for its difficult themes and messy form: George Grote set the tone in 1865 by writing, "It is neither clear, nor orderly, nor comparable in animation to the expository books of the *Republic*. . . . Every commentator of Plato, from Galen onwards, has complained of the obscurity of the *Philebus*."[7] Robert Bury concurred in 1897 by characterizing the *Philebus* as "harsh and rugged in style" and likening it to "a gnarled and knotted old oak tree."[8] Crombie calls it "obscure" and "a very precarious dialogue to interpret,"[9] while Gadamer notes the "famous problem" of its difficult transitions.[10] Guthrie comments that it is "on the whole lacking in dramatic interest" and calls it "a 'weary' dialogue" that tries readers with its "untidiness" and unclarity.[11] Davidson goes so far as to call it "one of Plato's oddest dialogues."[12]

However, the *Philebus* has always had its share of admirers. In the fifteenth century, Marsilio Ficino praised the dialogue as nothing less than "Plato's book on man's highest good," and had it read to his patron Cosimo de Medici on his deathbed.[13] In the nineteenth century, Schleiermacher wrote: "From the earliest times to the present, the *Philebus* has been regarded as one of the most important of the works of Plato, and also, as one of the most difficult."[14] More recently, Cynthia Hampton has defended Plato against charges of obscurity here by asserting "there is method in his (apparent) madness";[15] she also finds in this work a model of non-dichotomous thinking of great interest to current feminist thinkers.[16] Rosemary Desjardins goes so far as to call the *Philebus* "one of the most exhilarating . . . and important of Plato's dialogues."[17]

I acknowledge both sides of the debate: the *Philebus* is indeed often frustratingly dense and obscure. It lacks the wit and the dramatic force of many other dialogues. As readers we often feel lost in the twists and turns of the argument. But the *Philebus* has an often overlooked discursive strength, which lies in its determinant way of addressing plurality. This feature enacts the new methods and demonstrates the benefits of dialectical revision and stylistic repetition (as distinguished from mere repetitiveness), which together make possible the reconciliation between the one and the many, the limit and the unlimited. While many problems remain, the dialogue is not as hopelessly disjointed as it may at first appear. By paying attention to the dialogue form itself, the movements back and forth of the conversation, we allow the form and the content to illuminate each other. A close reading of the opening sections foreshadows the challenges and methods of the whole, highlights the contrasts with the *Parmenides*, and suggests connections with Aristotle.

From the start, the language of the *Parmenides* lacks a certain determinacy: no one questions or further defines Zeno's opening hypothesis that if things are many, they must be both like and unlike (127e). Socrates, whom Plato here presents as young and naive, quickly sees that by showing the impossibility of plurality Zeno allies himself with his teacher Parmenides, but he fails to ask in what sense Zeno means the terms "things," "many," "like," and "unlike." Socrates does, however, immediately distinguish between the plurality of things and the oneness of forms: "What he is proving is that *something* is many and one, not that unity is many or that plurality is one" (129d).[18] But it is this very distinction that gets him into trouble, because he cannot adequately revise it. An absence of careful revisions leads to a polarization of the positions.

When questioned by Parmenides, Socrates asserts he is certain that there is a form of beauty and goodness; "puzzled" about whether there is a form of man, fire, or water, and then about "hair or mud or dirt or any other trivial and undignified objects" (130c), he says at first a form for them would be absurd, but then wonders whether "what is true in one case may not be true in all" (130d). Socrates continues: "Then, when I have reached that point, I am driven to retreat, for fear of tumbling into a bottomless pit of nonsense" (130d). Parmenides replies that this is "because you are still young . . . and philosophy has not yet taken hold of you so firmly as I believe it will someday" (130e). Socrates obviously cannot reconcile "just the things we see" with the forms we know, the many with the one, the particular with the universal. His uncertainty shows in his language itself: he does not know what to say and fears the possibility of saying nothing at all.

Socrates does not challenge Parmenides on the "part theory" of how the many things share in the one form (131a–b), on the appropriateness of the analogy between the day and the sail (131b–c), or on the "third man" argument. If one looks at largeness itself and the many large things "in the same way in your mind's eye, will not yet another unity make its appearance—a largeness by virtue of which they all appear large?" (132a). Both the problem of divisibility and that of the infinite regress result from thinking of the forms as like sensible objects; yet thinking of them in the opposite way, as completely abstract and removed, proves even worse. Socrates accepts, again without question, that "no such real being exists in our world," since "how could it then be just by itself?" (133c). As illustrated by the example about "mastership itself" and "slavery itself," in contrast to any particular master or slave (133e), the forms of that "other world" of the gods have no significance for ours, and we cannot know the gods' world nor they ours.

As a result of these difficulties, "the hearer is perplexed," left in a state of utter ἀπορία (135a). Socrates notes the strangeness of an argument denying the gods knowledge, yet makes no move to criticize it (134e). Parmenides does not insist on the truth of this argument, but stresses that only "a man of wide experience and natural ability" willing to work through "a long and remote train of argument" could realize the intelligibility and relevance of the forms, and only a "still more remarkable" person could lead someone else to this view (135b). Yet without the stable being of the forms, there is no language or thought: as Parmenides explains, someone who has "nothing on which to fix his thought" will in the end "completely destroy the significance of all discourse" (135c). When confronted with the question, "What are you going to do about philosophy then?" the baffled Socrates can only say: "I can see no way out at the present moment" (135c).

This moment of ἀπορία results from both too many and too few repetitions: too many broad oppositions made quickly, and too few precise distinctions made carefully. The more theoretical, abstract side of this problem and the more concrete, discursive side reinforce each other: one does not know what to think because one lacks the terms, and one does not know what to say because one lacks the concepts. The discourse rushes on at a bewildering pace. To borrow the language of the *Philebus*, we could describe this dialogue as an unhappy, ill-harmonized mixture. The *Parmenides* differentiates the one and the many at first insufficiently, so that the forms become things, then too extremely, so that the world splits in two. The distinctions here range between the determinant or the limited (πέϱᾶς) and the indeterminate or the unlimited (ἄπειϱόν), but they do not show any middle path between them: they are distinct enough to show the problem but too vague to show its solution. Just as we do not know the metaphysical status of the one and the many, so too we do not know their discursive status: How should we bring these many conflicting, ill-defined terms into an intelligible harmony, a real dialogue? At this point we may feel some of Socrates' confusion at the relation of the one and the many, and thus his "fear of tumbling into a bottomless pit of nonsense."

Parmenides, noting something "noble and inspired" in Socrates' love of argument, advises him to submit himself "to a severer training in what the world calls idle talk and condemns as useless" (135d). The language of ontology is necessarily difficult and unconventional, and not meant for everyone.[19] Parmenides then recommends Zeno's example of supposing that everything that *is* equally *is not*. In our supposing, for instance, first that there is, then that there is not, a plurality, the language itself takes on the most basic plurality, that of being and non-being, and then considers the consequences. But this method does not stop to consider a middle way between being and non-being (that is, becoming), or to examine the different senses of "is" and "is not."[20] This language, while technically brilliant, actually puts itself at risk by considering only the extremes and missing the revisions of being and of speaking that would define the space in between.

Socrates is daunted by this enterprise, and Parmenides says he is "frightened of setting out, at my age, to traverse so vast and hazardous a sea" (137b). Indeed, it is such a sea: in considering the consequences of whether there is or is not "the one itself," Parmenides ends by fragmenting any unity of meaning or speaking—a deeply ironic position for one who wants to assert precisely that unity. The discourse ceases to be a dialogue and becomes an extremely dense, esoteric series of paradoxes in which repetition only confuses the issue and distinctions collapse as soon as they are made.[21] This sea of λόγοι culminates in utter equivocation:

> It seems that, whether there is or is not a one, both that one and the others alike are and are not, and appear and do not appear to be, all manner of things in all manner of ways, with respect to themselves and to one another. (166b)

Yet at the same time we learn, "If there is no one, there is nothing at all" (166b). We are left blocked in a state of ἀπορία when the dialogue concludes simply, "Most true." One is tempted to say that since there is no coherence to the discourse, there is no coherence to the meaning either. Of course, that may be exactly the point, intended to provoke the reader to take the problem further. At any rate, this enigmatic language never questions the stark binary oppositions between "is" and "is not," between the one and the many, and never investigates a middle way between them. The *Parmenides* as a whole discusses and demonstrates both the one and the many but without any revisions that might promise to reconcile them.

With the *Philebus*, the reader feels in surer hands from the start. Socrates is reassuringly back in control, here in his familiar role of older, wiser mentor of younger participants.[22] Strikingly, this is the only dialogue typically regarded as late in which Plato casts Socrates in the leading role; the dialogue thus yokes together the Socratic search for a specifically *human* good with the Platonic interest in dialectics, ontology, and methodology. Yet the dialogue that ends in agreement begins with competition: starting from a preestablished rivalry between intelligence and pleasure as the good, Socrates repeatedly cautions and chastises Protarchus. Socrates himself sets up the opposition by saying that "knowledge [φρόνησις] wins over pleasure, and pleasure loses" if he can prove his point (12a), and that he will need "different armament" to continue the fight for intelligence (23b8). Protarchus in response says that pleasure has "been defeated as if knocked down" and has "fallen in her fight for victory" (22e5–6). But Socrates also suggests that "we can reach a like position if each side makes some concessions to the other" (13d), and adds: "For we are not contending here out of love of victory for my suggestion to win or for yours," but are instead acting together "as allies in support of the truest one" (14b5–7). This tension between competition and cooperation plays a positive role: neither the language nor the issues should come too easily at first, for both must work out their tensions in due time and measure.[23] Repetition in this dialogue plays a positive role: the gradual reevaluation of positions and methods serves to overcome initial antagonisms.

Socrates' first words already indicate the subtler, more self-reflective nature of the language. He advises Protarchus to consider both positions carefully and reformulate the thesis he inherits from Philebus, and he then summarizes them again to define the debate clearly (11a–c). Socrates also moves from pleasure as the good "for all creatures" to intelligence and knowledge as the good "to all who can attain them" (11b4–8), and thus turns the discussion to specifically human concerns. But after this restatement of a foregoing discussion, the question changes: Socrates proposes that "if it should turn out that there is another possession" better than either pleasure or knowledge (11d10), then these two would become rivals for second place, each claiming the responsibility for the higher good (22d–e). By assuming as given the simple opposition between hedonism and intellectualism, but then complicating the issue, the *Philebus* imposes further determinacy on an old problem.[24] Plato does not simply have Socrates repeat the critique of hedonism, which he has presented elsewhere, but moves beyond it by revising and retesting it.[25] What is inherited is already reexamined; both the question posed and the method used are more complex. But obviously much work lies ahead. The two initial categories are unexamined conglomerates in need of more determination: "to enjoy . . . to be pleased and delighted, and whatever else goes together with that kind of thing" is one conglomerate, and "knowing, understanding, and remembering, and what belongs with them, right judgment and true calculations" is the other (11b–c).

The reader notes right away the absence of "our fair Philebus" (11c7) as defender of his cause: "I absolve myself of all responsibility and now call the goddess as my witness" (12b). Philebus gives only his name to the dialogue.[26] His silence signifies that the bodily pleasure in which he believes cannot, even need not, make an argument for itself. Philebus is thus consistent with his own hedonism; as Gadamer writes in

The Idea of the Good in Platonic-Aristotelian Philosophy, "the pleasure principle has a kind of obvious predominance, unlimited and overpowering" for which it would be contradictory to give a rational account (105). Philebus proves to be as ἄλογος, as irrational and inarticulate, as the physical pleasures he defends. By bowing out of the pleasures of argument, he fits proleptically into Socrates' later characterization of a fully irrational life as subhuman, or "mollusk"-like (21d).

Intellectual pleasures, on the other hand, reveal themselves precisely in such discussion and debate. Simply because it takes place in a philosophical dialogue, the rivalry is already biased toward intellectual activities. Protarchus, in taking over the position, cannot escape this implicit bias, and does not even represent the strongest proponent of hedonism.[27] He shares Socrates' fundamental assumption of the rationality of the cosmos (28d–e), and he sometimes misses a chance to defend his cause.[28] But his more moderate stance can also be seen as another sign that this dialogue is a search for—and indeed a demonstration of—a middle path between the narrowly cerebral and the crudely hedonistic extremes.

The search for such a path leads Socrates to reflect on naming. Should Aphrodite's true name be Pleasure (ἡδονή), as Philebus holds?[29] By what names dare we address the gods? Socrates expresses "a more than human dread" at renaming the gods, but asserts confidently of pleasure: "If one just goes by the name, it is one single thing, but in fact it comes in many forms [μορφας] that are in some way even quite unlike each other" (12c–d). In turning away from the divine personification and toward the human-given name, Socrates at the same time turns to an ambivalence rooted in language: the name, as a unit, implies the entity is a one, while it may really be plural in its kinds. But naming can also let us determine plurality. The pleasure of sobriety may be the opposite of the pleasure of silliness (to use his example), yet both go by the same name; this tension demands a reexamination of the nature of pleasure. In this sense names implicitly contain the one and the many within themselves: a name can both unify things into a class and differentiate them into particulars and subclasses.

Plunged into the problem of the one and the many, we immediately see how the nuances of language can both complicate and clarify this problem. Protarchus at first cannot understand either the conceptual or the linguistic distinctions; his "common sense" objections slow down the dialogue but also allow needed distinctions to arise. He insists at first on the unity of pleasure: "How could pleasure not be, of all things, most like pleasure?" (12e). Socrates replies that this refusal to differentiate makes them join the ranks of "the most incompetent and at the same time newcomers in such discussions" for attempting to prove that "the most unlike thing is of all things most *like* the most unlike" (13d). Plato thus recollects for the reader Zeno's first hypothesis in the *Parmenides*. But whereas the *Parmenides* ends in utter ἀπορία, the *Philebus* seeks a complex solution to the one/many problem. Socrates now accepts that "all together, the branches of knowledge will seem to be a plurality, and some will seem quite unlike others" (13e9–10). If he excluded this possibility, he would not be "a worthy partner in a discussion" (14a1). Plurality, both in word and thought, must be fully acknowledged. Significantly, the speakers here for the first time agree on something: to examine all the variations of each candidate (14b). The turn toward the plurality within each unity anticipates the new methods to come.

Now turning full-face to the "amazing" or "wondrous" (θαυμαστὸν; 14c9), even "monstrous" (τέρατα; 14e) statement that the many is one or the one many, Socrates again stresses, as he did at the start of the *Parmenides,* that to say a produced thing is both many and one does not raise problems, but to say so of a non-perishable thing does: "Zealous concern with divisions of these unities and the like gives rise to controversy" (15a6–7). Socrates here gives man, ox, beauty, and the good as examples of this constant category of the forms, whereas the young Socrates of the *Parmenides* had doubts whether to assert forms for the first two. Perhaps this shift evidences Parmenides' prediction that when philosophy takes hold of Socrates, he "will not despise any of these objects then" (*Parmenides* 130e). As we will see, Plato in the *Philebus* shows Socrates the pathway home, toward the οἶκός, "downwards" from the ideal One to the world of plurality in which we dwell.

The *Philebus* runs right into the tangle of problems presented in the *Parmenides:* How can each unit remain firmly itself while being found in an indeterminate number of particulars? Does each unit remain "always one and the same" but become "dispersed and multiplied," or does it somehow stay whole but become "entirely separated from itself" (15b–c)? Yet the same problem receives a different treatment here: "It is these problems of the one and the many . . . that cause all sorts of difficulties [ἀπορία, literally "blocked passage"] if they are not properly settled, but promise progress [εὐπορία, "good passage"] if they are" (15c).[30] The reader again hears Plato's implicit criticism of, and improvement upon, the method of Zeno and Parmenides. As Dorothea Frede says, "The Socrates of the *Philebus* has clearly profited from the lesson he was taught by old Parmenides."[31] The approach here differs in the interlocutors' explicitness about the problem, their patience in enumerating, distinguishing, and of course *repeating* its aspects, and their awareness of their own language—indicating their self-consciousness, or better, Plato's, about method.

In the *Philebus*, the language of reconciliation through repetition explicitly calls attention to itself. Socrates says outright: "It is through *discourse* [ὑπὸ λόγων] that the same thing flits around, becoming one and many in all sorts of ways" (15d4–5). This concise statement highlights what is both bewildering and awe-inspiring about language—its "'immortal and ageless' condition" (15d8).[32] In language, the tension between the one and the many works itself out on several levels; just as names can both separate and unify things, language too can multiply itself (more and more words, definitions, distinctions) while still remaining itself a unity (one grammar, one dialogue). This oneness branching out into the many has ontological as well as linguistic significance, since for the Greeks λόγος encompasses both speech and thought.

As in the *Parmenides*, youth and age play a role in thought and speech. Socrates says of this one/many feature of language: "Whoever among the young first gets a taste of it is as pleased as if he had found a treasure of wisdom. He is quite beside himself with pleasure," which eventually leads to confusion (15e). This remark connects thought with the pleasure of the immature delight in mental gymnastics. Socrates has to steer the dialogue clear of "childish" proofs (13d6) and "commonplace puzzles" that are "no longer even worth touching" (14d5–7). Protarchus, faced with these affronts, at first reacts defensively by reminding Socrates "we are all young"; he then seeks to "remove this kind of disturbance from our discussion in a peaceful way" (16a5–b). But Protarchus must suffer many more rebuffs and upsets in order to learn and to mature; he learns through a *positive* repetition. At first, Protarchus objects to Socrates' way of "plunging us into difficulties and repeating questions" (20a). Yet later, Protarchus welcomes Socrates' suggestion to review categories "one by one, for memory's sake" (27b–c) and he asks for yet another reminder (31c–d).[33] By the end, Protarchus accuses pleasures of resembling "children who don't possess the least bit of reason" (65c6). Dialectical revision proves crucial to the maturing process.

The λόγος must follow a long, rough path of repeating and refining questions to move toward the gradual reconciliation of the questioner and the questioned. Even Socrates has problems in his method of searching for truth. He remains devoted to the finest method (καλλίων ὁδὸς), although "it has often escaped me and left me behind, alone, and helpless [ἄπορον]" (16b5–7). It is easy to explain but hard to practice. A theoretical explanation will not suffice; the problems of the one and the many, the determinant and the indeterminate, must work themselves out equally in the *practice* of language.

In the new method of classification, described as a Promethean gift from gods to humans (16c5), the central concepts of determinacy and indeterminacy come to the fore and guide the rest of the discussion. Socrates claims this heavenly gift is responsible for every discovery in every realm: "Whatever is said to be consists of one and many, having in its nature limit [πέρας] and unlimitedness [ἀπειρίαν]" (16d). We should take each thing and posit one form (ἰδέαν), then two or three, "until it is not only established of the original unit that it is one, many, and unlimited, but also how many kinds it contains" (16d5–7). Only when we have made each enumeration should we identify the plurality as unlimited. This careful, patient method of classifying allows, in fact necessitates, cooperation between the one and the many. The one (as genus) contains the determinacy of the many species potentially within it; similarly, the many contains oneness within it as the unity of classes and species. This method, then, is the gods' gift of classifying beings, a way to "inquire and learn and teach one another" (16e2–3). It is a gift that must be honored through use; as Protarchus remarks, "there is no taking back a gift properly given" (19e).[34]

To honor the gift, then, Socrates has to put it into practice: he gives specific, determinate examples to illustrate a general point, and to give shape to the indeterminate mass of particulars. Such accounting for the areas between the one and the many renders the language truly philosophical, in contrast to the eristic method of contemporary "clever ones" (σοφοὶ) who "make a one haphazardly and make it many times faster or slower than they should" in jumping straight from the one to the indeterminate plurality (17a5).[35] Again we hear an implied critique of Zeno and Parmenides, who do seem to offer only one extreme or the other, an absolute one or an unknowable indeterminacy. Then there are those who know only the indeterminacy: "The boundless [ἄπειρόν] multitude in any and every kind of subject leaves you in boundless [ἄπειρόν] ignorance, and makes you count for nothing and amount to nothing" (17e5–6). This of course indicates Philebus, whom Plato has speak here on cue: "But of what use is all this talk [λόγος] to us, and what is its purpose?" (18a). Given the importance of language, it is not accidental that the illustration focuses on speech: vocal sounds appear at first to lie on an indeterminate continuum, but can in fact be classified and enumerated (vowels, consonants, and mutes), until we realize "the one link that somehow unifies them all . . . the art of literacy" (18d).[36] Language contains both πέρᾶς and ἄπειρόν within itself.

Armed with these flexible discursive skills, the dialogue progresses to a similarly flexible theoretical aim: defining the good life as "a life that results from the mixture" of pleasure and intelligence (22a).[37] Protarchus concedes that if we had no thought or memory, we would not even be aware of our own pleasure; that would be the life of a mollusk or other shellfish (21b–d). A life of only thought, without any pleasure, is not desirable either. Pleasure and thought have become rivals for determining this mixture. Since the speakers have learned how to determine the middle ground through classification, they can now determine the middle way as the best human life.

In the midst of this discussion, Socrates urges Protarchus (and the reader) to be patient, since "a long discussion [λόγος]," and a hard one, still awaits them:

> For it seems that, in the battle about the second prize for reason, a different device [ἄλλης μηχανῆς] will be needed, different armament, as it were, from that used in our previous discussion, though it may partly be the same. (23b5–9)

This "different device" turns out to be a further taxonomy to reconcile unity and plurality. Amid the critical debate over the relation between this passage and the earlier one on the divine gift, my own position is that the repetition of the terms πέρας and ἄπειρόν, as well as the phrase "partly be the same," suggest at the very least an important connection between the two passages.[38] The "different armament" revives the earlier method of collection and division, while expanding the senses of limit and the unlimited. Plato "repeats" the section on dialectical method, but with a twist, in order to unfold it gradually and dialogically to his readers.

In the fourfold analysis of everything in the universe—the indeterminate or unlimited (ἄπειρόν), the determinant or the limit (πέρας), the mixture (σύμμιξις) of the two, and the cause (αἰτία) of the mixture—the first three are scattered and must each be rounded up "into a unity again, in order to study how each of them is in fact one and many" (23e7). Pleasure, at least when understood in the common physical sense, belongs to the indeterminate class. Philebus, fittingly, makes his point here again: "How could pleasure be all that is good if it were not by nature boundless [ἄπειρόν] in plenty and increase?" (27e7–9). Socrates counters: "Nor would pain be all that is bad, Philebus!" By contrast, the determinant class imposes definite relations: "The kind that contains equal and double, and whatever else puts an end to the conflicts there are among opposites, making them commensurate and harmonious by imposing a definite number [ἀριθμός] on them" (25e).[39] For example, a temperature described simply as "too hot" or "too cold" remains indeterminate until we measure a distinct degree that imposes a limit on it. The mixed class is praised as producing harmony in everything from good climate to good character, while the cause of order and cycles in the universe "has every right to the title of wisdom and reason" (30c7).

The successfully blended life itself repeats the fourfold scheme, especially of course the newly elevated category of the mixture. Gadamer holds that the theory of the four kinds provides the ontological ground for the good life as mixed: "Only when the mixture is no longer thought of as a diminution and clouding of the pure, true, and unmixed, but as a genus of its own" can the mixed category, in the cosmos or in the soul, be seen as the good (*Idea of the Good*, 113). This mixture provides a middle way between "is" and "is not," namely, the realm of becoming. Plato has Socrates describe this third class with the important phrase, γένεσιν εἰς οὐσίαν (26d8).[40] Being and becoming must themselves be blended with measure. The new methods lead to a new understanding of both ontology and ethics. As Günter Figal summarizes:

> The Good is the unity of πέρας and ἄπειρόν. This unity can only be the fortunate coincidence of the two principles in which form retains its harmonious proportions in the midst of becoming, and the ephemeral nature of becoming comes to anchor in form (94).[41]

Intelligence, as the cause of the mixture, grants the proportion that the mixture needs to become stable. The new discursive methods of reconciling the one and the many allow the mixed class, and the mixed life, to come into focus as the good.

Despite the more flexible language, there are still many difficult moments in the complex arguments. The different senses of pleasure are not always clear, as for instance when Socrates switches between Philebus' coarse physical pleasures and those of learning. We have not, of course, delved into the detailed analyses of pleasure and pain, or true and false pleasures. Yet even after recognizing the problems, we still may conclude that the method of repetition contributes to the reconciliation that the dialogue eventually achieves. As Socrates reminds us just before the mixing of thought and pleasure, "the proverb fits well here that says that good things deserve repeating 'twice or even thrice'" (60a).[42] The speakers repeat not only phrases but equally methods, enacting both the divine gift of classification and the fourfold ontological scheme. In this way all the many different kinds of pleasure—true and false, intellectual and physical, pure and mixed—can become differentiated without losing relation to each other, or to the dialogue as a whole.[43]

Thanks to such repetitions, the more the *Philebus* makes things many, the more in the end it makes things one. The plurality of language, held in check by its own measure, allows for this eventual resolution. Protarchus finally denounces pleasure as "the greatest impostor" and elevates reason as the closest thing to truth (65c–d). But thought and pleasure have gone beyond their initial antagonism: pleasure can be seen as more limited, determined, and intellectual. Neither side alone can be completely self-sufficient.[44] To emphasize the practical, the dialogue concludes with three mentions of οἶκός (61b, 62b–c, 64c), of house and home as the concrete dwelling of the human good: inexact types of knowledge must be included in the mix so that we can find our way home in the world.

The good then cannot simply be *one* pure being but rather a harmonized combination of *many:* a trio, understood as "a conjunction of three: beauty, proportion, and truth," accounts for the goodness of the good mixed life (65a1–5). This mixture within a mixture is, as Guthrie says, "a trinity in unity." It cannot be just "an unconnected medley" (or "mishmash," as Benardete says, or "hotch-potch" as Gosling says), but must involve "measure and proportion [μέτρου καὶ τῆς συμμέτρου]" (64d10–e2). Such harmony, as we have seen, requires repeated testing through dissonance and disagreement. Philebus, the nonrational representative of non-bounded pleasure, cannot share in this resolution because he refuses to mature or to learn the pleasures of λόγος. But Socrates' last speech, repeating one of his first distinctions, concludes that such a thoughtless sort of pleasure properly belongs to animals; to humans belongs the "love of argument that is constantly revealed under the guidance of the philosophic muse" (67b6–8).

The whole dialogue, then, once it finds the proper way of overcoming dichotomies, both argues for and demonstrates a thoughtful pleasure, a pleasurable thought. In this sense, the *Philebus* belongs to the mixed category itself. The dialogue portrays πέρας and ἄπειρόν not as starkly opposed but as necessarily mixed in this special sense, as the defining limit and what needs such defining. To illustrate the point, the dialogue begins and ends with the indeterminate, talk we do not hear; as Protarchus remarks at the very end, "There is still a little missing, Socrates" (67b11). In *The Tragedy and Comedy of Life,* Benardete suggests that the "unbounded *Philebus* represents something essential about philosophy, that it is an activity that cannot have a beginning or an end of a strictly determined kind" (88). Further, Gadamer links the ontological category of the indeterminate to the ethical challenge of achieving the right mixture:

Because of the *apeiron*, human life can never be absolutely successful; rather it always runs the risk of miscarrying and must forever
be wrested from its tendency to sink into a measurelessness even so
extreme as that of the unconscious and torpid life of an oyster [or mol-
lusk] (*Philebus* 21d).[45]

Along different lines, Christopher Smith notes that after classification,
"we are to let the whole thing lapse *eis to apeiron*, into the infinite and
indefinite," and that the Platonic method of question and answer itself
proceeds without *peras*, or as Smith puts it, "indeterminately, unend-
ingly, inconclusively."[46] Against such an indistinct background, determination carves out meanings through constant repetition and revision.

By contrast, in the *Parmenides*, the act of repeating only sets us
further adrift in the vast and dangerous sea of λόγος. Both the thought
and the language lack any harmonious mixture, any middle way, any
mediation between the one and the many, the "is" and the "is not." The
inflexibility of these positions reduces argument to a series of paradoxes
and puzzles, a choice between two untenable extremes. Repetition in
this case leads only to incompatibility. In the *Philebus*, on the other
hand, the act of repeating allows revision to function as a *re*-vision of
the problems. It is true that such repetition produces many upsets and
many unconnected pieces. But the very "untidiness" gives it a surprising
strength to reconcile the many and the one, the indeterminate and the
determinant, becoming and being.[47]

Plato's deliberately open-ended approach in this dialogue leads
us to brief concluding thoughts on Aristotle's relation to his mentor. As
Aristotle states at the beginning of the *Nicomachean Ethics*, ethics cannot
be an exact science, so it suffices "to indicate the truth roughly and in
outline" (1094b20–21).[48] Further, Aristotle makes the idea of a plurality
within a unity central to both ethics and ontology; as he famously says,
" 'good' has as many senses as 'being' " (1096a23–24). His categories can
be seen as a determinate way of doing justice to these many senses, while
still maintaining one focal sense. Aristotle's criticism of the Platonic
Idea of the Good, that we cannot achieve or practice it (1096b33), loses
its sting against the *Philebus*, which presents the good as specifically human and attainable.[49] And surely Aristotle was aware that the problem of
"two worlds" was already developed by Plato himself in the *Parmenides*.[50]
Finally, we sense that Plato's implicit reconciliation of being and becoming develops into Aristotle's more explicit interest in γένησις (becoming), κίνησις (change or motion), δύναμις (potentiality) and ἐνέργεια
(activity or actuality) and their relation to οὐσία (being).

Given such resonances, should we regard the *Philebus* as an "Aristotelian" dialogue? Did Plato's most famous student influence the move-

ment of his dialogues? Or did Plato show Aristotle a new method toward a measured plurality? To what extent is Aristotle still fundamentally Platonic in his orientation to ethics? While a full discussion of such questions goes beyond the scope of this paper, let us stress that Aristotle does acknowledge his debt to his mentor and build upon his work. In the *Nicomachean Ethics,* for instance, Aristotle says that with the turn away from a single, transcendent Good to a plurality of human goods, "the argument has by a different course reached the same point" (1097a24). Then Aristotle's real target would not be Plato per se (at least not the Plato of the *Philebus*), but rather certain misinterpretations of the good as transcendent and "otherworldly," misinterpretations which Plato himself has anticipated. Perhaps this explains why Aristotle hesitates before launching his critique and does not name Plato directly, but rather the "Platonists" or "friends of the forms."[51]

In its emphasis on practice, the *Philebus* anticipates the Aristotelian "golden mean" in the motif of the harmonious mixture of two elements. As Robert Dostal notes:

> This notion of the "mix" in the *Philebus* also serves . . . as the basis for defending Plato against Aristotle's critique concerning the unity of the good in the *Nicomachean Ethics.* The mix requires measure. From this it is a short step to Aristotle's virtuous mean. (294)[52]

The new category of mixture demands a language of re-vision and a method of reconciliation. As I have tried to show, it is not only Socrates who adopts a "different device" in the *Philebus* but equally Plato, in criticizing dichotomies and moving toward a more complex unity, a more plural oneness, a more attainable pathway toward finding our way home. In this sense we can say the final agreement—hard won through repetitions—on the mixed life does to a large extent successfully reconcile the one and the many in both thought and speech.[53]

Notes

The epigraph for this chapter is taken from Plato, *Philebus,* trans. Dorothea Frede, in *Plato: Complete Works,* ed. John M. Cooper (Indianapolis: Hackett, 1997), 398–456.

1. As Gadamer writes: "The interpretive method that is appropriate to the *philosopher* Plato is not that of clinging fast to his definitions of concepts and developing his 'doctrine' into a uniform system . . . instead, it is to retrace, as a questioner, the course of questioning that the dialogue presents and to describe the direction in which Plato, without following it, only points" (Hans-

Georg Gadamer, *Plato's Dialectical Ethics: Phenomenological Interpretations Relating to the Philebus*, trans. Robert Wallace [New Haven: Yale University Press, 1991], 10–11). He analyzes "the unity of dialogue and dialectic which *only* the *Philebus*, out of all Plato's literary works, presents in this way" (15). See also Gadamer's influential treatment of modern method in *Truth and Method*, trans. Joel Weinsheimer and Donald Marshall (New York: Continuum, 1994).

2. Gadamer, *Plato's Dialectical Ethics*, 112–13.

3. For a contrasting approach to the question of reflexivity in this dialogue, see Christopher Smith, "The (De)construction of Irrefutable Argument in Plato's *Philebus*," in *Does Socrates Have a Method? Rethinking the Elenchus in Plato's Dialogues and Beyond*, ed. Gary Alan Scott (University Park: Pennsylvania State University Press, 2002), 199–216.

4. I follow A. E. Taylor here in viewing the *Parmenides* as "a dialogue clearly presupposed by the *Philebus*" (introduction to *Philebus and Epinomis*, trans. A. E. Taylor [London: Nelson and Sons, 1956], 49). For a range of interpretations of the *Parmenides*, see Robert S. Brumbaugh, *Plato on the One: The Hypotheses in the Parmenides* (New Haven: Yale University Press, 1961); Constance Meinwald, *Plato's Parmenides* (New York: Oxford University Press, 1991); Mitchell Miller, *Plato's Parmenides: The Conversion of the Soul* (Princeton: Princeton University Press, 1986); and Kenneth Sayre, *Parmenides' Lesson: Translation and Explication of Plato's Parmenides* (Notre Dame: University of Notre Dame Press, 1996).

5. The search to find the right expression to do justice to the thought manifests itself as one of the most pressing issues for Plato. In the *Phaedo*, for instance, Socrates makes the point dramatically: "To express oneself badly is not only faulty as far as the language goes, but does some harm to the soul" (115e). Significantly, the same dialogue contains several mentions of pleasure and pain: Socrates says they are "like two creatures with one head" (60b) and that violent pleasure and pain weld body and soul together (83d), while his followers feel a mixture of pleasure and pain upon seeing him for the last time (59a) (translated by Grube, in Cooper, ed., *Plato: Complete Works*).

6. Seth Benardete, *The Tragedy and Comedy of Life: Commentary on Plato's Philebus* (Chicago: University of Chicago Press, 1993), 240.

7. Georg Grote, *Plato and the Other Companions to Socrates*, vol. 2, trans. John Murray (London: John Murray, 1865), 584.

8. Robert Gregg Bury, *The Philebus of Plato* (Cambridge: Cambridge University Press, 1897), ix.

9. I. M. Crombie, *An Examination of Plato's Doctrines*, vol. 2 (New York: Humanities, 1963), 252.

10. Hans-Georg Gadamer, *The Idea of the Good in Platonic-Aristotelian Philosophy*, trans. P. Christopher Smith (New Haven: Yale University Press, 1986), 104.

11. W. K. C. Guthrie, *A History of Greek Philosophy*, vol. 5 (New York: Cambridge University Press, 1978), 198, 238–39.

12. Donald Davidson, "Gadamer and Plato's *Philebus*," in *The Philosophy of Hans-Georg Gadamer*, ed. Lewis Hahn (Chicago: Open Court, 1997), 423. One can of course acknowledge both the strengths and the weaknesses of the dialogue, as Hackforth does: "Nobody would claim for the *Philebus* the architec-

tural mastery displayed in the *Phaedo* and the *Republic;* on the other hand, the formlessness of the work has often been exaggerated" (R. Hackforth, *Plato's Examination of Pleasure* [Cambridge: Cambridge University Press, 1945], 10). Mark Moes, following Robert Brumbaugh's interpretation of the *Republic,* suggests that the *Philebus* has a symmetrical structure: ABCDE—EDCBA (Mark Moes, *Plato's Dialogue Form and the Care of the Soul* [New York: Peter Lang, 2000], 125).

13. *The Philebus Commentary,* ed. and trans. Michael Allen (Tempe: Center for Medieval and Renaissance Studies, 2000), 72 and 1.

14. *Introductions to the Dialogues of Plato,* trans. William Dobson (New York: Arno, 1973), 309.

15. Cynthia Hampton, *Pleasure, Knowledge, and Being: An Analysis of Plato's Philebus* (Albany: State University of New York Press, 1990), 12.

16. Cynthia Hampton, "Overcoming Dualism: The Importance of the Intermediate in Plato's *Philebus,*" in *Feminist Interpretations of Plato,* ed. Nancy Tuana (University Park: Pennsylvania State University Press, 1994), 225n27.

17. Rosemary Desjardins, *Plato and the Good* (Leiden: Brill, 2004), 17.

18. Translated by Cornford, in Cooper, ed., *Plato: Complete Works.*

19. When Heidegger writes of the "harshness" (*die Härte*) of any language that poses the question of being, he turns to Plato's *Parmenides* as a classic example (Martin Heidegger, *Being and Time,* trans. John Macquarrie and Edward Robinson [New York: Harper and Row, 1962], 34; *Sein und Zeit* [Tübingen: Max Niemeyer, 1953], 39).

20. Guthrie calls this duality Parmenides' "familiar weapon, the 'either-or' dilemma" (*History of Greek Philosophy,* 50), and notes that without this ambiguity in the key terms, the contradictions would not result (55).

21. Of course, this language still has value as "a series of dialectical exercises" to train the young philosopher, as Guthrie suggests (*History of Greek Philosophy,* 53).

22. As Benardete puts it, what seems "peculiarly Socratic" in this dialogue is "the subordination of all cosmological speculation to the issue of the human good"; but he also rightly notes "the strangeness of the *Philebus*'s Socrates" (*Tragedy and Comedy of Life,* 89–90).

23. Benardete suggests that Protarchus' request to repeat points "again and again [εἰς αὖθίς τε καὶ αὖθις]" (24e, the passage quoted at the beginning of this paper) dramatically combines limit and unlimited: "Without their present 'dissonance,' there would have been no dialogue. . . . Protarchus chose dissonance when he did not choose mind. He now proposes an unlimited number of repetitions; he means, presumably, repetitions mixed with rephrasings and fresh examples" (*Tragedy and Comedy of Life,* 147).

24. As Guthrie writes: "By this dramatic device of a dialogue before the dialogue Plato shows plainly that he has no intention of treating us to yet another refutation of the naive hedonistic equation of pleasure and the good. . . . With the question 'what place can be assigned to pleasure in the good life, and what sorts of pleasures can there find admission?' he breaks new ground" (*History of Greek Philosophy,* 202).

25. For an overview of such critiques (in *Protagoras, Gorgias, Phaedo,* and *Republic*), see Dorothea Frede, "Disintegration and Restoration: Pleasure and

Pain in Plato's *Philebus*," in *The Cambridge Companion to Plato,* ed. Richard Kraut (Cambridge: Cambridge University Press, 1996), 425–63.

26. Benardete renders the name as "Lover of Youth" (*Tragedy and Comedy of Life,* 1); Gosling understands it as "an invention of Plato's, translatable as 'Loveboy'" (*Philebus,* trans. J. C. B. Gosling [London: Oxford University Press, 1975], x).

27. As Frede notes, "one cannot reform a Callicles or a Philebus, so it is better not to try. But one can get far with those who, like Protarchus, are ready to listen" ("Introductory Essay" to the *Philebus,* lxxi). Sayre renders the name Protarchus as "priority of principle" (*Plato's Late Ontology: A Riddle Resolved* [Princeton: Princeton University Press, 1983], 118). Moes suggests that Plato presents the two characters "as personified powers or components of a typical self," with Philebus as the appetitive part of the soul and Protarchus as the spirited part, open to reasoning (*Plato's Dialogue Form,* 156).

28. Guthrie suspects that with this assumption, "Protarchus has given away his case from the start, and one can imagine a satirical smile on the face of the listening Philebus" (*History of Greek Philosophy,* 215).

29. Later, Socrates will assert against Philebus that Aphrodite "imposes law and order and limit" on our excessive, boundless pleasures (26b–c).

30. Gadamer describes the *Parmenides* as the *aporia* of the mixture of the one and the many, and the *Philebus* as the *euporia* of this mixture (*Plato's Dialectical Ethics,* 118–19).

31. "Introductory Essay" to the *Philebus,* trans. Frede, lxx.

32. Frede describes "immortal and ageless" as a customary epithet of the gods and cites Homer, *Iliad,* 8.539 (*Philebus* 5d8n1).

33. As Frede notes, "the repetitions indicate not only that Protarchus is not much used to such debates, but that the distinction itself is a novel one" (*Philebus* 31c–dn1).

34. For more on the gift in Greek philosophy, see Gary Alan Scott's "Socrates as Student: The Contrast Between a Market and a Gift Economy" in his *Plato's Socrates as Educator* (Albany: State University of New York Press, 2000). See also my essay "The Ethics of Generosity and Friendship: Aristotle's Gift to Nietzsche?" in *The Question of the Gift,* ed. Mark Osteen (New York: Routledge, 2002), 118–31.

35. The sophists and rhetoricians of the time seized upon the ambiguities of language without defining the terms in between the one and the many. Since Protarchus was interested in Gorgias, this influence is probably a target of this passage.

36. The mention of the Egyptian god Theuth in this passage (18b–d) invites comparison with the passage on Theuth as the inventor of writing in the *Phaedrus* (274c ff.), the occasion for Plato's famous (and ironic) critique of writing.

37. As Gadamer discusses, this notion of mixture is meant metaphorically, not literally as a recipe or *technē* of living (*Idea of the Good,* 110–11). Crombie notes the odd sense of blending here: intelligence seems to be both an ingredient in the mixture, and the measure of it (*Examination of Plato's Doctrines,* 1:254).

38. For more on the relation between these two methodological passages,

see the studies by Frede cited above, as well as Constance Meinwald, "Prometheus's Bounds: *Peras* and *Apeiron* in Plato's *Philebus*," in *Method in Ancient Philosophy*, ed. Jyl Gentzler (Oxford: Clarendon, 1998), 165–80; and Gisela Striker, *Peras und Apeiron: Das Problem der Formen in Platons Philebos* (Göttingen: Vandenhoeck and Ruprecht, 1970).

39. There is a strong Pythagorean influence on Plato's understanding of limit and the unlimited. However, while the Pythagoreans leave such pairs contrasted in their Table of Opposites (one/many, odd/even, right/left, male/female), Plato seeks to overcome such dichotomies through the intermediary. As Cynthia Hampton writes, the divine method of the *Philebus* "provides a nondualistic model for how ultimate reality is related to sensibles," one of interest to feminist readers who seek to challenge the gender bias typically found in pairs of opposites ("Overcoming Dualism," 225). Hampton reminds us that in the *Symposium* Plato has Diotima teach the lesson of the intermediate, and that it is not accidental that she is a woman ("Overcoming Dualism," 223–24).

40. Frede translates this as "a coming-into-being"; Benardete, as "genesis into being"; Crombie, as "process leading to stability"(*Examination of Plato's Doctrines*, 2:432); Gadamer, as "Werden zum Sein" (*Dialectical Ethics*, 138).

41. Günter Figal, "The Idea and Mixture of the Good," in *Retracing the Platonic Text*, ed. John Russon and John Sallis (Evanston: Northwestern University Press, 2000), 85–95.

42. For the other places Plato repeats this proverb on repetition, see Benardete (*Tragedy and Comedy of Life*, 75). Plato's word ἐπαναπολεῖν (*Philebus* 60a), "to repeat yet again," invites comparison with the related word ἀναπολήσῃ, "to turn up the ground again, repeat, revise, reconsider" (*Philebus* 34c). See also the word ἐπαναλαμβάνων, "to take up again, resume, repeat," at *Gorgias* 488b, *Phaedrus* 228a, and *Theaetetus* 169e.

43. As Guthrie summarizes, "The crude question: 'Is pleasure good or bad?' is unreal until one has answered the further questions: 'What sort of pleasure?' and 'Pleasure in what?'" (*History of Greek Philosophy*, 200).

44. The movement from "a clear-cut either-or" to a balance of the two sides "makes human practice the theme," as Gadamer explains (*Idea of the Good*, 30).

45. Hans-Georg Gadamer, *Dialogue and Dialectic: Eight Hermeneutical Studies on Plato*, trans. P. Christopher Smith (New Haven: Yale University Press, 1980), 155.

46. Smith, "(De)construction of Irrefutable Argument," 216.

47. This last point reveals a movement in the dialogues traditionally regarded as late. Crombie explains this shift as one in which "*genesis* or becoming can develop into *ousia* or being," and the transient can become stable and permanent (*Examination of Plato's Doctrines*, 2:422). Guthrie also concludes that while the difference still holds, in the "late" dialogues "it seems to be a question less of contrasting Being with Becoming than of distinguishing grades of Being" (*History of Greek Philosophy*, 232).

48. Aristotle, *Nicomachean Ethics*, trans. W. D. Ross, in *The Complete Works of Aristotle*, ed. Jonathan Barnes (Princeton: Princeton University Press, 1984).

As Guthrie acknowledges, this untidiness may be a certain "lack of precision which Plato himself singles out as the mark of real knowledge" (*History of Greek Philosophy*, 238).

49. As Guthrie writes, this dialogue "offers us not the slightest hint of a culmination in any mysterious Form of the Good, transcending knowledge, truth and even existence" (*History of Greek Philosophy*, 201).

50. As Gadamer puts it, "it is almost absurdly obtrusive to the modern reader that the late Plato of the *Parmenides* seems every bit the equal of Aristotle in criticizing the doctrine of the ideas" (*Idea of the Good*, 9).

51. For more on these questions, see Gadamer's essays "Plato's Unwritten Teaching" and "*Amicus Plato Magis Amica Veritas*," in *Dialogue and Dialectic*, as well as the debate between Cynthia Hampton (*Pleasure, Knowledge, and Being*) and Kenneth Sayre (*Plato's Late Ontology*). For Aristotle's reports of Platonic mathematics in relation to the *Philebus*, see *Metaphysics*, Alpha 6, trans. W. D. Ross, in *Plato: Complete Works*.

52. Robert Dostal, "Gadamer's Continuous Challenge: Heidegger's Plato Interpretation," in *The Philosophy of Hans-Georg Gadamer*, ed. Lewis Hahn (Chicago: Open Court, 1997), 289–307.

53. This essay has a long history (one topic, many revisions). It began as a paper written for a graduate seminar with Sarah Waterlow Broadie, which was then awarded the Cooper Prize in Greek Philosophy at Yale University in May 1993. For stimulating ways of interpreting the *Philebus* overall, I acknowledge the series of lectures given by Günter Figal at the Collegium Phaenomenologicum, Citta di Castello, Italy, in July 2002. I also thank Walter Brogan for inviting me to lead a seminar on this dialogue during the Collegium. Finally, I am grateful to James E. Berg and Gary Alan Scott for recent careful readings and helpful suggestions.

8

Is There Method in This Madness? Context, Play, and Laughter in Plato's *Symposium* and *Republic*

Christopher P. Long

> Though this be madness, yet there is method in't.
> Shakespeare, *Hamlet*, act 2, scene 2

Where there is madness in Plato, method lurks. In its modern guise, method is designed to establish philosophy as a science by determining procedures in advance that ensure objectivity. Modern method permits no madness. Yet another, older, less rigid, but no less rigorous sense of method resonates in the Greek word μέθοδος, which means "a following after" and points not to a fixed set of rules but to a path, an ὁδός, a way. Although he has no method in the modern sense, Plato surely has a way, a path of thinking that finds expression not in a metaphysical system of doctrines, but in living dialogues between individual characters animated by an erotic desire to weave the ideas of the good, the beautiful, and the just into the fabric of human community. By writing this erotic desire, this madness, into the dialogues, Plato at once subverts the authority of his own texts and infuses them with an openness that not only resists calcification into dogma but also provokes the very critical, philosophical attitude modeled in the dialogues themselves.

To discern this method of madness in Plato, we must attend to the madness of which Socrates speaks in the *Phaedrus:* it is not the madness of mental deficiency, or of divine prophecy, or indeed of poetic inspiration; rather, it is the madness associated with eros that playfully awakens human souls to the life of philosophy and touches on something of the truth.[1] Dimensions of this sort of erotic madness can be found in the dramatic contexts in which the dialogues are situated, in the playful spirit with which they are enacted and the laughter that often resonates through them. Ironically enough, these dimensions of erotic madness take on methodological import in precisely those dialogues that many commentators identify with the "middle period" of Plato's thinking—the period in which Plato allegedly moves away from his teacher, Socrates, and develops the metaphysical system associated with "Platonism."[2]

In what follows, I trace the method of madness at work in two dialogues usually associated with this "middle period"—the *Symposium* and *Republic*—by highlighting three strategies Plato uses to subvert dogmatism, inspire critical self-reflection, and model the sort of philosophical activity capable of transforming the world of human community. The first is a distancing strategy. The concrete contexts in which Plato situates the dialogues establish critical distance in two interrelated ways. On one hand, these contexts distance Plato from his own writing in such a way that every attempt to ascribe unequivocally any of the views brought forth in the dialogues to Plato himself is confounded. On the other hand, the dramatic contexts render ambiguous the manner in which the text is received, generating a distance between text and reader that demands critical consideration. Thus, the contexts undermine the authority of both author and text in such a way that the reader is forced to approach the text with precisely the heightened presence of mind with which Plato expects the philosopher to engage the world. The second strategy is grounding: by situating the dialogues in specific social and political contexts with real historical characters who defend positions of great currency, Plato is able to ground philosophy firmly in the contingent world of human community. This gives the philosophical ideas presented in the text a sense of urgency, legitimacy, and particularity that mitigates against the attempt to distill from them an abstract set of universal doctrines. The third strategy is demonstrative: the play, irony, and laughter found in the dialogues add determinate philosophical content to the discussions themselves. This sort of play is demonstrative in the sense that it shows what cannot be said either directly by any of the characters or by the author himself. Together the distancing, grounding, and demonstrative strategies are aspects of a highly sophisticated methodological approach that both circumvents a range of metaphilosophical problems and fosters the sort of philosophical openness that lies at the heart of Plato's teaching.

As Charles Griswold has suggested, modern treatises on method are metaphilosophical insofar as they seek to address the very conditions under which rigorous philosophical investigation can be undertaken.[3] Thus, in prefaces and prolegomena, modern philosophers, speaking

CHRISTOPHER P. LONG

in their own names, seek to philosophize about how to philosophize, to reason about the limits of reason. In so doing, however, they inevitably either fall into an infinite regress—for metaphilosophical reasoning remains itself a form of philosophical reasoning—or beg the question—for the metaphilosophical principles they allegedly discover are presumptively posited as the very objective principles they seek.[4] This sort of philosophizing before beginning to philosophize is absent in Plato because it is unnecessary. Philosophy has always already begun at the very beginning of a Platonic dialogue. There is no question begging because the metaphysical principles are always introduced hypothetically and couched within a determinate context that undermines every attempt to render them objective and universal. There is no infinite regress because these contexts carry with them their own set of themes and assumptions and so provide their own starting points. Yet for all this, there remains the demonstrative dimension of the dialogues in which something like a Platonic position begins to reveal itself not through what is said directly by any of the characters, but through what the action of the dialogues themselves shows.

To borrow Wittgensteinian vocabulary: the *Symposium* and *Republic* show what cannot be said.[5] They embody a philosophical openness that is irreducible to systematic dogma. This openness is at the core of Plato's method. To focus philosophically on the playful dimensions of Plato's writing is thus not to deny that Plato has a definitive teaching; rather, it is to recognize that this teaching itself had to be expressed in a playful manner. By delineating how the distancing and grounding methodological strategies dovetail with the playful dimensions of the *Symposium* and *Republic*, a method in Plato will begin to come into focus that not only addresses important metaphilosophical concerns regarding beginnings in philosophy, but also establishes a powerful—because fundamentally open—philosophical position.

The *Symposium*

No Platonic dialogue is embedded in a more complex, compelling, and puzzling context than the *Symposium*. It belongs, with the *Theaetetus* and *Parmenides*, to a small subset of dialogues related by a narrator who is not portrayed as being present at the original discussion itself. By nesting the dialogue in a series of secondary recitations, Plato allows the authority of the text to be called into question.[6] The *Symposium* is unique among these dialogues insofar as it is received through the recollection of not one, but two fanatical disciples of Socrates: Aristodemus and Apollodorus.[7] Although this could be a sign, as Bury suggests, of the reliable accuracy of the accounts—for the disciple learns the words of the master by rote—it also implicitly calls into question the very objectivity of the story itself; for the fanatic is an unstable character with an ulterior motive: to cultivate the reputation and authority of the master.[8] By having the original conversation mediated by not one, but two, fanatical disciples of Socrates, Plato at once distances his audience from the original conversation and forces us to consider the contingencies of its provenance.

This distancing strategy is part of an implicit critique of zeal that compels us to be on guard against the very speeches we are about to encounter. In the opening passages of the *Symposium*, Apollodorus is the very paradigm of a zealot whose life is miserable precisely because he is only able to mimic the words of his master, not live the life he idealizes. This is *shown* at the beginning of the dialogue. In an echo of the opening passage of the *Republic* in which Polemarchus, "catching sight [of Socrates] from afar" (κατιδὼν οὖν πόρρωθεν), sends his slave to order Socrates to stop as he is headed homeward from Piraeus, the *Symposium* begins with Glaucon "catching sight of me [Apollodorus] from afar" (κατιδών με πόρρωθεν) as Apollodorus was going up to town from his home in Phalerum.[9] Glaucon calls out to Apollodorus, saying, "Phalerian, you, Apollodorus, will you not wait?" (172a4). Apollodorus tells us explicitly that in addressing him this way, Glaucon is making a joke.[10] Whatever the specific nature of the joke, there is play in it and a little restraint.[11] Of course, restraint here does not rise to the level of the playful coercion found at the beginning of the *Republic*, for Apollodorus, unlike his master, is quite willing, if not downright eager, to remain and satisfy Glaucon's desire to hear about the words spoken at Agathon's that evening in 416 B.C.E.

Phalerum is a port city just east of Piraeus. So the path Apollodorus takes at the start of the *Symposium* mimics that of Socrates in the *Republic*—they are both going up to Athens. Symbolically, however, they move in opposite directions, for Socrates is homeward bound (οἴκαδε, *Republic* 327b1), whereas Apollodorus is moving away from his home (οἴκοθεν, *Symposium* 172a2), or, perhaps more significantly, from his own nature. The superficial similarity between Socrates and Apollodorus eclipses a deeper difference. While Socrates responds with playful irony to Polemarchus, Apollodorus earnestly seeks to set the record straight first with Glaucon and then with a group of unnamed businessmen, for he has made it his "concern to know each day what he [Socrates] says and does" (172c). Socrates speaks in his own voice; Apollodorus only mimics the words of others.

The claim to know precisely the words and actions of Socrates gives the account that Apollodorus will present the aura of verisimilitude. This aura is reinforced first by the assertion that Apollodorus heard it directly from Aristodemus, who was there, and second, by the claim that Apollodorus questioned Socrates and received his agreement about some of the things he heard from Aristodemus (173b1–5). Yet what Plato offers with one hand, he takes away with the other. For precisely *which* of the things he heard received the Socratic imprimatur and exactly how far Aristodemus is to be trusted remains unclear. Indeed, Plato has Apollodorus tell us specifically that Aristodemus, who went around, like Socrates, barefoot, was one of the most devoted lovers of Socrates at the time. This suggests, however, that perhaps the accounts heard here are somehow tainted by the erotic madness of the fanatic and ought not to be received without a certain skepticism.

Our critical awareness of the dubious provenance of the λόγοι we are about to be presented is further reinforced by the personality Apollodorus exhibits in his initial exchange with the group of unnamed businessmen who ask him to relate the speeches. He has all the haughtiness of the dogmatist confident in the path he has chosen, and his contempt for the "rich men of business" is surpassed only by his own self-loathing. As Benardete puts it, "he knows he is despicable along with everyone else, and only Socrates is exempt from reproach."[12] Although he is clearly eager to relate the story they request, Apollodorus feigns being somewhat put upon to repeat it—"If it is necessary to tell you as well, then that is what I must do" (173c; see also *Republic* 328b3)—in order to afford himself the opportunity to belittle their wretched mode of existence. His unnamed companion remains somewhat above this rude treatment, exhibiting a degree of self-restraint and an erotic desire for the philosophical account worthy of Socrates himself. He claims that Apollodorus is always calling everyone, including himself, miserable, everyone, of course, save Socrates. He goes on to add: "Where you caught this nickname 'maniac,' *I* do not know. However, you are always like this in your speeches, angry at yourself and at others, except Socrates" (173d).[13] Apollodorus then attempts to draw his companion into a Socratic discussion by asking if he is so crazy and out of his mind to criticize his own life and the lives of all who do not adequately pursue philosophy. The companion, however, does not want to engage Apollodorus on this level, preferring to hear the speeches of others recited from memory. Apollodorus does not resist, and one has the sense that he would himself prefer to recite the speeches than engage in a rigorous Socratic dialogue in which he might have to think for himself. Here Apollodorus is made to do what the fanatic does best: mimic the words of others.

Yet Plato does not simply allow us to accept the veracity of this mimesis at face value. The "noble dissembling" of Platonic irony forces us to be on guard against the words received from Aristodemus and recited by Apollodorus.[14] This is reinforced by a final comment Plato puts into the mouth of Apollodorus before beginning the first speech on eros: "Everyone of them spoke, but Aristodemus did not remember everything, nor did I remember everything he said. But I will tell you the things that seemed to me most worthy of remembering from each of the speeches" (177e–178a). This rather offhanded comment takes on enormous significance in light of our consideration of the characters of Apollodorus and Aristodemus, for it alerts the careful reader again to the tenuous nature of the accounts that are about to be recited.[15] Plato engages here in a strategy of equivocation designed to heighten the critical awareness of all who encounter his text. By distancing himself and the reader from the speeches, Plato forces us into a mode of critical self-reflection even as the content of the text is being presented.

If the figures of Apollodorus and Aristodemus manifest one dimension of the distancing strategy of Plato's method in the *Symposium*, they, along with the constellation of figures who participate in the discussion of eros, contribute to the grounding strategy as well. As familiar followers of Socrates, Apollodorus and Aristodemus do not speak as strangers—they present themselves to us as living beings each with a peculiar history of his own. Thus, the *Symposium* is not simply narrated by a disembodied voice, but by two dedicated students of Socrates himself. As we have seen, this cannot but color our reception of the accounts they present. All of the other characters who speak in the *Symposium* too come with important political legacies that cannot be ignored, for they serve to ground the content of the dialogue in a determinate political context.

Chief among these figures, of course, is Alcibiades, whose charming good looks and political acumen had brought him in 416—the dramatic date of the dialogue—to the height of his political influence.[16] Yet Plato situates the dialogue just one year before the greatest shame of Alcibiades' career: the destruction of the herms on the night before Alcibiades commanded the ill-fated expedition to Sicily in 415. Indeed, two other important speakers in the dialogue, Phaedrus and Eryximachus, were accused of complicity in the destruction of the herms and sent into exile. For their part, Agathon and Pausanias seem to have left Athens to take up with the tyrant Archelaus of Macedonia.[17] As for the political legacy of Aristophanes, his comic poetry was held in part responsible for the accusations against Socrates that led ultimately to his death sentence at the hands of the Athenian democracy.[18] By bringing figures with such histories together in the *Symposium*, Plato implicitly enjoins us to consider the relationship between eros and politics. This becomes strikingly obvious when the speech given by Diotima through Socrates is brought into relation to that offered by Alcibiades. A consideration of these two speeches and their relation to one another not only lends insight into the methodological significance of Alcibiades' political background, it also illustrates the sophisticated way in which Plato brings the distancing and grounding strategies together to significant demonstrative effect: it at once shows something important about Plato's method and illustrates the substantive philosophical stance Plato seeks to establish.

If Leo Strauss is correct in characterizing the comical as that which treats the impossible as possible, then the speech Diotima gives through Socrates on eros is high comedy indeed.[19] It represents nothing less than the impossible possibility that a human being could come to possess a "pure, clear and unmixed" vision of the beautiful itself and become, as Diotima puts it herself, "a friend of the gods" (212a). The comedy is, however, tragic as well, for it represents human beings as divine, thus transgressing the fundamental Delphic principle to "know thyself," that is, to know one's position as a mortal and not madly to presume pure access to things divine. However, the tragicomic dimensions of the speech are eclipsed if the distancing and grounding strategies Plato deploys in presenting it are not recognized and the speech is taken as straightforward Platonic doctrine. In fact, Plato distances himself from the speech in two ways, first by putting it into the mouth of Socrates and second by having him insist that it is received from a priestess, Diotima. The religious aura of the speech is reinforced by Socrates' own purified figure: he has arrived at Agathon's fresh from a sort of inspired trance, beautified and wearing socks (174a–175c).[20] This complex, multilayered distancing strategy has a twofold effect. It at once disassociates Plato from the ideas presented in the speech and implicitly alerts the audience to be on guard against its mystical, nonrational, and perhaps even hyperbolic dimensions. If these textual clues are not heeded, the authoritative aura of the speech could give rise to a profoundly unphilosophical sort of erotic madness that is incapable of recognizing its own finitude—the height of tragic hubris.

Precisely this danger is embodied in the figure of Alcibiades, who appears suddenly after Diotima's speech. He is drunk and crowned with a wreath of ivy and violets—symbols of both Dionysus and Athens, madness and politics.[21] He provokes laughter in all who apprehend him (212c–e). Alcibiades' appearance is grounding insofar as it draws us back to the concrete world of lived experience and the eros for individual persons after the speculative heights reached by Diotima.[22] The grounding effect of Alcibiades' appearance, however, anticipates a deeper way in which the speech he gives is grounding, for the comic λόγοι of Alcibiades are necessarily couched within the context of his ultimate rejection of philosophy and his profound political failure. Somehow the two are *shown* to go together. Thus, however comic the speech of Alcibiades may be, ultimately it is a tragedy; for Alcibiades, whose tragic flaw is an unphilosophical sort of erotic madness, seeks precisely what he is unprepared to have: a direct relationship with Agathon, the man whose very name suggests τὸ ἀγαθόν, the good.

The real political dangers endemic to the sort of hubris Alcibiades embodies are explicitly shown by Plato in a playful vignette that concludes the dialogue. In this performance, Socrates, Agathon, Alcibiades, and ultimately Aristophanes play a game of musical chairs that seems, at first glance, a mere trifle, but in fact has important implications for our understanding of the entire dialogue. The stage for this game is already set at the beginning of the dialogue when Socrates first arrives and is playfully invited to sit to the right of Agathon, so, as Agathon says, "by touching [ἀπτόμενος] you I may profit from the wisdom that just occurred to you on the porch; for it is clear that you found it and are holding it [ἔχεις]" (175c–d). Socrates takes his seat disavowing the possibility that wisdom could be transferred through touch. This at once anticipates the sort of touching Alcibiades seeks to engage in with Socrates in order to come to possess something of his spiritual beauty, and, of course, the rather ridiculous claim that Diotima makes that a human being can "lay hold of" (ἐφαπτομένῳ) and possess the truth (212a).

Later, when Alcibiades enters the party, his crown of ribbons blocks his view of Socrates sitting next to Agathon. In fact, Socrates himself moves over when he sees Alcibiades (213b). This results in a seating arrangement in which Alcibiades is situated between Socrates and Agathon. And although Alcibiades leaps up in surprise upon recognizing Socrates (213b), this seating arrangement seems to be maintained until the end of Alcibiades' speech. At which point, Agathon remarks that Alcibiades' reclining between him and Socrates has the effect of separating them (222e). Thus begins a little game.

Alcibiades proposes the following positions:

| Alcibiades | Agathon | Socrates |

This would have the effect of placing him and Socrates equidistant from the most beautiful man at the party, the man whose name evokes the good itself. Alcibiades' hubris drives his proposal, for he believes himself justified in claiming equal access to the good with Socrates. To this Socrates responds: "But that is impossible" (222e). And although the reason Socrates explicitly gives for this is that it would mean that Agathon would have to praise him again, the deeper implication is that Alcibiades, having rejected philosophy and turned to popular politics, is unprepared for such close proximity to the good. In contrast to Alcibiades' proposal, Socrates suggests that Agathon recline on the other side of him, thus setting up the following positions:

| Alcibiades | Socrates | Agathon |

Here Socrates would not only have to praise Agathon, but also, like Eros himself, he would be situated between the human and the divine, between the politician addicted to the unhealthy eros associated with narcissistic popularity and the divinely inspired, beautiful tragic poet. Yet even this configuration is not actualized in the dialogue; for just as Agathon moves to recline by Socrates, a crowd of revelers interrupts him and the party descends into erotic chaos. The anarchy of human eros literally disrupts Socrates' attempt to establish a fixed relationship with the good and to situate himself firmly between it and the political (223b). Once the chaos subsides and the upsurge of erotic energy gives way to the peaceful predawn rising of the morning light, a new constellation emerges:

| Agathon | Aristophanes | Socrates |

After the others have gone home, these three remain "drinking from a large bowl, from left to right" with Socrates trying to convince them that the same person could write both tragedy and comedy (223c).[23] Here Aristophanes replaces Socrates as the mediating figure, and the comic recognition of human finitude is made to stand between Socrates and the good. If Agathon symbolizes not only the good itself, but also the very search for wholeness expressed in tragic poetry, the seating order would then show what Plato himself cannot explicitly say: seek the good, but beware of the delusion that you possess it. The erotic search for the good that animates human life must always be tempered by a humble, indeed a comic, recognition of human finitude. The darkness of this latter recognition gives way at the end of the dialogue to the hope that perhaps even through comedy something of the good may be weaved into the fabric of human community.

This playful manipulation of the seating arrangements illustrates how Plato brings together the distancing, grounding, and demonstrative strategies in an attempt to show what he cannot say without falling into a rigid, self-defeating sort of dogmatism. Rather than offering a logical argument for the validity and importance of pursuing the good in human life, he shows the power and beauty of this pursuit in all its concrete complexity. Without being didactic, the demonstrative strategy has a sort of protreptic effect. It enjoins a critical and reflective approach to the core project of philosophy: to translate the good, the beautiful, and the just into the contingent world of human community. From this perspective, the distancing and grounding strategies serve an important moderating role, for they systematically subvert the thoughtless fanaticism that often accompanies this attempted translation.

The *Republic*

The methodological subversion of fanaticism links the *Symposium* to the *Republic*. On the face of it, the two dialogues seem diametrically opposed. The one, set in the city, speaks of private things; the other, set outside the city in the Piraeus, addresses political things; the one is saturated with eros—in it there is sexual innuendo, eating, and ultimately drinking, while the other is peculiarly devoid of eros—in it sex is firmly regulated and a promised meal is preempted by philosophical conversation. The *Symposium* allows divine madness to enter the human world; the *Republic* imposes divine rationality on the human community; the one is playful, the other serious.[24]

Upon further investigation, this superficial opposition gives way to a deeper affinity. This has already been intimated by the discussion of the opening passages of the *Symposium* in which an echo of the *Republic* is heard. Strangely enough, Apollodorus' response to having been stopped by a certain "Glaucon" along the road to Athens at the start of the *Symposium* lacks the playfulness of the response Socrates makes to Polemarchus' slave who orders him and Plato's brother, another "Glaucon," to wait at the beginning of the allegedly more serious *Republic*.[25] While the opening scene of the *Symposium* reveals the dangerous fanaticism that runs just beneath its surface playfulness, the opening scene of the *Republic* uncovers a dissembling playfulness that subverts its own idealistic seriousness. In the *Republic,* this playfulness serves the same methodological function that the nested narratives served in the *Symposium:* it establishes critical distance and alerts us to be on guard against taking the λόγος about to be presented too seriously.[26]

While the *Republic* is narrated by Socrates himself, his authority is constantly undermined by playful irony. Distance here is established by embedding the account not in a nexus of testimony with ambiguous credibility, but in an atmosphere of mock coercion that constantly runs the risk of becoming frighteningly serious. So the *Republic* begins, quite literally, with Socrates being held against his will. After pointing out that Socrates and Glaucon are outnumbered, Polemarchus says: "Be either stronger than these men or remain." To which Socrates responds, "Does there not remain yet one other possibility; let us persuade you that it is necessary for us to go" (327c9–11). Polemarchus suggests that this is impossible if they refuse to listen, but in the end, Adeimantus and Polemarchus do in fact use persuasion to convince Socrates to stay—Adeimantus tempting him with a novel torch race on horseback, and Polemarchus with the erotic possibilities of dining with many young men. Socrates relents, though that he remains somewhat unwilling is heard in his last statement of this opening scene: "But if it is so resolved [εἰ δοκεῖ], this is how we must act" (328b3).[27] The phrase Socrates deploys here—εἰ δοκεῖ—gestures to the vocabulary the Athenian Assembly used when it announced that it had passed a law.[28] Although this decree establishes the ad hoc political community around which the action of the *Republic* takes place, the founding of the polis is not without coercion.[29] And while these opening passages obviously prefigure the complex set of political questions concerning the relationship between force and justice addressed in the *Republic*, methodologically they introduce a dimension of coercion that infuses the entire discussion of the *Republic* with an aura of ambiguity.

Here again, Plato's distancing strategy is manifest. The straightforward acceptance of the ideas presented in the text is undermined by the atmosphere of coercion in which they appear. This atmosphere is not limited to the opening scene, but pervades the entire dialogue. Coercion already underlies Thrasymachus' bestial attack on Socrates in book 1 (336b; see also 354a–b). Book 2 begins with Socrates thinking he "has been released from the argument" only to have Glaucon and Adeimantus pull him back to defend the just against the unjust life (357a–b). Socrates recognizes his predicament: he is caught between the urgent need to come to the defense of justice and the recognition of his own incapacity to mount a definitive apology (368b–c). As in the *Symposium*, Socrates is here shown to occupy the in-between position of eros: he is drawn toward justice and yet aware of the finitude that keeps it beyond his grasp. The entire discussion of books 2–4 of the *Republic* in which Socrates founds a series of progressively more rationally ordered cities is determined by this erotic position. The irony is, of course, that these cities win their rational stability only as they are systematically purged of eros.

At the start of book 5, coercion drives the discussion to its most perverse extremes. In a scene that echoes that of the opening passages of the dialogue, Polemarchus takes hold of Adeimantus' cloak and asks if they should let Socrates go (449b–c). They then proceed to insist upon a more detailed account of the economy of eros Socrates means to impose upon the citizens of the just city.[30] The passage is rife with the authoritative vocabulary of political coercion. Adeimantus says: "That which you heard has been resolved by us [δέδοκται ἡμιν]: not to release you until you have gone through all these things just like the rest" (449d–450a). Glaucon adds his "vote" and Thrasymachus claims it is a "resolution" they all support. To this Socrates responds: "What a thing you have done by arresting me" (450a5). This detention forces Socrates to discuss not only the manner in which eros is to be thoroughly regulated in the imagined city, but also to introduce the most radical and hubristic suggestions of the entire dialogue. Chief among these is the proposal that there will be no perfect justice until "either philosophers rule in the cities or those now called kings are able to philosophize genuinely and adequately, and political power and philosophy coincide in the same place" (473d). The claim is that cities will succumb to the vagaries of human eros so long as their leaders remain determined by eros. The solution is to replace erotic leaders with purely rational philosophers, beings who are "able to grasp what is always the same in all respects" (484b). This, of course, is the height of hubris. To ascribe such godlike capacities to mere human beings is to fail to "know thyself," a failure, according to the *Philebus*, worthy of laughter.[31]

Indeed, Socrates offers this, the so-called third wave, "even if, just like an uproarious wave, it is going to drown me in laughter and ill-repute" (473c6–7). This is not simply a dramatic flourish. It serves, rather, an important methodological function: to force those who hear what follows to be on guard against the speech about to be offered.[32] Laughter, which appears throughout the *Republic* despite its being banned from the just cities established in speech (388e5ff.), is present even at the highest and most striking moment of the dialogue, when Socrates introduces the "good beyond being." Socrates reports that to this "Glaucon quite ridiculously [μάλα γελοίως] said, 'Apollo, what a demonic excess.'" To which Socrates himself responds: "You are responsible for compelling me to tell my opinions about it" (509b–c). Of those present, only Glaucon is capable of laughing with, as opposed to at, Socrates. Thus, it is with Glaucon that Socrates introduces the most radical and ridiculous suggestions of the *Republic*, suggestions that he is willing to present only to one who is capable of laughing. At the beginning of book 5, it is Glaucon more than Adeimantus, Polemarchus, or Thrasymachus—men who show themselves to be incapable of philosophical laughter—who lends Socrates the courage to proceed although he is concerned that his speech will be misunderstood, that is, taken seriously as established dogma when Socrates himself says that he is presenting arguments at a time when he is "in doubt and seeking" (450e1). Glaucon laughs and reassures Socrates that they will release him if they are affected in a discordant way by his argument (451b).

By inscribing the most radical suggestions set forth in the *Republic* in an atmosphere of coercion and laughter, Plato distances both himself and Socrates from the determinate content of the suggestions themselves. The distancing strategy here is similar to that deployed in the *Symposium* when it was Diotima, rather than Socrates in his own voice, who spoke of the vision of beauty itself.[33] Here, as there, however, the point is not to reject the truth of what is presented under the conditions of coercion, laughter, or divine revelation, but to instill an erotic desire for the beautiful and the good in those who hear, while at the same time reinforcing the recognition that the definitive possession of either is not within the purview of mere mortals. This is accomplished by the very mode in which these ideas are expressed.

In the *Republic* as in the *Symposium,* Plato reinforces this sense of the contingency of things human by not only grounding the action of the dialogue in a specific context, but also by making Socrates engage specific individuals, each with a peculiar personality of his own. Socrates speaks differently to different people. Thus, for example, with the wealthy old Cephalus, Socrates gently stirs him up by asking about eros in old age and pushing him to consider the role of money in a good, just, and pious life (328b–331d); with Thrasymachus, he is more forceful, compelling him to blush with embarrassment for his inability to counter an argument that itself lacks logical rigor (350d).[34] However, this aspect of the grounding strategy comes most clearly into focus when the personalities of the two brothers, Glaucon and Adeimantus, are juxtaposed. Adeimantus is earnest, his personality sober, serious, and calculating. He seeks rational order and demands from Socrates an account through which a powerful person will be "made willing to honor justice and not laugh when he hears it praised" (366c). This Socrates provides by founding with him in speech a city of absolute rational order, cleansed of the anarchic turmoil of eros. Thus, the most radical purges of the city in speech are accomplished by Socrates in conjunction with Adeimantus.[35] The exception is the discussion of music, which Socrates takes up with Glaucon, who is characterized as both erotic and musical.[36] Music, however, links the rational and the erotic in a way that is inherently dangerous to a city founded exclusively on principles of rational order. Because Glaucon alone of those present is capable of reflectively joining together the rational and the erotic, he emerges as the interlocutor with whom Socrates speaks when the most important themes of the dialogue are introduced.

Glaucon becomes the central figure of the dialogue only after proving himself capable of a kind of philosophical play that tempers the serious business of rational argumentation with an erotic desire that prevents reason from calcifying into dogma. Unlike Adeimantus, who seeks unequivocal answers in rational order, Glaucon is satisfied with no dogma; unlike both Apollodorus and Aristodemus in the *Symposium*, Glaucon is no fanatical disciple. Rather, he sees the play of Socrates' approach and seeks to join with him in it. This is demonstrated not only by Glaucon's ability to laugh with Socrates, but also by Socrates' decision to focus his pedagogy firmly on Glaucon during the discussion of the Divided Line, the allegory of the Cave, and the "song of dialectic" (532a). By directing his educational efforts toward Glaucon and introducing him to this "song" which must proceed hypothetically rather than dogmatically, Socrates is able to force Glaucon to recognize both his own erotic desire to know and its limitations. Glaucon, like Socrates, finds himself in the erotic position of the philosopher who appreciates at once how hard it is to accept Socrates' assertion that there is, in fact, the good, the just, and the beautiful, and how difficult it is not to accept these things (532d). He has in some sense recognized the profound philosophical importance of positing the good, the just, and the beautiful as erotic principles that drive human beings to pursue a better, more just, and beautiful embodied existence.

Here Plato's grounding strategy dovetails with the demonstrative strategy to profound philosophical effect. As Eva Brann has suggested, the only city founded in *deed* as opposed to merely in speech in the *Republic* is the community established between Socrates and Glaucon.[37] The establishment of this community is demonstrated by the very action of the dialogue, which is directed throughout toward the conversion of Glaucon's soul by Socrates. This is the political core of the *Republic*, established in book 1, when Socrates breaks off his taming of Thrasymachus to focus Glaucon's attention on the profound choice he must make—to live a just or unjust life (347e)—and reinforced by the Myth of Er in book 10, when Socrates calls out Glaucon by name (618b9ff., 621b9ff.) as he tells the fate of those who fail to choose the life of justice. Thus the *Republic*, like the *Symposium*, shows what it cannot argue for in exclusively rational terms: the just life is spent attempting to weave a vision of the good, the beautiful, and the just into the human community by engaging in dialogue with others. Here philosophy emerges not as an abstract obsession with a set of metaphysical problems divorced from the human world, but as a fundamentally political activity that seeks to nudge this world in the direction of the good by combining the demand for rational responsibility with an erotic passion for truth and justice.

The methodological approach operating in the *Symposium* and *Republic* itself supports this substantive vision of philosophy. The distancing strategy provokes critical reflection and the heightened presence of mind such a conception of philosophy requires. The grounding strategy anchors philosophy firmly in the contingent world of human community and mitigates against the tendency to divorce ideas from the concrete contexts in which they arise. For its part, the demonstrative strategy models the complex process by which the good, the beautiful, and the just are translated into this world without falling into a dangerous, unreflective dogmatism. And although we have only traced this method in two dialogues, its path is discernible throughout Plato's writings. In the *Phaedo,* for example, the distancing strategy appears in the way the dialogue is received through the voice of Phaedo as he tells it to Echecrates, in its use of myth, and in the Pythagorean atmosphere in which it is situated; the grounding strategy is found in the decisive political and human context that surrounds the death of Socrates; and the demonstrative strategy is manifest in the way the failures of the rational arguments for the immortality of the soul are themselves negated by the earthly immortality that the spirit of Socrates wins in the telling and retelling of the story itself. To one degree or another these strategies can be seen operating in all the dialogues; for they are part of a method that substantively determines the philosophical stance Plato seeks to inspire. Method for Plato is not, as it is for the moderns, designed to divorce philosophy from the very real contingencies of human existence so as to set it on the pure path of science. Rather, it embraces madness by allowing this contingency to animate the very life of philosophy. Though this be method, yet there is madness in it.

Notes

1. *Phaedrus* 265b, in Plato, *Platonis Opera,* vol. 2 (Oxford: Oxford University Press, 1901). The central importance of madness—and specifically the distinction between divine and human madness—to our understanding of how the Platonic method provokes philosophical reflection on the beautiful and the good has been well articulated by David McNeill. See David McNeill, "Hu-

man Discourse, Eros, and Madness in Plato's *Republic*," *Review of Metaphysics* 55, no. 2 (2001).

2. The division of the dialogues into three periods—early, middle, and late—is as well known as it is problematic. For a thorough discussion of the trends of the last two hundred years of scholarship on Plato, including this developmentalist position, see Gerald A. Press, "The State of the Question in the Study of Plato," *Southern Journal of Philosophy* 34, no. 4 (1996). For an excellent, convincing critique of all attempts to definitively establish the precise chronology of the dialogues, see Jacob Howland, "Re-Reading Plato: The Problem of Platonic Chronology," *Phoenix* 45, no. 3 (1991). For a strong statement of the position that the "middle" dialogues, including the *Republic* (books 2–10) and the *Symposium*, expresses truly Platonic as opposed to Socratic philosophical doctrines, see Gregory Vlastos, *Socrates: Ironist and Moral Philosopher* (Ithaca: Cornell University Press, 1991).

3. See Charles L. Griswold Jr., "Plato's Metaphilosophy: Why Plato Wrote Dialogues," in *Platonic Writings, Platonic Readings*, ed. Charles L. Griswold Jr. (New York and London: Routledge, 1988).

4. Griswold, "Plato's Metaphilosophy," 149.

5. Ludwig Wittgenstein, *Tractatus Logico-Philosophicus* (London and New York: Routledge, 1981), prop. 4.1212.

6. The *Theaetetus* recovers something of its authority in the written word set down by Euclides immediately after hearing the story from Socrates, and more, when Euclides edits the text with corrections garnered from Socrates himself. The *Parmenides* is more subject to the vagaries of human memory than the *Symposium*, for not two, but three narrators stand between us and the original conversation. See *Theaetetus* 143a; *Parmenides* 126a–127a; *Symposium* 172a–174a.

7. In the term "fanatic" resonates the Latin *fanum*, "temple." It is used here to evoke the degree to which both Aristodemus and Apollodorus are possessed by a sort of deity or demon, indeed, the demonic character of Socrates.

8. R. G. Bury, *Symposium of Plato* (Cambridge: W. Heffer and Sons, 1973), xvi. For the position that the accounts of the two fanatics render the text less reliable, see Stanley Rosen, *Plato's Symposium*, 2nd ed. (New Haven: Yale University Press, 1987), 10–11.

9. *Republic* 327b1; *Symposium* 172a3. The Greek text for the *Republic* is from Plato, *Platonis Opera*, vol. 4 (Oxford: Oxford University Press, 1992). For the *Symposium*, see Bury, *The Symposium of Plato*. While translations are my own, I have consulted Bloom in translating passages from the *Republic* and Cobb and Benardete in translating those from the *Symposium*: Plato, *The Republic of Plato*, 2nd ed., trans. Allan Bloom (New York: Basic Books, 1991); William S. Cobb, *The Symposium and the Phaedrus: Plato's Erotic Dialogues* (Albany: State University of New York Press, 1993); and Plato, *Plato's Symposium*, trans. Seth Benardete, with commentary by Allan Bloom and Seth Benardete (Chicago: University of Chicago Press, 2001).

10. There is some debate concerning the nature of this joke. For various suggestions, see Bury, *Symposium of Plato*, 1–2. Cobb suggests that it plays on the

formal mode of address normally used in the courts; not unlike the pseudo-civility practiced in the U.S. Congress when speaking of the "gentleman from Pennsylvania." See Cobb, *The Symposium and the Phaedrus*, 179.

11. Rosen emphasizes the importance of restraint here; Rosen, *Plato's Symposium*, 12–13n30.

12. Plato, *Plato's Symposium*, 180.

13. There is considerable controversy as to whether the nickname is μαλαχός (softy, gentle one) or μανιχός (madman, maniac). Bury reads the latter, Benardete and Cobb, the former. While Cobb is correct to point out that the play between gentleness and violence is at work in the dialogue, this of itself does not necessarily justify μαλαχός. However, μαλαχός does seem appropriate for Apollodorus, given his incessant crying in the *Phaedo;* see 59a8 and 117d5. This latter reference speaks not only of Apollodorus' weeping, but of his being vexed or angry (ἀγαναχτῶν). Being "soft" and being "mad" in the sense of having lost rational control of oneself would have been closely linked in the Greek psyche. Bury's case for μανιχός draws on Apollodorus' response to the companion in which iterations of both μαίνεσθαι (to be mad) and παραίειν (to wander from one's senses) occur. He claims that the thought is: "Though I do not know exactly why you got the nickname 'fanatic'—yet in your speeches at any rate you do something to justify the title." See Bury, *Symposium of Plato*, 6.

14. For a discussion of Platonic irony as "noble dissembling," see Leo Strauss, *On Plato's Symposium* (Chicago: University of Chicago Press, 2001), 33. The distinction between Platonic and Socratic irony is made clear by Drew Hyland: Socratic irony occurs where the dissembling words and intentions are attributable to the figure of Socrates; Platonic irony, on the other hand, occurs in the action, structure, or setting of the dialogues Socrates could not control. See Drew A. Hyland, *Finitude and Transcendence in the Platonic Dialogues* (Albany: State University of New York Press, 1995), 91.

15. Gary Scott has recognized the importance of the "general lack of care for handling the narration" these characters embody. See Gary Alan Scott, *Plato's Socrates as Educator* (Albany: State University of New York Press, 2000), 181n.

16. Plato tells us the exact date of the drama of the dialogue by having Apollodorus report that the symposium took place when Agathon won the prize with his first tragedy (173a). This sort of explicit dating is part of the grounding strategy as well.

17. See Debra Nails, *The People of Plato: A Prosopography of Plato and Other Socratics* (Indianapolis: Hackett, 2002), 9.

18. See *Apology* 18a ff.

19. Leo Strauss, *The City and Man* (Chicago: University of Chicago Press, 1964), 62. For a detailed discussion of the comic dimensions of this speech, see Richard Rojcewicz, "Platonic Love: Dasein's Urge Toward Being," *Research in Phenomenology* 27 (1997): 108–12.

20. For a discussion of the ritualistic dimensions of Socrates' outfit, see Rojcewicz, "Platonic Love," 109.

21. For the recognition that the wreath of ivy and violets represents both Dionysus and Athens, see Rojcewicz, "Platonic Love," 111.

22. Scott recognizes the grounding function of Alcibiades' speech when he writes: "It makes concrete and particular the Eros that had become quite abstract in Diotima's speech, and it returns the conversation to the everyday world of human concerns." See Scott, *Plato's Socrates as Educator*, 120–21.

23. Rosen contends: "The phrase 'from left to right' suggests that Aristophanes is now between Agathon and Socrates." See Rosen, *Plato's Symposium*, 325.

24. The deep and complex relationship between the *Republic* and *Symposium* has been recognized by Strauss. See Strauss, *On Plato's Symposium*, 19. His student, Stanley Rosen, further determines the nature of this relationship along the lines outlined here. See Stanley Rosen, "The Role of Eros in Plato's *Republic*," *Review of Metaphysics* 18 (1965): 452–75.

25. Because the dramatic date of the *Republic* is ambiguous, it remains unclear whether the "Glaucon" referred to in the *Symposium* is Plato's brother who appears in the *Republic*. Friedländer recognizes that the name "Glaucon," even if it is not Plato's brother, calls the *Republic* to mind. He claims: "The scene at the beginning of the *Republic* is reminiscent of the *Symposium* in its very words." See Paul Friedländer, *Plato: The Dialogues, Second and Third Periods*, vol. 3 (Princeton: Princeton University Press, 1969), 6.

26. There is a long history of interpretations that fail to recognize the function of the playfulness of the *Republic*. One of the best expressions of this tradition is found in Popper's *Open Society and Its Enemies*, which sees the philosopher king of the *Republic* as "Plato himself, and the *Republic* is Plato's own claim for kingly power." Popper goes on to assert that the *Republic* is "meant by its author not so much as a theoretical treatise, but as topical political manifesto." See Karl Popper, *The Open Society and Its Enemies*, vol. 1 (Princeton: Princeton University Press, 1943), 153. The presumption that the *Republic* is a political treatise in the modern sense, or, more radically, a manifesto, are anachronisms that fail to recognize the ambiguities Plato wrote into the text itself.

27. These words: "Ἀλλ' εἰ δοκεῖ, . . . οὕτω χρὴ ποιεῖν" are parroted in the *Symposium* by Apollodorus': "εἰ οὖν δεῖ καὶ ὑμῖν διηγήσασθαι, ταῦτα χρὴ ποιεῖν" (173c).

28. Plato, *Republic of Plato*, 441.

29. John Sallis recognizes that Socrates establishes a community by turning force into persuasion. See John Sallis, *Being and Logos: Reading the Platonic Dialogues*, 3rd ed. (Bloomington: Indiana University Press, 1996), 322.

30. Recognizing the importance of coercion at the start of book 5, Jacob Howland suggests that Adeimantus and Polemarchus envision themselves as the noble guardians who will receive the full pleasure of erotic procreation in the city Socrates establishes in speech. See Jacob Howland, "The *Republic*'s Third Wave and the Paradox of Political Philosophy," *Review of Metaphysics* 51, no. 3 (1998): 646.

31. *Philebus* 48a–e.

32. See *Symposium* 189a–b, when Eryximachus says to Aristophanes: "Although you are supposed to be giving a speech, you make jokes and force me to be on guard against your speech in case you say something funny, when you should come out and speak in peace." Saxonhouse has highlighted the comic atmosphere of book 5 of the *Republic*. See Arlene W. Saxonhouse, "Comedy in Callipolis: Animal Imagery in the Republic," *American Political Science Review* 72, no. 3 (1978): 888–901. Hyland contends that the second and third waves introduced in book 5 are fundamentally comic; Rowe agrees, though for very different reasons. See Hyland, *Finitude and Transcendence*, 59–86. See also Christopher Rowe, "The Good, the Reasonable and the Laughable in Plato's *Republic*," in *Laughter Down the Centuries*, ed. Siegfried Jäkel and Asko Timonen (Turko: Turun Yliopisto, 1997).

33. A similar distancing strategy is at work in Aspasia's speech in the *Menexenus*. See Christopher P. Long, "Dancing Naked with Socrates: Pericles, Aspasia and Socrates at Play with Politics, Rhetoric and Philosophy," *Ancient Philosophy* 23 (2003): 49–69.

34. See Sallis, *Being and Logos*, 356.

35. For a discussion of just how radical these purges are, see Bernard Freydberg, *The Play of the Platonic Dialogues*, Literature and the Sciences of Man 12 (New York: Peter Lang, 1997), 86ff.

36. Glaucon is characterized as erotic at 474d, as musical at 398e. The link between music and eros is established at 403c. For a good discussion of the importance of Glaucon's erotic nature, see Sallis, *Being and Logos*, 400–401. See also Jacob Howland, *The Republic: The Odyssey of Philosophy* (New York: Twayne, 1993), 102.

37. Brann writes: "The philosopher's city is coming into being while Socrates and Glaucon converse—*the primary political act is the 'conversion' to a philosophical education of one youth by one man*." See Eva Brann, "The Music of the Republic," *Agon* 1 (1967): 24. Sallis seems to draw on Brann's interpretation in his own reading of the *Republic*. See Sallis, *Being and Logos*, 312–455.

9

Traveling with Socrates: Dialectic in the *Phaedo* and *Protagoras*

Gerard Kuperus

In this essay, I argue that Socratic or Platonic[1] dialectic is not a method that follows rigid structures as is suggested by, for example, the model of the elenchus.[2] Although the Greek word μέθοδος (*meta hodos*) refers to the established or public road (*hodos*), a road that is already there, I argue that unlike this traditional *methodos*, Platonic dialectic is a method that is open; it does not develop through a specific plan. There is not a blueprint or a standard formula that is used by either Socrates or Plato. Encountering a dialogue therefore requires flexibility of the interlocutors, and most of all of the reader. In the following, I discuss the *Phaedo* and the *Protagoras*, two dialogues that do not follow the model of the elenchus. The method of the *Protagoras* might appear as a variation of the elenchus, but is in fact a radically different model: Socrates and Protagoras exchange positions. Their discussion evolves around the question of which method to use in that very discussion. As I will argue, the exchange of positions that takes place during this dialogue is related to the change in method: the sophistic method of monologues and a method that involves dialogue, respectively. The other main dialogue discussed in this essay is the *Phaedo,* in which—if we want to use this term—a complete reversal of the model of the elenchus is at work. For, it is not Socrates who proves that his interlocutors' definition of *x* is false; the interlocutors themselves show the limitations of their own theory.

Instead of using the model of the elenchus, I will provide an alternative terminology with which dialectic can be described as what I call an "open" method. More precisely, the Platonic corpus itself offers us such an alternative terminology in metaphors that refer to labyrinths and navigation, metaphors that in the *Phaedo* and the *Protagoras*—as I will argue—symbolize the Platonic method.[3] Both *navigators* and philosophers deal with "things" that are not ready to hand (navigators with stars, the wind, and the days of the year, the philosopher with the ideal forms), and both are dealing with these eternal truths within a world that is characterized by change or flux. In relating philosophy and navigation, the guiding question will be: What exactly is the similarity between navigating through the sea and navigating through a dialogue? The metaphor of the *labyrinth* refers to difficulties in finding a way.[4] The labyrinth appears implicitly in the *Phaedo* in a reference to the myth of Theseus and the Minotaur. As I argue, the labyrinth is a symbol for philosophical issues discussed in the dialogue. The architectural structure of the labyrinth is (re)constructed by different arguments and gestures made by the participants of the dialogue, as well as by the narrative structure. We, as readers of the Platonic dialogue, enter this labyrinth of ways and non-ways, through which we somehow have to find our way. In discussing this second metaphor I will provide a brief account of some of the arguments of the *Phaedo*, focusing upon the methodological proceedings. As I will argue, the construction and reconstruction (through the reader) of a dialogue is similar to building a labyrinth. Likewise, finding a way through the arguments of a dialogue is comparable to finding a way through a labyrinth.

Finding a Method: From Sophistry to Socratic Dialectic in the *Protagoras*

The *Protagoras* is one of the few Socratic dialogues dealing explicitly with method. Socrates' discussion with the sophist Protagoras leads us, in the middle of the dialogue, into a crisis about which method is going to be used. Although this is the pinnacle of the discussion, the issue of method is already foreshadowed from the very beginning of the dialogue. Prior to the meeting with Protagoras, Socrates warns Hippocrates, who wants to take classes with the famous sophist, against the dangers of sophistry and asks Hippocrates his famous "what" question: "About *what* does the sophist make one a clever speaker?"[5] This is a question Hippocrates cannot answer, and with which Socrates points to the heart of the problem: the sophist is not concerned with any issue in particular, but simply makes one a clever speaker. His technique or method, "the *how*" of his teachings, is not different from *what* he teaches. The sophist is simply a persuader, a technician without a field of expertise. Accordingly, someone who is being taught by a sophist becomes a clever speaker who can persuade others.

After Hippocrates and Socrates have met Protagoras, one of the first things Protagoras tells them is that he himself does "not conform to the method" many other sophists make use of.[6] Others often "disguise" their art (τέχνη) by making use of other arts—such as poetry, mystic rites, music, or even athletics—as outer coverings. Protagoras does not cover the art of sophistry, since "the multitude, of course, perceive practically nothing, but merely echo this or that pronouncement of their leader."[7] The great sophist is concerned here with the fact that most people simply repeat what their teacher tells them, without perceiving the art or technique (techne) that was used to get to such a pronouncement. To cover up the art of sophistry with other technai involves the danger of making this process even harder to perceive. Protagoras, instead, wants to make the method as transparent as possible. This "open method" is a civic science (πολιτικήν τέχνην) with which he teaches virtue, or assists others in order to become good.[8]

Socrates, on the other hand, does not think that it is possible to teach others to become good, and thus Protagoras has to defend his techne. He does so by giving a couple of long discourses, which—in the middle of the dialogue—makes Socrates say: "If someone addresses me at length I forget the subject on which he is talking."[9] This remark about Socrates' bad memory is the beginning of a discussion on which method to use. Socrates questions Protagoras' description of his "open method"—his art without outer coverings. Socrates implicitly claims that Protagoras' sophistry is not transparent at all, since his speeches are so long that his audience simply forgets what he is even talking about. Protagoras replies by stating that if he would "argue simply in the way my opponent demanded, I should not be held superior to anyone nor would Protagoras have made a name among the Greeks."[10] The two face a real crisis here, in which Socrates even attempts to leave the scene. The intervention of Callias, Alcibiades, Critias, Prodicus, and Hippias is needed to keep Socrates and Protagoras in dialogue, or rather to get them into a true Socratic dialogue. Alcibiades states the dilemma and the solution as follows: "If Protagoras confesses himself inferior to Socrates in argumentation [διαλεχθῆναι], Socrates has no more to ask: but if he challenges him, let him discuss [διαλεγέστω] by question and answer; not spinning out a lecture on each question—beating off the arguments, refusing to give a reason, and so dilating until most of his hearers have forgotten the point at issue."[11] Protagoras is here characterized as the person who gives long speeches and Socrates as the person who is good in argumentation. The transition to the Socratic method is then a transition to dialectic, or dialogue, a transition to question and answer.

The dialectical method is enforced in the second half of the dialogue in a discussion of "being" and "becoming." In interpreting a poem of Simonides, one of Socrates' claims is that "to become good, indeed, is hard, though possible, but to be good is impossible."[12] One cannot simply be good, but one actually has to do things in order to become good. Virtue can only be pursued or taught through praxis. This praxis seems, for Socrates, first of all, to be actively involved in a dialogue. Virtue cannot be learned by simply listening to someone else; one needs to develop one's own knowledge by actively participating in a dialogue. Virtue thus cannot be taught by Protagoras' *technē*—in which one listens to long monologues—but if it is teachable, then it can be taught by way of dialectic. I will further develop this distinction between *technē* and dialectic in the discussion of the *Republic* below.

The discussion about being and becoming eventually leads to a reversal of the positions of Protagoras and Socrates: at the end of the dialogue, Socrates believes that virtue can be taught, while Protagoras doubts this. This reversal of positions can be explained as follows: Socrates does not think that virtue can be taught if Protagoras' method is used. If virtue can be taught, it is only possible by way of dialectic, that is, by a process of becoming. Protagoras, on the other hand, seems to be convinced by Socrates that virtue cannot by taught by his method, that is, by sophistry, but he does not want to commit himself to dialectic. This reversal of positions has, in a sense, been anticipated by Socrates at the beginning of their discussion when he stated that "even you [Protagoras], though so old and so wise, would be made better if someone taught you what you happen not to know."[13] Socrates here already emphasizes the theme of becoming. Protagoras *can* be made better, he can become better, and at the end of the dialogue *is* made better by Socrates, who showed him something he did not happen to know, namely that virtue cannot be taught, at least not with the sophistic method.

Since Socrates and Protagoras have reversed positions, they both have appropriated the position of the other, and in doing so their positions are still opposed to one another. This makes Socrates say: "What strange [ἄτοποί] creatures you are, Socrates and Protagoras."[14] This strangeness, this not being designated to a particular place (*atopos*), emerges at the end of the dialogue, but it is precisely what makes the dialogue possible in the first place. If the interlocutors are not willing to change their positions, a process or development is impossible. The interlocutors have to be willing to relocate themselves, to change topos, in order to make a dialogue possible. Openness to other positions, which we could call strangeness, can be considered as a condition for the possibility of Socratic dialectic.

Navigation: How to Distinguish
Ways from Non-Ways

After the interlocutors in the *Protagoras* have decided to use the Socratic method—a crucial point in the dialogue—an important image comes to the fore when Hippias, who is also a sophist, advises Socrates and Protagoras, and says to Protagoras that he must not "let out full sail, as you run before the breeze, and so escape into the ocean of speech leaving the land nowhere in sight."[15] Protagoras should shorten his speeches so that his listeners do not get lost in his ocean of speech. Protagoras' "escape into the ocean" is again an indication that his method is not open or transparent. The listeners lose sight of land, the starting point of the discussion, and get lost in the ocean, the long speech. This image of philosophy as a voyage through the sea is one of the many references to the sea and navigation within the Platonic corpus. This might appear to be insignificant in the works of someone who lived close to the sea, but its occurrence at this point in the dialogue is striking: Plato here makes a reference to sailing and the possibility of being lost in the ocean of speech at a decisive point in the dialogue where the way how to proceed is decided. Is there a similarity between sailing a ship through the sea and making one's way through a dialogue? Is doing dialectic an art of navigation? In the following I will discuss this metaphor in more detail by looking into some other remarkable uses of the imagery of sailing and navigation within the Platonic corpus.

In book 6 of the *Republic* we do find one of the most concrete references to navigation[16] when Socrates likens the government of a city to that of a ship.[17] This "allegory of the ship"—as I will call it—describes the situation of the captain of a ship who does not have a decent knowledge of navigation to begin with. When a sailor persuades the captain to turn over the helm to him, the situation on the ship becomes even worse, since the sailors do not know "that for the true pilot it is necessary to pay careful attention to year, seasons, heaven, stars, winds and everything that's proper to the art."[18] Additionally, the sailors do not consider navigation to be something learnable. Instead, they consider that person most knowledgeable who is able to persuade the captain to turn over the helm, and thus gain control of the ship. From this perspective the true pilot—the one who actually pays careful attention to the year, seasons, heaven, stars, and winds—is thought to be a mere stargazer.

This allegory symbolizes how people in the city think about philosophers: similar to navigators, philosophers deal with intangible objects.

Their methods of navigating—through life or through the sea—raise suspicion precisely because both are dealing with intangible objects. On the ship, as well as in the city, it is considered more important to persuade others than to look behind the immediate world of experience. The sailor who is good at persuading others represents the sophist who can teach how to persuade others, but cannot teach how to become good citizens, or how to navigate through the problems of life. The navigator, on the other hand, is looking at that which is eternal in order to determine the right course of the ship in situations that are always different. Similarly, the philosopher observes "that which is eternal and not wandering between the two poles of generation and decay."[19] Philosophers are "those who are capable of apprehending [ἐφάπτεσθαι] that which is eternal and unchanging."[20] As the apprehension of the position of the stars has a practical application for the navigator, the apprehension of the ideal realities does, for Socrates, have a practical application since it allows one to establish "the laws of the beautiful, the just and the good."[21] The knowledge of the forms (eidē) can guide us in determining the right course in a life in which everything is constantly changing.[22]

However, the application of this knowledge is something different than dialectic, that is, the process by which one can gain this knowledge. Knowledge of *the things that are* cannot be gained through leaving hypotheses untouched, but one needs to be able to give an account of them.[23] The dialectical "process of inquiry" destroys or does away with hypotheses "up to the first principle itself in order to find confirmation there."[24] We could say, then, that dialectic and navigation do have in common that they both deal with intangible, eternal things within a world that is in constant flux. However, the navigator already has knowledge of these intangible things and applies this knowledge when he determines the best course for the ship. The philosopher, on the other hand, still has to gain knowledge of the forms. Dialectic is a way by which we can gain such knowledge, that is, proceed to the first principles. In the *Protagoras* we found a distinction between the sophistic *technē* and (philosophical) dialectic. In the *Republic*, it becomes clear that dialectic is not completely separated from *technai*, which "can be described as assistants and helpers in the turning around of others."[25] The process of dialectic, therefore, can make use of *technai*, but is itself not a *technē*. Since it is a destruction of hypotheses and a search for the truth, it can be described as a journey of which the path is to be determined as we go along, here expressed with the image of navigation.

In the *Protagoras* we found the metaphor of sailing at a crucial point in the dialogue, when the method with which to proceed was being determined. This metaphor is also used in the *Phaedo* when Socrates narrates his educational "autobiography," and turns to his famous "second sailing."[26] In the prelude to this journey Simmias introduces the idea of finding the strongest vessel, that is, *logos,* to travel with. This idea appears in the context of the discussion of the immortality of the soul. Simmias admits that it is "either impossible or very difficult to acquire clear knowledge about these matters in this life."[27] What we can do instead, when we cannot find the truth—in this case the truth concerning the immortality of the soul—is to find the human *logos* that is "best and hardest to disprove."[28] One has to embark upon this *logos* "as upon a raft, sail upon it through life in the midst of dangers, unless he can sail upon a stronger vessel, some divine revelation [λόγου θείου], and make his voyage more safely and securely."[29] Sarah Kofman discusses the crossing of a sea as a path that has to be found each time as if for the first time: "The sea is the endless realm of pure movement, the most mobile, changeable and polymorphous of all spaces, a space where any way that has been traced is immediately obliterated, which transforms any journey into a voyage of exploration which is always unprecedented, dangerous and uncertain."[30] It is this unprecedented, dangerous, and uncertain voyage we are making with Socrates in the *Phaedo.* In Socrates' characterization of this voyage he reiterates Simmias' idea of finding the best possible *logos:* "I put down as hypothesis whatever account [λόγον] I judge to be mightiest."[31] One could say then that the best possible or the mightiest *logos* has to serve as a vessel with which we can travel through the sea, that "mobile, changeable and polymorphous" space in which each way is immediately erased. There is not one way to go through the dialogue or the sea; there is, rather, a manifold of possibilities. These ways are not established, but are rather ways that still have to be found, or even still need to be created. This idea of a plurality of possible ways and the creation of these ways is emphasized in Socrates' "autobiography" (96a–102a) that leads into the second sailing.[32] Just like Protagoras, Socrates now tells us that he does not use the method of others. Instead, he has "randomly smushed together [εἰκῇ φύρω] another way [τρόπον]."[33] This way is then introduced as the "second sailing," a nautical term referring to the use of oars due to a lack of wind. The wind, possibly a metaphor for a divine truth, is failing for Socrates, and he has randomly smushed together another method while crossing through the sea. The strongest vessel he can find to make this voyage is the theory of the forms. The journey itself, that is, the dialogue, can make this vessel even stronger.

GERARD KUPERUS

The Dialectical Labyrinth: From
Pythagorean Opposites to Socratic *Logos*

In the last part of this paper I discuss the dialogue, or voyage, in more
detail by focusing on another metaphor, namely the labyrinth. This image is evoked in the beginning of the dialogue when Phaedo starts his
narration of the circumstances surrounding Socrates' death, by mentioning "a vow" the Athenians made to Apollo "to send a mission every
year to Delos" if the fourteen youths and maidens were saved.[34] Phaedo
refers here to the myth of "Theseus and the Minotaur," according to
which the Minotaur (the bull of Minos, a creature half man, half bull)
is the result of the greed and selfishness of King Minos of Crete. When
he did not sacrifice the most beautiful bull of his herd to the gods, as he
should have done, the gods took revenge by letting his wife, Pasiphae,
fall in love with the bull, and after she mated with the bull, the Minotaur was conceived. Minos asked Daedalus (who first helped Pasiphae
to trick the bull, in order to mate with it) to build a labyrinth in which
the beast could be kept. To keep the Minotaur satisfied, Minos ordered
the city-states that were occupied by the Cretans to sacrifice every year
a particular number of young people to the beast. The Athenians were
asked to sacrifice fourteen youths and maidens every year. Fortunately,
Theseus appeared at the right time, and traveled with the fourteen to
Crete. Once there, Ariadne, the daughter of Minos, fell in love with
Theseus and told him how to get out of the labyrinth (according to some
accounts of this myth, she told him to use a thread). With her advice, he
manages, after killing the Minotaur, to find the way out of the labyrinth
and to save the fourteen youths as well as himself.[35]

Since Theseus had saved the fourteen, the Athenians sent a mission to Delos every year, as Phaedo tells us. This mission happened to
have started on the day before Socrates' trial. Since the city had to keep
itself pure, and could not execute anyone during the trip of the ship to
Delos and back, and since this trip sometimes takes a long time "when
contrary winds detain it . . . Socrates passed a long time in prison between his trial and his death."[36] Here, right at the outset of the dialogue,
is thus another reference to traveling by boat, and the difficulties such a
journey can involve, such as contrary winds.

After referring to the myth, Phaedo introduces us to fourteen of
Socrates' friends who are present in the prison. This number of friends—
the twice seven (*dis hepta*), as Phaedo says[37]—is another reference to the
myth in which fourteen youths and maidens are saved by Theseus.[38] If we
were to map the myth upon the *Phaedo,* we could interpret the fourteen
friends as being saved by Socrates, while Ariadne symbolizes Phaedo,

who gives us a thread in the form of the discourse, as a sort of "father of our debate [πατὴρ τοῦ λόγου]."[39] Such an interpretation would become immediately problematic when we try to imagine Socrates as being a Theseus, the hero who kills the Minotaur. Theseus kills a symptom or symbol of greed and selfishness, while Socrates attempts to hunt down the real causes of such a symptom.[40] Instead of interpreting the *Phaedo* as a philosophical copy of the myth, I will focus here on the image of the labyrinth as a metaphor for the dialectical structure.[41]

The first actual argument in the discussion of the immortality of the soul—or the first way in the labyrinth of discourse—is the argument that opposites generate one another. This argument, given by Socrates, is in fact a Pythagorean (or Ionic) conception of nature, and for that reason it is strongly supported by Simmias and Cebes, the two main interlocutors in the *Phaedo,* who are both loyal to the Pythagorean theories. Socrates argues here as follows: if something becomes smaller it must have been greater, otherwise it could not become smaller.[42] A similar movement between opposites can be found in sleeping and waking, since waking up is a transition from sleeping to being awake.[43] Again, something similar must be at work in the process of dying and being born. Dying is merely a transition from one state to the other, and birth is the return to the other state: being alive. Everything has to take part in this circular movement between contraries, for if there was a movement in only one direction, that is, a generation "forward in a straight line without turning back or curving, then . . . in the end all things would have the same form."[44] Everything that lives would die, and if life did not generate from the dead, but from the living, everything in the end would die.[45] Assuming that everything living can die, the source of life cannot be something living, otherwise it could die as well, and without this source everything would end up dead. The source of life, therefore, has to be something dead.

Although this theory is interesting, it is questionable how it can contribute to a discussion about the immortality of the soul. Why does Socrates bring up this "physics of circularity"? As Gadamer writes: "What is striking about the proof is that it is obviously unsuited to prove the point which it is supposed to prove."[46] How can this argument prove that there is something immortal, something continuous that remains somehow the same in this cycle? For it is Socrates' claim that the soul does not *perish* when the body dies, but even *flourishes* when it departs from the body.

To answer this question we will need to understand the structure of the arguments of the *Phaedo,* which I will lay out in the following, starting with the anamnesis theory. This theory is discussed after the initial argument of the circular movement between opposites. It is strik-ing that this anamnesis theory is not introduced by Socrates, who is—as we are reminded here in the *Phaedo*—"fond of saying, that our learning is nothing else than recollection."[47] Instead, anamnesis is brought into the discourse by Cebes. It is important to note that first Socrates makes a Pythagorean argument, and then Cebes, a Pythagorean, introduces a Socratic argument. We could then suggest that it is Socrates' strate-gic plan, or method, to introduce the theory of opposites not because he agrees with it, but to entice his interlocutors into the dialogue, and more importantly to let them introduce the arguments that will eventu-ally dismiss the theory of contraries. We could describe Socrates here thus again as strange or out of place (*atopos*). With this strange position in which he takes up the Pythagorean doctrine he can, as an infiltrator, attack the theory from the inside, or rather let his interlocutors attack the theory. In this way Socrates himself does not argue against their theory, but he will force his opponents to question and eventually dis-miss their own metaphysical understanding of reality. Socrates in this way sets up a labyrinth through which his interlocutors—as well as he himself—have to find a way, which often involves taking some steps back and making a redirection.

The first redirection is given by the theory of anamnesis, brought up by the Pythagorean Cebes. It is eventually Socrates himself who ex-plains this theory in more detail, by discussing first of all the example of equality. He argues here that we can recognize that two things are equal to one another because we know equality itself, or "equality in the abstract."[48] We have not learned this abstraction from the sensible objects, since they all fall short of equality itself. "It appears that we must have acquired it [equality] before we were born."[49] The soul acquired these ideas or forms in the purest existence of the soul, that is, in its existence without the disturbances of the body. The use of these forms, such as in the recognition of the equality of two things, is a recollection, an anamnesis, of this knowledge.

Socrates' example of the equal itself (αὐτο τὸ ἴσον) might be con-sidered odd here, since equality is a comparison of two different things, and therefore seems to imply a relativity.[50] The good, the beautiful, or the circle itself appear to be purer examples of these ideal forms. The example of equality has, however, another function here. It is a hint by Socrates or Plato that points us to the fact that the dialogue has made a turn. We have left the path we were on with the theory of opposites; the interlocutors have turned into an alternative way in the labyrinth. Instead of a change between opposites, we are now looking for some-thing that remains the same (*isos*), something that does not perish, and so escapes the physics of circularity. The dialogue is thus making a move from the opposites to something equal, a move from the Pythagorean discourse to the Socratic-Platonic *logos*. Socrates has opened the door to the two Pythagoreans by letting them hear what they wanted to hear. This door is now slowly dismissed by the Pythagoreans themselves. In doing so they assist Socrates in creating the maze of arguments and counterarguments. Once in this labyrinth, there is no way back, that is, the entrance through which one came does not provide an exit. Socrates has dragged them (and us) into the labyrinth, from which no escape is possible.

Yet Socrates wants to drag Simmias and Cebes even further into the labyrinth. After Simmias and Cebes suggest that it is only proven that our soul existed before birth (with the anamnesis theory), and not that it will also exist after we die, Socrates provokes the two by stating: "It has been shown, Simmias and Cebes, already . . . if you will combine this conclusion with the one we reached before, that every living being is born from the dead."[51] Socrates, of course, knows that the immortality of the soul is not proven by combining the anamnesis theory with the theory of contraries, but wants to hear from his interlocutors what is lacking in their own theory—the theory of opposites. The only true Socratic method to accomplish this is by ironically stating that the answer already has been given.

The final move of this strategy is made with Socrates' silence after he has presented his arguments on visibility and invisibility: "Socrates himself was *apparently* [ἐφαίνετο] absorbed in what had been said."[52] Socrates' apparent absorption can be read as an invitation to Cebes and Simmias—a didactic trick—to again let *them* ask the questions. Socrates will apparently have to defend himself, but in fact remains the master. He guides the others by letting them interrogate him, which is in fact an interrogation of their own ideas. The Pythagoreans thus interrogate the Pythagorean theories; a self-reflection through the medium Socrates. This idea is emphasized another time after Socrates' silence, during which Simmias and Cebes start to talk to one another. Socrates seizes his way to complete his strategic move, and asks them whether there is any incompleteness in what has been said. He adds:

> If you are perplexed [ἀπορεῖτον] about all this, do not hesitate to speak up yourselves and go through it if it appears to you that it could have been said better. And what is more, do not hesitate to take me along with you [συμπαραλαβεῖν] if you think you will fare better [εὐπορήσειν] in my company.[53]

Important here are the words *aporos* and *euporos*, the first being a negation of *poros*, the second being a confirmation (in the sense of good or well) of *poros*. *Poros* is a way through or over, a passage, but also a re-source. *Poros* is opposed to *hodos*, a (public) road that is clearly laid out. A *poros* is, instead, a way that has to be found. An aporia is the impos-sibility of finding this way, or a non-way in the labyrinth, here translated as "being perplexed." Since *poros* also means wealth or resource, we can also understand aporia as a lack of resources. *Euporos* can then be trans-lated as having good or better resources, or being better able to find a way. What is suggested here is, first of all, that the way is still to be found or even has to be created (no *hodos* is available). I will return to this sug-gestion in the conclusion. Second, this passage suggests that together with Socrates, his two interlocutors will be more resourceful in their attempt to find a way. In other dialogues Socrates is often presented as a resource without resources. He is the philosopher who is wise because he knows he does not know. This lack of resources is precisely his re-sourcefulness, because this forces his interlocutors—who mostly *think* they know—into a dialogue. Here in the *Phaedo* his method is different: he presents a theory that is proving the opposite of what it is supposed to prove, but by doing this he makes the others more resourceful, makes it possible for them to find ways. Socrates thus lacks resources, but in a different way than by simply not knowing—as is the case in many other dialogues—since he at least provides us with a theory, suggesting that he knows something.[54] Even while he is being questioned himself, Socrates is nevertheless the guide in the philosophical labyrinth, since he is—as described above—enticing the others in questioning their own theory; Socrates thus leads the others through the dialectical process.

After Simmias compares the soul to the tuning of the lyre, Cebes compares the soul to a weaver who can wear out many cloaks but who will eventually die himself as well. Cebes' argument is referring precisely to the lack of continuity that is provided by the theory of opposites: it only provides a continuous movement, without the possibility of stability in this flux. Cebes therefore rightly suggests that the soul might last longer than the body—as the weaver lasts longer than his cloaks—but at some point the soul might perish as well. It is interesting that Cebes' coun-terargument, as opposed to the easily dismissed argument of Simmias, is never referred to as an aporia. This might indicate that Cebes' argu-ment is in fact not an aporia precisely because it provides a new way, and shows us that in fact the idea of a circular physics was not the right way; it blocked the way, or was a dead end. The weaver argument problematizes the theory of opposites and, as such, is not a blockage, not an aporia. Instead, the theory of opposites is now considered to be an aporia while the new theory provides new ways, opens up new possibilities. This new voyage is Socrates' "second sailing," which is first of all Socrates' own attempt to find "the cause of generation and decay" after Anaxagoras and others disappointed him. Second, it is a new way within the dialogue to prove the immortality of the soul, after Cebes has shown that the first attempt (the theory of opposites) did not lead us anywhere but was—so to speak—a roadblock. Third, as discussed above, the ideal realm of forms—Socrates' own sailing—is the best possible *logos* for Socrates. Approximating the divine truth, it is the most secure and safest vessel to cross the sea, or the best way one can find through the labyrinth.

The development of the above-described arguments shows that the labyrinth of ways and non-ways is in a constant flux: ways turn out to be non-ways; non-ways can become ways. The flux of the dialogue can be intimidating. As discussed in the *Republic*, the *Protagoras*, and the *Phaedo*, many people develop a fear of dialectic. This is a fear of falling into a labyrinth like Tartarus, described at the end of the *Phaedo*.[55] Tartarus is a labyrinth in which no progress is possible; no distinction can be made between better and worse ways, since every way will lead back to the same point. This is the fear that one can have of philosophy: the fear of not being able to get anywhere; the fear of not getting out, or the fear of not finding anything stable, but only a flux in which navigation is impossible.

Socrates addressed this problem earlier in the *Phaedo* after Simmias and Cebes gave their arguments and everyone—including Echecrates, to whom Phaedo narrates the last day of Socrates' life—seemed to be at a loss about the direction that they now had to take. They first thought Socrates' arguments were sound and stable, but now Simmias' and Cebes' arguments, which dismiss the earlier arguments, are very convincing as well. Echecrates phrases the fear of a flux in which nothing is stable by asking, "What argument shall we believe henceforth?"[56] Before discussing Simmias' and Cebes' arguments, Socrates first—as if he hears Echecrates' question in the frame dialogue—discusses with Phaedo the possibility of misology, hatred of arguments. Socrates wants to prevent us from thinking that "there is nothing sound and sure in anything, whether argument or anything else, but all things go up and down, like the tide in the Euripus, and nothing is stable for any length of time."[57] In a dialogue such as the *Phaedo* we encounter many conflicting arguments, and consequently we could easily become either relativists or postmodernists, or—as Socrates fears—misologists, for whom there is no possibility of a *logos* that is "true and sure and can be learned."[58] What we are left with then is dialectic itself, in which one does not argue in the way "quite uncultured persons" do, who "do not care what the truth is in the matters they are discussing, but are eager only to make their own views seem true to their hearers."[59] Instead of this persuasion of others, the true dialectician wants to convince himself. Yet precisely this "selfish attitude"—as Socrates calls it—requires a partner with whom to talk things through. In order to find one's way one needs company. Socrates himself is the ultimate example of this "need for company." It is true that Socrates is a guide who leads the others into and somehow through the labyrinth, and as this guide he is resourceful for others, but in order to be this guide Socrates too needs company; he needs dialogue. He can only be resourceful in the company of others; he can only find his way by way of a dialogue.

Conclusion: The Dialectical Voyage

The need for dialectic is emphasized in the *Protagoras,* when Socrates cites Homer: "When two go together, one observes before the other; [*Iliad* 10.224] for somehow it makes all of us human beings more resourceful [εὐπορώτεροι] in every deed or word or thought."[60] This "going together" that makes us more resourceful is in the *Protagoras* an opposition of positions of the interlocutors that leads to a reversal of their positions. Protagoras is made "better"—he becomes more resourceful—by learning from Socrates that virtue cannot be taught by way of long monologues. In the *Phaedo* the interlocutors "go together" since Socrates takes up the theory of his opponents. In this way Cebes is able to dismiss his own metaphysical ideas through an ingenious dialectic in which he revalues his own values. The Pythagorean theory of opposites is an aporia, is therefore dismissed, but is at the same time at work within the dialogue as a non-way that provides a way precisely in being a non-way. In a sense, we could say, the Socratic-Platonic dialogue is the embodiment of the physics of circularity, discussed in the theory of opposites. Although dialectic—like navigation—looks at a world beyond the physical movement between opposites, dialectic itself does belong to the world of flux. The reversal of positions in the *Protagoras,* and, in the *Phaedo,* the presentation of the theory of opposites, which in the end is not supported by any of the interlocutors, are precisely examples of this flux or circular movement. Through dialectic—a philosophical navigation—a way can be found through the movement of ways and non-ways that one (either as a reader or as an interlocutor) encounters in a dialogue.

The image of the labyrinth shows us that to run into an aporia is not only a running into a blind alley, but is rather a redirection indicating a detour, or to start all over again. In this way poverty—the poverty of an argument—becomes resourcefulness. Similar to *poros,* in the myth told by Diotima in the *Symposium,* who can only be resourceful in the company of *penia,* Socrates can only be resourceful in the company of poor arguments that do not prove what they are supposed to prove. In the *Phaedo* he provides poor arguments, and by doing so he makes his interlocutors much more resourceful than they could ever have been without his company. Socrates' poverty is his resourcefulness. This ambiguous resourcefulness, though, works only in the company of others; he is in need of a partner.[61] Dialectic is a *logos* in which one can change positions in an attempt to find a way through the labyrinth. As a philosophical navigator the dialectician establishes, or smushes together, a way as he goes along. The labyrinth through which one tries to find a way is thus itself established in the process of doing dialectic. By way of questioning the different theories, hypotheses will be destroyed in order to make progress. In finding and constructing a path, the dialectician constructs the labyrinth, and in doing so he or she gazes at intangible things in order to determine a course that will hopefully lead in the right direction. What we learn from Socrates is *not* primarily some *logos,* some theory, account, or doctrine. We rather learn the method to get to such an answer, that is, dialectic, the process of finding ways (*poroi*), finding non-ways (aporias), and finding new ways through a labyrinth.

This paper started with the presumption that there is such a thing as a Platonic or Socratic method. Here at the conclusion of this paper, the question should be answered whether dialectic indeed is a method, and what sort of method this is. What exactly have the metaphors of sailing and navigation told us about Plato's method, besides that the dialectical process could be described as a journey? First of all, we have seen that, specifically in the *Phaedo* and *Protagoras,* Plato lets Socrates entice his interlocutors in the dialogue. The dialogue is a labyrinth in which the interlocutors and the readers of the text become entangled. Plato lures his readers by presenting several conflicting theories and arguments. These conflicts (and the urge to resolve them) draw the reader into the dialectical process.

Second, I have discussed how that dialectical process is analogous to navigation. Philosophizing by way of dialectic is not a standard procedure that can be learned and applied. It is, rather, a method that is always different, depending upon the circumstances. The ocean of speech is constantly changing, and as the navigator adapts to the movement of the stars, the seas, and the winds, so should the philosopher adapt to the movement of the arguments.

The way in which the philosopher finds "truth" has been shown to be not an established path or road, not a *hodos.* The dialogue lays out a journey as a *poros,* a path that has to be created while it is being taken, an endeavor closely resembling sailing through the ocean, which is never the same. As a metaphor for dialectic, navigation tells us that dialectic is applied differently each time it is used.

Can dialectic then be called a *meta ta hodos*, or *methodos*? For if there is a lack of a standard way (*hodos*), dialectic is never a standardized journey. Dialectic as navigation is a finding of the way, either through a sea that is constantly changing, or through a labyrinth in which a way or resource (*poros*) can become a non-way (aporia) and vice versa. Human beings can approximate the truth by trying to find the best possible vessel to cross the sea, and this vessel is, for Plato, dialectic. Dialectic is both the development of this vessel and this very vessel itself. The metaphor of the labyrinth similarly has illustrated that the unfolding of the dialogue itself is the construction of a multiplicity of ways and non-ways. It is thus my claim that the development or construction of the dialogue lacks a standard method. Method is not preestablished, but the result of dialectic, the dialogue itself, can once it is established be called a method, that is, a thinking through of different positions either with a real or an imaginary partner.

Notes

1. This essay reexamines the question of Socratic-Platonic dialectic by taking into account the dramatic and literary context of the dialectic at work in the *Protagoras* and *Phaedo*. Hence, this paper discusses Socratic-Platonic dialectic.

2. The elenchus is often used in describing the Socratic dialectical method. This model in its simple form can be sketched as follows: Socrates lets one of his interlocutors pose a definition of *x*, after which Socrates will interrogate the interlocutor up to the point where the latter has to admit that his definition was, indeed, wrong and that he does not know what *x* is. This model of the elenchus can indeed be found in some dialogues—I think especially in the "early" dialogues. Discussions of this model are often focused upon the outcome of the elenchus: scholars such as Gregory Vlastos argue that the outcome is positive, that is, there is an actual result (see, for example, Vlastos's article "The Socratic Elenchus: Method Is All," in *Socratic Studies*, ed. Myles Burnyeat [Cambridge: Cambridge University Press, 1994], 1–36). Others argue that there is no positive outcome possible, and that only a deprivation of knowledge can be acknowledged (see, for example, Richard Robinson's *Plato's Earlier Dialectic* [Oxford: Clarendon, 1953]). For an elaborate discussion of these positions, see Francisco Gonzalez, *Dialectic and Dialogue: Plato's Practice of Philosophical Inquiry* (Evanston: Northwestern University Press, 1998), 1–16.

3. Metaphors referring to sailing and navigation are used throughout the Platonic corpus. It lies beyond the scope of this paper to discuss all these refer-

ences, although I have attempted to include all sailing and navigation metaphors that refer to method.

4. The term "way" is—I would say—one of the crucial terms in John Sallis, *Being and Logos: Reading the Platonic Dialogues*, 3rd ed. (Bloomington: Indiana University Press, 1996). Sallis's "way" leads out of the city and back into it, up and down. Although the "way" I describe is not first of all one of *logos* or—to or from—"being," it can indeed be characterized by such a double directionality in the sense that the ways of philosophizing are never stable and can even change from ways into non-ways.

5. Plato, *Protagoras*, in *Plato II: Laches, Protagoras, Meno, Euthydemus*, trans. W. R. M. Lamb, Loeb Classical Library (Cambridge: Harvard University Press, 1977), 312e (my emphasis).

6. *Protagoras*, 317a.

7. *Protagoras*, 317a.

8. *Protagoras*, 319a.

9. *Protagoras*, 334d.

10. *Protagoras*, 335a. This reference to Protagoras' reputation hints at one of the problems the two are struggling with in the entire dialogue: Who is giving the class, or leading the discussion, Protagoras or Socrates? So far, obviously, Protagoras has been the teacher, since he gives long monologues. A transformation to the Socratic method is therefore a serious threat to Protagoras, who might lose control over the discussion, which again might hurt his reputation.

11. *Protagoras*, 336c–d.

12. *Protagoras*, 344e.

13. *Protagoras*, 318b.

14. *Protagoras*, 361a.

15. *Protagoras*, 338a.

16. Unfortunately, we do not know exactly what the Greeks knew about navigation. In Homer's *Odyssey* the ships seem to be navigated more by the gods than anything else. However, we have to take into consideration that the stars and the winds are not necessarily differentiated from the gods. In the *Nicomachean Ethics*, Aristotle characterizes navigation, along with ethics and medicine, as an art that does not have "exact precision" and in which "the agents themselves have to consider what is suited to the circumstances on each occasion" (2.2.4). The passage from the *Republic* that I discuss here gives us a more concrete indication about how they actually navigated.

17. Plato, *Republic*, in *The Republic of Plato*, 2nd ed., trans. Allan Bloom (New York: Basic Books, 1991), 488b–489a.

18. *Republic*, 488d.

19. *Republic*, 485b.

20. *Republic*, 484b.

21. *Republic*, 484d.

22. Although this is speculative, we could assume that the metaphor of sailing through the sea refers to Heraclitus' idea of flux.

23. *Republic*, 533c.

24. *Republic*, 533c.

25. *Republic*, 533d.

26. Plato, *Phaedo*, in *Plato I: Euthyphro, Apology, Crito, Phaedo, Phaedrus*, trans. H. N. Fowler, Loeb Classical Library (Cambridge: Harvard University Press, 1971), 99d.

27. *Phaedo*, 85c.

28. *Phaedo*, 85c.

29. *Phaedo*, 85d.

30. Sarah Kofman, "Beyond Aporia?" in *Post-Structuralist Classics*, ed. Andrew Benjamin (New York: Routledge, 1988), 10. Originally published in French as *Comment s'en sortir?* (Paris: Éditions Galilée, 1983).

31. Plato, *Phaedo*, in *Plato's Phaedo*, trans. Eva Brann, Peter Kalkavage, and Eric Salem (Newburyport: Focus Classical Library, 1998), 100a.

32. Much has been written about this "autobiography." Reale identifies it in his magnificent *Toward a New Interpretation of Plato* as "one of the most famous and magnificent passages that Plato has left us" (Giovanni Reale, *Toward a New Interpretation of Plato*, trans. John R. Catan and Richard Davies [Washington, D.C.: Catholic University of America Press, 1997], 95). Even though what is at stake here in the dialogue are causes of generation and destruction, I do not want to focus here on causality, as discussed, for example, by Sallis (*Being and Logos*, 38–44) and Gonzalez (*Dialectic and Dialogue*, 188–208). Instead, I want to emphasize the change in method that is symbolized by the "second sailing."

33. *Plato's Phaedo*, 97b.

34. *Phaedo* 58b.

35. Much more can be said about the myth, but since it is not certain which version(s) of the myth was/were known to Plato, I have tried to summarize the basic elements of the story.

36. *Phaedo*, 58c.

37. *Phaedo*, 58a–b.

38. In fact, there are more people present in the prison, but only fourteen people are named here by Phaedo. Interestingly, the fourteen names are, when Phaedo enumerates the names, grouped in a set of seven Athenians, two additional Athenians, and five foreigners. This could be seen as another reference to the "twice seven."

39. Plato, *Symposium*, in *Plato III: Lysis, Symposium, Gorgias*, trans. W. R. M. Lamb, Loeb Classical Library (Cambridge: Harvard University Press, 1996), 177d.

40. Socrates is not the slave doctor, but rather the "free-born doctor" of the *Laws*. He is the free-born doctor who tries to find the real cause of such illnesses, the origin from which nature unfolds (ἀρχῆς καὶ κατὰ φύσιν [*Laws*, 720d]).

41. In the whole Platonic corpus the word "labyrinth" is used only once, at least explicitly: "At this point we were involved in a labyrinth: when we supposed we had arrived at the end, we twisted about again and found ourselves practically at the beginning of our search, and just as sorely in want as when we first started on it" (*Euthydemus* 291b–c). The image of the labyrinth here suggests

the difficulty, or in fact the impossibility, of finding ways that lead to the truth. In the two dialogues discussed here we can find a similar idea. In the *Protagoras* Socrates and Protagoras are at the end of the dialogue still opposed to one another, and in the *Phaedo* we are left with nothing more than good hopes about the immortality of the soul.

42. *Phaedo,* 70e.

43. *Phaedo,* 71c.

44. *Phaedo,* 72b.

45. *Phaedo,* 72c.

46. Hans-Georg Gadamer, *Dialogue and Dialectic: Eight Hermeneutical Studies on Plato* (New Haven: Yale University Press, 1980), 25.

47. *Phaedo,* 72e.

48. *Phaedo,* 74e.

49. *Phaedo,* 75c.

50. *Phaedo,* 74a.

51. *Phaedo,* 77c.

52. *Phaedo,* 84b–c (my emphasis).

53. *Plato's Phaedo,* 84c–d.

54. It is this peculiar character of Socrates to which Kofman alludes in her "Beyond Aporia?" when she makes her famous analysis of the figures of *poros, penia,* and *eros* as we find them in Diotima's speech in the *Symposium.* Eros is the child of *poros* and *penia; poros* is the father, the resourceful, who has possibilities to find ways; and *penia* is the mother, who is poor. The child of these parents, eros is "[n]either mortal nor immortal, Love is a daemon, an intermediary being. Neither wise nor ignorant, he is a philosopher" (Kofman, "Beyond Aporia?" 26).

55. *Phaedo,* 111c–114c.

56. *Phaedo,* 88d.

57. *Phaedo,* 90c.

58. *Phaedo,* 90c.

59. *Phaedo,* 91a.

60. *Protagoras,* 348d.

61. We can see this, for example, in the *Symposium* where Socrates is supposed to give a eulogy, but starts off with a short dialogue with Agathon. He eventually does give a eulogy on love, but in the form of an (imaginary) dialogue with Diotima. In order to give an account, to provide a *logos,* Socrates thus needs dialectic, possibly even with an imaginary interlocutor. Since his imaginary eulogy can be seen as a continuation of his dialogue with Agathon, we find here again a reversal of positions in which Socrates adopts the position of Agathon, and Diotima adopts Socrates' position.

10

In Plato's Image

Jill Gordon

And a wolf is very like a dog, the wildest like the tamest of animals. But the cautious man must be especially on his guard in the matter of resemblances, for they are very slippery things.
Sophist 231a

Next we must declare the most important benefit effected by [the eyes], for the sake of which god bestowed them upon us. Vision, in my view, is the cause of the greatest benefit to us, inasmuch as none of the accounts now given concerning the Universe would ever have been given if men had not seen the stars or the sun or the heaven. . . . From these we have procured philosophy in all its range, than which no greater boon ever has come or will come, by divine bestowal, unto the race of mortals.
Timaeus 47a–b

Plato's images are among the most powerful and alluring ever contrived: the cave dwellers of the *Republic* sit in shackles before the shadows cast on the cave wall, prevented from turning their heads toward the real source of those images; the unruly, winged horse of the *Phaedrus* resists the bridled control of the charioteer and therefore fails to ascend to the heights; Socrates, the midwife in *Theaetetus,* aids in the birth of ideas and disposes of those ideas delivered stillborn or unfit; Aristophanes relates the story in the *Symposium* of our origins as double-sided humans, two joined as one, cartwheeling around with our other halves in erotic bliss; philosophy is depicted as medicine for the soul when it is in ill health; Alcibiades flaunts his striking and seductive beauty; and we might even say that Socrates flaunts his ugly visage.[1] These images form so integral a part of the dialogues that the philosophical importance of Plato's image-making demands investigation.[2] And yet several dialogues contain passages in which interlocutors seem to throw into question the moral and epistemic value of image-making, and to denigrate what is visible in comparison to what is purely intelligible. Plato's own use of images therefore compels us to reckon with a deeply entrenched view of "Platonic metaphysics" and to broaden our common conceptions of Plato's method.

It is widely accepted that Plato subscribes to some metaphysical system that involves two realms or kinds of being which are hierarchically arranged, and two kinds of apprehension or knowledge that correspond to the two kinds of being. The superior kind of being comprises things-in-themselves, or forms, which are real, eternal, and unchanging. Furthermore, the realm of the forms is the invisible realm, and so the forms cannot be known through the senses. They are known, if they can be known at all, through reason, independently of the senses, emotions, or passions. Finally, purely rational knowledge of the forms constitutes true philosophical enlightenment. Inferior to the forms, in this same view of "Platonic metaphysics," are the phenomena of human experience. We apprehend the phenomena through our senses, and they are in constant flux. Sensation, passion, and emotion, which necessarily accompany human experience since we are embodied creatures, hinder clear understanding. The phenomena are not wholly real but are imitations or mere images of the forms. When we grasp the phenomena, therefore, we perceive only images of reality. Our apprehension of these phenomena or images falls far short, at best, of philosophical wisdom.[3]

If this two-realm metaphysics is an accurate depiction of Plato's metaphysical commitments and of his commitment to philosophy's residing in the realm of pure reason, then we might question why Plato did not himself maintain the level of discourse in his philosophical works by offering only rational argumentation for philosophical positions; why would he sully his own work with lowly, unphilosophical, or anti-philosophical images? If to appeal to what is best philosophically is to appeal to what is purely rational, why didn't Plato just write arguments?

While the dialogues are consistent with a commitment to the two-realm metaphysical view, they are not consistent with a view of philosophy as a purely rational enterprise. To the contrary, the dialogues never fail to appeal to our visual senses, forcing us to see and to create images in our minds.[4] Plato draws repeatedly from the phenomena of human experience, asking us to understand philosophical ideas through the finite, mutable objects of our experience. And beyond our sense experience, Plato relies on the fancy of our imagination to create other worlds and images. Plato's use of images and his implicit belief in their potential for good effect, as evidenced by his pervasive and artful use of them, compel us to ask why Plato chose to use images as he does and why they are such an effective tool for his project. I will argue that the dialogues are, therefore, paradigms of image-making as an avenue for philosophical insight.

The Evidence of the *Phaedo*

The *Phaedo* happens to be a major source for passages that seem to denigrate the senses in comparison to reason, and is therefore an appropriate locus for reopening the investigation of the traditional understanding of Plato's metaphysical commitments, his methods, and just what role vision and images might actually play in philosophy. While the *Phaedo*, on the surface, appears to support the traditional understanding of "Platonic metaphysics" and philosophy as a purely rational enterprise, it actually provides clear evidence that this understanding needs re-vision.

Set in Socrates' jail cell only hours before he drinks the hemlock, *Phaedo* focuses appropriately on the immortality of the soul. Near the beginning of the dialogue, Socrates claims that the philosopher tries as far as is possible to live a life in which body and soul are separate. The philosopher shuns the so-called pleasures of the body such as eating, drinking, and sex. Moreover, he thinks little of personal adornment in clothes, shoes, and the like. In this way, the philosopher lives toward and desires death insofar as death is the separation of body and soul. "The philosopher more than other men, separates the soul from communion with the body" (65a). Socrates then reasons that anyone who shuns the body would have to shun the senses, since the sense organs are bodily organs:

> Would not that man do this [i.e., separate soul from body] most perfectly who approaches each thing, so far as possible, with the reason alone, not introducing sight into his reasoning nor dragging in any of the other senses along with his thinking, but who employs pure, absolute reason in his attempt to search out the pure, absolute essence of things, and who removes himself, so far as possible, from eyes and ears, and, in a word, from his whole body, because he feels that its

companionship disturbs the soul and hinders it from attaining truth and wisdom? Is not this the man, Simmias, if anyone, to attain to the knowledge of reality? (66a)

At this point in the dialogue Socrates has thus established the threefold dichotomy: body and soul; senses and reason; objects of human experience and things-in-themselves. As the traditional view of "Platonic metaphysics" would have it, these pairs are wholly disjunctive, but when the story of recollection is introduced, the dichotomies demand a closer look. The story of recollection reveals remarkable means of connecting the elements in each pair, ontologically and epistemically. It therefore contains important clues about the role that images play in linking the two realms.

The story of recollection tells us that before the soul's embodiment or birth, it knew the realities. Upon birth it forgets these truths, and if we are to learn them at all, we must recollect them. Socrates tells us that various things in our experience can remind us of other things. For example, seeing the lyre can remind us of the one who plays it; seeing the cloak worn by a lover can remind us of our lover; seeing a picture of Simmias can remind us of Simmias. When we perceive one thing, it calls to our minds some other thing. The item recalled can be like and/or unlike the item which stimulated its recall. We are then induced to analyze the recollection to see what relationship obtains between the thing recalled and the item that brought it to mind, and we evaluate the likeness or difference between the two (72e–74a).

> "Now see," said [Socrates], "if this is true. We say there is such a thing as equality. I do not mean one piece of wood equal to another, or one stone to another, or anything of that sort, but something beyond that—equality itself [αὐτὸ τὸ ἴσον].[5] Shall we say there is such a thing, or not?"
>
> "We shall say that there is," said Simmias, "most decidedly."
>
> "And do we know what it is?"
>
> "Certainly," said he.
>
> "Whence did we derive the knowledge of it? Is it not from the things we were just speaking of? Did we not, by seeing equal pieces of wood or stones or other things, derive from them a knowledge of equality itself, which is another thing? . . . Then," said he, "those equals are not the same as equality itself."
>
> "Not at all, I should say, Socrates."
>
> "But from those equals," said he, "which are not the same as equality itself, you have nevertheless conceived and acquired knowledge of it?"

> "Very true," he replied.
> "And it is either like them or unlike them?"
> "Certainly."
> "It makes no difference," said he, "Whenever the sight of one thing brings you a perception of another, whether they be like or unlike, that must necessarily be recollection." (74a–d)

What makes this passage remarkable is its claim that we can come to know the realities from the objects of human experience in the process called recollection. By using our senses—in this case, sight—we can come to know something of things-in-themselves. Socrates even claims that "it is impossible to gain this knowledge [of reality], except by sight or touch or some other of the senses" (75a)! By perceiving, we are reminded of, and we recover, the realities our souls once knew. The objects of our experience and the things-in-themselves are both like and unlike, so we glimpse the realities insofar as they are similar to the images before us, and at the same time we recognize that the images before us are not the realities themselves, are unlike them in fundamental ways.

Recollection thus provides the link between all three dichotomies: senses and reason are linked by recollection, since we rely on our senses in order to grasp what we might later reason about, namely, the realities; objects of experience and things-in-themselves are linked by recollection, since we recall the things-in-themselves through the objects of our experience; and body and soul are linked through recollection, since the senses and the intelligence necessarily work together in that activity. This means, incidentally, that recollection is therefore what allows embodied souls to be integrated beings. Most important, what becomes clear when we take these aspects of recollection together is that recollection is what makes philosophy possible. We *can* have access, and we can *only* have access, to the things-in-themselves through our dim images of them in this realm because of the links recollection makes possible.

The *Phaedo*, then, portrays philosophical investigation taking place *between* the realms of sense and intellect, and so the exclusivity of the two realms in the traditional "Platonic" metaphysical dualism needs to be reexamined. Socrates' explicit commitment to the study of the objects of human experience, and to the sensible faculties as a means for investigating the realities, that is, as a means of philosophical investigation in the genuine learning process of recollection, remains incongruous with the traditional view. The two realms are necessarily linked, and philosophical inquiry into the nature of reality must necessarily take place within the realm of appearances. The reason why it must take place there is central to the *Phaedo*.

There is strong evidence in the *Phaedo*, and in other dialogues, as I shall show, that rather than being an escape from this embodied life, philosophy is a way of coping from within it. That is, philosophy is a way of directly addressing our human condition with courage and intelligence. The *Phaedo*, in this way, offers a radically different conception of philosophy than the traditional "Platonic" interpretation of it as purely rational activity carried out beyond the human realm. Socrates makes it clear that the human life is one of embodiment which necessarily limits the capacities of the soul; and in particular, the body limits the soul's access to things-in-themselves. Note the frequency of Socrates' qualifications in the passages discussed above regarding the philosopher's limitations: "so far as possible," "if anyone can," "so far as he was able." The *Phaedo* offers a conception of philosophy as a human activity carried out within—and because of—our limitations, and images are a part of philosophy.

Our first indication that philosophy might be the remedy for human limitation occurs at a critical juncture in the drama. Socrates speaks of the immortality of the soul—literally on his deathbed—in response to Simmias' and Cebes' challenge to the fearless manner in which he faces his fate (63a–b). The young men have objections to Socrates' arguments, although they are hesitant to make them on account of Socrates' "present misfortune" (84d); they fear the consequences if philosophy cannot meet their objections. Simmias nevertheless musters his courage to ask his question, explaining that despite the difficulty of knowing certain things, one must attempt the discovery nonetheless. Simmias' brief prologue to his own objection introduces a metaphor: human life is carried out in rough waters where there is danger all around. We need beliefs and ideas to help us stay afloat, but it is difficult, if not impossible, to know which of those ideas are to be believed. We should cling to that vessel which serves us best, that belief which best stands the test of dialectic and, holding fast to it, make our way the best we can (85b–d). To question, as Simmias is doing, is to take courage in this difficult situation, and philosophy is the means by which we test the worthiness of our own vessels and perhaps leave them behind when we have found sturdier craft. In any case, our plight is risky and uncertain, and philosophy provides the life raft.[6]

Properly steeled with philosophy on their side, Simmias and Cebes make their objections, which appear to present formidable challenges to Socrates' arguments. Significantly, their objections each take the form of an image. Simmias likens the soul to a harmony and the body to a lyre, asking whether the soul might be destroyed with the body just as the harmony is destroyed along with the lyre (85e–86d). Cebes uses the image of the old weaver and his cloak, which is left behind after the weaver's death. Cebes claims that even though the weaver has had many cloaks prior to this last one, we cannot infer by its existence that the weaver, the longer lasting of the two, is still alive because the cloak still exists (87b–88b). Plato draws our attention to the self-conscious use of images when he has Cebes say that, like Simmias, he too is in need of an image in order to express his objection (87b; εἰκόνος γάρ τινος, ὡς ἔοικεν, κἀγὼ ὥσπερ Σιμμίας δέομαι). The *Phaedo* thus indicates that images can play a role in posing formidable philosophical questions.

Just as Simmias faced asking difficult questions, so now Socrates faces answering difficult questions, and the *Phaedo* recommends philosophy as the courageous choice in both cases. In fact, Socrates must assuage some of the anxiety of those who now fear that philosophy is not a match to meet these formidable objections.[7] Socrates' cure for the anxiety of the interlocutors amounts to an admonition never to tire of the pursuit of an argument and, furthermore, when philosophy fails, never to blame the argument, but to see the failing in ourselves. We must not become misologists, haters of argument, but we must maintain trust in philosophical argument, even when it seems to betray us (89c–91a). One might object that Socrates is saying exactly the opposite of what I want to establish, since he claims that our faith ought to remain in argument. Socrates' view, however, implies that arguments will necessarily fail us. What comes through strongly in these passages is again the fundamental limitation of human beings. Despite the occasional failure of argument, we ought not let that deter us from the life of philosophy. Socrates' cure for anxiety, while assuring us that we ought to remain faithful to philosophy, at the same time warns us of our limitations.

And while the participants in this dialogue look to philosophy for preservation in the seas of uncertainty, philosophy is not, as it is practiced in the *Phaedo*, pure argumentation, nor an appeal to reason, separate from other faculties. Near the beginning of the dialogue, Socrates describes his discussion of the soul and the afterlife as telling stories (μυθολογεῖν, 61e), and he prefaces his defense that he is right not to grieve at death by saying that he hopes (ἐλπίζω) to go to a good fate, "though I should not dare to assert this positively; but I would assert as positively as anything about such matters that I am going to gods who are good masters" (63c). The entire setup for Socrates' views on the immortality of the soul is therefore couched in non-conclusive, speculative terms. And after having presented his views on the immortality of the soul, Socrates finds it necessary once again to attenuate: "There are still many subjects for doubt and many points open to attack, if anyone cares to discuss the matter thoroughly" (84c).

The largest portion of the dialogue contains what might be called "arguments" for the immortality of the soul and Socrates' response to objections to those arguments. But even these arguments are not enough, ultimately, to convey what Socrates says really lies at the heart of his belief that the soul is immortal, namely, the necessity of becoming "as good and wise as possible" (107d). Since the final justice meted out to good and bad souls appears to be as important, if not more important, than the mere immortality of the soul, Socrates completes the dialogue with a description of the journey of the soul in the afterlife and of the worlds it might come to inhabit (107b–115a). To demonstrate the importance of *how* we live our lives, the arguments for the immortality of the soul must be supplemented by more images and stories. Death can not simply be the separation of body and soul. If only that, death would be an escape and "a boon to the wicked" (107c). Regarding the truth of the story Socrates tells about the world and the fate of the soul, his last words on the subject are again about human risk and uncertainty:

> Now it would not be fitting for a man of sense to maintain that all this is just as I have described it, but that this or something like it is true concerning our souls and their abodes, since the soul is shown to be [φαίνεται οὖσα] immortal, I think he may properly and worthily venture to believe; for the venture is well worthwhile. (114d)

None of what Socrates contributes to this dialogue would seem to be an appeal to pure reason or rational argumentation. He presents ancient stories and myths, and he presents them tenuously in keeping with his commitment to human limitation. What are the most likely candidates for pure argumentation in this dialogue—the "proofs" for the immortality of the soul—are flanked by disclaimers as to their demonstrative truth, and are in need of supplemental stories that supply essential elements of Socrates' view.

The *Phaedo* presents three points clearly: that we must look to images of reality in order to learn about reality itself, that humans are fundamentally limited, and that we ought to maintain faith in philosophy. Moreover, that its three primary interlocutors make their most acute philosophical points through images has something important to say to us. The dialogue in its entirety encourages, through its telling of the story of recollection, the use of our senses in the service of philosophical inquiry. For human beings, learning entails looking to images in the midst of our philosophical argumentation. It is not a foolproof method; it will fail us at times, and it might lead us astray, but in the end it is all that we embodied, limited beings have. And, for the sake of our souls, now and ever after, the risk is worthwhile.

The Evidence of Other Dialogues

That human beings are inherently limited, that philosophy is the appropriate medium for human inquiry due to our limitations, and that philosophy needs therefore to be carried out to some extent through images, are pervasive ideas in the Platonic corpus. I do not intend here to give a full interpretation of any particular dialogue, or to provide an exhaustive treatment of all discussions about philosophy, human limitation, and the use of images; rather, I mean to present enough evidence to establish that these ideas appear frequently and consistently in the dialogues and are fundamental to Plato's project.[8]

The *Apology* provides testimony that human limitation is the bedrock of Plato's project insofar as it sets out in the clearest, most poignant fashion the meaning of Socratic ignorance. Socrates remains outstanding among other humans because he recognizes his ignorance while others do not recognize theirs. What makes Socratic ignorance "Socratic" therefore is nothing that mitigates the ignorance, but is instead the open and explicit recognition of the ignorance itself—the laying claim to that ignorance, which is a necessary propaedeutic for philosophy.[9] The two terms, "Socratic" and "ignorance," when put together, present both a universal human condition and a particularized human ideal: Socratic *ignorance* is emblematic of the universal human condition since all humans are alike in their ignorance, but *Socratic* ignorance is also representative of an ideal for humans who need to recognize and admit their ignorance and yet aspire to philosophize.

The *Symposium* addresses the human aspiration to philosophize, and it can be read as a dialogue that attempts to bridge the gulf between human ignorance and pure, enlightened wisdom. The language of Diotima's speech, for example, is filled with references to mediation, to finding a middle path, to navigating between two realms, and of the limited being who wants nonetheless to ascend to truth.[10] Our limitation implies that we cannot achieve pure rationality, nor need we remain flailing in the depths, but we can aspire to a middle path. Philosophy guides us in that middle path, steering away from ignorance, navigating toward wisdom, but forever remaining between the two. In one brief but telling passage Diotima responds to one of Socrates' questions:

"Who then, Diotima," I asked, "are the lovers of wisdom, if they are neither the wise nor the ignorant?"

"Why, a child could tell by this time," she answered, "that they are the intermediate sort, and amongst these also is Eros. For wisdom has to do with the fairest things, and Eros is a love directed to what is fair; so that Eros must needs be a friend of wisdom, and, as such, must be between wise and ignorant." (204a–b) [11]

Eros, in his capacity as lover of wisdom, that is, in his capacity as philosopher, is of the intermediate type between wisdom and ignorance. If Socrates is a philosopher, and there is plenty of evidence in this dialogue (and others) that Socrates loves wisdom and the beautiful but does not possess them, then we ought to take note that Diotima's method of teaching Socrates about eros is through an image: the ladder of ascent. The language here, however, would seem to preclude reading Diotima's speech as simply a method of ascent that was, strictly speaking, recommended and possible for humans. The language is consistent with a view of humans as fundamentally limited, and Diotima puts forward philosophy as the practice reserved for those who love wisdom and the beautiful, but who do not possess them. Furthermore, Socrates, the lover of wisdom, who claims to have learned much from the wisdom of Diotima, learned first from question and answer and then from the beautiful image she created for him.[12]

An even more compelling image in the *Symposium* is drawn by Aristophanes, and this image tells the story of human incompleteness (189c–191d). Long ago, we were beings which we would now consider "double," with four legs and four arms, two sets of genitals, and two faces, joined together back to back. Each such being exhibited great strength, vigor, and joy. We were, in that state, complete. These beings had such "lofty notions" that they "conspired against the gods," scheming to assault them in "high heaven." So, in anger the gods split these beings asunder, ensuring that forever they would be doomed to seek their other halves for completeness. As Drew Hyland describes this symbolic representation of human limitation, we are consequently "bound to strive to overcome that incompleteness we experience."[13]

Like the *Symposium*, the *Phaedrus* also tells the tale of erotic impulses toward wisdom. It is further linked to the *Symposium* insofar as it contains a myth that has many similarities to Diotima's ladder. The story and image of the charioteer, like Diotima's ladder, tells the tale of the lover ascending to the heights. Oddly enough, though, the *Phaedrus* also relies on recollection and so has important links to the *Phaedo*. Socrates begins his story of the charioteer by saying that he cannot give a direct account of the nature of the soul, but will instead provide an image.

He pays particular attention to the manner in which the soul can and should be discussed, claiming that it should not be through discourse, but through image:

> Concerning the immortality of the soul this is enough; but about its form we must speak in the following manner. To tell what it really is would be a matter of utterly superhuman and long discourse [διηγήσεως], but it is within human power to describe it briefly in an image [ἔοιϰεν]; let us therefore speak in that way. (246a) [14]

To make images is a human thing. The distinction between godly or superhuman discourse and human image-making serves as a frontispiece to the image of the charioteer and his team of horses which represents the human soul. Socrates implies that image-making is fundamental to human discourse—even philosophical discourse about the most important of issues.

Socrates persistently reaffirms the distinction between what is peculiarly human and what is superhuman through the images he creates in *Phaedrus*. The soul can sprout wings that help it to soar to the gods' dwelling place and to glimpse the realities there. While the gods clearly make the ascent to the realities and dwell there, seeing reality, the plight for humans is quite different. "Such is the life of the gods; but of the other souls, that which best follows after God and is most like [εἰϰασμένη] him, raises the head of the charioteer up into the outer region and is carried round in the revolution, troubled by the horses and hardly beholding the realities" (248a). The description continues (through 248d) with language clearly stating that the charioteer will necessarily fail in his attempts to reach the realities. The image of the charioteer who is trying to control the two horses—one noble, the other troublesome—depicts a human attempt to ascend to the realities, entities which Socrates clearly demarcates as lying beyond human capacity. The horses continue to give humans trouble, even in the best of human circumstances, bound as we are beneath the gods. Thus the *Phaedrus* underscores our limitation.

But just when Socrates introduces human limitation into the myth of the afterlife in *Phaedrus*, he also introduces recollection, which provides a strong link to passages in the *Phaedo* that portray the importance of images for philosophy. An entire menagerie of souls are introduced into the myth of the afterlife in *Phaedrus*, differentiated and hierarchically arranged by the degree to which each soul has glimpsed the realities. Clearly there are several types of souls beyond any human, that is, embodied, souls (248a–c), but the best type of human soul is the soul of a philosopher or a lover of beauty, and all human souls glimpse what they once knew by means of recollection (249b).

> It is not easy for all souls to gain from earthly things a recollection of those realities, either for those which had but a brief view of them at that earlier time, or for those which, after falling to earth, were so unfortunate as to be turned toward unrighteousness through some evil communications and to have forgotten the holy sights they once saw. Few then are left which retain an adequate recollection of them; but these when they see here any likeness [ὁμοίωμα] of the things of that other world, are stricken with amazement and can no longer control themselves; but they do not understand their condition, because they do not clearly perceive. Now in the earthly copies of justice and temperance and the other ideas which are precious to souls there is no light, but only a few, approaching the images [ὁμοιώμασιν] through the darkling organs of sense, behold in them the nature of that which they imitate [τοῦ εἰκασθέντος], and these few do this with difficulty. (249e–250b) [15]

The earthly likenesses are dim compared to the realities, but are dim reminders nonetheless. Human access to the realities comes from things in this world that are images of the realities. What is needed is simply the right use of the aids of recollection (249c). Furthermore, the philosopher's vision—a vision of objects of human experience that reveals dim glimpses of reality, not direct vision of reality—will be difficult and rare. In this manner the *Phaedrus* echoes elements of *Phaedo* in which we learn that we gain understanding of things-in-themselves (for example, the equal) from objects of our experience (for example, two sticks of equal length).

The *Sophist* also treats images, and eventually points to their role in philosophical discourse. The Eleatic Stranger and young Theaetetus, in their complex and at times circuitous conversation, weave together discussions of images (roughly 235b–236d, 239c–d, 264c ff.) and the possibility of not-being (roughly 237c, 239d–264b). A formulation of the ontological status of not-being emerges from their conversation, explaining how non-being helps render philosophical discourse possible, and delineating the role of images as part of that discourse.

The Stranger and Theaetetus are confronted with the nature of negation and falsehood and the puzzle of what-is-not. They are plagued by the sophistic claim that falsehood is utterly impossible, since not-being could neither be conceived nor uttered since it has no part of being and is therefore nothing (236e–237a, 260c–d). The motivation for their search lies in the difficulty they face if they claim that the sophist deals with false discourse or creates false images. Image-making, when done according to the true proportions of the thing imitated, is simply called "likeness-making" (εἰκαστικήν), and the Stranger and Theaetetus accept this kind of image-making as, at the very least, neutral (235d). But there is another category of image-making which produces appearances, not likenesses, which is called "fantastic art" (φανταστικήν) and contains an element of falsehood (236c), and this type of image-making concerns the sophist. (Note that the discussion of the possibility of false language is rooted first in the possibility of false *images*. This undermines contemporary treatments of this dialogue that cast the problem of not-being exclusively in terms of language, in terms of how false *propositions* can or cannot correspond to the world. Clearly it is not necessarily or exclusively a problem of language that Plato is concerned with here, since false images initiate the investigation.) [16]

They therefore embark together on a mission the Stranger sets for himself: "I shall have to . . . contend forcibly that after a fashion not-being is and on the other hand in a sense being is not" (241d). The larger aim here is to establish that discourse of all kinds—speech, opinion, conceptualization, and image-making—participates both in being and not-being. That is, discourse exists (participation in being) and yet there is such a thing as negative and false discourse (participation in not-being) which is distinguishable from positive or true assertion of being. Without that, discourse, at least meaningful discourse, is impossible. So the very existence of philosophical or any other type of meaningful discourse depends on the mixture of being and not-being, and it depends on the distinction between truth and falsity and the distinction that parallels it between true likenesses and fantastic appearances.

In establishing that discourse is necessarily a mingling of being and not being, the Stranger and Theaetetus now allow for the possibility of falsehood. So the position of the Stranger in the *Sophist* is consistent with that espoused by Diotima in the *Symposium*, which places philosophy in the position of medium between two worlds. In the former case philosophy lies between being and not-being, and in the latter case between the fullness of divine reality and the poverty of human want. The possibility of falsehood that comes with the mingling of being and not-being, while it certainly brings with it the promise of philosophical discourse, carries with it significant consequences.

> Our object was to establish discourse [τὸν λόγον] as one of our classes of being. For if we were deprived of this, we should be deprived of philosophy, which would be the greatest calamity; moreover, we must

at the present moment come to an agreement about the nature of discourse, and if we were robbed of it by its absolute nonexistence, we could no longer discourse; and we should be robbed of it if we agreed that there is no mixture of anything with anything. . . . But if falsehood exists, deceit exists. . . . And if deceit exists, all things must be henceforth full of images and likenesses and fancies [εἰδώλων τε καὶ εἰκόνων ἤδη καὶ φαντασίας]. (*Sophist*, 260a–c)

This conception of philosophy precludes its dealing with pure being or with the realities directly, and roots philosophy firmly in a mixture of being and not-being. The boon to mankind from the mingling of being and not-being is philosophical discourse, and the price we pay is the possibility of deceit. But somewhere between the benefit of philosophical discourse and the price of deceit lie images. Philosophy is described as mixing the realms of being and not-being, so it must contain images since it cannot contain the realities. Furthermore, by the very reasoning used by the Stranger, it would not be warranted to assume that since these images are not-real that they are therefore completely unreal. We know from several instances in this dialogue that there are two kinds of images, those that imitate reality and are ca lled true images and those that do not imitate reality and are called false images.[17] It is more than plausible that the true images are those that point us, in comparing likeness and unlikeness, toward the realities and must therefore be a proper constituent of philosophical discourse.[18]

The *Timaeus* sets up the entire world of human experience as an image of some other world, after which it is patterned.[19] Timaeus then plays on the etymological link between "likenesses" as an ontological entity and "likelihood" as an epistemological category, arguing that since humans must deal with an image or copy (εἰκασία) we must accept that our account will only be likely (εἰκός).[20] Human limitation lies at the root of Timaeus' account, and he tells us that we must forever deal in images. We "are but human creatures," and as such we must accept our epistemological limitations.

Since what we experience as humans is an image of reality, then it would seem to be of paramount importance both to recognize that fact and to understand the difference between the images and the original. Two of the necessary conditions for turning toward the things-in-themselves are recognizing their existence and understanding (albeit in a limited capacity) their difference from what we sense and experience. These conditions would be satisfied through the activity of investigating likeness and unlikeness between image and reality, and to do that one must recognize the distinction between image and reality. As limited beings we might use images to ascend to the realities, but we cannot confuse the two. We cannot change our finite, limited existence, but we must still be aware of and turned toward what lies beyond. To confuse one's sensations and experiences with the realities that cause them would prohibit one from seeking out those underlying realities, which is exactly the kind of bondage depicted metaphorically in the *Republic*'s story of the cave dwellers.

The *Republic* is perhaps the dialogue singly most responsible for the condemnatory view of images and image-making imputed to Plato. Ironically, it is also the source of the most vivid and memorable images Plato created. In addition to its description of the cave and its unfortunate denizens, the dialogue in its entirety is predicated on an analogy between justice in the city and justice in the soul. And even further, this analogy is itself introduced by way of yet another image:

> "So, since we are not clever persons, I think we should employ the method of search that we should use if we, with not very keen vision, were bidden to read small letters from a distance, and then someone had observed that these same letters exist elsewhere larger and on a larger surface. We should have accounted it a godsend, I fancy, to be allowed to read those letters first, and then examine the smaller, if they are the same."
>
> "Quite so," said Adeimantus; "but what analogy to this do you detect in the inquiry about justice?"
>
> "I will tell you," I said: "there is a justice of one man, we say, and, I suppose, also of an entire city? . . . Is not the city larger than the man? . . . Then, perhaps there would be more justice in the larger object and more easy to apprehend." (368d–e)

The dim vision of the investigating party is emblematic of our human limitation or ignorance.[21] Our ignorance necessitates that we look to one image which is more easily seen or understood in order to understand another. The entire method of the *Republic*, in its effort to see justice in the soul by first seeing justice in the city, is based on looking at likenesses in order to learn about the object of inquiry.

The simile of the sun is likewise intended to help the interlocutors understand the form of the Good by way of another powerful image. Socrates puts off discussing the nature of the Good directly because he may not be able (μὴ οὐχ οἷός τ' ἔσομαι, 506d) to explain the Good. Instead he offers "what seems to be the offspring of the good and most nearly made in its image" (ὃς δὲ ἔκγονός τε τοῦ ἀγαθοῦ φαίνεται καὶ ὁμοιότατος ἐκείνῳ, 506e).[22] We are left to wonder whether Socrates, or any embodied being, would ever be able to explain the nature of the realities, and whether the image of the sun is therefore the most philosophically appropriate means for helping the young men understand the nature of the Good after all.

But images play a more important—even crucial—role in the *Republic*, philosophically speaking. As Socrates reveals in his conversation with Adeimantus, the primary activity of the philosopher, as depicted in the *Republic*, is to imitate noble images!

> "For surely, Adeimantus, the man whose mind is truly fixed on eternal realities has no leisure to turn his eyes downward upon the petty affairs of men, and so engaging in strife with them to be filled with envy and hate, but he fixes his gaze upon the things of the eternal and unchanging order, and seeing that they neither wrong nor are wronged by one another, but all abide in harmony as reason bids, he will endeavor to imitate [μιμεῖσθαι] them and, as far as may be, to fashion himself in their likeness and assimilate himself [ἀφομοιοῦσθαι] to them." . . . "If then," I said, "some compulsion is laid upon him to practice stamping on the plastic matter of human nature in public and private patterns that he visions there, and not merely to mold and fashion himself, do you think he will prove a poor craftsman of sobriety and justice and all forms of ordinary civic virtue?" "By no means," he said. "But if the multitude become aware that what we are saying of the philosopher is true, will they still be harsh with philosophers, and will they distrust our statement that no city could ever be blessed unless its lineaments were traced by artists who used the heavenly model?" "They will not be harsh," he said, "if they perceive that." (500b–e)

It is through the faculty of vision that the philosopher is connected to the realities and, relying on his vision, he creates, in the manner of the artist or craftsman, imitations of what he sees. Plato uses the language of vision and plastic, artistic creation. Not only does the philosopher mold his own soul in this manner, but when compelled to rule the polis, he "stamps out on the plastic matter of human nature" the virtues and character needed in the citizens.[23] Likewise, the Socratic project, with respect to the interlocutors, and the Platonic project, with respect to reader and audience, could be conceived of in similar terms as molding or making impressions on souls.[24] Note again the subtle concessions in the passage above made to the limitations of the person whose gaze is fixed on the realities. Even that person endeavors to imitate the realities "as far as may be" and consequently that person's soul becomes ordered and divine "in the measure permitted to man."

Near the end of book 9 of the *Republic,* Glaucon comes to understand the purpose of the images Socrates has drawn, the image of the
ideal city and the corresponding soul.

> "I understand," [Glaucon] said, "You mean [the wise man] will [take
> part in politics] in the city whose foundation we have now gone
> through, the one that has its place in speeches, since I don't suppose
> it exists anywhere on earth."
>
> "But in heaven," I said, "perhaps a pattern [παράδειγμα] is laid up
> for the man who wants to see [ὁρᾶν] and found a city within himself
> on the basis of what he sees. It doesn't make any difference whether
> it is or will be somewhere. For he would mind the things of this city
> alone, and of no other." (592a–b)[25]

The image of the just city is that to which the wise person looks when
modeling his or her own soul. We model our souls on the ideals, as those
ideals are represented in and through images. The images' imaginary
status is irrelevant for Socrates, since as long as there is the ideal image
to gaze at, the wise person's attention can be fixed and focused, and the
just life can still be glimpsed. Glaucon's reply—"It is likely" (Εἰκός)—to
Socrates' claim that the image of the city is a model to look at for the
wise man, is not an insignificant end to book 9. Glaucon's reply again
links, as did the *Timaeus,* the need to look to images (εἰκών) for human
understanding and the epistemological status of human understanding
as merely likely or probable (εἰκός).

The significance of these passages, however, seems to be to help
the young men to avoid confusing reality and image, to avoid being
deceived about which is which. The images themselves are not (meta-
physically) evil or bad, since the philosopher or the wise man need both
original and image to do what they do, and they must see and understand the difference between the two. Instead of condemning images
and image-making, Socrates seems to condemn the individual who mistakes images for reality. Deception is foremost on Socrates' mind:

> When anyone reports to us of some one, that he has met a man who
> knows all the crafts and everything else that men severally know and
> that there is nothing that he does not know more exactly than anybody
> else, our tacit rejoinder must be that he is a simple fellow who appar-
> ently has met some magician or sleight-of-hand man and imitator and
> has been deceived by him into the belief that he is all-wise, *because of
> his own inability to put to the proof and distinguish knowledge, ignorance and
> imitation.* (598d, my emphasis)[26]

Socrates' life mission, as he describes it in the *Apology*, is at its core to "put to the proof and distinguish" knowledge from ignorance. And what sets Socrates apart from others is not that he has knowledge, nor that he is not ignorant, but that he is not deceived about the difference between these two states. Socrates is not speaking in these passages simply about the dangers of painting or poetry, but more generally about those who are deceived about the nature of reality—the kind of deception that the cave dwellers epitomize. They believe that all reality dances across the cave wall in shadow. Socrates exhorts the two young men to be the sort of people who can distinguish knowledge from ignorance (or at least who are not easily deceived), to understand when they see imitation that it is imitation, and to cast their glance from the imitation to the original.

Socrates' admonition of Adeimantus and Glaucon in these passages brings us back around again to the reason for the discussion of poetry in the city in the first place. The two boys relied heavily and exclusively on the poets to support their view that the unjust life is rewarding and fulfilling as long as one's injustices go unpunished. The particular imitators on which Glaucon and Adeimantus relied to make their case show the unjust human life to be worth living, and Socrates is warning the young men to be wary of their own deception. They need to investigate through dialectic, to "put to the proof," just what the poets say in order to find out whether it is a true imitation or not.

Even if Glaucon and Adeimantus have been persuaded that the images that these specific poets have created are not imitations of what is true, they need not reject imitation per se. Instead they can take up the multifarious and beautiful images created by Socrates which cast their glance at the true originals. Adeimantus and Glaucon can gaze upon the cave dwellers, the Divided Line, the image of the sun, the analogy of soul and city, and other images in the dialogue, and they can reconsider philosophically in light of those images whether the just life is worth living. And since the entire discussion of the *Republic* has been a dialectic investigation of what the just life is and whether it is worth living, they are being asked to trade bad images for good ones, but images nonetheless.

The *Republic*, that behemoth work of education, learning, politics, virtue, and the societal role of philosophy and philosophers, is the single largest source of the most intricate and beautiful images Plato created. And it too portrays images as appropriate vehicles for important philosophical endeavors. Given these brief but highly significant examples from the *Republic*, it is difficult to imagine taking the criticisms that occur in that dialogue as criticisms of image-making itself. Plainly, images are not only legitimate and useful, but are a part of the human manner of proceeding philosophically.

In a consistent way, therefore, many dialogues portray a decided emphasis on the limitations of humans, yet they urge the interlocutors and the reader to philosophize and to take up the philosophical life. If we are to take that urging seriously, there must be an avenue to philosophical insight open to limited beings such as ourselves. What that avenue might be lies right before our eyes, exemplified in the dialogues themselves: not merely arguments to higher truths, but images that attract our gaze and turn us toward philosophy.

The Philosophical Effect of
Images and Image-Making

When we see images and recognize them as such, we see similarity and dissimilarity (see *Phaedo* 76a). It is the image's very unlikeness to its intended object—its otherness—that stimulates comparison. This makes it interesting, captivating. We look also for the basic similarity that makes the image an image of something. We then move dialectically between the two, seeing further similarities and dissimilarities along the way. We are moved to consider the qualities of the image, what the corresponding qualities of the original must be, why there is this difference, what the significance of the difference is, and how the unlike could be like. Real learning comes from the deeper exploration of images (metaphors, analogies, myths) in which the several details of image and original are compared. Clearer and detailed pictures emerge from which one can gain complex understanding of both objects under view. Neither is an image an exact likeness of its original, nor are its differences from the original plainly obvious. The richness of an image, and therefore its philosophical value, are appreciated only on reflection. We must work with the image, turn it over in our minds, see it from many perspectives—some of them not our usual perspectives—and we must think about what the image is and what it is not.

Let us look at one example of an image and its original to see how the phenomenon of examining that image takes place. Late in the *Symposium*, the drunken Alcibiades relates the tale of his failed seduction of Socrates. He tells the assembled party that he will create an image of Socrates in order to praise him (οὕτως ἐπιχειρήσω, δι᾽ εἰκόνων, 215a).

> [Socrates] is likest to the Silenus-figures that sit in the statuaries'
> shops; those, I mean, which our craftsmen make with pipes or flutes

in their hands: when their two halves are pulled open, they are found
to contain images of gods. (215a–b)

As Alcibiades draws out the details of this simple image, we see both
similarity and difference. Like the satyr, Socrates has bulging eyes
and a pushed-up nose; but unlike Silenus, Socrates has beauty as well.
Like the satyr, Socrates is a figure who associates himself with erotic
objects—young, beautiful men; but unlike the satyr, as Alcibiades' failure to lure him into bed indicates, Socrates' erotic liaisons are not in-
dulged through sexual activity. Like Marsyas, Socrates has great power
to enchant his listeners, although not with a flute, but rather with his
words. We learn from this image that Socrates' external appearance be-
lies what is inside, that he is complex. We learn that his grotesque face
contrasts with the beauty of his soul. We learn that the Many can be
deceived if they fail to open him up to see what is inside. And finally, we
learn that opening him up to examine his life and his soul might reveal
glimpses of the divine.

In a brief space, this simple image manages to convey a detailed
and complex picture of Socrates. It is therefore not at all like the image-
making Socrates describes flippantly in the *Republic* as walking around
holding up a mirror to everything (596d–e). A mirror held up to Socrates
would tell us less than this rich image. Recall that an image has both
likeness and unlikeness. A mirror simply reflects exactly what is put before it, whereas an image, properly constructed, can induce us to see a
richness in the objects before us and to gain insight into the object and
its original that might not be plainly evident. Is this enough for us to
hold out hope, therefore, that images can lead to truth and philosophical insight? Yes. Alcibiades says as much, in fact, just before introducing
the image cited above:

> The way I shall take, gentlemen, in my praise of Socrates, is by simili-
> tudes [δι' εἰκόνων]. Probably he will think I do this for derision; but
> I choose my similitude for the sake of truth [τοῦ ἀληθοῦς ἕνεκα], not
> of ridicule. (215a)

The evidence here and elsewhere conspires to compel us to take seriously Alcibiades' view that images can serve truth.[27]

We are reminded, too, of the likeness and unlikeness between
Meno and his slave which I examine elsewhere.[28] Socrates created the
image of the slave speaking before large crowds, lecturing on falsehoods
and misconceptions about geometry. Meno and the reader are meant to
see the exact manner in which Meno's lectures on virtue are the same
and yet different from this image. They are similar insofar as each is an

act of ignorance, but they are different insofar as Meno's slave has admitted his ignorance. They are similar insofar as both are shameful acts committed by ignorant people, but they are different insofar as the geometrical falsehoods are more easily correctable. In order to correct his ignorance, Meno must engage in dialectic which is risky and personally difficult in ways that geometry lessons are not. The reader and Meno gain important insights into virtue, knowledge, and ignorance by close examination of the image of the slave's public lectures and its original instance in Meno's lectures on virtue.

If the Platonic dialogues urge the use of images in the service of good philosophy, then what can be concluded about the traditional view of "Platonic metaphysics"? That there are two distinct realms—of things-in-themselves and of the objects of human experience—seems clear enough. But that pure reason, leading to insight into the forms, is to be identified with philosophy, is not supported by the texts. Reason alone as an avenue to enlightenment is not a possibility for humans. Philosophy, the very tool necessary for limited, embodied persons, mediates between the two realms for those beings necessitated to dwell in one alone but with aspirations to understand the other. In this capacity, philosophy certainly includes arguments, but it relies as well on images in the form of myth, analogy, metaphor, and the like. Pure reason is left to the gods; philosophy is left to humans.

A renewed look at Plato's metaphysics reveals surprising results. Even the forms—the eternal, unchanging bearers of reality—and the disembodied rationality that can grasp the forms are themselves images.[29] It has perhaps escaped our notice that even these stories that are spun throughout the dialogue are imagistic, and what has traditionally passed for Plato's metaphysics and his epistemology are themselves composed of images. We have perhaps neglected to see that even these things called "forms" take shape in our imagination in ways other than their ascribed reality. They are meant to have no physical manifestation and yet they are presented to us and are taken up into our cognition as shapes, forms, literally "that which is seen."[30] Furthermore, we must imagine another world beyond our own, this realm of the things-in-themselves, this reality which is different from our lived experience and yet similar, and we must construct it from our fancy or imagination, furnish it with conceptions drawn from our own limited experience. And Plato expects us truly to have some access to this reality from the images he creates and from the images he compels us to create for ourselves. Ultimately, all of Plato's images are addressed to an audience firmly and necessarily grounded in human phenomena and are meant to turn us toward philosophy. Does this imply that ultimately we are only relegated to images? Perhaps yes. But fortunately we have philosophy. If we take seriously that this world is a mere image of the reality it imitates, then indeed we must forever deal in images. It is the human lot.[31]

We might now have a bit more insight into Plato's use of images. He is providing the link for limited humans to the realities. Just as looking at two equal sticks can help us to recollect the reality of equality itself, so also other perceptions and images can aid in our recalling many other truths. Imperfect as this is, and even risky as it is, this is the avenue open for embodied beings such as ourselves. Plato faces the task of urging us to philosophy when he knows that we can only practice it as the limited beings that we are. How do you urge one to philosophy in the face of the guarantee that arguments will fail? Knowing the power of images and image-making, Plato is induced to choose them as appropriate media for moving us in certain directions. Plato is infamous for "his" critique of poets and image-makers. Yet he is the poet and image-maker extraordinaire. While he puts warnings about the use of these devices in the mouths of his interlocutors, at the same time he places those very devices alongside the warnings. A full understanding of the dialogues cannot overlook this fact.

In order to understand the power and the risk of images, I return to the epigraphs that frame this chapter. The first, from the *Sophist*, seems to warn us away from resemblances by evoking a sense of danger. The wildest of animals, the wolf, might very well look to us like the tamest, the dog. Mistaking one for the other could have dire consequences. The second epigraph, from the *Timaeus*, praises our vision, which is responsible for philosophy "in all its range, than which no greater boon ever has come or will come, by divine bestowal, unto the race of mortals." There would appear to be some tension between the meaning of the two passages. On the one hand, we put ourselves in danger if our vision is not keen enough to distinguish between like things, the dog and the wolf. And on the other hand, our vision, a gift from the gods, is of the greatest benefit to us and has procured philosophy into our midst. I hope that my argument has shown that these two claims are not truly contradictory, despite the tension between them; instead they convey the essence of the dialogues' presentation of vision and image. Images and vision are at the same time risky and of great benefit to us. It is our vision that casts our gaze toward philosophy, but it is also our vision that can drag us down into the mire. What accounts for the difference between these two activities is the object of our gaze. Plato's dialogues provide the kinds of resemblances that humans need in order to steer clear of danger, the images that cast our eyes toward philosophy.

Notes

1. This essay is taken from chapter 6 of my book, *Turning Toward Philosophy: Literary Device and Dramatic Structure in Plato's Dialogues* (University Park: Pennsylvania State University Press, 1999). Unless noted otherwise, I use the translations from the Loeb Classical Library.

2. There are many ways to think of images. As the few brief examples cited in the opening paragraph indicate, some images in the dialogues are what we call metaphors; some are more properly considered analogies; and some are woven into the fabric of what we consider myths or allegories. In addition, some are what we might call "fictional" stories, and in some cases these images take the form of plastic artifacts. The Platonic texts support the grouping of these various instances under the single heading "image" insofar as these several devices are referred to as εἰκών throughout the corpus and denote likenesses of one kind or another. Plato's language surrounding the use of images includes, as well, various cognates of "image" such as εἴδωλον and εἰκασία. I hope to point to a link between images and the role of vision in Platonic metaphysics by drawing attention to the further connection to "that which is seen" and "form" (εἶδος). The semantic correlate to "image" would be παράδειγμα—the pattern or model after which a likeness may be produced. I will cite the Greek terms being used in the many examples that follow in order to underscore the unity of the semantic field in which these terms are placed by Plato. There are even further links when one considers the term "mimesis" (μίμησις), which describes the relationship between an image and its original, between εἰκών and παράδειγμα.

3. For dialogues that are plausible sources for this view, see, for example, *Phaedo* 65a–67b, 79a; *Republic* 509c–511e, 514a–518b, 597e–603b; *Sophist* 234b–236e, 264c–266e.

4. While I have chosen to focus on images and the visual aspects of the dialogues, some of the conclusions at which I arrive could apply to the senses more generally and their role in the Platonic corpus. For example, it can be argued that the aural is also central to Socratic interactions, that "hearing" is central to teaching and it makes the "seeing" of images possible. Hence one might proceed cautiously in privileging seeing or the sense of sight. I am indebted to Gary Alan Scott for bringing this important point to my attention.

5. Fowler translates this phrase as "equality in the abstract." I prefer the more literal translation "equality itself" for my purposes here.

6. Both Socrates and Plato are confronted with the task of urging others to engage in philosophical inquiry when there is a risk that in this life we might not find answers to our deepest questions.

7. I have omitted a discussion here of the role of fear in the *Phaedo* and the dramatic shift from the jail cell back to the framing conversation between Phaedo and Echecrates, which occurs just at the point in the dialogue when that fear over the possible failure of philosophy is most palpable (88c–89b). These are discussed in detail in *Turning Toward Philosophy*.

8. Gadamer makes a similar case regarding the consistent message in the

dialogues about human limitation and the role of vision. Gadamer, in *Dialogue and Dialectic: Eight Hermeneutical Studies on Plato,* trans. P. Christopher Smith (New Haven: Yale University Press, 1980), 99–100ff., enumerates and explains four means of communicating a thing, none of which guarantees that the thing will then be "known": the word or name of a thing (*onoma*); the explanation or conceptual determination of a thing (*logos*); the appearance, illustrative image, example, or figure of a thing (*eidolon*); and the knowledge or insight itself of that thing. Gadamer is then careful to warn us that we must not see these four ways as an ordered ascent, culminating in knowledge of the good. All attempts to see them as such "are completely mistaken" (111). Ultimately, pure knowledge or the "life of pure theory" is not attainable for humans. Of the third means of communication, Gadamer says, "Examples, of course, are one of the necessary media in which true knowledge is presented" (115), and he further argues for the need for all four types: "For they all serve to make one more 'dialectical,' to educate one's vision for the thing itself" (122). Our human limitations are, according to Gadamer in another work, "an essential characteristic of man's humanity" in light of which "Plato always sees man's existence . . . which means that he presents them as defined by the process of going beyond them. Man is a creature who transcends himself" (Hans-Georg Gadamer, *Plato's Dialectical Ethics: Phenomenological Interpretations Relating to the Philebus,* trans. Robert M. Wallace [New Haven: Yale University Press, 1991], 4–5). See also Aryeh Kosman, "Silence and Imitation in the Platonic Dialogues," in *Methods of Interpreting Plato and His Dialogues,* ed. James C. Klagge and Nicholas D. Smith (Oxford: Clarendon, 1992), which has close links to this section.

9. See also, for example, *Meno* 84a–b; *Theaetetus* 210c.

10. This position is argued in detail by Luce Irigiray, "Sorcerer of Love: A Reading of Plato's *Symposium,* Diotima's Speech," trans. E. Kuykendall, in *Feminist Interpretations of Plato,* ed. Nancy Tuana (University Park: Pennsylvania State University Press, 1994), 181–95.

11. I have translated φιλοσοφοῦντες as "lovers of wisdom" instead of Lamb's "followers of wisdom" and I have rendered ἔρως as "eros" rather than "love."

12. Socrates claims specifically at *Symposium* 201e that Diotima questioned him, and at 203b Diotima embarks on a long story (Μακρότερον μέν, ἔφη, διηγήσασθαι).

13. Drew Hyland, *Finitude and Transcendence in Plato's Dialogues* (Albany: State University of New York Press, 1995), 118. See his full discussion of Aristophanes' speech at 111–37.

14. Fowler's translation uses "figure," but I have used "image" in order to be consistent with all the translations of the same cognate elsewhere in this chapter.

15. Charles L. Griswold Jr., *Self-Knowledge in Plato's Phaedrus* (New Haven: Yale University Press, 1986), 144: "The gods of this myth do seem to be (among other things) idealized human types who serve the crucial purpose in the story of helping articulate the notion that we are imperfect in specific ways." Griswold also sees in *Phaedrus* "the possibility of reflection on its own status qua written work. This is in keeping with the view that the written word is an 'image'

of the spoken (276a8–9) and the assumption that the image is to be understood relative to its original" (219).

16. As an example of many such propositional treatments of these passages, see David Wiggins, "Sentence, Meaning, Negation, and Plato's Problem of Non-Being," in *Plato I: A Collection of Critical Essays,* ed. G. Vlastos (Notre Dame: University of Notre Dame Press, 1978); G. E. L. Owen, "Plato and Not-Being," in *Plato I: A Collection of Critical Essays;* and even, in some measure, Stanley Rosen, *Plato's Sophist: The Drama of Original and Image* (New Haven: Yale University Press, 1983). The dialogue contains clear statements that the falsehood under consideration is not only linguistic. See, for example, *Sophist* 235d ff., 260c.

17. In addition to the passage cited above, see *Sophist* 235d–f and 264c–267b.

18. The Stranger, unfortunately, never fully addresses the metaphysical status of the true images, as Rosen says in *Plato's Sophist,* 147, 152–53.

19. See also *Cratylus* 423 and 430ff., in which words and language are discussed as imitations of reality.

20. At least five various forms of these terms occur in the brief passage at *Timaeus* 29b–d. See also H. S. Thayer, "Plato on the Morality of Imagination," *Review of Metaphysics* 30 (June 1997): 594–618, esp. 615–16; and Gadamer, *Dialogue and Dialectic,* 120.

21. Hyland, in *Finitude and Transcendence,* reads the *Republic* in its entirety as a treatment of human limitation and philosophy as the means to transcend that limitation; he intends for his reading of the *Republic* to create a perspective for reading the entire Platonic corpus as well.

22. Paul Shorey translates ὁμοιότατος ἐκείνῳ as "most nearly made in its likeness."

23. The objection that vision and artistic craft are mere metaphors for, respectively, the kind of knowing that the philosopher has of the realities and of the work he must do to fashion the souls of good citizens, helps to underscore my point about the need for images. Socrates' chosen way for expressing the understanding of the philosopher and the political task before him is through these images. Philosophy needs the use of images to do its work.

24. See the discussion on the semantic and philosophical significance of "making" and "doing" in chapter 3 of my *Turning Toward Philosophy,* 76ff. This is one more way in which we are made into philosophers.

25. Plato, *The Republic of Plato,* trans. Allan Bloom (New York: Basic Books, 1968).

26. See also *Republic* 598c and 598e regarding Socrates' concern with deception rather than imitation itself. See also *Phaedrus* 261e–262d: "Then he who is to deceive another, and is not to be deceived himself, must know accurately the similarity and dissimilarity of things" (262a).

27. See Martha Nussbaum, *The Fragility of Goodness: Luck and Ethics in Greek Tragedy and Philosophy* (New York: Cambridge University Press, 1988), 185ff. She addresses the issue directly of Alcibiades' claim to tell the truth but, contrary to my position here, she sees the telling of truth through images as disallowed by philosophy. Jean-François Mattéi, "The Theater of Myth in Plato," in *Platonic*

Writings, Platonic Readings, ed. Charles L. Griswold Jr. (University Park: Pennsylvania State University Press, 2002), 66–83; and Gerald Press, "Knowledge as Vision in Plato's Dialogues," *Journal of Neoplatonic Studies* 3 (1995): 61–89, present views consistent with those I present here. See also my "Eros and Philosophical Seduction in *Alcibiades I,*" *Ancient Philosophy* 23 (2003): 11–30.

28. Gordon, *Turning Toward Philosophy.*

29. See Aristotle, *Metaphysics* 1.9.12: "To say that the Forms are patterns, and that other things participate in them, is to use empty phrases and poetical metaphors [τὸ δὲ λέγειν παραδείγματα αὐτὰ εἶναι καὶ μετέχειν αὐτῶν τἆλλα κενολογεῖν ἐστὶ καὶ μεταφορὰς λέγειν ποιητικάς]." I agree with Aristotle wholeheartedly that these are poetical metaphors, but *not* that they are empty phrases.

30. H. Liddell and R. Scott, *Greek-English Lexicon* (Oxford: Clarendon, 1985). Thanks again to Gary Alan Scott for putting the fine point on this.

31. I have been asked on several occasions whether I am making Plato out to be a postmodern figure. Such a conjecture seems off the mark. To say that humans must always deal with images is not to say that there are nothing but images, i.e., that there is no truth or reality. The purpose of images is to help us to ascend toward some higher reality or truth. There is some reality to which we aspire and of which we can fall short. Indeed, it is embedded in what it means to be an image that it is an image *of something.*

Appendix: Dramatic Dates of Plato's Dialogues

Dialogues with Dramatic Dates in Socrates' Lifetime (470/469–399 B.C.E.)

Parmenides	(Socrates very young)	450–445
Alcibiades I	(Alcibiades not yet twenty)	433
Charmides	(Socrates returns from Potidea)	432
Protagoras		
Republic	(Thracian goddess unveiled)	430
Laches	(Delium retreat)	424
Symposium	(Agathon's victory)	416
Ion	(Ephesus' revolt)	412
Gorgias	(Socrates' council service)	later than 406
Euthydemus	(Alcibiades dead)	later than 404
Meno	(winter 402)	402
Theaetetus	(Socrates says he must go to King Archon's office)	399
Sophist	(the day after *Theatetus*)	399
Statesman	(same day as *Sophist*)	399
Euthyphro	(Socrates on way to King Archon)	399
Apology		399
Crito	(Socrates in jail)	399
Phaedo	(Socrates' execution)	399

Dialogues That Give No Indication of Dramatic Date

Lysis
Cratylus
Phaedrus
Laws
Hippias Major
Hippias Minor
Timaeus
Philebus

Primary source: Diskin Clay's *Platonic Questions: Dialogues with the Silent Philosopher*

Works Cited

Annas, Julia. *Platonic Ethics, Old and New.* Ithaca: Cornell University Press, 1999.

Aquinas, Thomas. *Summa Theologica* 1–2ae.

Aristophanes. *Comediae.* Ed. F. W. Hall and W. M. Geldart. Oxford: Oxford Classical Texts, 1970.

Aristotle. *Metaphysics.* Trans. Hugh Tredennick. Loeb Classical Library. Cambridge: Harvard University Press, 1989.

———. *Nicomachean Ethics.* Trans. David Ross, rev. J. L. Ackrill and J. O. Urmson. Oxford: Oxford University Press, 1998.

Baracchi, Claudia. *Of Myth and Life and War in Plato's Republic.* Bloomington: Indiana University Press, 2002.

Beaty, Michael, and Anne-Marie Bowery. "Cultivating Christian Citizenship: Martha Nussbaum's Socrates, Augustine's *Confessions,* and the Modern University." *Christian Scholar's Review* 31 (2003): 21–52.

Benardete, Seth. *The Tragedy and Comedy of Life: Commentary on Plato's Philebus.* Chicago: University of Chicago Press, 1993.

Benson, Hugh. *Socratic Wisdom.* New York and Oxford: Oxford University Press, 2000.

Blondell, Ruby. "Letting Plato Speak for Himself." In *Who Speaks for Plato? Studies in Platonic Anonymity,* ed. Gerald A. Press. Lanham: Rowman and Littlefield, 2000.

———. *The Play of Character in Plato's Dialogues.* Cambridge: Cambridge University Press, 2002.

Bloom, Allan. *Love and Friendship.* New York: Simon and Schuster, 1993.

———, trans. *The Republic of Plato.* New York: Basic Books, 1968. 2nd ed., 1991.

Bolotin, David. *Plato's Dialogue on Friendship.* Ithaca: Cornell University Press, 1979.

Booth, Wayne. *The Rhetoric of Fiction.* 2nd ed. Chicago: University of Chicago Press, 1983.

———. *A Rhetoric of Irony.* Chicago: University of Chicago Press, 1974.

Bowery, Anne-Marie. "Recovering and Recollecting the Soul." In *Plato's Forms: Varieties of Interpretation,* ed. William A. Welton. Lanham: Lexington Books, 2003.

———. [Anne-Marie Frosolono]. "Thus Spoke Augustine: An Analysis of the Relationship Between Language and Spirituality in the *Confessions.*" *Contemporary Philosophy* (1993): 4–7.

Brann, Eva. "The Music of the Republic." *Agon* 1 (1967): 1–117.

Brickhouse, Thomas C., and Nicholas D. Smith. "The Socratic Elenchos?" In *Does Socrates Have a Method? Rethinking the Elenchus in Plato's Dialogues and Beyond*, ed. Gary Alan Scott. University Park: Pennsylvania State University Press, 2002.

Brumbaugh, Robert S. *Plato on the One: The Hypotheses in the Parmenides*. New Haven: Yale University Press, 1961.

———. *Platonic Studies of Greek Philosophy*. Albany: State University of New York Press, 1989.

———. "The Purpose of Plato's *Parmenides*." *Ancient Philosophy* 1 (1980): 39–48.

Burger, Ronna. "Plato's Non-Socratic Narrations of Socratic Conversation." In *Plato's Dialogues: The Dialogical Approach*, ed. Richard Hart and Victorino Tejera. Lewiston: Edwin Mellen, 1997.

———. *Plato's Phaedrus: A Defense of a Philosophical Art of Writing*. Birmingham: University of Alabama Press, 1980.

Burnyeat, Myles. "Socratic Midwifery, Platonic Inspiration." *Bulletin of the Institute of Classical Studies* 24 (1977): 7–16.

———. "Sphinx Without a Secret." In *Plato: Critical Assessments*, ed. Nicholas D. Smith, vol. 1. New York: Routledge, 1998.

Bury, Robert Gregg. *The Philebus of Plato*. Cambridge: Cambridge University Press, 1897; repr. 1973.

———. *The Symposium of Plato*. Cambridge: W. Heffer and Sons, 1973.

Caldwell, Richard, trans. *Hesiod's Theogony*. Cambridge: Focus Information Group, 1987.

Carrick, P. *Medical Ethics in Antiquity*. Boston: D. Reidel, 1985.

Chance, Thomas. *Plato's Euthydemus: An Analysis of What Is and What Is Not Philosophy*. Berkeley: University of California Press, 1992.

Clay, Diskin. *Platonic Questions: Dialogues with the Silent Philosopher*. University Park: Pennsylvania State University Press, 2000.

———. "Reading the *Republic*." In *Platonic Writings, Platonic Readings*, ed. Charles L. Griswold Jr. New York and London: Routledge, 1988.

Cobb, William S., trans. *The Symposium and the Phaedrus: Plato's Erotic Dialogues*. Albany: State University of New York Press, 1993.

Coby, Patrick. *Socrates and the Sophistic Enlightenment: A Commentary on Plato's Protagoras*. Lewisburg: Bucknell University Press, 1987.

Cochrane, Charles Norris. *Thucydides and the Science of History*. New York: Russell and Russell, 1965.

Cohn, Dorrit. "The Poetics of Plato's *Republic:* A Modern Perspective." *Philosophy and Literature* 24 (2000): 34–48.

Craig, Leon Harold. *The War Lover*. Toronto: University of Toronto Press, 1994.

Crombie, I. M. *An Examination of Plato's Doctrines*. 2 vols. New York: Humanities, 1963.

Damasio, Antonio. *Descartes' Error: Emotion, Reason, and the Human Brain*. New York: Avon Books, 1994.

Davidson, Donald. "Gadamer and Plato's *Philebus*." In *The Philosophy of Hans-Georg Gadamer*, ed. Lewis Hahn. Chicago: Open Court, 1997.

Desjardins, Rosemary. *Plato and the Good*. Leiden: E. J. Brill, 2004.

De Strycker, Emile. "The Unity of Knowledge and Love in Socrates' Conception of Virtue." *International Philosophical Quarterly* 6 (1966): 428–44.

Dorter, Kenneth. *Plato's Phaedo: An Interpretation.* Toronto: University of Toronto Press, 1982.

Dostal, Robert J. "Gadamer's Continuous Challenge: Heidegger's Plato Interpretation." In *The Philosophy of Hans-Georg Gadamer,* ed. Lewis Hahn. Chicago: Open Court, 1997.

———, ed. *The Cambridge Companion to Gadamer.* Cambridge: Cambridge University Press, 2002.

Dubner, Steve. "Calculating the Irrational in Economics." *New York Times.* [Online]. June 28, 2003.

Ficino, Marsilio. *The Philebus Commentary.* Ed. and trans. Michael Allen. Tempe: Arizona Center for Medieval and Renaissance Studies, 2000.

Figal, Günter. "The Idea and Mixture of the Good." In *Retracing the Platonic Text,* ed. John Russon and John Sallis. Evanston: Northwestern University Press, 2000.

Frede, Dorothea. "Disintegration and Restoration: Pleasure and Pain in Plato's *Philebus.*" In *The Cambridge Companion to Plato,* ed. Richard Kraut. Cambridge: Cambridge University Press, 1996.

———. "Introductory Essay" to *Philebus.* Trans. Dorothea Frede, ed. John M. Cooper. Indianapolis: Hackett, 1993.

Frede, Michael. "Plato's Arguments and the Dialogue Form." In *Methods of Interpreting Plato and His Dialogues,* ed. James C. Klagge and Nicholas D. Smith. Oxford Studies in Ancient Philosophy supplementary volume. Oxford: Clarendon, 1992.

Freydberg, Bernard. *The Play of the Platonic Dialogues.* Literature and the Sciences of Man 12. New York: Peter Lang, 1997.

Friedländer, Paul. *Plato: The Dialogues, Second and Third Periods.* Trans. Hans Meyerhoff, vol. 3. Princeton: Princeton University Press, 1969.

Gadamer, Hans-Georg. *Dialogue and Dialectic: Eight Hermeneutical Studies on Plato.* Trans. P. Christopher Smith. New Haven: Yale University Press, 1980.

———. *The Idea of the Good in Platonic-Aristotelian Philosophy.* Trans. P. Christopher Smith. New Haven: Yale University Press, 1986.

———. *Plato's Dialectical Ethics: Phenomenological Interpretations Relating to the Philebus.* Trans. Robert Wallace. New Haven: Yale University Press, 1991.

———. *Truth and Method.* 2nd ed. Trans. Joel Weinsheimer and Donald Marshall. New York: Crossroad, 1989.

Geier, Alfred. *Plato's Erotic Thought: The Tree of the Unknown.* Rochester: University of Rochester Press, 2002.

Gifford, Mark. "Dramatic Dialectic in *Republic* Book 1." *Oxford Studies in Ancient Philosophy* 20 (2001): 37–52.

Gonzalez, Francisco J. *Dialectic and Dialogue: Plato's Practice of Philosophical Inquiry.* Evanston: Northwestern University Press, 1998.

———. "Plato's *Lysis:* An Enactment of Philosophical Kinship." *Ancient Philosophy* 15 (1995): 69–90.

————, ed. *The Third Way: New Directions in Plato Studies*. Lanham: Rowman and Littlefield, 1995.

Gordon, Jill. "Eros and Philosophical Seduction in *Alcibiades I*." *Ancient Philosophy* 23 (2003): 11–30.

————. *Turning Toward Philosophy: Literary Device and Dramatic Structure in Plato's Dialogues*. University Park: Pennsylvania State University Press, 1999.

Greene, David. *Man in His Pride: A Study of the Political Philosophies of Thucydides and Plato*. Chicago: University of Chicago Press, 1950.

Griswold, Charles L., Jr. "Plato's Metaphilosophy: Why Plato Wrote Dialogues." In *Platonic Writings, Platonic Readings,* ed. Charles L. Griswold Jr. New York and London: Routledge, 1988.

————. *Self-Knowledge in Plato's Phaedrus*. New Haven: Yale University Press, 1986.

————, ed. *Platonic Writings, Platonic Readings*. New York and London: Routledge, 1988.

————, ed. *Platonic Writings, Platonic Readings*. University Park: Pennsylvania State University Press, 2002.

Grote, George. *Plato and the Other Companions of Sokrates*. 3rd ed. 3 vols. London: John Murray, 1865.

Guthrie, W. K. C. *A History of Greek Philosophy*. 6 vols. New York: Cambridge University Press, 1978.

Hackforth, R. *Plato's Examination of Pleasure*. Cambridge: Cambridge University Press, 1945.

Haldane, John. "Medical Ethics: An Alternative Approach." *Journal of Medical Ethics* 12 (1986): 145–50.

Halperin, David. "Plato and the Erotics of Narrativity." In *Methods of Interpreting Plato and His Dialogues*, ed. James C. Klagge and Nicholas D. Smith. Oxford Studies in Ancient Philosophy supplementary volume. Oxford: Clarendon, 1992.

Hampton, Cynthia. "Overcoming Dualism: The Importance of the Intermediate in Plato's *Philebus*." In *Feminist Interpretations of Plato,* ed. Nancy Tuana. University Park: Pennsylvania State University Press, 1994.

————. *Pleasure, Knowledge, and Being: An Analysis of Plato's Philebus*. Albany: State University of New York Press, 1990.

Harris, William. *Ancient Literacy*. Cambridge: Cambridge University Press, 1989.

Harrison, Paul. *The Disenchantment of Reason: The Problem of Socrates in Modernity*. Albany: State University of New York Press, 1994.

Havelock, Eric. *A Prologue to Greek Literacy*. Cincinnati: University of Cincinnati Press, 1971.

Heidegger, Martin. *Being and Time*. Trans. John Macquarrie and Edward Robinson. New York: Harper and Row, 1962.

Howland, Jacob. *The Republic: The Odyssey of Philosophy*. New York: Twayne, 1993.

————. "The *Republic*'s Third Wave and the Paradox of Political Philosophy." *Review of Metaphysics* 51 (1998): 633–57.

————. "Re-Reading Plato: The Problem of Platonic Chronology." *Phoenix* 45, no. 3 (1991): 189–214.

Hyland, Drew. *Finitude and Transcendence in Plato's Dialogues.* Albany: State University of New York Press, 1995.

———. *The Virtue of Philosophy: An Interpretation of Plato's Charmides.* Athens: Ohio University Press, 1981.

Irigiray, Luce. "Sorcerer of Love: A Reading of Plato's *Symposium,* Diotima's Speech," trans. E. Kuykendall. In *Feminist Interpretations of Plato,* ed. Nancy Tuana. University Park: Pennsylvania State University Press, 1994.

Jaeger, Werner. "Aristotle's Use of Medicine as Model of Method in His Ethics." *Journal of Hellenic Studies* 77, pt. 1 (1957): 54–61.

———. *Paideia: The Ideals of Greek Culture.* Trans. Gilbert Highet, 3 vols. New York: Oxford University Press, 1944 [1971].

Kahn, Charles. *Plato and the Socratic Dialogue.* Cambridge: Cambridge University Press, 1996.

Kenny, Anthony. "Mental Health in Plato's *Republic.*" In *The Anatomy of the Soul: Historical Essays in the Philosophy of Mind.* Oxford: Basil Blackwell, 1973.

Klagge, James C., and Nicholas D. Smith, eds. *Methods of Interpreting Plato and His Dialogues.* Oxford Studies in Ancient Philosophy supplementary volume. Oxford: Clarendon, 1992.

Kofman, Sarah. "Beyond Aporia?" In *Post-Structuralist Classics,* ed. Andrew Benjamin. New York: Routledge, 1988.

Kosman, Aryeh. "Silence and Imitation in the Platonic Dialogues." In *Methods of Interpreting Plato and His Dialogues,* ed. James C. Klagge and Nicholas D. Smith. Oxford Studies in Ancient Philosophy supplementary volume. Oxford: Clarendon, 1992.

Lain-Entralgo, Pedro. *The Therapy of the Word in Classical Antiquity.* New Haven: Yale University Press, 1970.

Liddell, H., and R. Scott, eds. *Greek-English Lexicon.* Various editions. Oxford: Oxford University Press.

Lidz, Joel Warren. "Medicine as Metaphor in Plato." *Journal of Medicine and Philosophy* 20 (1995): 527–41.

Lloyd, G. E. R. *In the Grip of Disease: Studies in the Greek Imagination.* Oxford: Oxford University Press, 2003.

Lloyd, Genevieve. *Man of Reason: Male and Female in Western Philosophy.* Minneapolis: University of Minnesota Press, 1984.

Long, Christopher P. "Dancing Naked with Socrates: Pericles, Aspasia and Socrates at Play with Politics, Rhetoric and Philosophy." *Ancient Philosophy* 23 (2003): 49–69.

Mattéi, Jean-François. "The Theater of Myth in Plato." In *Platonic Writings, Platonic Readings,* ed. Charles L. Griswold Jr. University Park: Pennsylvania State University Press, 2002.

McNeill, David. "Human Discourse, Eros, and Madness in Plato's *Republic.*" *Review of Metaphysics* 55, no. 2 (2001): 235–68.

Meinwald, Constance, trans. *Plato's Parmenides.* New York: Oxford University Press, 1991.

———. "Prometheus's Bounds: *Peras* and *Apeiron* in Plato's *Philebus.*" In *Method in Ancient Philosophy,* ed. Jyl Gentzler. Oxford: Clarendon, 1998.

Miller, Mitchell. *The Philosopher in Plato's Statesman*. Boston: Martinus Nijhoff, 1980.

———. *Plato's Parmenides: The Conversion of the Soul*. Princeton: Princeton University Press, 1986.

———. *Plato's Parmenides: The Conversion of the Soul*. University Park: Pennsylvania State University Press, 1991.

Moes, Mark. "Mimetic Irony and Plato's Defense of Poetry in the *Republic*." *Journal of Neoplatonic Studies* 5, no. 1 (Fall 1996): 43–74.

———. "Plato's Conception of the Relations Between Moral Philosophy and Medicine." *Perspectives in Biology and Medicine* 44 (Summer 2001): 353–67.

———. *Plato's Dialogue Form and the Care of the Soul*. New York: Peter Lang, 2000.

Moors, Kent. "The Argument Against a Dramatic Date for Plato's *Republic*." *Polis* 7 (1987): 6–31.

Muecke, D. C. *The Compass of Irony*. London: Methuen, 1969.

Nails, Debra. *The People of Plato: A Prosopography of Plato and Other Socratics*. Indianapolis: Hackett, 2002.

Nehamas, Alexander. *The Art of Living: Socratic Reflections from Plato to Foucault*. Berkeley: University of California Press, 1998.

Newman, J. H. *An Essay in Aid of a Grammar of Assent*. Garden City, N. Y.: Image Books, 1955.

Nichols, Mary P. "Glaucon's Adaptation of the Story of Gyges and Its Implications for Plato's Political Teaching." *Polity* 17, no. 1 (Fall 1984): 34–36.

———. "Spiritedness and Philosophy in Plato's *Republic*." In *Understanding the Political Spirit: Philosophical Investigations from Socrates to Nietzsche*, ed. Catherine Zuckert. New Haven: Yale University Press, 1988.

Nietzsche, Friedrich. *Twilight of the Idols and the Anti-Christ*. Trans. R. J. Hollingdale. London: Penguin Books, 1990.

Nussbaum, Martha. *Cultivating Humanity*. Cambridge: Harvard University Press, 1997.

———. *The Fragility of Goodness: Luck and Ethics in Greek Tragedy and Philosophy*. New York: Cambridge University Press, 1988.

———. *Love's Knowledge: Essays on Philosophy and Literature*. New York: Oxford University Press, 1990.

———. *Poetic Justice: The Literary Imagination and Public Life*. Boston: Beacon Hill, 1995.

———. "Upheavals of Thought: The Intelligence of Emotions." *Graduate Faculty Philosophy Journal* 23 (2002): 235–38.

Owens, G. E. L. "Plato and Not-Being." In *Plato I: A Collection of Critical Essays*, ed. G. Vlastos. Notre Dame: University of Notre Dame Press, 1978.

Parkes, Malcolm. *Pause and Effect: An Introduction to the History of Punctuation in the West*. Berkeley: University of California Press, 1993.

Planeaux, Christopher. "Socrates, Alcibiades, and Plato's *Ta Poteideia*: Does the *Charmides* Have an Historical Setting?" *Mnemosyne* 52 (1998): 72–77.

———. "Socrates, an Unreliable Narrator? The Dramatic Setting of the *Lysis*." *Classical Philology* 96 (2001): 60–68.

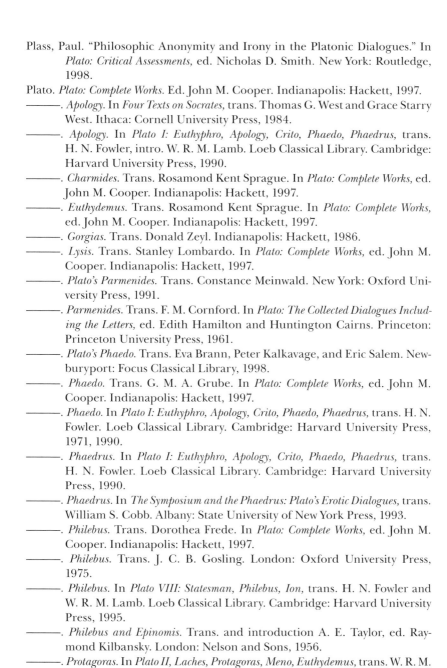

Plass, Paul. "Philosophic Anonymity and Irony in the Platonic Dialogues." In *Plato: Critical Assessments,* ed. Nicholas D. Smith. New York: Routledge, 1998.

Plato. *Plato: Complete Works.* Ed. John M. Cooper. Indianapolis: Hackett, 1997.

———. *Apology.* In *Four Texts on Socrates,* trans. Thomas G. West and Grace Starry West. Ithaca: Cornell University Press, 1984.

———. *Apology.* In *Plato I: Euthyphro, Apology, Crito, Phaedo, Phaedrus,* trans. H. N. Fowler, intro. W. R. M. Lamb. Loeb Classical Library. Cambridge: Harvard University Press, 1990.

———. *Charmides.* Trans. Rosamond Kent Sprague. In *Plato: Complete Works,* ed. John M. Cooper. Indianapolis: Hackett, 1997.

———. *Euthydemus.* Trans. Rosamond Kent Sprague. In *Plato: Complete Works,* ed. John M. Cooper. Indianapolis: Hackett, 1997.

———. *Gorgias.* Trans. Donald Zeyl. Indianapolis: Hackett, 1986.

———. *Lysis.* Trans. Stanley Lombardo. In *Plato: Complete Works,* ed. John M. Cooper. Indianapolis: Hackett, 1997.

———. *Plato's Parmenides.* Trans. Constance Meinwald. New York: Oxford University Press, 1991.

———. *Parmenides.* Trans. F. M. Cornford. In *Plato: The Collected Dialogues Including the Letters,* ed. Edith Hamilton and Huntington Cairns. Princeton: Princeton University Press, 1961.

———. *Plato's Phaedo.* Trans. Eva Brann, Peter Kalkavage, and Eric Salem. Newburyport: Focus Classical Library, 1998.

———. *Phaedo.* Trans. G. M. A. Grube. In *Plato: Complete Works,* ed. John M. Cooper. Indianapolis: Hackett, 1997.

———. *Phaedo.* In *Plato I: Euthyphro, Apology, Crito, Phaedo, Phaedrus,* trans. H. N. Fowler. Loeb Classical Library. Cambridge: Harvard University Press, 1971, 1990.

———. *Phaedrus.* In *Plato I: Euthyphro, Apology, Crito, Phaedo, Phaedrus,* trans. H. N. Fowler. Loeb Classical Library. Cambridge: Harvard University Press, 1990.

———. *Phaedrus.* In *The Symposium and the Phaedrus: Plato's Erotic Dialogues,* trans. William S. Cobb. Albany: State University of New York Press, 1993.

———. *Philebus.* Trans. Dorothea Frede. In *Plato: Complete Works,* ed. John M. Cooper. Indianapolis: Hackett, 1997.

———. *Philebus.* Trans. J. C. B. Gosling. London: Oxford University Press, 1975.

———. *Philebus.* In *Plato VIII: Statesman, Philebus, Ion,* trans. H. N. Fowler and W. R. M. Lamb. Loeb Classical Library. Cambridge: Harvard University Press, 1995.

———. *Philebus and Epinomis.* Trans. and introduction A. E. Taylor, ed. Raymond Kilbansky. London: Nelson and Sons, 1956.

———. *Protagoras.* In *Plato II, Laches, Protagoras, Meno, Euthydemus,* trans. W. R. M. Lamb. Loeb Classical Library. Cambridge: Harvard University Press, 1977.

———. *Protagoras*. Trans. Stanley Lombardo and Karen Bell. In *Plato: Complete Works*, ed. John M. Cooper. Indianapolis: Hackett, 1997.

———. *Republic*. Trans. Paul Shorey. In *Plato: The Collected Dialogues Including the Letters*, ed. Edith Hamilton, Huntington Cairns, and Lane Cooper. Princeton: Princeton University Press, 1963.

———. *Republic*. In *Plato VI: The Republic, Books 6–10*, trans. Paul Shorey. Loeb Classical Library. Cambridge: Harvard University Press, 1935.

———. *The Republic of Plato*. Trans. Allan Bloom. New York: Basic Books, 1968; 2nd ed., 1991.

———. *Sophist*. In *Plato VII: Theaetetus, Sophist*, trans. H. N. Fowler. Loeb Classical Library. Cambridge: Harvard University Press, 1987.

———. *Symposium*. Trans. Alexander Nehamas and Paul Woodruff. Indianapolis: Hackett, 1989.

———. *Symposium*. In *Plato III: Lysis, Symposium, Gorgias*, trans. W. R. M. Lamb. Loeb Classical Library. Cambridge: Harvard University Press, 1996.

———. *Plato's Symposium*. Trans. Seth Benardete, with commentary by Allan Bloom and Seth Benardete. Chicago: University of Chicago Press, 2001.

———. *Symposium*. In *The Symposium and the Phaedrus: Plato's Erotic Dialogues*, trans. William S. Cobb. Albany: State University of New York Press, 1993.

———. *Theaetetus*. Trans. John McDowell. Oxford: Oxford University Press, 1973.

———. *Theaetetus*. In *Plato VII: Theaetetus, Sophist*, trans. H. N. Fowler. Loeb Classical Library. Cambridge: Harvard University Press, 1921.

———. *Theaetetus*. In *Platonis Opera I*, ed. E. A. Duke, W. F. Hicken, et al. Oxford: Oxford University Press, 1995.

———. *Plato's Theaetetus*. Trans. Seth Benardete. Chicago: University of Chicago Press, 1986.

———. *Timaeus*. In *Plato IX: Timaeus, Critias, Cleitophon, Menexenus, Epistles*, trans. R. G. Bury. Loeb Classical Library. Cambridge: Harvard University Press, 1989.

Popper, Karl. *The Open Society and Its Enemies*. Vol. 1. Princeton: Princeton University Press, 1943.

Press, Gerald A. "Continuities and Discontinuities in the History of *Republic* Interpretation." *International Studies in Philosophy* 28, no. 4 (1996): 61–78.

———. "Knowledge as Vision in Plato's Dialogues." *Journal of Neoplatonic Studies* 3 (1995): 61–89.

———. "The State of the Question in the Study of Plato." *Southern Journal of Philosophy* 34, no. 4 (1996): 507–32.

Ranasinghe, Nalin. *The Soul of Socrates*. Ithaca: Cornell University Press, 2000.

Randall, John H. *Plato: Dramatist of the Life of Reason*. New York: Columbia University Press, 1970.

Rankin, H. W. "A Modest Proposal About the *Republic*." *Apeiron* 2, no. 1 (November 1967): 20–22.

Reale, Giovanni. *Toward a New Interpretation of Plato*. Trans. John R. Catan and

Richard Davies. Washington, D.C.: Catholic University of America Press, 1997.

Reeve, C. D. C. *Philosopher-Kings: The Argument of Plato's Republic.* Princeton: Princeton University Press, 1988.

Robb, Kevin. *Literacy and Paideia in Ancient Greece.* Oxford: Oxford University Press, 1994.

———. "Orality, Literacy and the Dialogue Form." In *Plato's Dialogues: The Dialogical Approach,* ed. Richard Hart and Victorino Tejera. Lewiston: Edwin Mellen, 1997.

Roberts, Robert. *The Schooled Heart.* Cambridge: Cambridge University Press, 2003.

Robinson, Richard. *Plato's Earlier Dialectic.* Oxford: Clarendon, 1953.

Rojcewicz, Richard. "Platonic Love: Dasein's Urge Toward Being." *Research in Phenomenology* 27 (1997): 103–20.

Roochnik, David. *Beautiful City: The Dialectical Character of Plato's Republic.* Ithaca: Cornell University Press, 2003.

———. *Of Art and Wisdom: Plato's Understanding of Techne.* University Park: Pennsylvania State University Press, 1996.

Rosen, Stanley. *Plato's Sophist: The Drama of Original and Image.* New Haven: Yale University Press, 1983.

———. *Plato's Symposium.* 2nd ed. New Haven: Yale University Press, 1987.

———. "The Role of Eros in Plato's *Republic.*" *Review of Metaphysics* 18 (1965): 452–75.

Rowe, Christopher. "The Good, the Reasonable and the Laughable in Plato's *Republic.*" In *Laughter Down the Centuries,* ed. Siegfried Jäkel and Asko Timonen. Turko: Turun Yliopisto, 1997.

Rudebusch, George. "Plato's Aporetic Style." In *Plato: Critical Assessments,* ed. Nicholas D. Smith, vol. 1. New York: Routledge, 1998.

Rutherford, R. B. *The Art of Plato.* Cambridge: Harvard University Press, 1995.

Ryle, Gilbert. *Plato's Progress.* Cambridge: Cambridge University Press, 1966.

Saenger, Paul. *Spaces Between Words.* Stanford: Stanford University Press, 1997.

Sallis, John. *Being and Logos: Reading the Platonic Dialogues.* 3rd ed. Bloomington: Indiana University Press, 1996.

Saxonhouse, Arlene W. "Comedy in Callipolis: Animal Imagery in the Republic." *American Political Science Review* 72, no. 3 (1978): 888–901.

Sayre, Kenneth. *Belief and Knowledge: Mapping the Cognitive Landscape.* Lanham: Rowman and Littlefield, 1997.

———. "A Maieutic View of Five Late Dialogues." In *Methods of Interpreting Plato and His Dialogues,* ed. James C. Klagge and Nicholas D. Smith. Oxford Studies in Ancient Philosophy supplementary volume. Oxford: Clarendon, 1992.

———. *Parmenides' Lesson: Translation and Explication of Plato's Parmenides.* Notre Dame: University of Notre Dame Press, 1996.

———. *Plato's Late Ontology: A Riddle Resolved.* Princeton: Princeton University Press, 1983.

Schleiermacher, Friedrich. *Introductions to the Dialogues of Plato.* Trans. William Dobson. New York: Arno, 1973.

Schmid, W. Thomas. *Plato's Charmides and the Socratic Ideal of Rationality.* Albany: State University of New York Press, 1998.

Scott, Gary Alan. *Plato's Socrates as Educator.* Albany: State University of New York Press, 2000.

———, ed. *Does Socrates Have a Method? Rethinking the Elenchus in Plato's Dialogues and Beyond.* University Park: Pennsylvania State University Press, 2002.

Sheen, Fulton. *God and Intelligence in Modern Philosophy: A Critical Study in the Light of the Philosophy of Saint Thomas.* New York: Longman's, Green, 1925.

Simon, Bennett. *Mind and Madness in Ancient Greece: The Classical Roots of Modern Psychiatry.* Ithaca: Cornell University Press, 1978.

Slater, Philip. *The Glory of Hera: Greek Mythology and the Greek Family.* Princeton: Princeton University Press, 1968.

Small, Jocelyn. *Wax Tablets of the Mind.* New York: Routledge, 1997.

Smith, Nicholas D., ed. *Plato: Critical Assessments.* Vol. 1. New York: Routledge, 1998.

Smith, P. Christopher. "The (De)construction of Irrefutable Argument in Plato's *Philebus.*" In *Does Socrates Have a Method? Rethinking the Elenchus in Plato's Dialogues and Beyond,* ed. Gary Alan Scott. University Park: Pennsylvania State University Press, 2002.

Snyder, H. Gregory. *Teachers and Texts in the Ancient World: Philosophers, Jews, Christians.* New York: Routledge, 2000.

Solomon, Robert. "The Joy of Philosophy: Thinking Thin Versus the Passionate Life." *Review of Metaphysics* 55 (2002): 876–78.

———. "Reasons for Love." *Journal for the Theory of Social Behavior* 32 (2002): 115–44.

Stern, Paul. *Socratic Rationalism and Political Philosophy: An Interpretation of Plato's Phaedo.* Albany: State University of New York Press, 1993.

Strauss, Leo. *The City and Man.* Chicago: University of Chicago Press, 1964.

———. *On Plato's Symposium.* Ed. Seth Benardete. Chicago: University of Chicago Press, 2001.

Striker, Gisela. *Peras und Apeiron: Das Problem der Formen in Platons Philebos.* Göttingen: Vandenhoeck and Ruprecht, 1970.

Svenbro, Jesper. "The Interior Voice: On the Invention of Silent Reading." In *Nothing to Do with Dionysus? Athenian Drama in Its Social Context,* ed. John Winkler and Froma Zeitlin. Princeton: Princeton University Press, 1990.

Szlezák, Thomas. *Reading Plato.* Trans. Graham Zanker. New York: Routledge, 1999.

Tarrant, Harold. "Chronology and Narrative Apparatus in Plato's Dialogues." *Electronic Antiquity* 1, no. 8 (1994).

———. "Orality and Plato's Narrative Dialogues." In *Voice into Text,* ed. Ian Worthington. Leiden: Brill, 1996.

———. *Plato's First Interpreters.* Ithaca: Cornell University Press, 2000.

Tejera, Victorino. *Rewriting the History of Ancient Greek Philosophy.* Westport: Greenwood, 1997.

Tessitore, Aristide. "Plato's *Lysis:* An Introduction to Philosophic Friendship." *Southern Journal of Philosophy* 28 (1990): 115–32.

Thayer, H. S. "Plato on the Morality of Imagination." *Review of Metaphysics* 30 (June 1997): 594–618.

Thesleff, Holger. "The Early Version of Plato's *Republic.*" *Arctos* 31 (1997): 149–74.

———. "The Philosopher Conducting Dialectic Plato's Dialogues. In *Plato's Dialogues: New Studies and Interpretations,* ed. Gerald A. Press. Lanham: Rowman and Littlefield, 1993.

———. *Studies in Platonic Chronology.* Commentationes Humanarum Litterarum 70. Helsinki: Societas Scientiarum Fennica, 1982.

Thornton, Bruce. "Cultivating Sophistry." *Arion* 6, no. 2 (1998): 180–204.

Too, Yun Lee. *The Pedagogical Contract: The Economies of Teaching and Learning in the Ancient World.* Ann Arbor: University of Michigan Press, 2000.

Toulmin, Steve. *Return to Reason.* Cambridge: Harvard University Press, 2001.

Van Der Ben, N. *The Charmides of Plato: Problems and Interpretations.* Amsterdam: B. R. Grüner, 1985.

Vegetti, Mario. *La Medicina in Platone.* Venice: Il Cardo Editore, 1995.

Vlastos, Gregory. *Socrates: Ironist and Moral Philosopher.* Ithaca: Cornell University Press, 1991.

———. "The Socratic Elenchus: Method Is All." In *Socratic Studies,* ed. Myles Burnyeat. Cambridge: Cambridge University Press, 1994.

Waugh, Joanne. "Neither Published nor Perished: The Dialogues as Speech not Text." In *The Third Way: New Directions in Platonic Studies,* ed. Francisco J. Gonzalez. Lanham: Rowman and Littlefield, 1995.

West, Elinor J. M. "Plato's Audiences, or How Plato Replies to the Fifth-Century Intellectual Mistrust of Letters." In *The Third Way: New Directions in Platonic Studies,* ed. Francisco J. Gonzalez. Lanham: Rowman and Littlefield, 1995.

Wiggins, David. "Sentence, Meaning, Negation, and Plato's Problem of Non-Being." In *Plato I: A Collection of Critical Essays,* ed. G. Vlastos. Notre Dame: University of Notre Dame Press, 1978.

Wittgenstein, Ludwig. *Tractatus Logico-Philosophicus.* New York: Routledge, 1981.

Woodruff, Martha Kendal. "The Ethics of Generosity and Friendship: Aristotle's Gift to Nietzsche?" In *The Question of the Gift: Essays Across Disciplines,* ed. Mark Osteen. New York: Routledge, 2002.

Xenophon. *Memoirs of Socrates.* Harmondsworth: Penguin Books, 1990.

Zuckert, Catherine. "Hermeneutics in Practice: Gadamer on Ancient Philosophy." In *The Cambridge Companion to Gadamer,* ed. Robert J. Dostal. Cambridge: Cambridge University Press, 2002.

———. "Plato's *Parmenides:* A Dramatic Reading." *Review of Metaphysics* 51 (1998): 875–906.

———, ed. *Understanding the Political Spirit: Philosophical Investigations from Socrates to Nietzsche.* New Haven: Yale University Press, 1988.

Index

254

Asclepius, 53, 73n36, 107n33
askēsis (asceticism, training, spiritual
  exercise), xxii
Aspasia, 192n33
Assembly, Athenian, 16
Athenian character, xvi, 37n19
Athenian Stranger, xiv, 63, 71n17,
  72n28, 74n39
Athens in Thucydides' *History*, 20–29
audience
  and distancing strategy, 175
  and emotional responses, 103
  in *Euthydemus*, 91
  invitation to participate, 28–31
  and narrative markers, 83, 90
  Socrates as character, 98–99
  for Thucydides, 17, 18–23, 24, 33
aviary, image of, 151n39

balancing opposed accounts, 17, 30–31
being and becoming
  in *Philebus*, 154–56, 167
  in *Protagoras*, 196
belief (*doxa*) vs. knowledge, 6–8, 10–11
beloved. *See* lover-beloved relationship
blushing, 94

Callias, 90, 94, 149n21
care for the young (*paideia*), 51
care of the self, xxii–xxiii
care of the soul/mind, 44, 52, 53
cause (*aitia*), xxvii, 131, 139, 164, 165
cave, allegory of the, 87, 187, 229
Cebes, xxv, 38n32, 43, 112, 201–5, 217–18
censorship and education of guardians,
  60, 74n42, 117–19, 120–21
Cephalus, xxxin16, 66, 86, 95, 186
Chaerephon, 83, 87, 99
characters in dialogues, ix, x–xi
  names of, xvi–xvii, xxxin16
  viewpoint of characters, xii–xiii
  see also names of specific characters, e.g.,
  Glaucon
charioteer, image of, 124, 212, 221–22
Charmides, 38n30, 94
Charmides (dialogue)
  elenchus in, 27
  emotion expressed in, xxvi, 94, 95, 102
  erotic dimensions, 93
  medical model, 48, 66, 75n46, 80n81

narrative frame, 87–88
Socrates as character, 97, 98
chronology, compositional, xvi, 175,
  189n2. *See also* developmentalism
chronology of dramatic events, 239
classification in *Philebus*, 154, 163–64,
  167
Clinias, 90, 93, 94
coercion in *Republic*, 184–85
cognitive powers, 6–7
comedy and tragedy in *Symposium*, 116–17
Corcyrean dispute in Thucydides, 22
Corinthian embassy in Thucydides, 20–
  23, 24
Cratylus (dialogue), 27, 28
Critias (dialogue)
  elenchus in, 28
  and emotional responses, 94, 96, 98,
  107n31
  medical model, 48, 66, 80n81
Crito, 90–92, 95, 97, 98–99, 101–2, 107n33
Crito (dialogue), xxxn12, 82, 99
Critobulus, 91
cross-examination, 94. *See also* elenchus
  (refutation)
Ctesippus, 90, 93, 108n34

deception. *See* falsehood and deception
Delphic oracle, 37n25, 39n34, 99, 137,
  149n23
demonstrative strategy in *Symposium*,
  xxviii, 175, 181–83, 188
denial of wisdom. *See* Socrates: admis-
  sions of ignorance
developmentalism, xvi, 66, 189n2. *See
  also* chronology, compositional
dialectic, theory of
  fears of, 205
  and the Good, 158
  images, 206–7, 208
  openness to other positions, 196
  in *Philebus*, 153
  and synoptic ability, 32–33
dialogical bondage in *Theaetetus*, 138–43
dialogue
  as genre, ix–x, xviii–xix, xxxin23
  as process, xxii
  see also logos (discourse)
Diomedes and Glaukos, myth of, 113,
  127n5

Dionysodorus, 90, 91
Diotima
  and antilogy, 31–32, 33, 172n39
  in *Apology,* 99
  and comedy, 180
  and grounding function, 191n22
  images in, 220–21
  and medical model, 73n33
  as muse, 116
  and poverty, 207, 211n54, 211n61
Dissoi Logoi, xix, xxxin16, xxxin19
distancing strategy in middle period
    works, xxviii, 175, 177–79, 184, 186,
    188
Divided line, image of, 7–8, 76n58,
    77n59, 81n88, 187, 229
dogmatism, 175–76, 183, 188
drama in dialogues, x–xiii
dramatic dialogues. *See* enacted
    dialogues
dramatic style in Thucydides, 29
dreaming, images of, 3–4, 7

Echecrates, 108n35, 205, 234n7
eichos (probable) reasoning
  in Plato, 26
  by Socrates, 38n28
  in Thucydides, 22, 25–26, 32, 38n27
eidos, eidē. See forms (*eidē*)
Eleatic Stranger
  and antilogy, 32
  and aporia, 109n45
  and image of Socrates, 133
  imagery, 121–22, 223–24
Eleatics and *Theaetetus,* 141
elenchus (refutation)
  contradiction in, 34
  and dialogue, 208n2
  and *Dissoi Logoi,* xxxin19
  and emotional responses, 95
  with holders of formulas, 26–27
  in psychic maieutics, 132
emotional experience
  in education of guardians, 118,
    128n14
  Socrates as character, xxvi, 98–103,
    107n31
  in Socratic philosophy, 92–96,
    109n41, 109n45
  see also laughter

enacted dialogues, 82, 99. *See also*
    Crito (dialogue); *Euthyphro* (dia-
    logue); *Gorgias* (dialogue); *Laches*
    (dialogue)
Ephialtes and Otos, myth of, 122,
    127n18, 128n18
equality and recollection, 202, 215, 233
Er, Myth of, 56, 60, 74n42, 87, 126, 187
eristics (disputation for its own sake),
    28, 35n4, 163
eros
  and the Good, 182–83
  and justice, 66–67
  and madness, 174–75
  and music, 192n36
  in narrative dialogues, 92–93
  in Platonic discourse, 79n80
  in *Republic,* 183–86
  in *Symposium,* xxxn15, 116–17, 122,
    179–83, 191n22, 221
  training of, 46–47, 50, 56, 61, 125
euporia
  in *Phaedo,* 203–4
  in *Philebus,* 161, 171n30
Euthydemus (dialogue), xvi
  elenchus in, 27
  emotional responses by Socrates, 95,
    97, 98–99, 101–3
  erotic dimensions, 93
  and labyrinth, 210n41
  narrative frame, 90, 91
Euthyphro (dialogue)
  aporia in, xvii–xviii
  emotional responses in, 95, 110n53
  narrative frame, 83
  reasoning with holders of formulas, 26

falsehood and deception
  and images, 228–29
  in *Protagoras,* 115
  in *Sophist,* 223–25, 268n16
  in *Theaetetus,* 137, 139
fanaticism in *Symposium,* 177–79, 183,
    189n7, 189n8, 190n13
fertility and psychic maieutics, 134–35,
    136–37
forms (*eidē*)
  and anamnesis, 202
  and antilogy, 28, 38n31, 38n32
  in Aristotle, 237n29

purpose of writings, xvi
unresolved difficulties in, xiv–xv
Platonic irony
    historical irony, 79n79
    in *Phaedrus*, 171n36
    in *Republic*, 185
    in *Symposium*, 175, 179, 190n14
    vs. Socratic irony, 103, 110n53
Platonic metaphysics, 213, 232–33
play
    and distancing strategy, 175
    in *Republic*, 4, 12, 14n4, 183
    in *Symposium*, 177, 181–83
pleasure, 158–61, 164–66, 169n5
plurality/unity dialectic, 156, 161–62.
    See also limited and unlimited, the
    (*peras/apeiron*)
poetry
    and emotion, 100–102
    and imitation, 5, 229
    in *Phaedrus*, 124–25, 129n24, 174
    and philosophy, x, xxiii, 86, 113–17
    in *Republic*, 76n56, 117, 229, 233
    in training of mind, 61
    underlying sense, 117–22
    see also Homer
Polemarchus, 66, 86, 117, 183–86
Polus, 30
Potidaean revolt in Thucydides, 22
poverty of argument, 206–7, 211n54
Prodicus, 89, 100, 102
Protagoras
    on dialectic, 16
    and emotional responses, 96
    erotic dimensions, 93
    orphaned *logoi* of, 135, 144, 149n21
    and self-knowledge, 141
    as teacher, 35n5, 209n10
Protagoras (dialogue)
    dialectic in, 193–96, 206
    emotion expressed in, 94, 100, 102
    Homeric allusions in, 114–15
    method in, xxviii–xxix
    narrative frame, 88–90, 89, 108n35
    Socrates as character, 97, 98
    virtue in, 151n41
Protarchus
    and language, 171n35
    name of, 171n27

in *Philebus*, 158–60, 162, 163–66
    and repetition, 171n33
psuchē in medical model, 43, 49, 50, 53,
    57, 66–67, 75n45
psychagogia (leading souls), 42–43, 62,
    65
Pythagoreanism, 83, 172n39. *See also*
    opposites, theory of

question-and-answer method
    in *Phaedo*, 203
    in *Philebus*, 167
    in Platonic dialogue, 64
    used against Protagoras, 195
    vs. other methods, 111

rational self-examination, 92, 108n40
reader. *See* audience
reading practices of ancient texts, 82–83
reason, 219, 232
recollection. *See* anamnesis
    (recollection)
reflection and psychic maieutics, 137–38
reflexivity, 153
refutation. *See* elenchus (refutation)
repetition as method
    and limits, 170n23
    in *Parmenides*, 157
    in *Philebus*, 155, 159, 162–63, 164,
    165–67
reported dialogues. *See* narrated
    dialogues
Republic (dialogue)
    emotional responses in, 94, 95, 102
    erotic dimensions, 93
    genre of, x
    images in, 3–14, 69n3, 126, 197,
    226–30
    medical model in, xxv, 45, 48–49,
    48–68
    methods in, xxviii, 183–88
    narrative frame, 86–87, 107n23
    poetry in, 76n56, 117, 229, 233
    question-and-answer in, 111
    Socrates as character, 97, 99
    rhetoric and medical model, 42–43

self-knowledge
    and medical model, 48–49

methodos, 112
 narration of, 104n3, 189n6
 psychic maieutics in, 130–38
 reasoning in, 27
Theodorus, 121, 141, 149n21, 150n30,
 150n31, 150n32
Theseus, image of, xvii, 194, 200–201
thought-experiments, 13
Thrasymachus, 66–68, 74n41, 86, 94
Thucydides, 16–26
 audience for, 28
 and medicine, xxv–xxvi, 62–63
 parallels with Plato, 77n65, 78n65
 role of speeches in, xxiv
Timaeus (dialogue), 225–26
Tiresias, imagery of, 119–20
truth (*sophos*) in medical model, 66, 67
"two going together" imagery in Homer,
 114–17, 206

unlimited, the. *See* limited and unlimited, the (*peras/apeiron*)

virtue (*aretē*)
 and *gymnastikē,* 51
 and images, 119–20, 227, 231–32
 and limits, 74n41
 medical model, 45–48, 53–56, 61, 67,
 74n42
 and reason, 109n40
 teachability of, 38n32, 196, 206
vividness in Thucydides, 16–17, 29

weaver, image of, 204–5, 218
wisdom as Socratic pursuit, xiii

Xenophon, xx, xxxin20, 48, 72n27

Zeno, 39n32, 155–57, 161, 163

Notes on the Contributors

Anne-Marie Bowery is an associate professor of philosophy at Baylor University. She also teaches in the Baylor Interdisciplinary Core and codirects the Summer Teaching Institute at Baylor. She has published several articles related to her work on Plato and Platonic pedagogy, and she is at work on a monograph that expands her chapter in this collection.

Bernard Freydberg is the author of *The Play of the Platonic Dialogues* and *Provocative Form in Plato, Kant, Nietzsche (and Others)*. He has written and lectured widely on Plato. His essay "Agon in the Platonic Dialogues" appeared in the journal *Iphitos*, and "Rewriting Homer and Aristophanes in the Platonic Text" appeared in *Rewriting the Platonic Text*. He is professor of philosophy at Slippery Rock University.

Jill Gordon is a professor of philosophy at Colby College in Waterville, Maine, and the author of *Turning Toward Philosophy: Literary Device and Dramatic Structure in Plato's Dialogues* and numerous articles on Plato, literary theory, and political philosophy.

Benjamin J. Grazzini received his Ph.D. from the New School for Social Research. His work focuses on the Platonic and Aristotelian texts and the history of their reception. His dissertation is an account of the problem of self-movement as it arises in Aristotle's physical, psychological, and ethical treatises. He is working on a study of the image of the wax block in relation to perception and memory in the Aristotelian tradition and medieval discussions of the intellect.

Phil Hopkins is an assistant professor of philosophy in the Department of Religion and Philosophy at Southwestern University. His research focuses on early Greek conceptions of cognition and language. He is completing a book on the epistemological significance and the relation of the expositional practices of several early Greek thinkers, from Thucydides to Plato.

Gerard Kuperus completed his dissertation on Hegel and is assistant professor at Saint Xavier University, Chicago. His areas of interest include phenomenology, German idealism, ancient philosophy (specifically Plato), and animal ethics.

Christopher P. Long is an associate professor of philosophy at Pennsylvania State University. He is the author of *The Ethics of Ontology: Rethinking an Aristotelian Legacy* and several articles on Plato, Aristotle, and other areas of Greek philosophy.

Mark Moes is an associate professor of philosophy at Grand Valley State University in Allendale, Michigan, where he teaches ancient philosophy and philosophy of history. He was trained in ancient philosophy and philosophy of mind under Kenneth Sayre at the University of Notre Dame. He is the author of *Plato's Dialogue Form and the Care of the Soul* and has published several articles on Plato. He is working on a book-length study of Plato's *Republic*, tentatively entitled *The Medicinal Rhetoric of Plato's Republic*.

Gary Alan Scott is an associate professor of philosophy at Loyola College in Maryland. He is the editor of *Does Socrates Have a Method? Rethinking the Elenchus in Plato's Dialogues and Beyond* and the author of *Plato's Socrates as Educator*. He also coauthored (with William A. Welton) the forthcoming *Erotic Wisdom: Philosophy and Intermediacy in Plato's Symposium*.

Nicholas D. Smith is the James F. Miller Professor of Humanities at Lewis and Clark College, where he has been since 1999. He is the author, coauthor, editor, or coeditor of over fifteen books, including *Socrates on Trial, Plato's Socrates, The Philosophy of Socrates,* and *The Trial of Socrates,* all with Thomas C. Brickhouse, as well as more than eighty journal articles and numerous translations and reviews on various topics in ancient philosophy, ancient literature, and epistemology.

Martha Kendal Woodruff is an associate professor of philosophy at Middlebury College. She received her Ph.D. from Yale University; she also studied for two years at Universität-Freiburg with a research grant from DAAD (German Academic Exchange Service). Her main areas of interest include ancient Greek and modern continental philosophy. She has published articles and book chapters on Plato, Aristotle, Nietzsche, and Heidegger. She is currently finishing a book manuscript, entitled *The Pathos of Thought: Aristotle and Heidegger on Mood, Poetry, and Philosophy.*